04

SEP 05.

97

97

05

90

22. NO

23. MAR 00

27. APR. 00

10. JUL

19. SEP

00

70000817927 5

D1492472

WELDING
Third Edition

JAMES A. PENDER
Technical Director
Tabor Park Secondary School
Scarborough, Ontario

HEREFORD AND WORCESTER
COUNTY LIBRARIES.

671·52

McGraw-Hill Ryerson Limited

Toronto Montreal New York Auckland Bogotá Cairo Guatemala Hamburg Lisbon London Madrid Mexico New Delhi Panama Paris San Juan São Paulo Singapore Sydney Tokyo

WELDING, Third Edition

Copyright © McGraw-Hill Ryerson Limited, 1986.
Copyright © McGraw-Hill Ryerson Limited, 1978.
Copyright © McGraw-Hill Company of Canada Limited, 1968.
All rights reserved. No part of this publication may be reproduced, stored in a retrieval system, or transmitted, in any form, or by any means, mechanical, electronic, photocopying, recording or otherwise, without the prior written permission of McGraw-Ryerson Limited.

ISBN 0-07-548953-8

6 7 8 9 0 D 5 4 3 2

Printed and bound in Canada

Cover and Book Design by Dave Hader

Cover Photo by Francisco Hidalgo/The Image Bank of Canada

Canadian Cataloguing in Publication Data

Pender, James A., date–
    Welding
Includes index.
ISBN 0-07-548953-8
1. Welding.   I. Title.
TS227.P45 1986   671.5′2   C85-099823-9

CONTENTS

PART 5

BASIC THEORY 251

PART 6

PRACTICAL ASSIGNMENTS 311

PREFACE

Like the second edition, this third edition of *Welding* is designed to assist beginning students with the basic principles of welding. Each chapter has been carefully reviewed, many have been expanded, and new chapters have been added to provide the student with a more thorough and comprehensive knowledge of welding fundamentals. Each section is followed by a short review, and each chapter concludes with a general review intended to provoke thought or encourage further exploration of the subject. Each chapter also contains lists of **Points to Remember** and **Words to Remember**, which reinforce the important points of the chapter and summarize key words that may be unfamiliar to the student.

In keeping with the emphasis on practical applications and to assist the student in developing more advanced skills, the number of practical exercises has been increased. Although these practical exercises are arranged in a specific, logical sequence, the instructor may easily reorganize their presentation in order to stress a particular area. **Part 6** of the text offers further practical applications, in the form of test assignments. These will prove invaluable in preparing students for work in the industry, as they are modelled on tests set by the agencies responsible for the testing of welders and welded joints.

Welding is a skill that will provide students with employment opportunities in many areas. The first chapter, "Welding as a Career", stresses the variety of work available to a welder, and will encourage students to research employment opportunities in their particular geographical area. In addition, welding courses may be given for specific trades by combining certain chapters of the book. For example, a course in auto body repair could be created by combining chapters on basic oxyfuel proce-

dures, braze welding and white metal welding, and GMAW. The oxyfuel chapters would be helpful in studying the sheet metal trade. Auto mechanics makes use of the basic procedures of arc welding and oxyfuel. For the machine-shop and small-engine repair trades, the chapters on nonferrous metals, metallurgy, and expansion and contraction will be useful reference material.

Safety aspects of welding have been highlighted throughout the book, including two chapters covering safety procedures to be followed when using oxyfuel equipment and arc welding equipment. Safety procedures appear at various points, to ensure that students become aware of the need to be safety conscious at all times.

Although this text deals with various welding processes, emphasis has been placed on the weld itself. Once students become aware of the importance of the careful study of the weld, they should notice the similarities in all welds, even if dissimilar equipment is used in the various processes involved. Here, the basic question is whether the metal melts or not. In other words, every weld represents a "fusion vs. nonfusion" situation. As students progress through the text, they will notice the similarities in the various techniques and processes and will eventually recognize that the newer processes are simply developments of arc and flame processes learned previously. For this reason, it is especially important that students practise with great diligence the basic exercises in the text.

The bead and weave basic welding techniques are explained fully. Emphasis has been placed on the fact that welds remain unaltered in all positions and change only in technique.

As in the second edition, references to pressures and amperages are omitted in general discussion for the following reasons:

1. The student is encouraged to work from manufacturers' charts. Alternatively, he or she could follow the industrial practice of setting equipment by sight and sound. This would also help the student to become more self-reliant.

2. In view of the wide variety of equipment on the market, the settings quoted may not correspond with those being used in a particular school. This could cause some discrepancy between the written instructions and the verbal directions from the instructor.

3. Equipment in constant use tends to become inaccurate. Gauge springs and tubes stretch slightly, and arc welding machines may lose accuracy in calibration. Equipment can easily be checked with a measuring instrument after it has been in use for a short time. These changes do not affect equipment performance, but could confuse a student if he or she were required to adhere to a definite setting. Instead, the student should find the correct settings by observing the flame and listening to the arc sound.

This edition also includes information and hints about special techniques and operations in a number of the chapters, in order to bring the student to an understanding of the latest developments in the welding field. Technical language and theory have been kept to a minimum. However, if students are involved in the practical application of the "how" of the subject, they may become curious about the "why" of it. Individual students should be encouraged to research areas that interest them. This research might then be used as a basis for discussion or a written essay. The following topics have proved to be successful ones:

Underwater welding and cutting
Salvage operations
Oxygen and its uses (other than welding?)
Related occupations
Making and using a home welding machine

Courtesy of Canadian Liquid Air Ltd.

Underwater repair work

Qualifications and earnings
Future trends (robotics)
Metal sculptures

The choice of suitable topics is limited only by the time available and the scope offered to the student. Projects expand a student's theoretical and practical knowledge. Whenever possible, and especially in senior grades, the students should be encouraged to choose their own projects and to work with a minimum of help from the instructor.

ACKNOWLEDGEMENTS

The author wishes to thank the following companies, who have been most generous in their assistance and cooperation in the preparation of this book.

For photographs and illustrations:

Canadian Liquid Air Ltd.
ESAB Ltd.
Hobart Brothers Company
The Lincoln Electric Company
Union Carbide Canada Ltd.
Ontario Hydro
Deloro Stellite
The Harris Calorific Company
The James F. Lincoln Arc Welding Foundation
Modern Engineering Company (MECO)
The American Welding Society
Cigas Products Ltd.

For articles from publications and works:

Articles on oxy-acetylene welding, cutting, and brazing:
- Union Carbide Canada Limited, *Oxy-Acetylene Handbook*, Second Edition, Linde Division.
- Modern Engineering Company (MECO), *Instruction Manual* (Service Bulletin #1)
- The Harris Calorific Company, *Instruction Manual*

The article on expansion and contraction and studding cast iron:
- The James F. Lincoln Arc Welding Foundation, *Metals and How to Weld Them*

The material on steel making:
- Stelco Inc.

The article on low hydrogen electrodes:
- ESAB Ltd., *Hints on the Use of O.K. Low Hydrogen Electrodes*

The material on hardsurfacing:
- Deloro Stellite
- Cigas Products Limited.

The author would also like to express his gratitude to his wife and family for their patience, help, and understanding, and to Mr. D. Richardson.

J.A.P.
March, 1986
Toronto, Ontario

METRICATION IN THE WELDING INDUSTRY

North America is gradually adopting the metric system of measurement, giving up its inch-pound (Imperial, U.S. Customary, etc.) units and means of measurement. The type of metric system being adopted is known as SI, from the French *Système Internationale*. This is the most advanced and simplest means of measurement yet devised. All Canadian institutions, including governments, industries, hospitals, and schools are now changing their operations, tools, and standards to SI.

Like all metric systems, SI is based on the convenience of decimal divisions. Most quantity units can be multiplied or divided by factors of ten to form multiples and submultiples of the original units. These factors are indicated by prefix names and symbols which attach to the original unit or its symbol. Common prefixes, with their meanings and symbols, are given below.

PREFIX	SYMBOL	MEANING
giga-	G	one billion
mega-	M	one million
kilo-	k	one thousand
hecto-	h	one hundred
deca-	da	ten
deci-	d	one tenth
centi-	c	one hundredth
milli-	m	one thousandth
micro-	μ	one millionth
nano-	n	one billionth

Proper SI style and conventions are, of course, followed throughout this text. Mass, for instance, is carefully differentiated from weight, which should always refer only to the force of gravity acting on a mass.

Conversion from one system of measurement to another involves several problems. Tools, materials, and products manufactured to old standard sizes must gradually be replaced. In order to do this, new standards and conventions for SI metric must be decided upon by both government and industry. For some industries, conversion is taking many years. People must also be educated in the new system, and markets for the new sizes must be found.

SI quantity units commonly encountered in welding and their symbols are given in the list on the facing page.

Today's student must expect to live and work in an SI metric world. To this end, this text presents the student with a fully SI learning experience. Yet, since the inch-pound sizes are still being used, students should also be aware of the old system. Therefore, this edition provides inch-pound measurements after some SI metric measurements. Should conversion tables become an absolute must, the student should refer to the CSA Metric Practice Guide 2234-1 or another set of precise SI conversion factors. As a guide only, the following conversion factors are offered to assist students in measuring and converting the units most commonly used in welding.

Length	Mass
1 mm = 0.03937 in. 1 cm = 0.3937 in. 1 m = 3.281 ft.	1 kg = 2.2046 lbs.
Pressure/Stress	**Gas Flow Rate**
1 MPa = 145.03 psi 1 kPa = 0.14503 psi	1 L/min = 0.41795 ft³/h

Quantity	Symbol	Unit
length	m mm	metre millimetre
area	m^2 mm^2	square metre square millimetre
volume (capacity)	m^3 dm^3 (L) cm^3 mm^3	cubic metre cubic decimetre (litre) cubic centimetre cubic millimetre
mass	g kg	gram kilogram
time	s, min	second, minute
electric current	A	ampere
electric potential	V	volt
electric resistance	Ω	ohm
temperature	K, °C	Kelvin or degree Celsius
frequency	Hz	hertz
force	N	newton
pressure	Pa kPa	pascal kilopascal
energy	J	joule
power	W	watt

THE WELDING INDUSTRY

WELDING AS A CAREER

1-1 THE SCOPE AND DIVERSITY OF WELDING

Welding plays a very important part in industry, and has such a great diversity of application that it would be difficult to name any metal industry that does not use welding to some degree. The AWS (American Welding Society) lists over 90 different welding and cutting processes. A welder could be employed on a production line performing simple tasks or working on skyscrapers, down a mine, or under the sea. (Figures 1-1 and 1-2 show two very different welding situations.) Although it is not possible to list all the areas or industries that use welding, the following list will give some indication of the diversity and scope of welding.

Oil and gas pipelines	Automobiles and motor-cycles
Oil rigs	
Construction	Shipbuilding and repair
Machine manufact-urers	Planes
	Space industry
Welding equipment	Scrap yards
Military equipment	Underwater salvage
Railroads and bridges	Sheet metal industry
Mines	Ornamental iron works

Courtesy of Miller Services

Figure 1-1   Gas tungsten arc welding (GTAW)

Courtesy of The Lincoln Electric Company

Figure 1-2
Welding at the control for
a rocket launch facility

CONSTRUCTION VERSUS PRODUCTION LINE

Welders working on construction, an example of a highly skilled area, would receive higher salaries than welders working on production lines. However, there are advantages and disadvantages to both types of work. The area in which you choose to work becomes a matter of personal choice and circumstances. In construction (see Figure 1-3), you may receive higher wages, but you would be required to work in less than ideal conditions, high in the air, on scaffolding exposed to the weather. Nevertheless, you would be performing a variety of tasks with a certain amount of freedom and responsibility. The work would or could involve some problem solving and decision making. On a production line (see Figure 1-4), wages are usually lower, but conditions would probably be better, with well-lit, clean, and ventilated work areas and modern equipment. A disadvantage is that many of the jobs are repetitive.

Courtesy of Hobart Brothers Company

Figure 1-3   Welding on a construction site

The Scope and Diversity of Welding   **3**

Figure 1-4
Welding on an auto-
mobile assembly line

Courtesy of Hobart Brothers Company

1-2 A WELDING EDUCATION

One can learn welding full-time at a technical or trade school and at community college, or part-time in evening classes in the local high school. Of course, you can also get on-the-job-training, often as an apprentice. It is possible to combine some of the above, by doing an apprenticeship and taking evening classes, for example. Some large companies employing many welders in production offer welding courses. These courses vary in length and content. Some are designed to train workers to perform simple production welding tasks in the shortest time possible. Others are intended to provide skilled welders with all-round knowledge, capable of supervising other workers.

SCHOOL-TO-WORK PROGRAMMES

The period required to train adequately skilled welders may vary from three to twelve months to as long as three years; the normal period of apprenticeship is 6000 hours. New programmes are being developed all the time by industry, government, and educational institutions, whereby students in high school can earn credits and

Courtesy of Canadian Liquid Air Ltd.

Figure 1-5   Welding on a cross-country pipeline

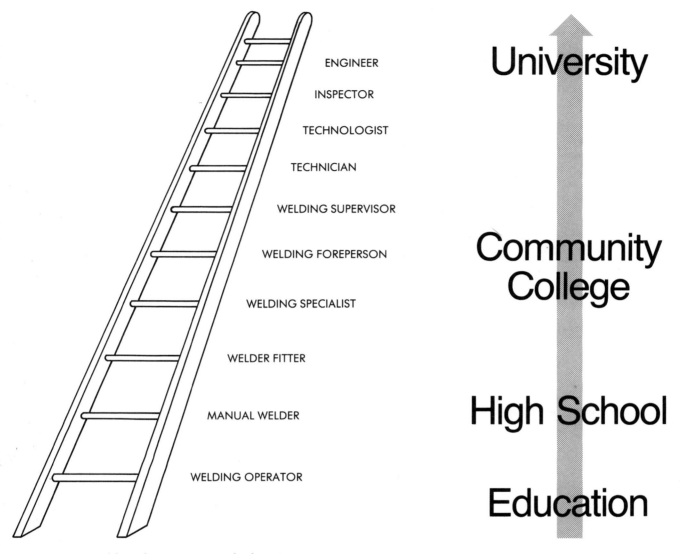

ENGINEER

INSPECTOR

TECHNOLOGIST

TECHNICIAN

WELDING SUPERVISOR

WELDING FOREPERSON

WELDING SPECIALIST

WELDER FITTER

MANUAL WELDER

WELDING OPERATOR

University

Community College

High School

Education

Figure 1-6   Ladder of experience and education

still have that time included in their apprenticeship training requirements. Students should check with their local high school counsellor, Canada Employment Centre, Department of Education, and, of course, their own instructor for further information on such programmes.

1-3 REQUIREMENTS FOR WELDING

Since lives may depend on the welds you produce, you will be required continually to pass **welding tests**. These

WELDING PROCESSES

FUSION

ARC WELDING (AW)

Atomic hydrogen welding ...	AHW
Bare metal arc welding	BMAW
Carbon arc welding.........	CAW
—Gas	CAW-G
—Shielded	CAW-S
—Twin	CAW-T
Electrogas welding..........	EGW
Flux-cored arc welding......	FCAW
Gas metal arc welding.......	GMAW
—Pulsed arc.............	GMAW-P
—Short-circuiting arc......	GMAW-S
Gas tungsten arc welding ...	GTAW
—Pulsed arc.............	GTAW-P
Plasma arc welding.........	PAW
Shielded metal arc welding	SMAW
Stud-arc welding..........	SW
Submerged arc welding	SAW
—Series.................	SAW-S

OXYFUEL GAS WELDING (OFW)

Air-acetylene welding........	AAW
Oxy-acetylene welding.......	OAW
Oxy-hydrogen welding.......	OHW
Pressure-gas welding	PGW

OTHER WELDING

Electron-beam welding.......	EBW
—High vacuum	EBW-HV
—Medium vacuum	EBW-MV
—Nonvacuum	EBW-NV
Electroslag welding..........	ESW
Flow welding................	FLOW
Induction welding...........	IW
Laser-beam welding	LBW
Thermit welding	TW

NONFUSION

RESISTANCE WELDING (RW)

Flash welding	FW
High-frequency-resistance welding....................	HFRW
Percussion welding	PEW
Projection welding	RPW
Resistance seam welding	RSEW
Resistance spot welding	RSW
Upset welding...............	UW

SOLID-STATE WELDING (SSW)

Coextrusion welding	CEW
Cold welding	CW
Diffusion welding	DFW
Explosion welding	EXW
Forge welding..............	FOW
Friction welding	FRW
Hot-pressure welding	HPW
Roll welding...............	ROW
Ultrasonic welding...........	USW

BRAZING (B)

Arc brazing	AB
Block brazing	BB
Diffusion brazing	DFB
Dip brazing	DB
Flow brazing	FLB
Furnace brazing	FB
Induction brazing	IB
Infrared brazing	IRB
Resistance brazing...........	RB
Torch brazing	TB
Twin carbon arc brazing	TCAB

SOLDERING (S)

Dip soldering................	DS
Furnace soldering	FS
Induction soldering	IS
Infrared soldering	IRS
Iron soldering	INS
Resistance soldering	RS
Torch soldering.............	TS
Wave soldering..............	WS

ALLIED PROCESSES

THERMAL CUTTING (TC)

OXYGEN CUTTING (OC)

Chemical flux cutting.........	FOC
Metal powder cutting	POC
Oxyfuel gas cutting	OFC
—Oxy-acetylene cutting	OFC-A
—Oxy-hydrogen cutting	OFC-H
—Oxy-natural gas cutting ..	OFC-N
—Oxy-propane cutting......	OFC-P
Oxygen arc cutting	AOC
Oxygen lance cutting	LOC

ARC CUTTING (AC)

Air-carbon arc cutting........	AAC
Carbon arc cutting...........	CAC
Gas metal arc cutting........	GMAC
Gas tungsten arc cutting......	GTAC
Metal arc cutting...........	MAC
Plasma arc cutting	PAC
Shielded-metal arc cutting	SMAC

OTHER CUTTING

Electron-beam cutting........	EBC
Laser-beam cutting	LBC

THERMAL SPRAYING (THSP)

Electric-arc spraying	EASP
Flame spraying..............	FLSP
Plasma spraying.............	PSP

Figure 1-7 Welding and applied processes

Figure 1-8 Welding careers

WELDING FOREPERSON	WELDER FITTER
WELDING TECHNOLOGIST	WELDING ENGINEER
WELDING OPERATOR	WELDING SUPERVISOR
MANUAL WELDER	WELDING SPECIALIST
WELDING TECHNICIAN	TECHNICAL WRITER
WELDING RESEARCH ENGINEER	WELDING SALES
WELDING JOB SHOP OWNER/OPERATOR	WELDING INSPECTOR (QUALITY CONTROL)
	WELDING INSTRUCTOR
WELDING DEVELOPMENT ENGINEER	

can range from very simple shop tests to controlled government tests. More than any other trade or craft, welders are tested and retested for the work they perform. Some of the more common tests will be described in parts 5 and 6 of this text.

UNIONS

Welders do not have a union of their own but, usually, because of the diversity of welding, many are members of unions appropriate to the industry in which they are engaged.

PERSONAL REQUIREMENTS

Anyone considering welding as a career should be in good physical health, possess good eyesight, and have good muscular control and a steady hand to perform the practical applications of welding. A skilled, knowledgeable welder will always find a place in industry, but only through study, enthusiasm, and constant practice does one truly become a craftsperson.

Among the areas of study most useful to anyone interested in pursuing a career in welding are metallurgy, blueprint reading, mathematics, science, physics, and chemistry. Students should not overlook the many industrial opportunities associated with the welding industry that require a knowledge of welding, but not the practical expertise. These include sales, laboratory work, quality control, and research.

POINTS TO REMEMBER

- Welding has a great diversity of application.
- The AWS lists over 90 welding and cutting operations.
- Career decisions require a lot of thought.
- There are many ways to learn the welding trade.
- Check the programmes in your area carefully before making a decision.
- Welders are tested and retested continually.
- A welder should possess good health, eyesight, and muscular control.
- A skilled welder will always find a place in industry.
- Study, enthusiasm, and practice make a good welder.

WORDS TO REMEMBER

diversity	industry	scope
construction	scaffolding	responsibility
supervising	union	certification
metallurgy	blueprint	research

REVIEW QUESTIONS

1. How many different processes does the AWS list?
2. Name three industries which use welding.
3. Compare the advantages and disadvantages of working on construction with the advantages and disadvantages of working on a production line.
4. Where can one learn welding?
5. What is the normal period of apprenticeship?
6. Do welders have a union of their own? Explain.
7. Why are welders continually being tested?
8. What qualities should a person entering the welding trade possess?
9. What area of study would be most useful to a person interested in a career in welding?
10. List some of the areas in which a person might be employed that are related to the welding trade.

2

WELDING HISTORY AND PROCESSES

2-1 WELDING HISTORY

It is difficult to obtain an accurate accounting of the true development of welding and the people involved because many similar experiments in welding techniques were being carried out in different countries at the same time. Experimenters in one country also had difficulty in communicating with experimenters of other countries in early times.

Although metalworking and the joining of metals goes back many centuries, it would appear that welding as we know it today began around the year 1900. (Figure 2-1 shows a welding patent issued shortly before that year.) However, it is interesting to note, in Table 2-1, the people of different nationalities and time periods who are connected in some way with the development of the welding process.

Coating. – Relates to a method of and apparatus for working metals in various ways by electricity, including a method of applying a fused metallic coating for ornamental or other purposes. A voltaic arc is formed by the approach of carbon to the part of the metal operated upon, the carbon usually forming the positive pole and the metal the other pole. The carbon, which may be solid or hollow, is fixed in an apparatus, one form of which is shown in the Figure. The frame A, having a jointed lever B to lower the carbon C, is insulated and supported on the plate or held in the hand. The frame may have wheels running on rails. The work may be supported on an insulated plate electrically connected. Layers of metal are formed by holding an insulated stick of metal in the electric arc. A coloured glass screen is provided to protect the eyes of the workmen.

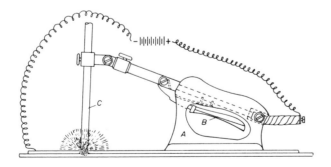

Courtesy of The Lincoln Electric Company

Figure 2-1
Copy of a British welding patent issued in 1885

TABLE 2-1 IMPORTANT WELDING PERSONALITIES

Name	Date	Nationality	Development
J. Priestley	1774	English	Heated mercuric oxide to produce oxygen gas
A. Volta	1800	Italian	Discovered that any two dissimilar metals connected by a substance that became a conductor when moistened would form a voltaic cell. The unit volt is derived from his name
Sir H. Davy	1801	English	Discovered that an arc could be created and maintained between two terminals
A.M. Ampere	1820	French	Was a pioneer in the field of electromagnetism. SI unit ampere is derived from his name
H.C. Oersted	1820	Danish	Established connection between electricity and magnetism
G.S. Ohm	1827	German	Discovered the resistance in an electric circuit. SI unit ohm is derived from his name
M. Faraday	1831	English	Obtained electricity from magnets. His experiments gave us the dynamo
E. Davey	1835	English	Discovered acetylene gas but its manufacture proved expensive
A. DeMeritens	1881	French	Actually joined lead battery plates with the carbon arc process
N. Bernardos and S. Olczewski	1885	Russian	Used carbon arc process for arc welding metals
N. Slavinoff	1888	Russian	Used first bare metal electrode for arc welding
H. Zerener	1889	German	First used twin carbon arc process

TABLE 2-1 IMPORTANT WELDING PERSONALITIES (cont'd)

Name	Date	Nationality	Development
C. L. Coffin	1892	American	Also credited with the use of first bare metal electrode, and the first spot welding process
T. L. Willson	1892	Canadian	Discovered an inexpensive method of manufacturing acetylene gas
H. Le Chatelier	1895	French	Discovered combustion of oxygen and acetylene gas
E. Fouch and F. Picard	1900	French	Developed first oxy-acetylene torch
O. Kjellberg	1907	Swedish	Developed first coated electrode for arc welding
N. Bernardos	1908	Russian	Developed an electro-slag process which is now becoming popular
O. Kjellberg	1914	Swedish	Improved on coated electrode
A. P. Strohmenger	1914	English	Developed the first asbestos wound electrode
H. M. Hobart and P. K. Devers	1930	American	Developed inert gas welding process
H. E. Kennedy, L. T. Jones, and M. A. Rodermund	1935	American	Developed submersion arc welding process
R. Meredith	1942	American	Developed first GTAW torch
not attributable	1948	not attributable	GMAW welding process was developed

2-2 WELDING PROCESSES

Welding is a process of joining metals. Although ancient methods of welding have hardly any resemblance to modern techniques, both ancient and modern processes fall into one of two categories. In the first type of welding, the pieces of metal are heated until they are molten and fuse together. This is called fusion welding. The second type involves heating the metals to a temperature below their melting point and bonding them with a molten filler metal or heating the metals until they are soft enough to hammer or press together. This is called nonfusion welding.

> Fusion welding is any process of joining metals that involves melting the base, or parent, metal (the metal which is being joined). Nonfusion welding is any process of joining metals that does not involve melting the base metal. (Nonfusion welding does not, of course, include bolting, riveting, or the use of any mechanical type of fastener.)

Figure 2-2 Blacksmith forging metals (FOW)

The earliest method of joining metals involved heating two pieces of metal in a blacksmith's fire until they were soft and pliable. The metal pieces were then hammered, or forged, together on an anvil and allowed to cool and harden (Figure 2-2). This process is rarely used today. The pieces of metal rested on a thick layer of coke while they were being heated and were kept as clean as possible. They were heated uniformly to the correct temperature. When the pieces were hammered together, the metals were not melted but were joined by the pressure of the hammering. Forging is therefore considered to be a type of nonfusion welding.

Near the beginning of the 20th century, another method of joining metals became popular. This method, called cast welding, was used to repair castings that were cracked or had flaws in them. Castings were made by pouring molten metal into moulds and allowing the metal to cool slowly, taking the shape of the mould. When a casting was found to be defective because of a crack or flaw, a smaller mould was formed around the defective area and molten iron was poured over the edges of the flaw again and again until the edges became molten. The mould was blocked, and the iron allowed to cool and become solid. This form of welding is a miniature casting operation; hence, the name cast welding. Because the molten metal being poured over the flaw eventually melted the surfaces and edges it came in contact with, this process can be classified as the first fusion welding process.

Neither forging nor cast welding proved very practical. Large pieces of metal could not be welded in a forge, and often the joints, or welds, were not strong and did not last. At about the same time that cast welding came into use, a better method of fusion welding was developed. It produced a permanent joint that was as strong as or stronger than the base metal. Welding technology and science have advanced so rapidly in recent years that it would be impossible to list the wide variety of welding processes in use today. However, all the current processes still fall into the category of either fusion or nonfusion welding.

2-3 FUSION AND NONFUSION WELDING

The two main processes in fusion welding are flame and arc welding. **Flame welding** processes use the heat of

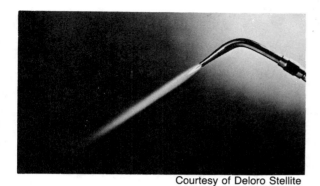

Courtesy of Deloro Stellite

Figure 2-3   Oxy-acetylene flame

ignited gases to melt or heat the base metal. Flame welding is usually done with an oxy-acetylene flame (Figure 2-3). This is called **oxy-acetylene welding** (OAW). However, mixtures of oxygen with fuel gases other than acetylene are now often used in industry. The general term **oxyfuel welding** (OF) refers to welding that makes use of any fuel gas. All these gases are highly explosive under certain conditions. A welder must be familiar with all the safety precautions to be taken. Flame welding will be discussed in Part 2, Oxyfuel Processes.

Arc welding (**AW**) processes use the heat created by an electric current to bring the base metal to the required welding temperature. The electric current is set up between the base metal and a wire, the electrode. This electrode is clamped in a special holder that the welder holds in his or her hand (Figure 2-4). The heat required to melt the base metal comes from the arc which is

created when a current of electricity jumps across the gap between the end of the electrode and the base metal. Both the base metal and the electrode are melted in this process. This was the process that Slavinoff used in 1888 (see Table 2-1). It has very limited application today in industry and is referred to as bare metal arc welding (BMAW).

Further developments produced shielding of the electrode by an inert gas or a granular flux and, in some processes, by a combination of both. Since molten metal often becomes brittle when exposed to air, the purpose of the shielding was to protect the weld. When a covering or coating is used on the electrode, it is called shielded metal arc welding (SMAW) (see Figure 2-5). Kjellberg is credited with developing in 1907 the first coated electrode for arc welding. If a granular flux is used to protect the electrode it is referred to as submerged arc welding (SAW). When an inert gas is used, it is referred to as

Courtesy of Hobart Brothers Company

Figure 2-5   Shielded metal arc welding (SMAW)

Courtesy of Canadian Liquid Air Ltd.

Figure 2-4   Carbon arc torch with twin electrodes

Fusion and Nonfusion Welding   **13**

Courtesy of Hobart Brothers Company

Figure 2-6   Shielded arc welding process using an inert gas (GMAW)

inert gas welding. The two most common inert gas welding processes are gas tungsten arc welding (GTAW) and gas metal arc welding (GMAW) (see Figure 2-6). These processes and their variations will be discussed in more detail in Part 3, Electrical Processes. Apart from forging, discussed in the previous section, there are two main types of nonfusion welding: resistance welding and soldering and related processes, including brazing and braze welding.

RESISTANCE WELDING

Resistance welding uses heat and pressure to join metal parts. The parts to be welded are clamped between two copper electrodes in a machine. The heat is generated by an electric current which flows through the point where the weld is to be made, that is, at the point where the electrodes touch the metal. Butt welding, spot welding, seam welding, and projection welding all involve the resistance process. The different names below refer to variations of resistance welding. Figure 2-7 shows how the processes are carried out.

In **butt welding** (upset welding—UW), the pieces to be welded are placed end to end so that the current flows across the joint.

In **spot welding** (resistance spot welding—RSW), the pieces to be joined are overlapped, and the current and pressure are applied to one spot only.

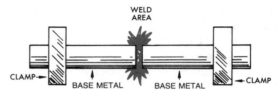

A Butt welding by the resistance method, or upset welding (UW)

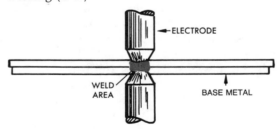

B Resistance spot welding (RSW)

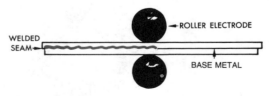

C Resistance seam welding (RSEW)

Figure 2-7   Resistance welding

14   Welding History and Processes

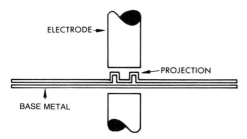

ELECTRODE →

→ PROJECTION

BASE METAL

D Resistance projection welding (RPW)

Figure 2-7   (cont'd)

In **seam welding** (resistance seam welding—RSEW), a rolling electrode makes spot welds at regular intervals along the seam. The spot welds can be made to overlap and form a watertight seam.

In **projection welding** (resistance projection welding—RPW), small bumps are made on one of the base metal surfaces. These bumps, or projections, are welded to another piece of metal by passing an electric current through them and applying pressure at the same time.

Although it is possible to weld fairly thick metals by the resistance welding method, it is more frequently used in the light metal industries, such as the sheet metal and automobile industries. One automobile manufacturer claims to use over one thousand spot welds in the making of a car. If one examines such items as refrigerators, stoves, washing machines, and heating and ventilating ducts, one can see many examples of resistance welding.

2-4 SOLDERING, BRAZING, AND BRAZE WELDING

In these processes, the base metal is never raised to its melting point. In soldering and brazing, the joint is produced by allowing capillary action to draw molten alloy metal into a gap between the pieces of metal being joined. The main difference between these two processes is the temperature at which the process is carried out. Braze welding, on the other hand, does not depend on capillary action. (Figure 2-8 shows one braze welding application.) The techniques used are similar to those used in fusion welding, but the base metal is not melted as in fusion welding. A full discussion of these processes is given in Chapter 9.

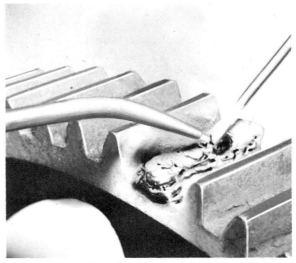

Courtesy of Union Carbide Canada Limited

Figure 2-8   Rebuilding a missing gear tooth with braze welding

These are all the types of welding processes that you will encounter in industry. In the next chapters, you will learn basic and then more complicated processes in these categories. By doing the exercises relating to each process, you will develop the skills needed to make strong, neat welds. Figures 2-9 to 2-11 on pages 16 and 17 show more applications of the welding processes you will learn in this book.

POINTS TO REMEMBER

• Welding as we know it today began around the year 1900.
• Welding is a process of joining metals.
• In fusion welding, the base (or parent) metal must be melted.
• In nonfusion welding, the base metal is not melted.
• In fusion welding, the two main processes are flame and arc welding.
• The three most common arc welding processes are GTAW, GMAW and SMAW.
• Molten metal often becomes brittle when exposed to air.
• The three main types of nonfusion welding are forging, resistance welding, and soldering and related processes.

Figure 2-9 Flame hardening a large shaft. Flame hardening, or quenching, is the heating and fast cooling (by air, water, or some other cooling medium) to produce a hard surface or skin on the metal.

Courtesy of Union Carbide Canada Limited.

Courtesy of Hobart Brothers Company

Figure 2-10 Welders working on a cross-country pipeline with a portable welding unit

Courtesy of Union Carbide Canada Limited

Figure 2-11   Flame priming a tank before painting. Flame priming is the heating of a unit prior to painting to remove rust and mill scale and to give better adherence to paint.

WORDS TO REMEMBER

fusion	forge	braze
nonfusion	butt	temperature
gas tungsten arc	spot	base metal
gas metal arc	seam	parent metal
shielded arc	projection	liquid
carbon arc	solder	molten

REVIEW QUESTIONS

1. What is welding?
2. Describe the work performed by a blacksmith.
3. Name the two categories into which all welding processes fall. What is the difference between these categories?
4. Which process uses the heat of ignited gases to melt the base metal?
5. What happens during the arc welding process?
6. In the arc welding process, how is the heat obtained?
7. What makes the shielded metal arc welding (SMAW) process different from others?
8. What do GMAW and GTAW have in common?
9. Name three resistance welding processes.
10. Where is the resistance welding process most frequently used?
11. Describe one nonfusion and one fusion welding process.
12. Compare the welding processes used before and after the year 1900.
13. Which process is represented by each of the following?

SMAW	RSW
AW	GMAW
UW	GTAW

OXYFUEL PROCESSES

3

SAFETY

Investigations by insurance companies and safety organizations have proven that welding is no more hazardous than any other trade or occupation. However, as in any other trade, there are certain precautions that must be taken to protect oneself and others. In this chapter, the focus is on general safety rules applying to all welding and cutting operations. Safety rules relating to specific welding techniques will also be discussed in detail throughout the book.

3-1 PERSONAL SAFETY

1. Always wear goggles when working with a lighted torch.
2. Wear gauntlet-type gloves made of heat-resistant material such as chrome leather.
3. Low-cut shoes or running shoes should not be worn. Regular safety footwear with steel toe caps should be worn.
4. Keep clothing free of oil and grease.
5. Do not allow clothing to become saturated with oxygen.
6. Wear fire-resistant clothing (apron, sleeves, leggings).
7. Keep sleeves rolled down, loose pockets closed, and pant cuffs turned down.

8. Always wear a helmet with the correct grade of filter lens. When using a hand shield (Figure 3-1) instead of a welding helmet, the same precautions still apply.

Courtesy of Lincoln Electric Company

Figure 3-1   Hand shield

9. Always check the lens in the helmet or shield for cracks before starting to weld.
10. Wear safety goggles when chipping slag from a weld.
11. Do not carry matches or liquid fuel lighters in your pocket.
12. Do not work with equipment that you suspect is defective. Report it immediately to your instructor.
13. Make sure that others are protected from arc welding rays before you start to weld.
14. When arc welding, never work in a damp or wet area.
15. Test for heat radiation by holding the palm of the hand above but not on the piece of metal. Do not touch the piece of metal even if it does not glow.

3-2 FIRE PREVENTION

Fires may occur where any welding or cutting operation is being performed if combustible material is allowed to come in contact with the arc, flame, spark, or hot slag. To prevent fires
1. Remove all combustible material from the welding or cutting area before beginning to work.
2. If combustible materials cannot be removed, provide fire barriers such as metal sheets or fire-resistant blankets and, if possible, have a fire watcher present.
3. Know the exact location of fire extinguishers before you begin to weld or cut.
4. Welding or cutting should not be performed in dusty, gassy areas, or areas where paint spraying is carried out. Explosions and fires could result.
5. Never do any welding or cutting on barrels, drums, tanks, or containers until they have been thoroughly cleaned and tested. You must be certain that all flammable residue has been eliminated in order to prevent explosion or fire.
6. Make sure that hollow assemblies are properly vented before welding or cutting into them, in order to prevent possible explosion.

3-3 VENTILATION

Since welding and cutting produce smoke, dust and fumes, all welding and cutting operations should be performed in well-ventilated areas. Many studies are being carried out on the types of fumes, gases, and other substances produced by the rod, flux, and base metal during the welding process. Vapours that arise from the process which may be changed into toxic compounds by the ultraviolet radiation in the arc itself are also under study.
1. Before beginning to weld or cut, ensure that ventilation is adequate to exhaust smoke, dust, and fumes, which could be health hazards.
2. Read and follow the precautions marked on labels for fluxes and filler metals.
3. Research the metal you are working on and take the necessary precautions with regard to fumes and proper ventilation.
4. An air supply respirator (Figure 3-2) is required in addition to normal ventilation when metals such as lead, brass, bronze, galvanized metals, cadmium, and mercury are being used.

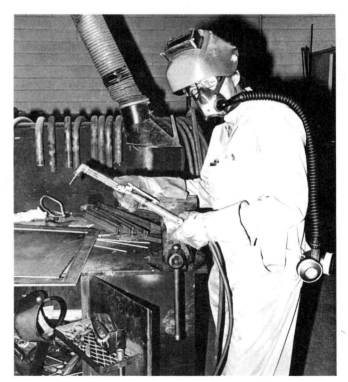

Courtesy of Ontario Hydro

Figure 3-2   Air supply respirator

5. Do not use a fuel-driven arc welding machine in a confined space unless the exhaust gases are vented outside the confined area.
6. When welding in a confined space, carbon monoxide may build up. Use an air supply respirator or have an air supply blowing into the confined space and have a watcher standing by at all times.

POINTS TO REMEMBER

- Welding is no more hazardous than any other trade if the appropriate precautions are taken.
- Certain kinds of clothing must be worn to ensure safety.
- The work area must never be damp or wet, and extreme caution must be taken if the work area is dusty or gassy.
- Equipment must be checked before use, and any that seems to be defective must be reported to the instructor.
- Remove all combustible materials from the work area before beginning to weld or cut.
- Know the exact location of fire extinguishers.
- Never work on barrels, drums, tanks, or containers until they have been cleaned.
- Vent all hollow assemblies before welding or cutting.
- Ensure that ventilation of the work area is adequate.
- Research the metal you are working on and follow the precautions marked on labels for fluxes and filler metals.

WORDS TO REMEMBER

combustible	fire-resistant	extinguisher
radiation	hollow	containers
ventilation	toxic	evolve
ultraviolet	fumes	vapours

REVIEW QUESTIONS

1. What safety precautions should be taken with goggles?
2. List five safety precautions to be taken with regard to clothing.
3. What precaution must be taken with respect to matches or fuel lighters? Why is this precaution taken?
4. What should one do if equipment seems to be defective?
5. How does one test for heat radiation?
6. List at least three safety precautions to be taken when doing arc welding.
7. How can fires start when welding or cutting is taking place?
8. How can one prevent fires before and during welding or cutting?
9. Why must a person pay particular attention to dusty, gassy areas when welding?
10. What precautions must be taken when welding tanks?
11. Why must hollow assemblies be vented before welding or cutting begins?
12. Why must there be adequate ventilation in the welding or cutting area?
13. Which metals require air supply respirators in addition to regular ventilation?

GASES USED IN WELDING AND CUTTING

4-1 NUMEROUS GASES

Many gases and gas mixtures are used in welding and cutting operations because industry is always looking for more efficient, more economical, and safer methods to use in all the welding and cutting jobs.

> Extreme caution must be used when working with any gas. The manufacturers' instructions should be followed carefully.

These gases are supplied as a gas (in gaseous form), in liquid form, or in solution. The cylinders are charged at 21°C (70° F). When a gas is compressed (not liquefied or in solution), the amount of gas in the cylinder is determined by reading the pressure gauge at 21°C (70°F).

(A difference in temperature can change the pressure reading on a cylinder gauge.) Liquefied gases or gases in solution are weighed before and after use to determine the amount of gas left in the cylinder. That is, the amount of gas in these cases is determined by mass, not pressure.

Welding and related industries use gases chiefly as **fuel gases** or **shielding gases**. In order to produce the flame necessary for welding, cutting, and heating operations, pure oxygen combined with a fuel gas will produce a great amount of heat. (The resulting mixture is called an **oxyfuel gas**.) Pure oxygen increases the speed and intensity of combustion. To protect a weld from contamination (by reacting with gases in the atmosphere), an inert gas such as argon or helium is used to shield the molten weld metal from the surrounding atmosphere. Many of these gases will be discussed in detail in the following chapters. Here, only a brief description is given of the main pure and mixed gases used in welding. A detailed discussion of oxygen and acetylene follows.

4-2 CHARACTERISTICS OF SEVERAL FUEL AND INERT GASES

FUEL GASES

Hydrogen gas. This is a colourless, highly flammable gas which is nontoxic and has no odour. Passing superheated steam over heated coke is a fairly common method of producing hydrogen gas. Because hydrogen gas is highly flammable when it is combined with oxygen under certain conditions, it can be a dangerous explosive when in mixture with oxygen.

Propane gas. This is a colourless, highly flammable, hydrocarbon fuel gas which has a low toxicity level and a faintly pungent odour. It is readily liquefied and is usually shipped in liquid form. An abundant fuel, it is used mostly for cutting and heating.

Acetylene gas. This gas is a colourless, highly flammable hydrocarbon fuel gas that is toxic and has a pungent garlic odour. Acetylene gas is produced by combining water and calcium carbide.

Natural gas is the most common of all fuel gases, and is usually found in areas where crude oil has been discovered. This gas is used mostly for heating and cutting. It is usually supplied to the work area by pipeline. The predominant hydrocarbon in natural gas is methane, which is colourless, odourless, and nontoxic, but it is flammable and can be explosive.

Propylene gas. Another hydrocarbon fuel gas, propylene is colourless, nontoxic, and has a pleasant odour, but it is highly flammable. It is obtained from petroleum.

The following gases are actually gas mixtures. The names shown are trade names.

MAPP gas. MAPP stands for methylacetylene, propadiene, and propylene. (Small amounts of other compounds also exist in this gas mixture.) It is normally supplied in liquid form.

Flamex gas. This is a compound of hydrocarbons used as an additive in propane and natural gas. It is also shipped in liquid form.

UCON 69. This is a liquefied hydrocarbon fuel gas, which is colourless and flammable, with a distinct odour.

INERT GASES

The following gases are used as shielding gases because they do not react with other elements. They are usually referred to as inert gases.

Argon. This is a colourless, nontoxic, nonflammable gas that has no odour. It is produced commercially today by fractional distillation of liquid air.

Helium. Like argon, helium has no colour or smell. It is nontoxic and nonflammable and is also obtained from liquid air.

Carbon dioxide. This is a colourless, slightly toxic, nonflammable gas with a faint odour, and a slightly acidic taste. As a liquefied gas, it is commonly known as dried ice. Technically, carbon dioxide is not an inert gas. It will react with other elements. However, since it is used as a shielding gas, it is sometimes referred to as being inert.

Gas mixtures. There are too many combinations of gas mixtures to mention here. Naming the uses of these combinations would fill one textbook alone. An example of a gas mixture, however, is the combination of argon with carbon dioxide. This mixture stabilizes the arc, reduces the weld spatter, and produces a wider, flatter weld bead in the GMAW process.

SHIPPING

Acetylene, hydrogen, and natural gas are shipped in a gaseous form, while propane, MAPP, Flamex, and others are shipped in liquid form. Because there are larger quantities of gas in cylinders containing liquid, there is less cylinder handling. This means that shipping gases in a liquefied form is the more economical method. Shipping of gas in any form must be done with care because of the possibility of explosion. However, many of the newer fuel gases have been found to be more stable than acetylene. Should a cylinder with one of these gases be dropped, bumped, or struck, it will not likely detonate. Unlike acetylene, they are very shock-resistant.

> All cylinders should always be handled with care. Mishandling can result in explosion.

4-3 COMPARING ACETYLENE WITH OTHER FUEL GASES

When in operation, many of the newer fuel gases are **safer** to use than acetylene because they have a much narrower explosive range and are therefore less likely to cause flashback or backfire. They also have a high pressure range. Acetylene at high pressure becomes very unstable. In fact, the law states that acetylene cannot be used at pressures in excess of 100 kPa (15 psi) gauge pressure. Because of this some industries are using the newer fuel gases instead of acetylene.

Another reason for replacing acetylene with newer gases is that these gases have better heat distribution in the flame. To understand the idea of heat distribution, it is necessary to know how burning (combustion) takes place when oxygen and a fuel gas are mixed and lit. As the gases issue from the torch, the flame burns in two distinct stages. The first, or primary, combustion stage is the **inner cone** of the flame, and the secondary combustion stage is the **outer envelope** (Figure 4-1). Heat is produced by the flame because of a chemical reaction.

Acetylene gas is produced from the reaction between calcium carbide and water: $CaC_2 + H_2O \rightarrow C_2H_2 + Ca(OH)_2$. When acetylene ($C_2H_2$) combines with oxygen ($O_2$), it produces $2CO$ (carbon monoxide) + H_2 (hydrogen). Both carbon monoxide and hydrogen are combustible gases. When combined with oxygen, they react to produce CO_2 (carbon dioxide) and H_2O (water) + heat:

$$\text{acetylene } (C_2H_2) + \text{oxygen } (O_2) \rightarrow \text{carbon dioxide} \ (CO_2) + \text{water } (H_2O) + \textbf{heat}$$

In the primary combustion stage, the acetylene first burns with the oxygen from the cylinder, to form carbon monoxide and hydrogen. These gases then unite with oxygen from the atmosphere, to form carbon dioxide and water vapour (second stage). Consequently, in this reaction, there is a loss of oxygen in the surrounding atmosphere. This reduces the tendency for the metal to become oxidized or contaminated.

The greatest amount of heat is produced at the top (or tip) of the inner cone. The heat distribution of an oxygen and fuel gas flame can be discovered by measuring the heat intensity (temperature in degrees celsius (°C) or degrees Fahrenheit (°F)) and the heat quantity (in British Thermal Units (BTUs)). The heat quantity of a flame is called its calorific value. Table 4-1 lists the calorific value in BTUs of acetylene and of some of the newer gases when they are combined with oxygen.

Note that although acetylene has a high temperature, and is high in BTUs at the primary stage, it does not have the highest total BTUs. This means that the secondary stage of the flame is cooler. In heating and cutting operations, the envelope (or secondary stage of the flame) provides the necessary preheat. As can be seen from Table 4-1 **the newer fuel gases produce hotter secondary flames**. They are therefore better for cutting and heating operations, according to the manufacturers. (Table 4-2 compares various characteristics of acetylene and the newer gases.) The oxy-acetylene flame, however, is a versatile and still widely used oxyfuel gas combination. It can be used for fusion welding (any metal), braze welding, heating and cutting, or any flame operation

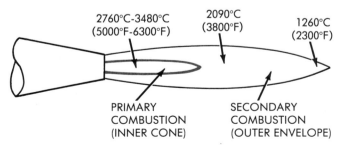

2760°C-3480°C (5000°F-6300°F)   2090°C (3800°F)   1260°C (2300°F)

PRIMARY COMBUSTION (INNER CONE)   SECONDARY COMBUSTION (OUTER ENVELOPE)

Figure 4-1   Primary and secondary combustion stages in the oxy-acetylene flame

TABLE 4-1 CALORIFIC VALUE OF VARIOUS OXYFUEL GASES

Fuel Gas	Temperature with Oxygen		BTUs		
	(°F)	(°C)	Primary	Secondary	Total
Acetylene	5720	3000	507	963	1470
Natural Gas	4800	2500	11	989	1000
MAPP Gas	5300	2780	517	1889	2406
Propane	5130	2680	255	2243	2498
UCON 69	5300	2760	444	1962	2406
Flamex	6000	3115	326	2280	2606

Courtesy of FLAMEX (a division of Cigas Products Ltd.)

TABLE 4-2 FUEL GAS DATA COMPARISON

Physical Property	1# Flamex 230 C.F. Natural Gas	1# Flamex 130 C.F. Propane	1# Flamex 9# Propane Pre-mix	(From MAAP Bulletins) MAAP Gas	Propane	(Oklahoma) Natural Gas	Acetylene
Shock Resistance	Completely Stable	Completely Stable	Completely Stable	Stable	Stable	Stable	Unstable
Explosive Limits							
% in oxygen	?	?	2.5 to 60	2.5 to 60	2.5 to 60	5.1 to 61	3.0 to 93
% in air	?	?	2.6 to 7.7	3.4 to 10.8	2.2 to 9.5	5.3 to 14	2.5 to 80
Max. safe regulator Press. — psi	Line	Cylinder	Cylinder	225 @ 130°F	Cylinder	Line	15 psi
Backfire tendency	Remote	Remote	Remote	Slight	Slight	Slight	Possible
Corrosive reaction hazards	Nil	Nil	Nil	Reacts with 67% copper-base alloy	Negligible	Negligible	Reacts with 67% copper-base alloy
SG liquid 60/60	N.A.	N.A.	0.516	0.576	0.507	N.A.	N.A.
SG gas-air 60/60	0.61	1.58	1.61	1.48	1.52	0.63	0.91
Vapor pressure psia @ 100°F	N.A.	N.A.	179	115	190	N.A.	685
Boiling point @ 760 MM	N.A.	N.A.	−45°F	−36 to −4	−43.7	N.A.	−184
Temp. with oxygen	6000°F	6000°F	6000°F	5301°F	4579°F	4600°F	5589°F

TABLE 4-2 FUEL GAS DATA COMPARISON (cont'd)

Physical Property	1# Flamex 230 C.F. Natural Gas	1# Flamex 130 C.F. Propane	1# Flamex 9# Propane Pre-mix	(From MAAP Bulletins) MAAP Gas	Propane	(Oklahoma) Natural Gas	Acetylene
Latent heat of vaporization BTU/LB. @ B.P.	N.A.	N.A.	179	227	183	N.A.	264 @ −116°F & 17.6 psi
Gross heating value BTU/LB. @ 25°C	22 500	22 780	21 436	21 100	21 484	20 160	21 460
Net heating value — BTU/LB.	20 500	21 080	20 445	?	19 768	19 172	17 457

References: *Handbook of Chemistry & Physics, Marks Mechanical Engr. Handbook, Phillips Petroleum Co. Bulletin, Matheson Gas Data Book.*
Courtesy of Cigas Products Ltd.

used in industry today. It is especially useful for fusion welding because of its hot inner cone. (In fusion welding, the hottest part of the flame is held close to the metal being melted.) Many industries and educational institutions still prefer the oxy-acetylene combination. Instructors often use oxy-acetylene, not only to demonstrate its joining capabilities on mild steel, but also as a very economical method for teaching students the basic manipulative techniques used in, for example, gas tungsten arc welding (GTAW).

TEST YOUR KNOWLEDGE

1. What do the letters MAPP stand for?
2. Which gases are shipped in liquefied form?
3. Why is it more economical to ship gas in a liquefied form?
4. What do the letters BTU stand for?
5. Why are other fuel gases apart from acetylene used in industry? Give two reasons.

4-4 OXYGEN

Oxygen is found in the atmosphere. The atmosphere, or air, is the covering of gases that surrounds the earth.

The two main ingredients found in air are oxygen and nitrogen. There are also small quantities of other gases, such as helium, argon, neon, and other inert gases. Oxygen as a free gas makes up approximately 21% of the earth's atmosphere.

An English chemist, Joseph Priestley, is credited with the discovery of oxygen in the year 1774. He first obtained the gas by heating red oxide of mercury (mercuric oxide). Others continued to experiment until, in 1884, **the liquid air process** was invented. This method allowed oxygen to be extracted from the air in large quantities at reasonable cost. Figure 4-2 shows a present-day oxygen plant.

THE LIQUID AIR PROCESS

Because air is a mechanical mixture of gases, the various gases can be drawn off. When air is subjected to very high pressures and very low temperatures, it becomes liquid. The gases which make up the air can also be liquefied. The various gases, however, are obtained at different temperatures when in the liquid form and can be collected by a process called distillation. They are stored in the liquid form in special containers, or are vaporized (made into gas) and compressed into cylinders.

Courtesy of Canadian Liquid Air Ltd.

Figure 4-2 An oxygen plant that produces 454 000 kg of oxygen each day

It is pure oxygen in the liquid form that powers the rockets and missiles with which we have begun to explore space. Compressed oxygen in cylinders is used in hospitals, in high-altitude flying, and in welding and cutting operations.

Another method of obtaining oxygen is the **electrolytic process**. This process separates the oxygen and hydrogen in water by means of an electric current. However, it is expensive and is profitable only if the hydrogen is also to be used. Most commercial oxygen is obtained by the liquid air method.

Oxygen can be obtained in three different forms: gas, liquid, and solid. As a liquid and a solid, oxygen has a pale blue colour and is paramagnetic (attracted by a magnet). It becomes liquid at $-183°C$ ($-298°F$) and solid at $-218°C$ ($-360°F$). Generally, oxygen is considered colourless, odourless, tasteless, and harmless.

However, it can be dangerous under certain circumstances.

> Oxygen should never be used to dust off clothing, nor should it be sprayed on an open cut. Clothing saturated wih oxygen becomes highly inflammable, and oxygen entering the blood stream can be fatal.

When oxygen unites chemically with another element, the reaction between them is called **oxidation**. If this oxidation takes place very rapidly, it produces heat and light and is called **combustion**. A rusty nail is an example of oxidation. However, the heat generated during the rusting process escapes easily because the rusting takes place slowly. On the other hand, if a metal, especially a hot metal, is brought into contact with pure oxygen, the rate of oxidation is much faster. This principle is used in oxyfuel cutting processes.

The principal value of oxygen to the welding trade is that, although oxygen does not burn, it will greatly accelerate (speed up) combustion. A tiny fire when exposed to pure oxygen will burn fiercely.

TEST YOUR KNOWLEDGE

1. Name the two gases used to form the oxy-acetylene flame.
2. What is the chief value of oxygen to the welding industry?
3. From where is oxygen obtained for use in welding and other areas?
4. By what process is most commercial oxygen obtained?
5. What other process can be used to obtain oxygen?
6. How was oxygen first obtained?

4-5 ACETYLENE

Acetylene gas is a chemical combination of two elements: carbon and hydrogen. It was first discovered by Edmund Davey in 1835, but his method of manufacturing the gas was very slow and expensive. In 1892, Thomas L. Willson, a Canadian inventor, was experimenting in his shop heating limestone and coke (soft coal) in an electric furnace. His experiment was a failure, but as he dumped the waste into a small creek behind his shop, a pollution practice that would not be tolerated today, a gas was given off. This gas proved to be acetylene gas. By accident he had discovered an inexpensive method of manufacturing acetylene gas.

TEST YOUR KNOWLEDGE

1. What two elements combine to form acetylene gas?
2. How was the inexpensive method of manufacturing acetylene gas discovered?
3. What two substances were heated in Willson's electric furnace?

ACETYLENE PRODUCTION

When limestone and coke are heated together in an electric furnace, they fuse, producing a new substance. This substance is called calcium carbide. When calcium carbide is brought into contact with water, acetylene gas is produced. There are two methods of manufacturing acetylene gas: water is added to carbide (Figure 4-3), or carbide is added to water (Figure 4-4). Either of these two methods produces what is known as **generated acetylene**. Because of the high temperatures generated, the possible ignition of the gases, and the need for cooling, the carbide to water method is preferred. The large volume of water eliminates these hazards. After the gas is generated, it is dried, purified, and stored in steel cylinders. It is then called **dissolved acetylene**.

An Acetylene Generator

The generating unit (when carbide is added to water) consists of a carbide hopper mounted on a feed chamber and a water tank. The carbide feed mechanism is driven by a water-powered engine. The water supply is regulated automatically, according to the gas consumption, and the calcium carbide is fed slowly and regularly into a large volume of water in the tank. This ensures complete decomposition of the calcium carbide and a high yield of acetylene gas.

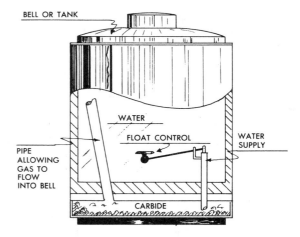

Figure 4-3   Water to carbide generator

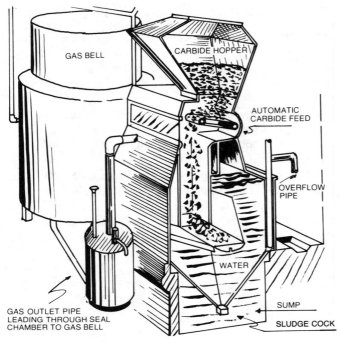

Figure 4-4   Carbide to water generator

When calcium carbide (CaC_2) is brought into contact with water, the reaction is instantaneous and the carbon in the carbide combines with the hydrogen in the water, forming acetylene (while the calcium combines with the oxygen to form slaked lime). The exhaust water from the engine is taken into the generating tank in such a way that it helps to circulate the water in the tank, stirring up the carbide deposit and keeping a uniform water temperature. This circulation also keeps the slaked lime in suspension. The lime is discharged with the overflow.

The chemical reaction between calcium carbide and water also causes considerable heating of the carbide. These high temperatures are undesirable, since they result in a lower gas yield. There is also a risk that the gases might ignite either because of the hot carbide or by the breaking down of the gas itself (polymerisation). (This simply means that the gas splits up into tarry substances and other gases, causing a sudden rise in temperature.) An important feature of good generation, therefore, is cooling. The rate of generation must also be carefully controlled, since rapid generation can result

in an impure gas. As the acetylene gas passes out of the generator and through the water, it is washed. It then proceeds through a drying unit and then a purification unit, finally emerging as a high-purity gas.

POINTS TO REMEMBER

- Oxygen is used with a fuel gas to produce a flame.
- There are a number of fuel gases.
- Many fuel gases are shipped in liquefied form.
- Flames burn in two stages.
- The hottest part of the flame is at the top of the inner cone.
- Acetylene gas is a chemical combination of carbon and hydrogen.
- The oxy-acetylene process may be used for any flame operation.
- The most common process of extracting oxygen is the liquid air process.
- When calcium carbide combines with water, it forms acetylene gas.
- Oxygen will greatly speed up combustion.

WORDS TO REMEMBER

fuel	chemical	oxidation
hydrogen	cone	carbon
propane	envelope	calcium carbide
acetylene	thermal	generated
FLAMEX	intensity	slaked
flashback	combustion	polymerisation
primary	unstable	unites
secondary	oxygen	extract

REVIEW QUESTIONS

1. Name three fuel gases.
2. How is hydrogen gas produced?
3. What measurements are used to measure heat?
4. Where is the hottest part of the flame located?
5. Which oxyfuel gas has the highest temperature?
6. Name two advantages that the newer fuel gases have over acetylene gas.
7. What makes the oxy-acetylene flame so versatile?

8. Name the different forms in which oxygen may be obtained.

9. What is the name of the process most used to produce oxygen?

10. Other than welding, name two other uses for pure oxygen.

11. Why is the electrolytic process not used to produce commercial oxygen?

12. How is calcium carbide produced?

13. What two methods are used to produce acetylene gas?

14. What is meant by the term *dissolved acetylene*?

15. Which method of generating acetylene gas is preferred?

BASIC EQUIPMENT FOR OXY-ACETYLENE

Before attempting to weld, it is necessary to understand the various pieces of equipment and their purpose. In order to ensure safe operation and prevent any possible explosion or injury to oneself and others, thorough familiarity with the equipment and with safety precautions is necessary.

5-1 BASIC EQUIPMENT

The basic equipment for oxyfuel welding is shown in Figure 5-1. It consists of

1. oxygen and fuel gas in cylinders
2. valves
3. regulators
4. hose
5. torch
6. tips

   All of the above equipment is designed with the one purpose in mind: to produce and control an oxyfuel flame. This chapter will refer specifically to the oxyacetylene flame, a common oxyfuel mixture.

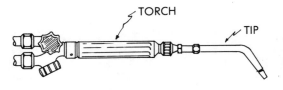

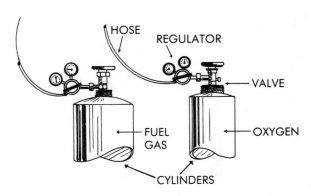

Figure 5-1   Basic equipment for oxyfuel welding

5-2 THE OXYGEN CYLINDER

Oxygen in a gaseous form (as a gas) is usually delivered to the consumer in steel cylinders (Figure 5-2). Large industries may require tank cars or huge cylinders of liquid oxygen and convert the liquid oxygen to gas as it is needed. Steel cylinders for normal use are manufactured in a variety of sizes, and the gas in them is compressed at 15 MPa (2200 psi) at 21°C (or 70°F, normal room temperature). The cylinders are hollow shells, specially constructed to withstand the extremely high pressure of the gas inside (Figure 5-3). They have **right-hand threads**.

THE OXYGEN CYLINDER VALVE

Figure 5-4 shows a typical oxygen cylinder valve. This valve should be opened all the way while the cylinder is in use to permit an unrestricted flow of gas and to act as a seal. A safety device is located on the valve opposite the regulator connection or outlet.

The safety device is in the form of a hexagonal nut

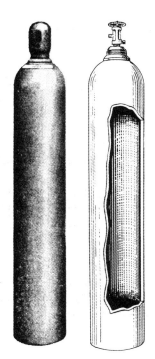

Courtesy of Union Carbide Limited

Figure 5-3   Internal construction of the oxygen cylinder

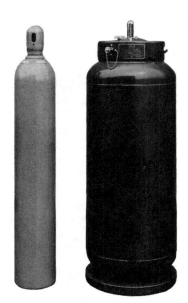

Courtesy of Union Carbide Canada Limited

Figure 5-2   Oxygen cylinders

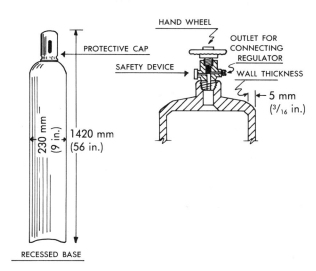

Figure 5-4   Oxygen cylinder valve

with small holes. Behind this nut is a disc made of special material which will burst if the pressure inside the cylinder becomes too great, allowing the gas to escape through the holes in the nut. If a cylinder is accidentally heated, the gas inside will expand, creating pressure on the cylinder. The safety device is installed for just such an accident.

> Care should be taken with oxygen cylinders. They should not be exposed to extreme heat. They should not be used as anvils, that is, hammered upon. They should **not be allowed to stand upright** unless they are fastened to a stationary object.

> Because of the high pressure inside a full cylinder, never stand directly in front of the outlet when opening the cylinder valve.

TEST YOUR KNOWLEDGE

1. What is the usual method of shipping oxygen?
2. What is the pressure in a full cylinder of oxygen?
3. Describe the safety device on an oxygen cylinder.
4. What is the purpose of this safety device?
5. Where is the safety device located?

5-3 THE ACETYLENE CYLINDER

The acetylene cylinder is usually shorter and wider than the oxygen cylinder (Figure 5-5). It is made in more than one section, while the oxygen cylinder is of one piece. It is not a hollow shell as is the oxygen cylinder, and it has **left-hand threads**.

Acetylene gas cannot be used at more than 100 kPa (15 psi).* If pressures higher than this are used, there is a danger of explosion. To prevent the danger of explosion and to allow a large quantity of gas to be stored, the acetylene cylinder is filled with a mixture of shredded asbestos, cement, and charcoal, or some similar mixture, in the form of a paste. The cylinder halves are then

Courtesy of Canadian Liquid Air Ltd.
Courtesy of Union Carbide Canada Limited

Figure 5-5   Acetylene cylinders

welded together, and the cylinder baked until the mixture dries.

The mixture inside the cylinder dries in a form like a honeycomb (Figure 5-6). A liquid called *acetone* is forced into the small compartments of this honeycomb arrangement. Acetone will absorb or dissolve 25 times its own volume of acetylene. The honeycomb arrangement has the advantage of localizing any decomposition that might result if a flame were accidentally played on the side of the cylinder.

> *The 100 kPa (15psi) reading given here and all other pressure readings given in this text represent *gauge* pressures, not *absolute* pressures. If your shop is still equipped with gauges calibrated in pounds per square inch, do not attempt to use acetylene gas at pressures greater than 15 psi.

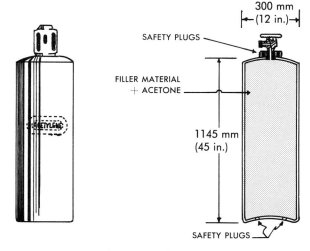

Figure 5-6   Acetylene cylinder

Unlike oxygen cylinders, cylinders that contain liquid acetone should always be stored **in an upright position**. If they are left on their sides, the acetone will flow into the cylinder valve and be drawn into the weld area. This will be harmful to the weld.

Acetylene gas is inflammable and highly explosive. Great care must be taken in handling the gas and the cylinders that contain it. This gas is mildly poisonous and can cause headache and nausea if inhaled for long periods of time.

SAFETY PLUGS

Like the oxygen cylinder, the acetylene cylinder has a safety device. This device is made of small machine bolts set into the steel shell of the cylinder. The number and location of the bolts vary, but there are usually at least four: two at the top and two at the bottom of the cylinder. The bolts are held in place by a special type of

Lead melts at 105°C (220°F), and the temperature of the oxy-acetylene flame is approximately 3315°C (6000°F). It is, therefore, very important to keep the flame away from the cylinders.

lead which melts at a temperature of 105°C (220°F). If the lead melts, the gas forces the bolts out.

Common problems for all cylinders are:
a. threads damaged by rough usage, or dirt on threads making connections impossible to seat properly, causing gas leakage;
b. safety discs or plugs, broken or leaking;
c. valve handles difficult to open or close;
d. the double-seating arrangement in some valves not seating properly and allowing gas to escape. (Figure 5-7 shows a valve with a double-seating arrangement.)

Any cylinder with suspected damage should be returned immediately to the supplier for repair, with an explanation of the problem. The cylinders are the responsibility of the manufacturer. No attempt should be made to repair the fault.

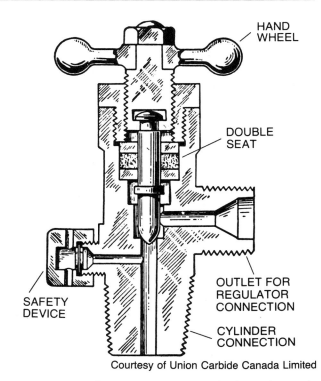

Courtesy of Union Carbide Canada Limited

Figure 5-7   High-pressure oxygen cylinder valve with double-seating arrangement

TEST YOUR KNOWLEDGE

1. Why must great care be taken when handling cylinders?
2. What term describes acetylene after it has been stored in cylinders?
3. Describe the differences between the oxygen cylinder and the acetylene cylinder.
4. What is the maximum pressure under which acetylene should be used?
5. What liquid is used in the acetylene cylinder?
6. How much acetylene can be dissolved by acetone?
7. Describe the safety device on the acetylene cylinder.
8. Why must the flame be kept away from the safety plugs on the acetylene cylinder?
9. Why are acetylene cylinders always stored in an upright position?
10. Describe the inner construction of an acetylene cylinder.

5-4 REGULATORS AND GAUGES

Regulators (Figure 5-8) are used in many different ways. For example, they are used by divers in underwater

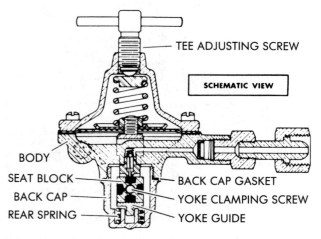

Courtesy MECO St. Louis, U.S.A.

Figure 5-8   Regulator

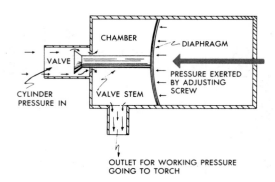

Figure 5-9   Principle of the single-stage regulator

equipment. The main purpose or function of a regulator is to reduce the very high pressure of the cylinder to a low, safe, working pressure and give an even, continuous flow of gas.

REGULATOR OPERATION

Figure 5-9 shows the action that takes place inside the single-stage regulator. The gas from the cylinder enters at the regulator connection and proceeds through the hose to the outlet connected to the torch.

The high-pressure gas enters the body of the regulator through a small nozzle controlled by a valve and flows into the chamber of the regulator. The pressure in the chamber rises until it is high enough to overcome the pressure of the spring. When this happens, the diaphragm is then deflected to the right and the valve, which is attached to it, closes and prevents any more gas from entering the chamber.

As the gas is withdrawn from the chamber by opening the torch valves, the pressure in the chamber falls below a certain point. The tension of the spring will deflect the diaphragm to the left again, reopening the valve. When the pressure of the spring and the pressure of the gas in the chamber are balanced, a constant flow of gas to the torch will result. The position of the diaphragm is controlled by a balance of forces between a compressed spring on one side and the pressure of the gas on the other. (Detailed illustrations of regulators appear in figures 5-10 and 5-11.)

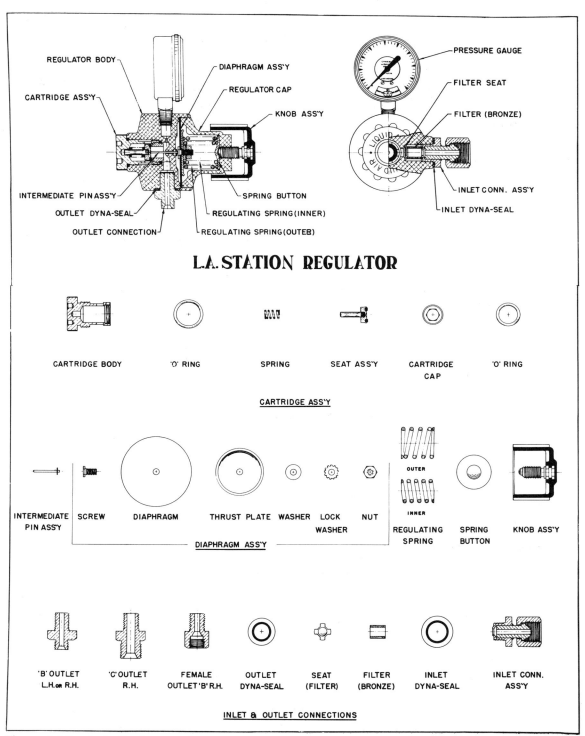

Figure 5-10   L.A. Station regulator

Courtesy of Canadian Liquid Air Ltd.

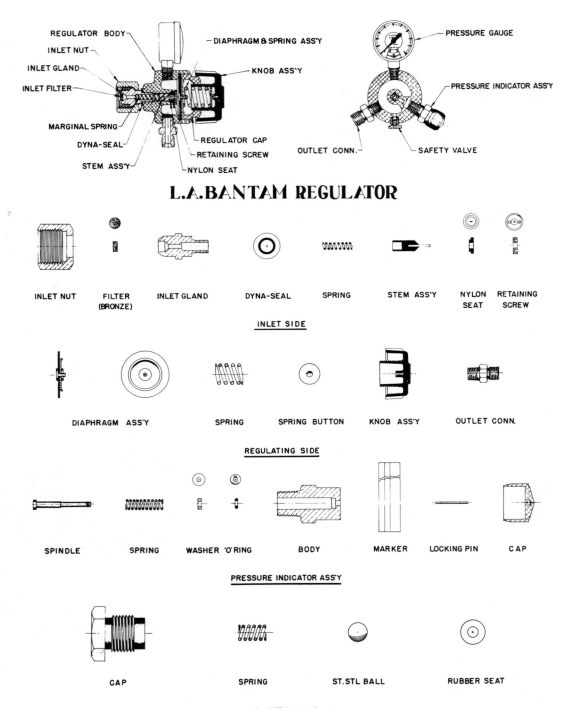

L.A.BANTAM REGULATOR

INLET SIDE

REGULATING SIDE

PRESSURE INDICATOR ASS'Y

SAFETY VALVE

Figure 5-11   L.A. Bantam regulator   Courtesy of Canadian Liquid Air Ltd.

Oil and grease must not touch the regulator. Hands, gloves, and tools must be free of oil and grease. When these substances come into contact with high-pressure oxygen, they decompose, forming carbon dioxide and water vapour. This combination can result in an explosion.

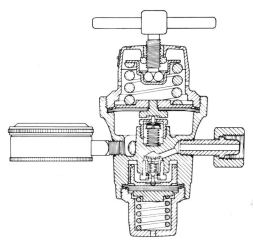

Courtesy of Union Carbide Canada Limited

If a pressure-adjusting screw is inserted to press on the end of the spring and vary the tension, any desired pressure can be obtained at the outlet. However, if the pressure-adjusting screw is turned **in** first and the cylinder valve then opened, the total pressure suddenly exerted against the average diaphragm of 4.5 cm² (7 sq. in.) is 106 MPa (15 400 psi). The impact usually results in severe damage to the regulator. Some manufacturers have installed a device to prevent this kind of damage from occurring.

It is important to check that the pressure-adjusting screw is turned out before opening the cylinder valve.

TEST YOUR KNOWLEDGE

1. What is the main purpose of a regulator?
2. Why should there never be oil and grease on or near a regulator?
3. Excluding welding, give an example of the use of a regulator.

TWO-STAGE REGULATORS

In a two-stage, or double-stage, regulator (Figure 5-12), the pressure reduction takes place in two stages. In the first stage, the tension of the spring is set by the manufacturer so that the pressure in the high-pressure chamber will be a certain fixed amount. In the second stage, the gas then passes from this chamber into a second reducing chamber that is supplied with a screw adjustment which makes it possible to obtain any desired pressure at the torch outlet (within the range of the regulator). There will be less fluctuation in the gas flow with a two-stage regulator than with a single-stage regulator. Figure

Courtesy of Canadian Liquid Air Ltd.

Figure 5-12   Two-stage regulator

5-13 gives a detailed view of a double-stage regulator. All parts of an assembled regulator are shown in Figure 5-14.

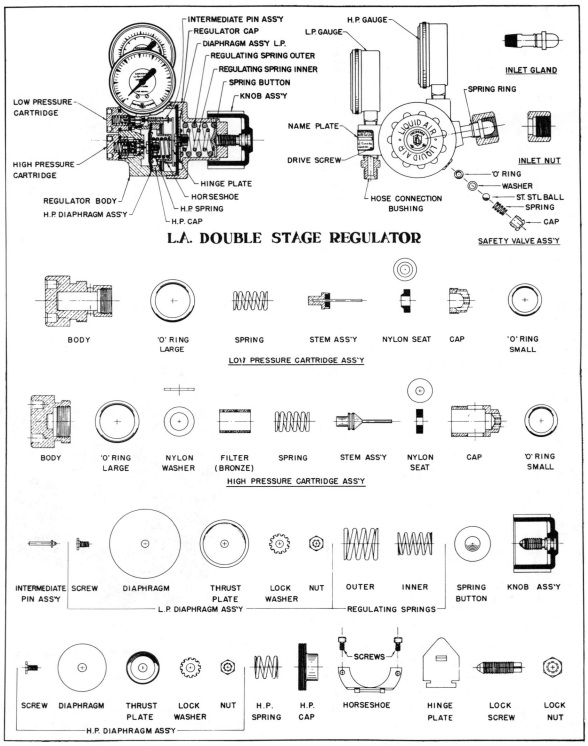

Figure 5-13   L.A. Double-stage regulator

Courtesy of Canadian Liquid Air Ltd.

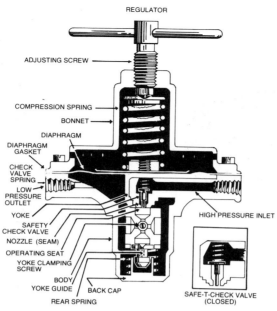

REGULATOR

ADJUSTING SCREW

COMPRESSION SPRING

BONNET

DIAPHRAGM

DIAPHRAGM GASKET

CHECK VALVE SPRING

LOW PRESSURE OUTLET

YOKE

SAFETY CHECK VALVE

NOZZLE (SEAM)

OPERATING SEAT

YOKE CLAMPING SCREW

BODY

YOKE GUIDE

REAR SPRING

BACK CAP

HIGH PRESSURE INLET

SAFE-T-CHECK VALVE (CLOSED)

Figure 5-14   Assembled regulator

Courtesy MECO St. Louis, U.S.A.

GAUGES

Oxygen and acetylene regulators are usually equipped with two gauges: one to indicate the pressure remaining in the cylinder and the other to indicate the pressure of the gas which is being delivered to the torch (Figure 5-15). Another type of regulator on the market is the one shown in Figure 5-16. This regulator does not have any gauges, and the working pressures are calibrated on the side.

Common problems with regulators are:

a. With the cylinder valve open and the pressure being adjusted, the needle of the gauge may jump erratically rather than moving steadily as pressure is increased. This could be an indication of diaphragm problems.

b. If the torch valve is closed and the pressure continues to increase on the gauge, it could be an indication that the valve seat is at fault.

c. If the needle of the gauge does not return to zero after the torch valve has been closed and the pressure released, it could indicate that the gauge mechanism has been damaged or sprung by the sudden release of high-pressure gas because the cylinder valve was opened too quickly.

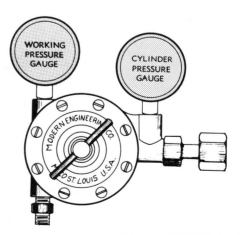

WORKING PRESSURE GAUGE

CYLINDER PRESSURE GAUGE

MODERN ENGINEERING CO.

ST. LOUIS U.S.A.

Courtesy MECO St. Louis, U.S.A.

Figure 5-15   Gauges

Courtesy of Canadian Liquid Air Ltd.

Figure 5-16   Regulator without a gauge

TEST YOUR KNOWLEDGE

1. Describe the purpose of the two gauges on the regulator.
2. What check should be made before the cylinder valve is opened?
3. Explain the difference between a two-stage and a single-stage regulator.

THE MANIFOLD SYSTEM

Many schools and industries use the manifold system, which consists of a number of cylinders connected and located at a central area (Figure 5-17). The gases are piped from this area to the various welding stations. This system has the advantage of leaving the working area around the welding stations free of cylinders. Because the acetylene gas must come out of the acetone solution, the flow of gas from an acetylene cylinder should

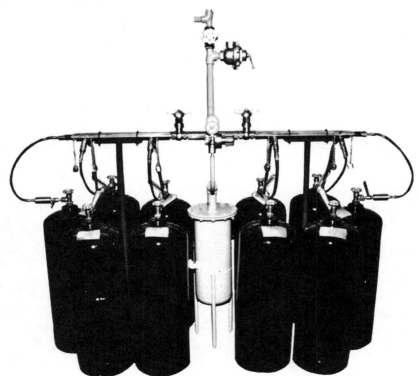

Courtesy of Canadian Liquid Air Ltd.

Figure 5-17   Acetylene manifold system

Courtesy of Union Carbide Canada Limited

Figure 5-18   Hose

not be more than 1/7 of the cylinder capacity. If it is greater, acetone will be drawn off with it. By using a manifold system, this problem is eliminated.

5-5 HOSES

Welding torches must be connected to the gas supply outlets with a good grade of hose (Figure 5-18). Acetylene hose is red; oxygen hose is green. The hose connections are threaded differently. The acetylene connecting nut has a left-hand thread, while the oxygen connecting nut has a right-hand thread. As a further precaution to prevent accidental interchange and to make identification easier, a groove is cut around the centre of the acetylene connecting nuts.

1. Never interchange hoses or fittings on hoses.
2. Test all hoses periodically for leaks by immersing them in water, using normal working pressure.
3. Do not let oil or grease come into contact with hoses.
4. Never use wire or tape to repair a hose. Wire will cut the hose, and tape is a poor substitute for proper repair.
5. Protect hose at all times from sparks and sharp objects.

5-6 WELDING TORCHES

The welding torch, sometimes called a blowpipe, has the following parts (figures 5-19 and 5-20):

1. **Two inlets** to supply oxygen and acetylene to the torch.
2. **Two needle valves** to control the flow of the gases and to make adjustments to the flame.
3. **A body** to which the inlets and valves are connected. This body is the part held by the welder.

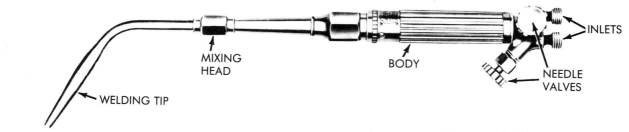

Figure 5-19   Welding torch

Courtesy of Union Carbide Canada Limited

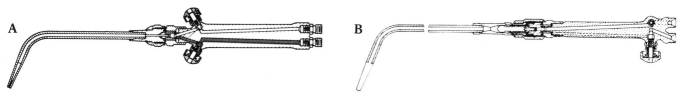

Figure 5-20   Welding Torches: internal views

Courtesy MECO St. Louis, U.S.A.

Hoses   **43**

Courtesy of Union Carbide Canada Limited

Figure 5-21   Injector torch

4. **A mixing head** to mix the gases in the correct amounts.
5. **A welding tip** to concentrate and direct the flame. The welding tips come in a variety of sizes, allowing the welder to obtain many different flame sizes using the same torch handle.

These torches are precision tools designed and constructed after careful study and should be treated as such. There are many types and designs of torches. However, all torches fall into two basic categories: the injector torch and the **medium-pressure** torch.

In the injector torch (Figure 5-21), the gases are mixed by means of an injector nozzle. The oxygen is at a much higher pressure than the acetylene. When the high-pressure oxygen passes through the nozzle, it draws in the correct amount of acetylene to produce the desired flame.

In the medium-pressure torch, the gases are mixed in a gas mixer. The most popular torch in this group is the equal- or balanced-pressure torch, in which the oxygen and acetylene are supplied at equal pressures and come together in the mixer in the correct amounts (see Figure 5-22). When the welding tip is changed, it is also necessary to change the mixer of the injector torch. In the equal-pressure torch, the mixer will serve all or a wide range of tips.

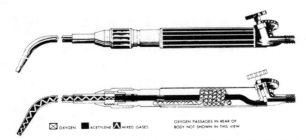

Courtesy of Union Carbide Canada Limited

Figure 5-22   Purox-W-201 balanced-pressure torch

When setting the pressures to be used with these torches, the standard procedure is as follows:

Injector torch. The acetylene pressure is set at 7 kPa (1 psi) or less. The oxygen pressure is usually stamped on the mixer that corresponds with the tip.

Equal-pressure torch. The pressure of oxygen and acetylene is set according to the tip size. For example, a number 1 tip would require the regulators to be set at 7 kPa oxygen and 7 kPa (1 psi) acetylene. Figures 5-23 to 5-26 show some of the types and designs of welding torches on the market today.

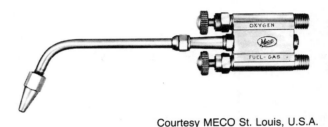

Courtesy MECO St. Louis, U.S.A.

Figure 5-23   Welding and brazing torch

TEST YOUR KNOWLEDGE

1. Name the two basic categories of torches.
2. What is another name for a welding torch?
3. Name the five basic parts of a welding torch.
4. Describe the method of mixing gases in each of the two basic types of welding torch.
5. What type of torch requires changing the tip only?
6. Why should a torch be treated with care?

Common problems with torches (including cutting torches and attachments):
a. When torch valves are closed, but pressure is still in hose, and a small amount of gas still issues from the torch tip, it may indicate that valves are not seating properly and should be repacked or replaced.
b. Normally the body and mixer of the torch require little maintenance unless they have been subjected to severe abuse. However, if excessive backfiring, flashback, or gas leaks are experienced, it indicates that the seating has dirt, nicks, or dents, or that the seal rings

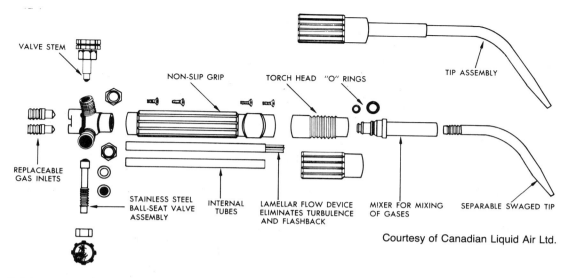

VALVE STEM

NON-SLIP GRIP

TORCH HEAD "O" RINGS

TIP ASSEMBLY

REPLACEABLE GAS INLETS

STAINLESS STEEL BALL-SEAT VALVE ASSEMBLY

INTERNAL TUBES

LAMELLAR FLOW DEVICE ELIMINATES TURBULENCE AND FLASHBACK

MIXER FOR MIXING OF GASES

SEPARABLE SWAGED TIP

Courtesy of Canadian Liquid Air Ltd.

Figure 5-24   Parts of a welding torch

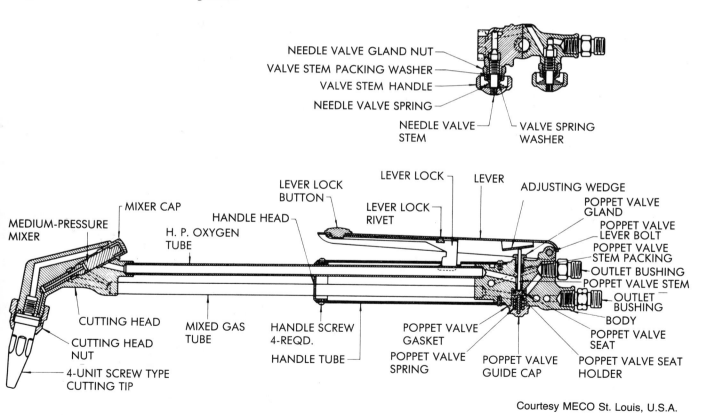

NEEDLE VALVE GLAND NUT

VALVE STEM PACKING WASHER

VALVE STEM HANDLE

NEEDLE VALVE SPRING

NEEDLE VALVE STEM

VALVE SPRING WASHER

LEVER LOCK BUTTON

LEVER LOCK

LEVER

ADJUSTING WEDGE

LEVER LOCK RIVET

HANDLE HEAD

MIXER CAP

MEDIUM-PRESSURE MIXER

H. P. OXYGEN TUBE

POPPET VALVE GLAND

POPPET VALVE LEVER BOLT

POPPET VALVE STEM PACKING

OUTLET BUSHING

POPPET VALVE STEM

OUTLET BUSHING

BODY

POPPET VALVE SEAT

POPPET VALVE SEAT HOLDER

CUTTING HEAD

CUTTING HEAD NUT

4-UNIT SCREW TYPE CUTTING TIP

MIXED GAS TUBE

HANDLE SCREW 4-REQD.

HANDLE TUBE

POPPET VALVE GASKET

POPPET VALVE SPRING

POPPET VALVE GUIDE CAP

Courtesy MECO St. Louis, U.S.A.

Figure 5-25   MECO cutting torch

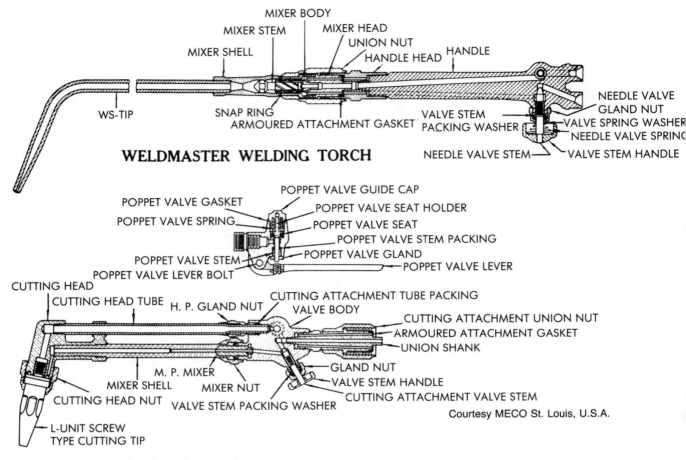

WELDMASTER WELDING TORCH

Courtesy MECO St. Louis, U.S.A.

Figure 5-26 Torch and cutting attachment

(sometimes called "O" rings) are damaged or missing.
c. An erratic flame issuing from the torch, after the usual cleaning procedures have been carried out, could be an indication of carbon build-up inside the mixer. This is usually caused by excessive backfiring. Backfiring in itself is an indication that the equipment is faulty and should be checked.

WELDING TIPS

Welding tips are usually made of soft copper and come in a variety of sizes. The size of the tip is determined by the diameter of the hole (orifice) at the end of the tip (Figure 5-27). Tip cleaners should be used to keep the hole clear. Care must be taken in cleaning the tip.

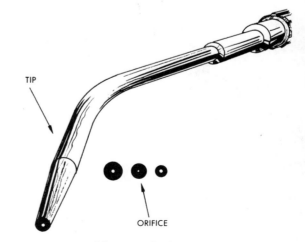

Figure 5-27 Welding torch tip

Although a large tip will release a greater amount of gas, the intensity of the flame will be the same. That is, the welding flame will be approximately 3315° C (6000°F) regardless of the size of tip used. To understand this look at Figure 5-28. Both kettles contain the same amount of water and are the same size and make. The temperature of the two flames is the same, but A has a much larger flame than B. Which of the two kettles will boil first? A is the correct answer. So with welding tips, a larger tip will heat the metal more quickly, but it will not make the metal any hotter.

Figure 5-28   Which of the two kettles will boil first?

The threads must be examined carefully before attaching the tip to the torch. A damaged thread can cause a leakage of gas, resulting in a fire or explosion. It can also ruin the torch body. It is important to avoid cross-threading the connection. Graphite or beeswax may be used to lubricate the threads, but not oil. The connections should be checked each time before the torch is used. Most connections require tightening by hand only.

TIP SELECTION

For best results, the proper tip size must be chosen. The proper tip size is determined by the thickness of the metal to be welded. If the tip is too large for the thickness of the metal, overheating will result, and the metal will be burned through. If this does happen, **do not** turn down the pressure, as this causes the flame to backfire or keep popping out. It can also damage the tip.

If the tip size is too small for the thickness of the metal, the metal will take a long time to melt (if it melts at all). **Do not** increase the pressure: this only causes a harsh, noisy flame, which will blow away from the end of the tip.

TIP CLEANERS

Only approved tip cleaners should be used to clean the welding tips. Two of the more popular types are shown in figures 5-29 and 5-30. They are designed to clean tips without enlarging the holes or scratching the smooth finish inside the tip.

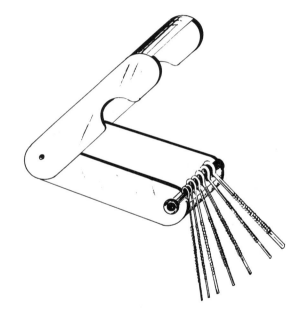

Figure 5-29   Welding tip cleaners

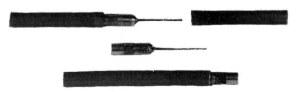

Courtesy of Union Carbide Canada Limited

Figure 5-30   Welding tip cleaning drills

TEST YOUR KNOWLEDGE

1. Describe the effects of using too large a tip.
2. Describe the effects of using too small a tip.

5-7 WELDING ACCESSORIES

WELDING GOGGLES

Goggles (Figure 5-31) protect the eyes from the glare of the flame, from flying sparks, and from hot metal. The goggles are made from heat-resistant material, are ventilated, and are very lightweight.

Welding goggles contain optical lenses manufactured in varying shades (usually green) to cut down the glare of the flame. Since these lenses are quite expensive, they are protected by a clear lens of plastic or glass. The goggles are equipped with an adjustable headband.

Courtesy of Canadian Liquid Air Ltd.

Figure 5-31   Welding goggles

1. You have only one pair of eyes; guard them well.
2. Wear goggles at all times when welding. See that they are clean.
3. Do not tie knots in the headband of the goggles.
4. Make sure that the clear lenses are inserted at the proper place.
5. Replace all broken or cracked lenses at once.

FRICTION LIGHTERS

Friction lighters (Figure 5-32) should always be used to light the torch.

A match or another torch should never be used. With a match, the hand is always close to the flame and may be severely burned. Using another torch for lighting could result in an explosion.

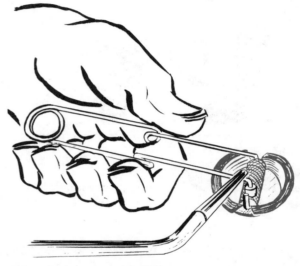

Figure 5-32   Friction lighter

WRENCHES

Wrenches of the correct size and design are supplied by the manufacturers of welding equipment (Figure 5-33). These wrenches should always be used, rather than adjustable wrenches.

Courtesy of Canadian Liquid Air Ltd.

Figure 5-33   Wrench

GLOVES AND MITTS

When large or heavy pieces of metal are welded, some heat radiation is given off. Whether a welder wears gloves or not is a matter of personal choice. Difficulty in holding and manipulating the welding rod may be experienced with gloves. If gloves are worn, however, they should be the gauntlet type and made of fire-resistant material (Figure 5-34).

> Gloves and mitts should be kept free of oil and grease and should not be used to handle hot metal.

Courtesy of Canadian Liquid Air Ltd.

Figure 5-34   Gloves and mitts

POINTS TO REMEMBER

- Oxygen and acetylene connections have different threads and must be stored differently.
- Cylinders must be handled with care.
- Safety plugs should not be tampered with at any time.
- Regulators are delicate instruments. Treat them with care.
- Tips must be handled with care.
- Use only approved cleaners for welding tips.
- Goggles are for your protection. Wear them.

WORDS TO REMEMBER

cylinders	safety plugs	injector
thread	gauge	orifice
pressure	manifold	goggles
regulator	blowpipe	

REVIEW QUESTIONS

1. List five safety precautions to be taken in handling cylinders.
2. What is the main purpose of a regulator?
3. What is the purpose of a manifold system?
4. What steps should be taken if you suspect that the equipment is defective?
5. What are some of the common problem areas associated with cylinders?
6. What precautions should be followed with a faulty cylinder?
7. Describe two common problems that can occur in regulators.
8. What faults can occur if a torch has a leaky valve?
9. What are some of the problems that might be indicated if excessive backfiring occurs?
10. Describe and state the purpose of the safety device on an oxygen cylinder.
11. Why should the pressure-adjusting screw be turned **out** before opening the cylinder valve?
12. Describe five differences between an oxygen cylinder and an acetylene cylinder.
13. Describe one application other than welding for which the oxy-acetylene flame can be used.
14. List the five basic parts of a welding torch, describing the purpose of each part.
15. Describe the two methods of mixing the gases in a welding torch.
16. What is the purpose of acetone in the acetylene cylinder?
17. Oil should never be used on a regulator. Explain.

CHAPTER

ASSEMBLING AND DISMANTLING FOR OXY-ACETYLENE: TYPES OF FLAMES

6-1   Steps in Assembling Oxy-Acetylene Equipment
6-2   Steps in Shutting Down and Disconnecting the Equipment
6-3   Lighting the Torch and Adjusting the Flame
6-4   Steps in Extinguishing the Flame
6-5   Types of Oxy-Acetylene Flames
6-6   Backfire and Flashback

Having studied the various pieces of equipment and their purpose, the next step is to assemble the equipment for use. This chapter will describe proper and safe methods of assembling and dismantling oxyfuel equipment. You will also find a description of the various types of flames and their effects on metal at the end of the chapter. This will be the first exercise in using the oxy-acetylene equipment and one which is very important. (Figure 6-1 shows one type of oxy-acetylene equipment.) As you work through this chapter, you should observe the effects of the different flames very carefully because the type of flame used can make the difference between a good weld or a poor weld.

6-1 STEPS IN ASSEMBLING OXY-ACETYLENE EQUIPMENT

In assembling and dismantling oxy-acetylene equipment, a routine must be followed. This routine is laid out step by step for your protection and to avoid damaging the equipment.

1. Secure the cylinders with a chain to a stationary object (Figure 6-2). Keep the cylinders upright.
2. Remove the valve protecting caps (Figure 6-3).
3. Blow out any dust in the regulator connection by **cracking**. Cracking means opening and closing the valve quickly. Note the position of the hands in Figure 6-4. Sometimes the valves stick and are difficult to turn. If this happens, place the hands as shown in the illustration and push down. At the same time, give a quick jerk in the direction of opening (counterclockwise).

Be sure that the cylinder is not pointing towards anyone. Keep it away from any open flame. Stand opposite to the side from which the high-pressure oxygen is released while cracking.

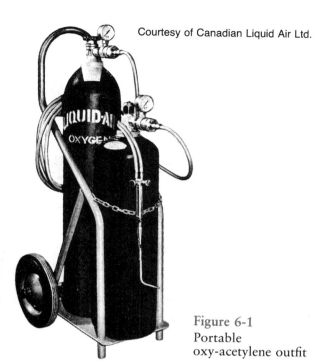

Courtesy of Canadian Liquid Air Ltd.

Figure 6-1
Portable
oxy-acetylene outfit

Courtesy of Union Carbide Canada Limited

Figure 6-2   Secure the cylinders with a chain

VALVE PROTECTING CAPS

Courtesy of Canadian Liquid Air Ltd.

Figure 6-3   Oxygen and acetylene cylinders

4. Check the cylinder and the regulator threads for damage. Attach the oxygen regulator to the oxygen cylinder. Attach the acetylene regulator to the acetylene cylinder (Figure 6-5). Remember to use the correct wrench. Remember also that acetylene connections have left-hand threads; oxygen connections have right-hand threads. Never force any connection. If difficulty is experienced, notify the instructor.

5. Check that the pressure-adjusting screw is turned out. Blow out any dust that may be in the regulator. This is done by opening the cylinder valve slowly, and then turning in the pressure-adjusting screw until a small amount of gas flows from the opening to which the hose will be attached (see Figure 6-6). Close the cylinder valve, and release the pressure-adjusting screw. Follow this routine with both regulators.

Courtesy of Union Carbide Canada Limited

Figure 6-4   Cracking cylinder valves. The operator is on the side of the outlet *opposite* to the side from which the high-pressure oxygen is released.

Courtesy of Union Carbide Canada Limited

Figure 6-5   Attaching the regulator

Courtesy of Union Carbide Canada Limited

Figure 6-6   Blowing out the regulator

Remember that acetylene gas is flammable. Do not release it near open flames or hot objects.

6. Attach the oxygen hose to the oxygen regulator, and the acetylene hose to the acetylene regulator (Figure 6-7). Check both connections for damaged threads beforehand.

Courtesy of Union Carbide Canada Limited

Figure 6-7   Attaching the hose

7. Attach the other end of the oxygen hose to the oxygen inlet of the torch, and the acetylene hose to the acetylene inlet of the torch. Again, check for damaged threads.

Remember that the **oxygen** hose is green and has **right-hand threads**; the **acetylene** hose is red and has **left-hand threads**.

8. Attach the welding tip to the torch.

Remember to check the threads for damage before attaching. Do not force and be careful not to cross-thread.

9. Open the oxygen cylinder valve and the acetylene cylinder valve slowly. Remember to open the oxygen valve all the way and the acetylene valve one and one-half turns.
10. Make sure that the torch needle valves are closed. Turn in the pressure-adjusting screws one at a time until the desired pressure shows on the gauges (Figure 6-8). The equipment is now correctly assembled and ready to be tested for leaks.

Courtesy Harris Calorific Company

Figure 6-8   Turning in the pressure-adjusting screws

Remember that if the cylinder valves are opened too quickly, the mechanism inside the gauge may become damaged, resulting in possible injury to yourself or to others.

TESTING FOR LEAKS

After the equipment has been assembled, it should be tested for leaks at the points shown in Figure 6-9.
A Oxygen cylinder valve
B Acetylene cylinder valve
C Oxygen regulator connection
D Acetylene regulator connection
E Oxygen and acetylene hose connections
F Oxygen and acetylene needle valves on torch

The soap solution for testing is applied to the points shown with a small brush. With the torch valves closed and the pressure applied, any leaks at the connection will show up in the form of small bubbles at the point where the gas is escaping.

If there are no leaks, wipe off the connections with a clean rag. If there are leaks, wipe off and tighten the connections, then reapply the solution. When you are sure that there are no more leaks, wipe off all connections with a clean rag.

Check with your instructor before testing to make sure that the proper precautions have been taken and that the equipment is ready for testing.
Be sure that hands and gloves are free of grease and oil.
Check the threads on connections for damage before assembly.
Use only an approved wrench.
Do not use unnecessary force with the wrench.
Be careful where you release unlit gases.
Do not open an acetylene cylinder valve more than one and one-half turns.
Check all connections for leaks.

Figure 6-9   Testing for leaks

Courtesy of Union Carbide Canada Limited

6-2 STEPS IN SHUTTING DOWN AND DISCONNECTING THE EQUIPMENT

1. Close the acetylene cylinder valve.
2. Close the oxygen cylinder valve.
3. Open the acetylene torch valve to drain the gas from the hose and the regulator.
4. Close the acetylene torch valve.
5. Release the acetylene pressure-adjusting screw. Turn the screw counterclockwise (to the left).
6. Open the oxygen torch valve to drain the hose and the regulator.
7. Close the oxygen torch valve.
8. Release the oxygen pressure-adjusting screw (as in step 5).
9. Dismantle the regulators, hose, torch, and tip.
10. Replace the valve protecting caps.
11. Store the equipment in the proper storage area.

6-3 LIGHTING THE TORCH AND ADJUSTING THE FLAME

This is the operation performed most often by the oxy-acetylene welder. It is essential to learn to do this safely, quickly, and efficiently. Two distinct methods are outlined for the safe and efficient lighting and adjusting of the torch.

Method A

1. Check that the equipment is properly assembled and the torch valves closed.
2. After observing the rules stated earlier, open the main valves, cylinder, or pipeline.
3. Set the gauges to the desired pressure by turning in the pressure-adjusting screws one at a time.
4. Hold the torch in one hand with the torch valves pointing up.
5. Hold the friction lighter in the other hand (Figure 6-10).

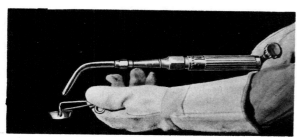

Courtesy of Union Carbide Canada Limited

Figure 6-10   Lighting the torch

6. Open the acetylene torch valve to the left, a 1/4 turn or less.
7. Hold the friction lighter close to the tip, and ignite the gas.
8. Open the acetylene torch valve all the way.
9. Open the oxygen torch valve all the way slowly.

Method B

1. Check that the equipment is properly assembled and that the torch valves are closed.
2. After observing the rules stated earlier, open the main valves, cylinder, or pipeline.
3. Pick up the torch, and open the acetylene torch valve all the way.
4. Turn the acetylene pressure-adjusting screw in until a small amount of gas flows from the tip.
5. Hold the friction lighter close to the tip and ignite the gas.
6. Continue to turn in the acetylene pressure-adjusting

screw slowly until the flame stops smoking and is about 3 mm to 5 mm (1/8 in. to 3/16 in.) away from the tip (Figure 6-11A).
7. Turn the acetylene torch valve back until the flame re-enters the tip, and stop.
8. Open the oxygen torch valve all the way.
9. Turn the oxygen pressure-adjusting screw in slowly, watching the flame closely. A bright inner cone will appear. This cone is called **a feather** (Figure 6-11B).
10. Continue to turn the oxygen pressure-adjusting screw in until the feather disappears, and stop. The flame which now appears is called a **neutral flame**. This type of flame is used for most welding operations (Figure 6-11C). Adding more oxygen will produce an oxidizing flame (Figure 6-11D).

Care must be taken in both these methods. If the acetylene is turned on too quickly, the flame might burn out of control. If the oxygen is turned on too quickly, the flame will be blown out.

Never point the flame towards any person or cylinder or pipeline or any material that is inflammable.

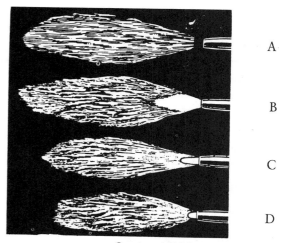

Courtesy MECO St. Louis, U.S.A.

Figure 6-11   Regulation of the flame

TEST YOUR KNOWLEDGE

1. Why is the acetylene torch valve opened only a 1/4 turn or less at first?
2. Why is the oxygen valve opened slowly?
3. What is the bright inner cone called?
4. At what point is the neutral flame obtained?

6-4 STEPS IN EXTINGUISHING THE FLAME

1. Close the acetylene torch valve all the way.
2. Close the oxygen torch valve all the way.
3. To close valves that are facing up, you should always remember to turn them to the right.

The acetylene torch valve should always be closed first to keep the tip free of carbon. Besides, if a torch has been in service for some time, the needle valves can become worn and difficult to close properly. If the oxygen torch valve is closed first and then the acetylene torch valve, there may be a small flame left burning at the tip, fed by the seepage of acetylene. When the acetylene is turned off first, the oxygen still flowing from the tip will blow out any small flame that remains, just as a match is blown out.

> Any sign that the needle valves are out of adjustment should be reported to the instructor immediately.

TEST YOUR KNOWLEDGE

1. Which valve should be closed first?
2. If the torch valves are facing up, in which direction should they be turned:
   a. to close them?
   b. to open them?
3. What is the purpose of allowing the oxygen to blow through the tip after the flame has been extinguished?
4. Why should the flame be kept away from cylinders and pipelines?

Figure 6-12 shows the names of the different parts of an oxy-acetylene flame. They will be used often in the following lessons, and it is necessary to be familiar with them.

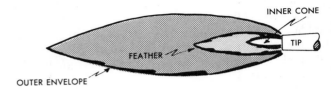

Figure 6-12   Parts of the flame

6-5 TYPES OF OXY-ACETYLENE FLAMES

Two methods are used by welders to determine whether or not the flame is ready to use.

Appearance

Acetylene burning in air has one long yellow flame and gives off large amounts of carbon (Figure 6-13A). The **carburizing or excess-acetylene flame** has **three** distinct parts: the outer envelope, the inner cone, and the feather (Figure 6-13B). The **neutral flame** has **two** parts: the outer envelope and the clear, well-rounded inner cone (Figure 6-13C). The **oxidizing flame** has two parts also: the outer envelope and a sharply-pointed inner cone (Figure 6-13D). The outer envelope is ragged at the end and has a purple colour. There is also a hissing sound from the tip. This hiss produces a harsh sound quite distinct from the sound of the soft, neutral flame.

A. Acetylene-in-air flame

B. Carburizing or excess-acetylene flame

Figure 6-13   Types of flames

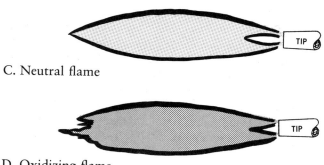

C. Neutral flame

D. Oxidizing flame

Figure 6-13 (cont'd)

Effect on Steel

Acetylene burning in air. This is the first flame that will be seen when the torch is lit. It is of little value to the welder, and when applied to a piece of steel, heats the steel very slowly and covers everything with carbon.

Carburizing or excess-acetylene flame. This is the second flame that will be seen. Oxygen has been added to the acetylene, but the feather in the centre shows that there is still too much acetylene. When this flame is applied to steel, it heats the metal much more quickly, but produces carbides which make the weld hard and brittle.

The neutral flame. This is the third and correct flame for welding steel. Just the right amount of oxygen has been added to the acetylene. When this flame is applied to steel, it heats the steel up even more quickly, but does not have any bad effect on the weld.

The oxidizing flame. This final flame indicates that an excessive amount of oxygen has been added. Although it is the hottest of the flames, when applied to a piece of steel it produces oxides which make the weld very brittle.

The **neutral** flame is the correct flame to use for most steel-welding operations. The carburizing and the oxidizing flame are used only in special situations. The flame shown in Figure 6-13A is not used at all for welding.

EXERCISE #1

In this exercise, you will see the effects of the different oxy-acetylene flames on steel. (These effects are also shown in Figure 6-14.)

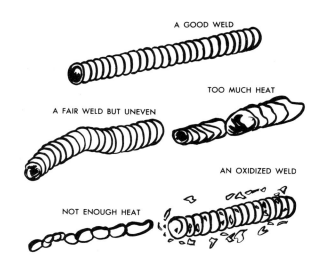

Figure 6-14 Effects of heat on steel

1. Light the torch, and obtain the acetylene-in-air flame. Apply it to a piece of metal. The metal will heat very slowly and be covered with carbon.
2. Adjust to the excess-acetylene flame, and apply this to the metal. Observe the puddle of molten metal that is formed. It will be cloudy with a white scum on top.
3. Adjust to a neutral flame. Apply this to the metal. Again observe the molten puddle. It will become clear and mirror-like.
4. Adjust to the oxidizing flame. Apply this to the metal. Once more, observe the molten puddle. It will boil and foam, and a great many sparks will be given off.

Practise this exercise until you can recognize the various flames both by appearance and by the effect they have on steel.

TEST YOUR KNOWLEDGE

1. Name the three parts of the flame.
2. Name the different types of flames.
3. Which one is the correct flame to use for most welding?
4. Why is the flame shown in Figure 6-13C the correct one to use?

5. What are the effects of an oxidizing flame on steel?
6. What are the effects of a carburizing flame on steel?
7. Which flame causes a scummy puddle?
8. Which flame causes a clear puddle?
9. Which flame causes a boiling or foaming puddle?

6-6 BACKFIRE AND FLASHBACK

There is a distinct difference between flashback and backfire. This difference must be clearly understood by anyone who is using oxy-acetylene equipment. Of the two, flashback is the most dangerous.

Sometimes when a person is welding, the torch flame appears to go out, and there is a loud snapping or popping noise at the tip. This is **backfire**. In addition, the torch will relight if the tip is accidentally brought too near the hot metal.

> If a backfire occurs, shut off the torch valves immediately and check the following points:
> 1. Has the tip been allowed to touch the metal? This is the most common cause with beginners.
> 2. Is there a piece of hot metal blocking the tip orifice?
> 3. Is the tip loose?
> 4. Is the tip overheated? Has it been held too close to the metal?

After checking these things, cool the tip in water with the oxygen blowing through the tip. Then have the instructor check the equipment.

When a **flashback** occurs, the flame goes out, and there is a loud squealing or hissing noise at the tip. This is usually accompanied by black smoke issuing from the tip.

> If a flashback occurs, shut off the torch valves (**oxygen first**) and the cylinder valves. Have the equipment checked by the instructor before proceeding any further.

In a flashback, the flame is actually burning inside the torch. If this continues, the flame could work its way back to the cylinders or the pipeline and cause a violent explosion. Oxygen will support the flame. It is for this reason that the oxygen valves are shut off first.

All oxy-acetylene equipment should have flashback arrestors installed. If they are not installed, they may be purchased from the manufacturer. Some torches, like the one shown in Figure 5-20B, are constructed with this in mind.

> The most common causes of flashback are:
> 1. Incorrect oxygen and acetylene pressures. This is the most common cause with beginners.
> 2. Touching the tip to the metal.
> 3. Using the improper method to light the torch.
> 4. Obstruction in the tip.

TEST YOUR KNOWLEDGE

1. Why is a flashback more dangerous than a backfire?
2. In the case of a flashback, why is the oxygen torch valve shut off first?
3. What should you do if a flashback does occur?
4. What should be done if a backfire occurs?
5. Give two reasons for the occurrence of a flashback.
6. State two faults that could cause a backfire.

POINTS TO REMEMBER

- Follow the steps laid out in this chapter when assembling and disconnecting the oxy-acetylene equipment.
- Test for leaks frequently.
- Using too much acetylene when lighting the torch may result in a badly burned hand.
- Too much oxygen added too quickly will blow out the flame.
- To extinguish the flame turn off the acetylene torch valve first.
- Do not point the flame towards anyone, a cylinder or pipeline or anything that is inflammable.

- The neutral flame is the correct flame to use.
- Flashback is more dangerous than backfire.
- If flashback or backfire occur, have the instructor check the equipment.
- For flashback **only**, shut off the oxygen torch valve first.
- Be careful not to let the tip touch the metal.

WORDS TO REMEMBER

cracking   oxidizing flame   flashback
neutral flame   backfire   feather

REVIEW QUESTIONS

1. Why should the cylinders be chained or fastened to a stationary object?
2. What is meant by cracking the cylinder valve?
3. What safety precautions should be observed when cracking a cylinder valve?
4. Why should the threads on the connections be checked for damage?
5. What is the difference between the oxygen and the acetylene hose with regard to
   a. colour?
   b. threads?
6. Describe the procedure used when testing the oxy-acetylene equipment for leaks.
7. What should you do if you find the equipment is faulty?
8. Why should you be careful about where you release the acetylene gas?
9. Why is the oxy-acetylene flame used for welding?
10. How many types of oxy-acetylene flames are there?
11. Which flame is used most often: neutral or oxidizing?
12. How many parts are there to a carburizing flame?
13. What is the difference between a neutral flame and an oxidizing flame?
14. The oxidizing flame is the hottest of the flames. Why then is it not used for welding steel?
15. What are the two methods used by a welder to determine whether or not the correct flame is being used?
16. Using the two methods above, describe the characteristics of a neutral flame.
17. Give the most common cause of
    a. backfire
    b. flashback
18. What is the main difference between flashback and backfire?

FUNDAMENTALS OF OXY-ACETYLENE WELDING

7-1   Lines of Fusion
7-2   Irregular Lines of Fusion
7-3   Welding Rods and Metal Thickness
7-4   Running a Bead with a Welding Rod

As in the case of any trade, you need to become familiar with some basic techniques before you can attempt actual welding operations. These fundamentals of welding are proper torch manipulation, control of the welding rod, and control of the molten metal. It is also important to be able to recognize defects in welds once they have been made.

Reading about these techniques and welding defects is only a first step. To become skilled, you need to practise making welds and spotting problems in them. The exercises in this chapter will give you the practice you need in welding both with and without welding rods.

7-1 LINES OF FUSION

RUNNING A STRAIGHT BEAD WITHOUT A WELDING ROD

When joining metals, some joints are assembled in such a manner that the actual base metal serves as a welding rod. Others require the addition of extra metal (filler metal) in the form of the welding rod. This first exercise

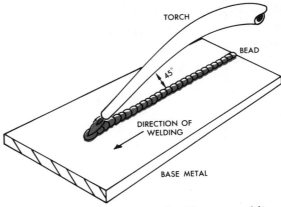

Figure 7-1   Running a bead without a welding rod

in oxy-acetylene welding will be done without a welding rod. The movement is basic to all oxy-acetylene welding operations and must be practised until it can be done skilfully. Figure 7-1 shows the movement.

EXERCISE #1

1. Obtain one piece of mild steel approximately

50 mm × 150 mm × 3 mm (or 2 in. × 6 in. × 1/8 in.).

2. Prepare the welding equipment. Remember to obtain a neutral flame.

3. Hold the tip of the inner cone about 3 mm (or 1/8 in.) above the metal, pointing it in the direction the weld is to be made. The angle between the torch and the metal should be approximately 45°.

4. Hold the flame in one spot until a puddle of molten metal about 6 mm (or about 1/4 in.) in diameter is formed.

5. Move the flame along the metal **slowly**, keeping the tip of the inner cone 3mm (or 1/8 in.) above the metal at all times. As the flame moves slowly forward, the puddle moves forward.

6. Watch the puddle carefully. If the torch is moved too quickly, the bead will become narrower, and the ripples will be pointed instead of round (Figure 7-2). If, on the other hand, the torch is moved too slowly, a hole will be burned in the metal.

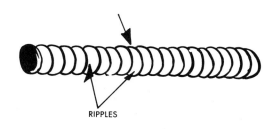

RIPPLES

CORRECT

Figure 7-3   A good speed maintained

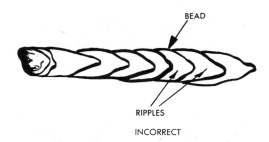

BEAD

RIPPLES

INCORRECT

Figure 7-2   Torch was moved too quickly

7. The correct speed is most important. Practise this exercise until you can run a straight bead with rounded ripples, no holes, and the same width along the entire length (as in Figure 7-3).

OTHER EXERCISES IN RUNNING A BEAD WITHOUT WELDING ROD

After becoming skilled at running straight beads without a welding rod, practise the following exercises. Observe the effects of each one.

EXERCISE #2

1. Start exactly the same way as in the previous exercise, but this time move the torch along the line of the weld with a small circular motion in a clockwise direction. In order to produce uniform beads (beads that are exactly the same), it is necessary to make exactly the same circular movement each time (Figure 7-4).

2. Again start the same way as before. This time, however, change the angle of the torch. Run a number of beads on the same piece of metal, changing the angle of the torch each time you make a new bead. Observe the results carefully. Note that the more the torch points straight down, the deeper the puddle sinks into the metal (Figure 7-5).

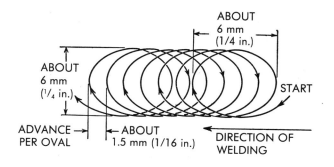

ABOUT 6 mm (1/4 in.)

ABOUT 6 mm (1/4 in.)

START

ADVANCE PER OVAL

ABOUT 1.5 mm (1/16 in.)

DIRECTION OF WELDING

Figure 7-4   Circular movement of torch

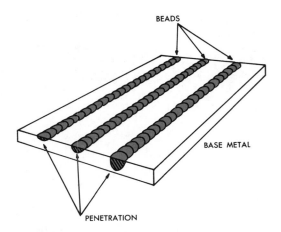

Figure 7-5   Penetration

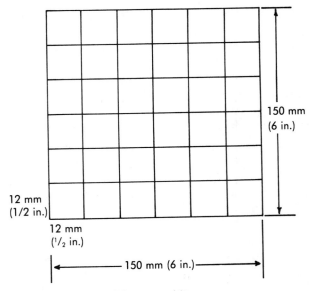

Figure 7-6   Initial layout of lines

7-2 IRREGULAR LINES OF FUSION

In industry, the welder is not always able to turn the metal around, nor are all welds straight lines of fusion (beads). The welder is required to manipulate the puddle in many different directions. The following exercise will help you develop skill in doing this.

EXERCISE #3

1. Obtain one piece of metal about 150 mm × 150 mm × 1.5 mm (6 in. × 6 in. × 1/16 in.).
2. With a ruler and chalk or soapstone, lay out lines as shown in Figure 7-6.
3. Draw a zigzag or irregular line connecting the corners of the squares, as shown in Figure 7-7.
4. Prepare the welding equipment, and proceed to weld along these irregular lines. Do not lift the torch, move the metal, or stop until each line is completed.

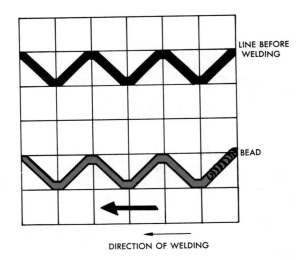

Figure 7-7   Layout for irregular lines of fusion and finished bead

TEST YOUR KNOWLEDGE

1. How far away from the metal should the tip of the inner cone be held?
2. What should the approximate diameter of the puddle be?
3. What happens if you move the torch too quickly?
4. What happens if you move the torch too slowly?
5. What are the characteristics of a good bead?
6. Describe the results produced when the angle of the torch is changed.
7. Why is it necessary for the welder to be able to manipulate the puddle in different directions?

7-3 WELDING RODS AND METAL THICKNESS

WELDING RODS

A welding rod is a filler metal used with the welding torch. In order to produce welds with the same qualities as the parent metal, the welding rods must be manufactured in as many varieties and types as there are metals. For welding steel, the most common type is the mild-steel rod with a copper coating.

The copper coating is merely a protection against rusting of the rod. All welding rods are identified by the letter R, followed by a combination of letters and numbers, such as RG45, RG60, RG65. The letter R stands for "rod"; the letter G indicates that it is used for gas welding; the numbers give the tensile strength of the deposited weld metal. (Deposited weld metal is the metal that has melted onto the base metal.)

For example:

R   indicates that it is a rod (as opposed to an electrode)

G   indicates that it is to be used for gas welding

60   gives the tensile strength as 60 000 psi

> **Note:** Under the metric system, this would read as 410 000 MPa.

The rod given in this example is a general all-purpose rod with good strength and ductility in deposited weld metal. (Ductility is the ability of a material to bend, flow, or be shaped without cracking.) Most gas welding rods are round and 900 mm (or 36 in.) long. The size of the welding rod is determined by measuring its diameter. The most common rod diameters are from 1.6 mm to 6.4 mm (about 1/16 in. to 1/4 in.). As a general rule, small diameter welding rods should be used for light-gauge metals and increasingly large diameter welding rods for thicker metals.

METAL THICKNESS

The term **gauge** currently refers to the thickness of a piece of metal manufactured to millimetre or inch sizes.

It is usually used in describing metals that are less than 3 mm (or 1/8 in.) thick.

For example:

- Metal that is 16 gauge is 1.5 mm (or 1/16 in.) thick.
- Metal that is 11 gauge is 3 mm (or 1/8 in.) thick.
- Metal that is 21 gauge is 0.8 mm (or 1/32 in.) thick.

> The higher the gauge number, the thinner the metal.

The Relationship between Metal Thickness and Welding Rod Size	
Metal Thickness	**Metal rod size**
1.5 mm (1/16 in.) or less	1.5 mm (1/16 in.)
3 mm (1/8 in.)	3 mm (1/8 in.)
2.4 mm (3/32 in.)	2.4 mm (3/32 in.)
4.8 mm (3/16 in.)	4.8 mm (3/16 in.)

For metals over 4.8 mm (3/16 in.) use a 6.4 mm (1/4 in.) welding rod.

7-4 RUNNING A BEAD WITH A WELDING ROD

When a bead is made without a welding rod, a depression or hollow is left on the surface of the metal. This hollow is called **penetration** and is caused by the puddle sinking into the metal. In order to fill this hollow and to bring the weld up to at least the surface of the metal, a welding rod is used.

Figure 7-8 shows the proper method of holding a welding rod. As the weld progresses, the welding rod is melting and has to be fed continually into the weld. By holding the welding rod as shown and with a little practice, it is possible to keep moving the welding rod down with the thumb and fingers.

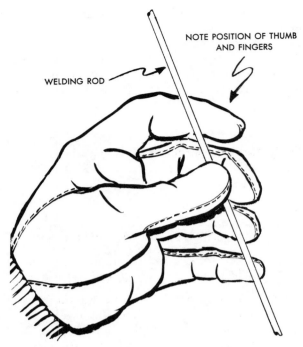

WELDING ROD

NOTE POSITION OF THUMB AND FINGERS

Figure 7-8   Proper position for holding a welding rod

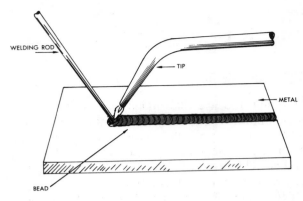

WELDING ROD

TIP

METAL

BEAD

Figure 7-9   Running a bead with a welding rod

EXERCISE #4

1. Obtain one piece of metal about 50 mm × 150 mm × 1.5 mm (2 in. × 6 in. × 1/16 in.)

2. Prepare the welding equipment.

3. Proceed as in the previous exercises to make a small puddle.

4. When the puddle is established, place the end of the welding rod in the centre of the molten puddle (Figure 7-9).

5. Be careful. If the rod is placed anywhere except in the centre of the molten puddle, it will stick to the metal.

6. If the welding rod does stick, do not try to pull it off. Simply hold the flame at the point where the rod is stuck, and it will melt off.

7. The same amount of welding rod must be added each time to produce a uniform weld.

8. The weld should look exactly the same as the

weld made without a welding rod, except that it will have a buildup above the surface of the metal (Figure 7-10).

9. Do not allow the metal from the welding rod to melt and then drop into the puddle. The rod must be placed in the centre of the puddle and allowed to melt.

10. Adding too much of the welding rod makes the weld build up too much. This can be done by dipping the rod too quickly into the puddle. Adding the rod too slowly makes the weld too flat.

11. Practise this exercise until a neat, smooth weld is obtained with an even amount of buildup above

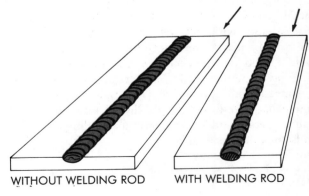

WITHOUT WELDING ROD   WITH WELDING ROD

Figure 7-10   These welds are similar.

Courtesy of Union Carbide Limited

Figure 7-11   A good weld

the surface. Usually 3 mm (or 1/8 in.) above the surface is sufficient; this is called **buildup** or **reinforcement**. Figure 7-11 shows an even amount of buildup. Also practise the exercise in Figure 7-7, but this time use a welding rod.

Figure 7-12   Welded irregular lines

EXERCISE #5

Another exercise that will improve welding skill is shown in Figure 7-12. Write your name on a piece of metal, using chalk. Light the welding torch, and follow the lines on the metal. Practise this exercise first with and then without a welding rod. This will further increase the manipulative skills necessary for welding. (Figure 7-13 shows different qualities of beads run with a welding rod.)

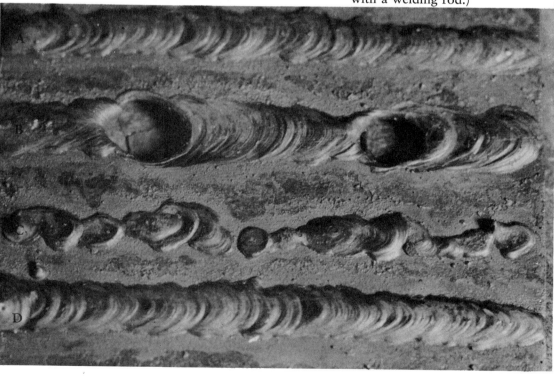

Figure 7-13
Sample beads made with a welding rod A and D are satisfactory, but not uniform. B had too much heat. C was run too fast.

Courtesy of Union Carbide Canada Limited

POINTS TO REMEMBER

- Always use a neutral flame.
- The angle between the torch and the metal should be 45°.
- The tip of the inner cone should be 3 mm (or 1/8 in.) above the metal at all times.
- If the torch is moved too quickly, the bead will become narrower.
- If the torch is moved too slowly, a hole will be burned in the metal.
- The correct speed is important.
- Welding rod size is determined by the measurement of its diameter.
- In general, small diameter welding rods should be used for light-gauge metals and larger diameter ones for thicker metals.
- Do not allow the metal to melt and then drop into the puddle from the welding rod.

WORDS TO REMEMBER

neutral	uniform	soapstone
bead	circular	diameter
ripples	irregular	gauge
puddle	fusion	penetration
		reinforcement

REVIEW QUESTIONS

1. Which flame is the correct one to use in these exercises?
2. What do narrow pointed ripples in the weld indicate?
3. What is meant by a uniform bead?
4. What is the correct distance between the inner cone and the metal?
5. When running a bead without a welding rod, what are the results of:
   a. moving the torch too quickly?
   b. moving the torch too slowly?
6. What causes the depression or hollow on the surface of the metal when a bead is run without a welding rod?
7. What is the term used to denote the thickness of the metal?
8. What is the purpose of a welding rod?
9. How is the size of a welding rod determined?
10. How are welding rods identified?
11. Give one example of welding rod identification.
12. What is the result of adding the welding rod too quickly?
13. Compare the characteristics of good welds made without a welding rod and with a welding rod.
14. What causes excessive buildup on the weld?

BASIC JOINTS

In most welding operations, it is rare to work on only one piece of metal. More often, at least two pieces are being joined together. In this chapter, you will learn how to assemble (or join) two pieces of metal, and several basic joints will be introduced. The proper assembly of joints is as important as using the correct flame and manipulating the torch and rod with skill. Incorrect set-up of a joint can ruin an otherwise perfect weld. In joining, and in other welding operations, penetration is also important.

Two more basic techniques will be learned as you study the basic welding joints: forehand and backhand welding.

8-1 AN OVERVIEW

Most welding that is done in industry consists of joining pieces of metal to form a particular shape: an automobile, a ship, or a train. There are only five basic joints, but there are many variations of these five joints.

Figure 8-1 shows a shipyard at night. There are thousands of joints on a ship this size and miles of welding. However, if we could examine this ship, we would find

Courtesy of The Lincoln Electric Company

Figure 8-1   Shipbuilding

that all the joints come under the heading of one of the five basic types:

1. corner joint
2. edge joint
3. lap joint
4. butt joint
5. tee joint

Figure 8-2 shows the planes that the pieces lie in to form a joint. Figure 8-3 illustrates the five basic joints. (In these illustrations, each piece of metal is called a "member".)

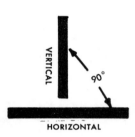

Figure 8-2   The horizontal position is parallel to the horizon. The vertical position is perpendicular to the horizon.

PENETRATION

The exercises that you did on running beads in Chapter 7 showed that the **angle of the torch** and the **speed of travel** affect the amount of penetration. In welding joints, the **gap** (or **distance**) between the two pieces of metal also affects penetration. There is too much penetration if

1. the angle of the torch is too high.
2. the speed of travel is too slow.
3. the gap or distance between the pieces is too wide.
  There is too little penetration if
1. the angle of the torch is too low.
2. the speed of travel is too great.
3. the gap or distance between the pieces is too small.

8-2 TACK WELDS

If two pieces of metal are merely placed in the joint design that is desired, they will fall apart or move out of alignment when the welding operation begins. To

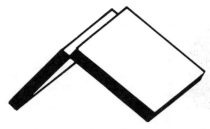

A. The corner joint is a joint between members located at right angles to each other.

B. The edge joint is a joint between the edges of parallel members.

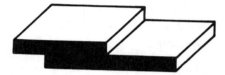

C. The lap joint is a joint between overlapping members.

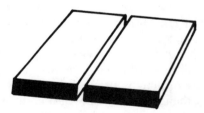

D. The butt joint is a joint between members lying in the same plane.

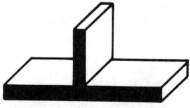

E. The tee joint is a joint between members located at right angles to each other.

Figure 8-3   The five basic joints.

prevent this, the pieces are held in position by what are called tack welds. Tack welds keep the metal from moving. They are small welds, approximately 12 mm (or 1/2 in.) in length, placed at different locations on the joint. Tack welds are usually made with a welding rod.

EXERCISE #1
STEPS IN MAKING A TACK WELD

1. Obtain two pieces of metal, each about 50 mm × 150 mm × 1.5 mm (or 2 in. × 6 in. × 1/16 in.)
2. Prepare the welding equipment, and obtain a welding rod.
3. Place the two pieces of metal flat on the welding bench side by side.
4. Light the torch and set it to obtain a neutral flame.
5. Apply the flame to one end of the pieces of metal.
6. Make a circular motion, about 12 mm (or 1/2 in.) in diameter, with the torch. Watch the metal carefully. A small molten puddle should appear on each piece.
7. Add the welding rod as it is done when running a bead. The metal from the welding rod should flow out and join the two puddles to form one large puddle.
8. If the puddles do not flow together at first, move them with the welding rod, and they will join.
9. Follow the same procedure at the other end of the joint and in the centre, making three tack welds (Figure 8-4).

The joint used here is the butt joint. Although this joint has been used to show the steps in tack welding, the same steps apply to **all** joints.

TEST YOUR KNOWLEDGE
1. What would happen if the joints were set in position without tack welds?
2. What is the usual length of a tack weld?
3. What is the purpose of a tack weld?
4. How are tack welds made?
5. What does the word "alignment" mean?

8-3 THE CORNER JOINT

When two pieces of metal are welded to form a small "tent", the joint is called a corner joint. A corner joint

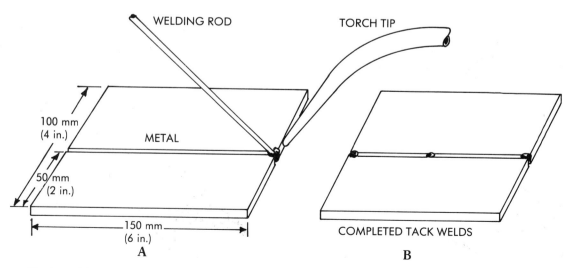

Figure 8-4   Tack welding a butt joint

may be welded with or without a welding rod. This joint is used in the manufacture of such items as boxes, tanks, and machine guards. Since the joint requires little preparation, it is widely used in industry. The weld should penetrate the entire thickness of the metal. The top and bottom of the weld should show smooth, even ripples.

TYPES OF CORNER JOINTS

Care must be taken when assembling a corner joint if full penetration is to be achieved. Note carefully the position of the pieces of metal in Figures 8-5, 8-6, and 8-7. Note also the results obtained by this positioning of the pieces.

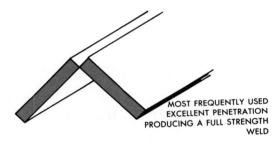

MOST FREQUENTLY USED
EXCELLENT PENETRATION
PRODUCING A FULL STRENGTH
WELD

Figure 8-5   Open corner joint

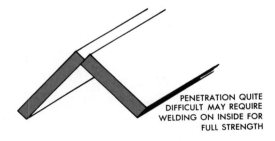

PENETRATION QUITE
DIFFICULT MAY REQUIRE
WELDING ON INSIDE FOR
FULL STRENGTH

Figure 8-6   Half-opened corner joint

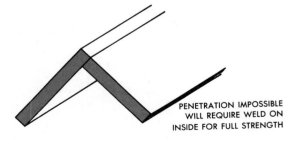

PENETRATION IMPOSSIBLE
WILL REQUIRE WELD ON
INSIDE FOR FULL STRENGTH

Figure 8-7   Closed corner joint

TEST YOUR KNOWLEDGE

1. Name the three types of corner joints.
2. Which one will provide the most penetration?
3. Which one will provide the least penetration?
4. Which one is used most frequently?
5. Which one will require welding from one side only to obtain full penetration?

EXERCISE #2
STEPS IN ASSEMBLING A CORNER JOINT

1. Obtain two pieces of metal, each about 50 mm × 150 mm × 1.5 mm (2 in. × 6 in. × 1/16 in.).
2. Prepare the welding equipment.
3. Obtain one piece of angle iron 50 mm × 200 mm (or 2 in. × 8 in.).
4. Place the angle iron on the welding bench. Set the two pieces of metal on either side of the angle iron as shown in Figure 8-8.
5. Make sure that the pieces are in alignment as in figures 8-5, 8-6, or 8-7.
6. Tack weld the joint in three places. Do not tack weld the metal to the angle iron.
7. Remove the joint from the angle iron and weld.

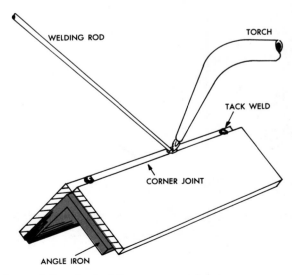

WELDING ROD

TORCH

TACK WELD

CORNER JOINT

ANGLE IRON

Figure 8-8   Assembling a corner joint

EXERCISE #3
STEPS IN WELDING A CORNER JOINT WITHOUT A WELDING ROD

1. Assemble two pieces of metal into a corner joint.
2. Tack weld the joint.
3. Make a molten puddle on both plates. Join the puddles by moving the torch slightly from side to side.
4. Move the puddle along the joint slowly to obtain good penetration. Penetration can be checked by turning the joint over after the weld is completed. The weld should look like the one shown in Figure 8-9.

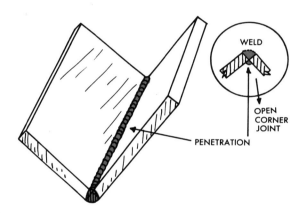

Figure 8-9   Penetration on a properly welded corner joint

EXERCISE #4
WELDING A CORNER JOINT WITH A WELDING ROD

1. Repeat steps 1 to 3 from Exercise #3.
2. While the flame is heating the metal, put the welding rod into the flame close to the joint.
3. When the welding rod is red hot, keep it at that temperature by moving it in and out of the flame. Once the molten puddle is established, dip the welding rod in and out of the puddle with a rhythmic motion. The addition of the welding rod builds up the weld so that the top of the weld is rounded instead of concave.

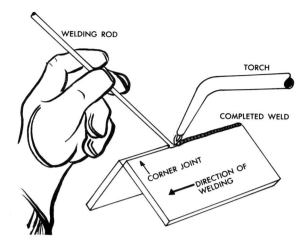

Figure 8-10   Welding a corner joint with welding rod

The same movements are performed in this operation as in running a bead with and without a welding rod. The only difference is that two pieces of metal are joined in this operation. Figure 8-10 shows this weld in progress. Figure 8-11 gives before and after views.

The dimensions of the metal may be changed, but the angle iron for tacking purposes should always have the same height as the smaller side of the metal. For example, if the metal measures 100 mm × 150 mm × 1.5 mm (or 4 in. × 6 in. × 1/16 in.) then the angle iron should be 100 mm × 200 mm (or 4 in. × 8 in.)

A. Before welding

Figure 8-11   Corner joint before and after welding

B. After welding

Figure 8-11   (cont'd)

TEST YOUR KNOWLEDGE

1. Why is it necessary to remove the joint from the angle iron before welding?
2. Why is the angle iron used to assemble the joint?
3. If two pieces of metal measured 150 mm × 150 mm × 1.5 mm (6 in. × 6 in. × 1/16 in.), what size of angle iron would have to be used?

8-4 THE EDGE JOINT

The edge joint is sometimes called a flange joint and is used most often on light-gauge metal. It can be welded with or without a welding rod. However, it is usually welded without a rod since the flange supplies enough filler metal for the joint. When finished, this joint will be similar in appearance to a butt joint (Figure 8-12).

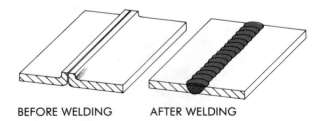

BEFORE WELDING   AFTER WELDING

Figure 8-12   Edge joint

EXERCISE #5
STEPS IN WELDING AN EDGE JOINT WITHOUT A WELDING ROD

1. Obtain two pieces of metal, each about 50 mm × 150 mm × 1.5 mm (or 2 in. × 6 in. × 1/16 in.).
2. Prepare the flange by bending it in a vise or in a sheet metal bending machine. Note that the depth of the flange is equal to the thickness of the metal (Figure 8-13).
3. Prepare the welding equipment.
4. Assemble the two pieces of metal as shown in Figure 8-13B, and proceed to tack weld the joint.
5. Start to weld at one end of the joint. Oberve the puddle closely until the flange metal melts.
6. Proceed to weld along the joint. Remember to move slowly in order to obtain good penetration.

For practice and to save time in making a flange, simply place the two pieces of metal side by side and proceed to tack and weld (Figure 8-14). All four edges

A   B

Figure 8-13   Flange

Figure 8-14   An alternative to making a flange weld

could be used for practice by turning the metal around each time. A C clamp will hold the pieces of metal in position during welding.

TEST YOUR KNOWLEDGE

1. What is another name for an edge joint?
2. Why is it unnecessary to use a welding rod on this joint?
3. Which other joint is similar to the completed edge joint?
4. On what type of metal is this kind of joint used most often?
5. Describe two methods of preparing a flange.
6. How can the depth of a flange be determined?
7. What other method can be used to replace the flange for practice?

8-5 THE LAP JOINT

The lap joint is used at times in place of the butt joint. Instead of the edges being brought together, they are overlapped. Oil fuel tanks contain many lap joints. The weld that is used to join the pieces of metal is called a fillet weld. It is necessary to use a welding rod for the lap joint.

EXERCISE #6
STEPS IN WELDING A LAP JOINT WITH A WELDING ROD

1. Obtain three pieces of metal, each about 50 mm × 150 mm × 1.5 mm (or 2 in. × 6 in. × 1/16 in.) and a welding rod.
2. Prepare the welding equipment.
3. Place two pieces of metal flat on the welding bench as though you were making a butt joint. Place another piece on top of the other two, half on each piece. This should leave an overlap of 25 mm (or 1 in.) as shown in Figure 8-15.
4. Tack weld at both ends, making sure that the pieces are close together. Use a C clamp, if neces-

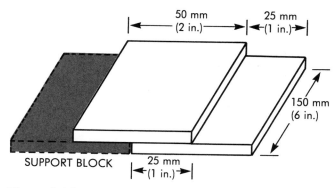

Figure 8-15   To assemble and tack weld a lap joint

sary, to ensure that there is no space between them. Only two pieces should be tack welded together. The third piece (the one shown in colour in Figure 8-15) is used only to support the top piece of metal and should not be tack welded.

5. Apply the flame to one end, and when both pieces of metal start to melt, insert the welding rod and form a molten puddle.
6. Use the same procedure as in making straight beads (Figure 8-16). However, be careful not to allow the top edge of the top piece of metal to melt away too fast. This is called **undercutting**.

Figure 8-16   Welding a lap joint

In order to avoid undercutting, the torch should be pointed more towards the bottom piece, and the welding rod should be kept at the top of the molten puddle (Figure 8-17). If there is a gap or space between the two pieces of metal, the top piece will melt away too quickly.

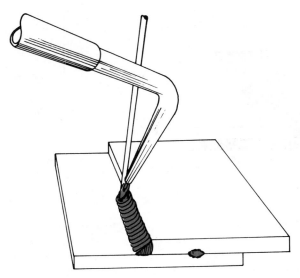

Figure 8-17　Preventing undercutting

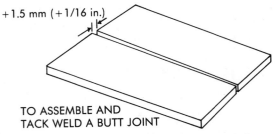

TO ASSEMBLE AND
TACK WELD A BUTT JOINT

Figure 8-18　Allowing for expansion and contraction

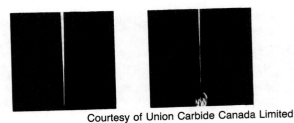

Courtesy of Union Carbide Canada Limited

Figure 8-19　Butt joint before and after applying heat

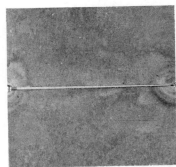

Courtesy of Union Carbide Canada Limited

Figure 8-20　Butt joint before welding

8-6 THE BUTT JOINT

The butt joint is the joint used most often in industry because it is easy to assemble. About 70% of all the joints used in industry are butt joints. A welding rod is always used for this joint. (Butt joints are sometimes called vee joints or single-vee butt joints because their edges form a vee. Chapter 23, Edge Preparation, gives more details.)

EXERCISE #7
STEPS IN WELDING A BUTT JOINT WITH A WELDING ROD

1. Obtain two pieces of metal, each about 50 mm × 150 mm × 1.5 mm (or 2 in. × 6 in. × 1/16 in.).

2. Obtain a welding rod.

3. Prepare the welding equipment.

4. Place the two pieces of metal on the welding bench side by side with the gap at one end 1.5 mm (or 1/16 in.) wider than at the other end, as shown in Figure 8-18.

5. Leave a gap between the two pieces of metal to obtain complete penetration. The reason for making the gap at one end 1.5 mm (or 1/16 in.) wider

is to allow for subsequent expansion and contraction. Figure 8-19 shows the effects of contraction. Apply one tack weld, and observe the difference in spacing before and after tack welding.

6. Make sure that the pieces are flat and aligned (Figure 8-20). Then tack weld in the usual manner.

7. After tack welding, start at one end of the joint and make a molten puddle. Add the welding rod, and proceed to weld along the joint (Figure 8-21).

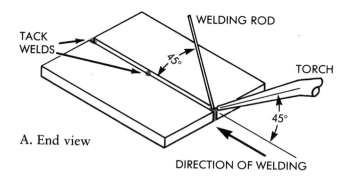

A. End view

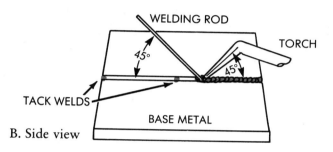

B. Side view

Figure 8-21   Correct position for welding a butt joint

8. Make certain that the molten puddle spreads equally on both pieces of metal and that it follows straight down the seam.

9. The angle of the welding rod and the torch should be approximately 45°.

10. After completing the weld, turn the piece over and check the underside. If the weld has been performed properly, the edges of the metal will not be visible, and the joint will have penetration (about 1.5 mm or 1/16 in.) all the way along.

8-7 FOREHAND AND BACKHAND WELDING

Two more basic techniques used in oxy-acetylene welding are forehand and backhand welding (Figure 8-22). (They are sometimes referred to as rightward and leftward welding.) The following directions are given for a right-handed person, someone who holds the torch in their right hand and a welding rod in their left hand.

This means that the joint is welded from the right side of the joint to the left. Anyone who is normally left-handed would reverse this welding procedure. So far, most of the practice welds discussed make use of the forehand technique (rightward). Exercise #8 will illustrate the backhand (leftward) technique.

A. Forehand (rightward)

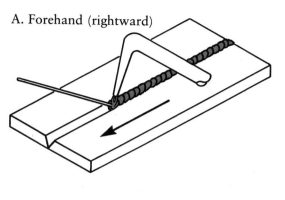

B. Backhand (leftward)

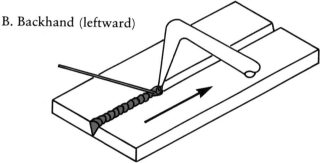

Figure 8-22   Forehand and backhand welding

EXERCISE #8
WELDING A BUTT JOINT USING THE BACKHAND TECHNIQUE

1. Obtain two pieces of metal each about 50 mm × 150 mm × 6 mm (or 2 in. × 6 in. × 1/4 in.).

2. Prepare the 150 mm (or 6 in.) edges at a 35° angle.

3. Obtain a 4.7 mm (3/16 in.) welding rod.

4. Prepare the welding equipment.

5. Assemble the pieces to form a single vee butt joint.
6. Set the torch to the correct pressure and light it.
7. Tack the weld joint at both ends.
8. For this exercise, it will be easier if the right-hand end of the butt joint is raised slightly, so that welding is performed uphill.
9. Preheat the tack weld at the left end of butt joint.
10. Hold the welding rod in the outer envelope of flame to preheat.
11. When a puddle starts to form, add the welding rod.
12. Use a semicircular motion with the welding rod.
13. Concentrate the flame at the bottom of the vee and move the puddle into the bottom of the vee to ensure penetration. Then concentrate the flame on the welding rod and move the molten puddle upward to fill the joint and supply the necessary reinforcement.
14. The torch should be held at a 45° to 60° angle and the rod at a 45° angle to the base metal.

In the beginning, overwelding and/or lack of penetration is not unusual because of rod and torch manipulation. With practice, however, these difficulties will soon be overcome. (See Figure 8-23.)

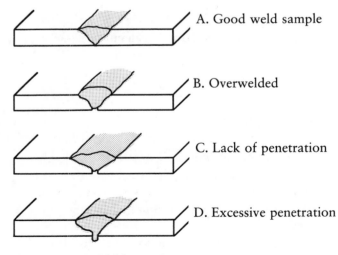

A. Good weld sample

B. Overwelded

C. Lack of penetration

D. Excessive penetration

Figure 8-23   Weld samples

Advantages of Backhand Welding
a. The welding rod does not prevent the flame from reaching the bottom of the vee joint as it can do in forehand.
b. Backhand welding is better than forehand for welding materials over 5 mm (3/8 in.) thick.
c. It is faster than forehand welding because of the preheating action of the flame being directed over the molten metal.
d. The welding flame covers the molten metal and prevents oxidation in the weld.
e. The molten metal in the puddle is thoroughly mixed by the welding rod and by torch manipulation.
f. Narrower grooves can be used in the vee preparation.

8-8 THE TEE JOINT

Like the butt joint the tee joint is widely used in industry. Approximately 30% of all joints used are tee joints. This joint looks like the letter "T" upside down. As with the lap joint, tee joints are connected by a fillet weld, and a welding rod is required for this joint.

EXERCISE #9
STEPS IN WELDING A TEE
JOINT WITH A WELDING ROD

1. Obtain two pieces of metal, each about 50 mm × 150 mm × 1.5 mm (2 in. × 6 in. × 1/16 in.).
2. Prepare the welding equipment.
3. Place one piece of metal flat on the welding bench. Place the second piece on top of the first, with edge-to-surface alignment (Figure 8-24).
4. Using an ordinary square, make sure that the vertical piece is in position at a 90° angle to the horizontal piece.
5. Clamp the pieces in this position using a C clamp with at least a 75 mm (or 3 in.) throat. Tack weld the joint at each end.

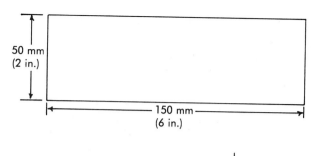

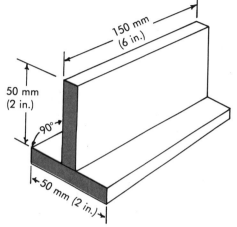

Figure 8-24 Assembling a tee joint

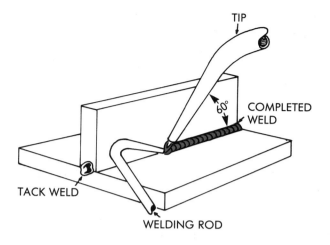

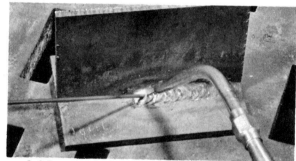

Figure 8-25 Welding a tee joint

6. Remove the C clamp and proceed to weld the joint.

7. Start at one end of the joint. Point the torch at a 60° angle to the horizontal piece.

8. Watch the metal closely. Both pieces should melt at the same time. If they do not, it may be necessary to change the angle of the torch slightly.

9. When a puddle has formed, add the welding rod as shown in Figure 8-25.

10. Move the welding rod slightly from the top to the bottom of the molten puddle in a zigzag motion (Figure 8-26A). At the same time, move the torch in a semicircular motion around the puddle (Figure 8-26B).

11. Avoid undercutting the vertical piece of metal by keeping the welding rod at the top of the molten puddle as much as possible.

A DIRECTION OF WELDING **B**
MOVEMENT OF WELDING ROD   MOVEMENT OF TORCH

Figure 8-26 Movement of torch and welding rod

POINTS TO REMEMBER

- A joint is made at the point where two pieces of metal come together.
- There are five different basic joints in welding.
- Penetration is affected by torch angle, speed of travel, and gap.
- The angle at which the torch is held is most important.

Welding a tee joint

- It is necessary to tack weld a joint.
- The height of the flange in an edge joint must be equal to the thickness of the metal.
- A gap between pieces in a lap joint will cause undercutting.

WORDS TO REMEMBER

horizontal	corner	undercutting
vertical	edge	tack weld
parallel	flange	butt
alignment	lap	tee
concave	fillet weld	

REVIEW QUESTIONS

1. How many basic joints are there?
2. Explain the meaning of the words "horizontal" and "vertical" as used in this chapter.
3. Give three factors that can result in too much penetration.
4. Give three factors that can result in too little penetration.
5. What are tack welds used for?
6. Describe the procedure used to tack weld a joint.
7. Give one example of a situation where a corner joint might be used.
8. What is the purpose of the angle iron in assembling a corner joint?
9. Why must care be taken when assembling a corner joint?
10. When preparing an edge joint using 1.5 mm (or 1/16 in.) metal, what would be the depth of the flange?
11. When making a lap joint, three pieces of metal are used. How many pieces are actually welded together to form the lap joint?
12. What is the name given to the weld used on a lap joint?
13. What is meant by the term "undercutting"?
14. In a lap joint
    a. How much of an overlap should the top piece have?
    b. Why would the use of a C clamp be necessary?
15. Which two joints use a fillet weld?
16. Which joint looks like a small "tent"?
17. Which joint looks like the letter "T" upside down?
18. Which joints can be welded without a welding rod?
19. In welding a tee joint, describe one method of avoiding undercutting a vertical piece of metal.
20. What is the main difference between running a bead with a welding rod and welding a joint without a welding rod?
21. After completing all the joints, prepare a list showing which ones were easy to weld, and which ones were easy to assemble. Give reasons for each one.

SOLDERING, BRAZING, AND BRAZE WELDING

Soldering, brazing, and braze welding (including bronze welding, or surfacing) are all nonfusion processes. (See Chapter 2.) They are used to join similar and dissimilar metals with a metal or alloy that has a lower melting point than the metals being joined. Although there are a number of similarities between these processes, there are differences that make each a distinct process in its own right.

9-1 THE DIFFERENCES

Soldering uses filler metals which melt at temperatures below 425° C (800°F), and it depends on capillary action to join the base metals. (Capillary action is the force that causes a liquid to rise against or to move away from a vertical surface.) Like soldering, brazing depends on capillary action, but its filler metals melt at temperatures above 425°C (800°F). Braze welding also uses filler metals which melt above 425°C (800°F), but it does not depend on capillary action at all. (See Figure 9-1.)

All of these types of welding have many applications. Developing skill in this area may open up opportunities in a number of fields. Automotive, auto body repair, and the sheet metal trades, for example, make extensive use of these types of nonfusion welding.

9-2 SOLDERING

This process is sometimes called **soft soldering** to distinguish it from brazing, which is sometimes called hard soldering. The temperature for soft soldering will depend on the composition of the filler metal being used. However, it will always be below 425°C (800°F). Soldering provides the fastest, easiest, and most inexpensive method of joining most metals.

SOLDERING IRONS

A basic soldering iron consists of a handle and a tip,

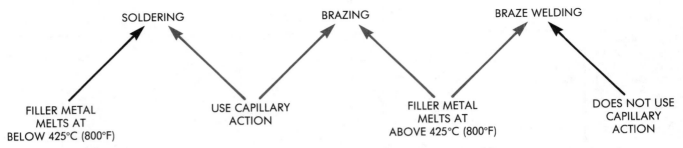

Figure 9-1 Similarities and differences between soldering, brazing, and braze welding

which is usually called a bit. The soldering iron may be heated by a number of methods. Its basic function is to carry heat and solder to the parts being joined. The bit, which is made of copper or copper alloy, can be purchased in a variety of sizes and weights. All bits, however, possess the same characteristics. They have a high thermal conductivity, they can resist scaling caused by high temperatures, and they resist corrosion from the soldering fluxes and alloys used in soldering. They also possess sufficient hardness to resist wear. Bits should never be overheated, and should be kept dressed and clean of scale.

SOLDERING ALLOYS

Most soldering filler metals (called solders) are alloys of tin and lead, the most common being 50/50 (50% tin/ 50% lead) and 60/40 (60% tin/40% lead). On occasion, solders may contain other elements such as zinc, cadmium, and silver. Alloys with a high tin content have a lower melting point, better wetting action, and more fluidity. But they are more expensive than alloys with a low tin content. These alloys can be obtained in bar form, as flux-cored wire, or as solid wire. The solid and flux-cored wire are also manufactured in a variety of geometric shapes for industrial applications, particularly furnace soldering.

FURNACE SOLDERING AND BRAZING

This process is used only when many parts are to be soldered or brazed. Whatever type of furnace is used (gas, electricity, etc.), close temperature control is essential to ensure consistently good results. The parts to

be joined are assembled, and the soldering or brazing material is preplaced at the joint to be connected. Then the entire assembly is placed in the furnace and heated. The soldering or brazing alloy is usually preformed to suit the outline of the joint. It may be in the shape of a flat strip, a washer, or a round ring. Furnace heating is not as widely used as some of the other heating methods. However, it has been found to produce consistent and satisfactory joints in many applications.

FLUXES

The main purpose of the flux is to remove oxides from the metal and to assist the solder to flow freely along the joint. There are three main types of flux: **chloride** (acid), **organic**, and **rosin**.

Chloride flux. Sometimes called acid, this flux is highly corrosive. It is effective on all common metals except aluminum and magnesium and it should not be used on electrical parts or assemblies where corrosion could create a problem.

Organic flux. This flux is much less corrosive than chloride because it quickly becomes inactive when exposed to heat. It then dries up and flakes off.

Rosin flux. This is a noncorrosive flux and is electrically nonconductive.

Fluxes can be purchased in paste, fluid, and/or powder form or they can be encased in the solder wire (commonly called flux-cored solder).

Different types of fluxes are used with different metals. Table 9-1 shows several metals and the fluxes that should be used with them. This table should be followed as a general guideline only. For more detailed information before you begin soldering, consult your instructor.

TABLE 9-1 METALS AND FLUXES

Metal	Flux Type
Aluminum	SP
Brass	N/C – C
Copper	N/C – C
Nickel	C
Steel	C
Tin	N/C – C
Zinc	C

Legend: SP – Special; N/C – noncorrosive; C – corrosive

CAPILLARY ACTION

The soldering process depends on **capillary action** to draw the molten filler metal of the welding rod into the joint. Consider what would happen if a glass tube with a very small bore, open at both ends, were inserted into a tank of water. The water would rise a certain distance in the tube, depending on the diameter of the bore (Figure 9-2A). This is capillary action. In soldering, the alloy acts as the water did in this example. Figure 9-2B shows the same effect when the tube is replaced by two glass plates sealed at the ends, with a slight separation between them.

Figure 9-2C shows what happens when the gap is widened. Similarly, as the gap between pieces of metal is widened, the soldering alloy will not penetrate an entire joint, regardless of the position of the metal pieces. This lack of penetration, of course, results in a weak joint and a waste of filler metal. However, if the gap is too small, the alloy will again fail to penetrate the joint.

JOINT DESIGN FOR SOLDERING

Wherever possible, a lap joint should be used for this welding process. A good rule of thumb to follow is to make the lap 1-1/2 times the thickness of the thinnest metal being joined. When joining metal tubing, a lap equal to the diameter of the inside tube should be sufficient. If a butt joint has to be soldered, a backing strip

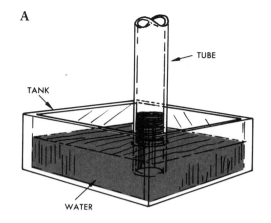

A

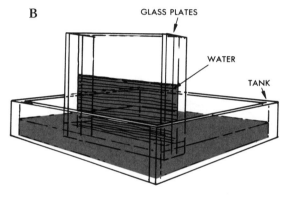

B

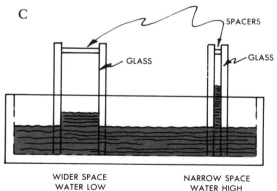

C

WIDER SPACE WATER LOW   NARROW SPACE WATER HIGH

Courtesy of Union Carbide Canada Limited

Figure 9-2 Capillary action

should be used if possible. Figure 9-3 shows correctly assembled lap and butt joints.

For the solder to flow properly, so that the capillary action will take place, the joint must be assembled with

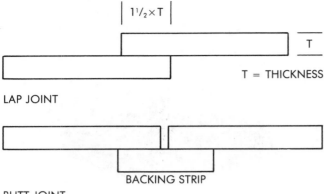

LAP JOINT

BUTT JOINT

Figure 9-3   Two joints suitable for soldering

a clearance or gap that is neither too large nor too small. A gap of 0.003 in. (0.08 mm) and 0.005 in. (0.12 mm) is appropriate.

PREPARING THE METAL

In order for the solder to wet or "tin" the surface, the metal must be perfectly clean. The flux is used to clean the metal, but it cannot do the job without some advance preparation. Before applying the flux, use an abrasive such as steel wool or emery paper or even an acid etching solution to ensure that the joint is clean.

When using acid, observe the strictest safety precautions. Never allow water to drop into acid, and do not let it touch any part of your body or clothing. If it does, wash the area immediately, and remove any affected clothing. If acid ever gets in your eyes, flush them out with water right away.

STEPS IN SOLDERING A JOINT

1. The metal must be clean.
2. Assemble the joint and check the gap between the pieces of metal. Spacing is important.
3. Apply flux sparingly, or use a flux-cored solder.
4. Apply heat with a soldering iron or torch.
5. Clean flux residue from the joint area. (Usually hot water and washing soda followed by a clear water rinse will be sufficient.)

TEST YOUR KNOWLEDGE

1. What is hard soldering?
2. What are the advantages of using alloys with a high tin content?
3. What is the main purpose of a flux?
4. Why should chloride flux not be used on electrical parts?
5. What is the best joint design for soldering?
6. Why is the gap or space between the pieces of metal important?
7. Why should the metal be cleaned?

9-3 SILVER BRAZING

Silver brazing has many other names such as silver soldering, hard soldering, and low-temperature brazing. This nonfusion process is quite a simple procedure. Almost all commercial metals, ferrous and nonferrous, can be silver brazed. The preparation and application are the most important points to be studied. The difference between **silver brazing** and **soldering** is that the silver brazing filler has a different composition, and a melting point above 425°C (800°F). While solder alloys are composed basically of tin and lead, silver brazing alloys consist of copper and silver (plus a few other elements), which have the higher melting points. The silver content may vary from 5% to 50%.

PREPARING THE METAL

The metal to be brazed must be absolutely clean. If the base metal is clean, the molten metal from the welding rod will flow over the cleaned area evenly and smoothly. The molten metal from the welding rod will not flow over an unclean area, but will tend to form in small balls on the surface of the base metal. The base metal may be cleaned by grinding, filling, or rubbing with steel wool. The method of cleaning used will depend on the amount of rust, mill scale, or paint on the surface of the base metal. The metal must be clean.

FLUX

The purpose of the flux is to chemically clean the base metal and to remove any impurities from the weld. It also allows the molten filler metal to flow more easily onto the base metal. The flux for silver brazing is supplied in a **paste form** and should be brushed onto both pieces of metal before joining. The ordinary commercial types of flux on the market are best. In an emergency, it is possible to use ordinary household borax mixed with hot water. The flux should always be removed from the completed weld because of its corrosive action. When welding copper to copper with silver braze, a flux is not necessary.

SILVER BRAZING RODS

Silver brazing alloy can be purchased in a variety of shapes, for example, as a rod, as a flat strip, or as a washer. The most commonly used form is the long, round welding rod. These alloys are expensive and should not be wasted. Only a small amount is required for a joint.

FLAME

A neutral to slightly carburizing flame should be used. In silver brazing, the flame should be moved continually in a circular motion, and the inner cone should not be held too close to the metal at any time. The metal is heated, not melted. Again, as in braze welding, a larger size tip should be used.

TEMPERATURE

It is not necessary to apply the flame directly to the brazing alloy. The heat from the base metal is sufficient to melt the alloy. The whole joint, not just one area, should be heated at one time. The flux will give a good indication of when the metal is hot enough for brazing. Near the brazing temperature, the flux will start to bubble, then it will become liquid. At this point apply the brazing rod. If the flux forms black patches, however, it indicates overheating.

JOINT DESIGN FOR SILVER BRAZING

In silver brazing, joint designs are limited, and gap or clearance is critical. To allow the capillary action to take place, the gap should be no less than 0.38 mm (0.0015 in.)

and no greater than 0.2 mm (0.008 in.). A lap joint is most suitable. An overlap that is three times the thickness of the thinnest metal used in the joint is usually sufficient. Where possible, all pieces should be flat and straight.

EXERCISE #1
STEPS IN SILVER BRAZING A LAP JOINT

1. Obtain three pieces of metal each about 25 mm × 50 mm × 1.5 mm (1 in. × 2 in. × 1/16 in.)
2. Prepare the welding equipment.
3. Select a tip according to the thickness of the metal.
4. Obtain silver brazing alloy and flux.
5. Clean the metal.
6. Apply the flux at the areas to be joined (Figure 9-4A).
7. Assemble the pieces of metal to form a lap joint (Figure 9-4B).
8. Light the torch and set for a neutral flame.
9. Proceed to heat the joint and the surrounding area.
10. Remember to keep the torch rotating in a circular motion.
11. Watch the flux closely:
    a. When heat is first applied to the flux, it will become white and powdery after bubbling.

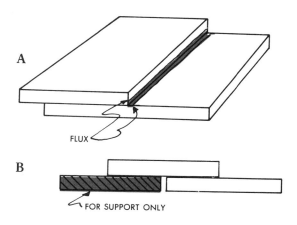

Figure 9-4   Lap joint

b. As more heat is applied, the flux will become fluid and will flow along the joint.

12. When the flux is molten and fluid, it is time to apply the brazing alloy.

13. Apply the silver brazing alloy to the joint a short distance from the flame. The alloy should melt and spread evenly along the joint. The flame must not be played on the silver brazing alloy at any time.

14. Use the flux sparingly because the brazing alloy will spread wherever the flux has cleaned the metal.

SAFETY

Apart from the normal safety procedures one should take when working with welding equipment, extra precautions should be taken in silver brazing. Some of the brazing alloys contain cadmium, which can produce dangerous fumes. Fluxes which have a fluoride base produce fumes which can also be dangerous.

> Read the manufacturers' labels very carefully and if any of the above are present, not only should the area be ventilated but a respirator or a mask with an independent air supply should be used (not just a filter mask).

Other metals that produce hazardous fumes are lead, zinc, mercury, and berrilium. The cleaning solvent which is used to clean the metal should be carefully washed off before brazing commences because its fumes can become toxic when exposed to heat.

TEST YOUR KNOWLEDGE

1. What is another name for silver brazing?
2. Which metals can be silver brazed?
3. What metals make up the basic silver brazing alloy?
4. What is the main purpose of the flux?
5. When brazing copper to copper, is it necessary to use a flux?
6. What is meant by capillary action?
7. Where does the heat come from that actually melts the brazing alloy?
8. What points must be observed with regard to the flame?
9. How does the flux help in indicating the temperature of the metal?

9-4 ALUMINUM SOLDERING AND BRAZING

Aluminum may also be soldered or brazed. The procedures for preparation, joint design, cleaning, and welding are similar to those used for silver brazing. Two unique problems exist in joining aluminum, however. These are the removal of the oxide coating and its high thermal conductivity.

The solder alloys for aluminum are zinc, tin, lead, and cadmium. The zinc base alloy has high strength and good corrosion resistance, but it requires high temperatures. This presents some problems in application and does not allow the use of noncorrosive organic fluxes. The tin base alloys provide medium strength and corrosion resistance, but they are easier to use than the zinc base alloys. Lead base alloys are not widely used. Cadmium base alloys are the best, but they are expensive.

Alloys for aluminum brazing are, of course, aluminum based rather than silver or copper based. The flux is usually a powder which is mixed to a paste with distilled water before application to the joint.

9-5 BRAZE WELDING

Braze welding is like silver brazing in that it uses filler metals that melt at temperatures above 425°C (800°F). However, it is a different process in most other ways. In silver brazing, the filler alloy is distributed through the joint by capillary action, whereas in braze welding the principles of fusion welding apply (except that the base metal is not melted). The two processes also differ in joint design and technique. The problems of limited joint designs and crucial clearance in silver brazing do not exist in braze welding. Almost any joint design can be braze welded, and spacing, though important for penetration, is not as critical.

The success of braze welding is based on the fact that the brass or bronze alloy used in the process will flow into properly prepared surfaces to produce an excellent bond. Although this welding process can be used on many metals, here the discussion and exercises will be confined to the braze welding of ferrous metals, such as steel, iron, or alloys of both.

PREPARING THE METAL

As in soldering and silver brazing, the metal to be braze welded must be absolutely clean and the same methods of cleaning may be used.

FLUX

The flux is also used for the same purpose as in soldering and silver brazing. It chemically cleans the base metal, removes any impurities from the weld, and allows the braze metal to flow more easily onto the base metal. There are two methods of applying the flux in braze welding:

1. Heat the welding rod, dip it in a powdered flux, and apply it to the weld area as required.
2. Use braze-welding rods to which a flux coating has already been applied.

TINNING

Prior to the actual braze-welding operation, a thin film of braze metal is applied to the area or joint to be brazed. This is called **tinning**. On properly cleaned, light-gauge metal, this tinning takes place as the braze weld is being applied. However, on heavier metal or veed joints, the entire area to be braze welded must be tinned before successive layers are applied. The metal **must** be tinned by one of these two methods.

BRAZE-WELDING RODS

There are many types of braze-welding rods. The most common rod used for welding ferrous metals is a copper/zinc alloy (called **brass**). This rod contains approximately 60% copper and 40% zinc to which may be added small amounts of silicon, tin, manganese, and iron. Each addition is designed to give the welding rod a desired characteristic, such as increased tensile strength, fewer fumes, greater ductility.

Extreme care should be taken in applying the flame in braze welding. If the welding rod is overheated, the zinc in the welding rod will boil out (volatilize). This not only ruins the weld, but the fumes can cause nausea. Therefore, when braze welding or welding brass, suitable arrangements for ventilation should be made, or a respirator should be worn. When zinc boils out, it appears as a white smoke (zinc oxide), and can be seen readily at the side of the weld area. The welding rod must not be overheated.

FLAME

The proper flame adjustment is essential for good results. As in most oxy-acetylene welding, the flame should be **neutral**. The tip size used is usually one size larger than the one used in fusion welding for the same thickness of metal. The correct flame must be used.

TEMPERATURE

The proper temperature for braze welding is reached when the base metal turns a **dull red** or just begins to glow. A little practice is required to recognize this. Of course, lighting conditions have to be taken into consideration. If the welding rod is applied before the base metal is hot enough, the braze metal will form into small balls on the surface of the base metal. On the other hand, if the base metal is too hot, the braze metal will boil and spread over a wide area, and be accompanied by white smoke at the side of the weld area.

TEST YOUR KNOWLEDGE

1. Why must the base metal be cleaned?
2. Name one method that can be used to clean the metal.
3. What is meant by tinning the base metal?
4. What is the result of overheating the welding rod?
5. How can the correct temperature for braze welding be recognized?
6. Which type of flame should be used to braze weld ferrous metals?

7. What is the purpose of the flux?

STEPS IN RUNNING A BRAZE-WELDED BEAD

Running a braze-welded bead is similar to running a bead with a welding rod in fusion welding. Care must be taken to have the bead uniform in height and width. The ripples should be evenly spaced also. However, it must be remembered that the base metal is not melted as in fusion welding. Study the examples shown in Figure 9-5 before starting to braze weld.

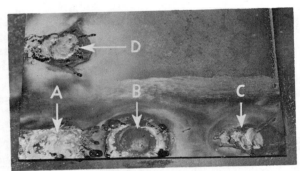

Courtesy of Union Carbide Canada Limited

Figure 9-5　Characteristics of braze welding
A. Correct tinning before welding
B. Too much heat (Note oxidized area in centre)
C. Not enough heat
D. Metal not clean

EXERCISE #2

1. Obtain one piece of metal about 50 mm × 150 mm × 1.5 mm (or 2 in. × 6 in. × 1/16 in.).
2. Obtain one braze-welding rod and flux if the rod is not prefluxed.
3. Grind or file the base metal until it is clean.
4. Place the metal on the welding bench.
5. Light the welding torch, remembering to obtain the correct flame.
6. Preheat the base metal in a straight line across the metal until it becomes a dull, red colour.
7. Apply the welding rod to the metal. If the braze

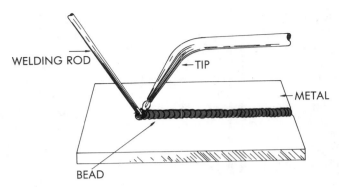

Welding a good braze-welded bead

metal spreads on evenly, without balling or fuming, proceed to tin all along the heated area.
8. After tinning the metal, proceed to weld a bead over the tinned area (Figure 9-6).
9. After this has been practised and the results observed, it will be seen that on light-gauge metal, such as 1.5 mm (or 1/16 in.), the two operations can be carried out as one. That is, if the metal is preheated and the rod applied, as soon as the molten brass puddle is formed, stroking the rod ahead slightly will tin the area in advance.

This latter method applies to light-gauge metals only. If veed joints are used, the joint must be tinned before the layers of bronze are applied. (Figures 9-7 and 9-8 show good and poor braze-welded beads.)

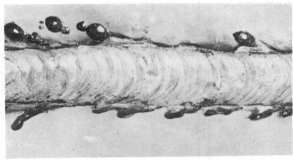

Courtesy of Union Carbide Canada Limited

Figure 9-7　A fairly good braze-welded bead. Dark particles at the side of weld are pieces of slag that have not been removed.

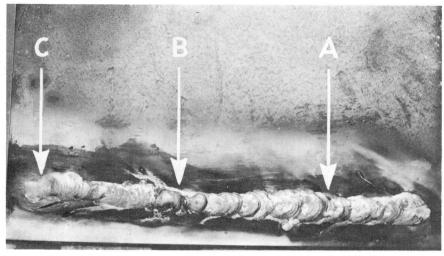

Courtesy of Union Carbide Canada Limited

Figure 9-8 Example of a poor braze-welded bead
A. Rod was added ahead of puddle
B. Rod was melted and dropped on top of metal
C. Overheated metal

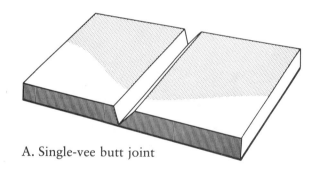

A. Single-vee butt joint

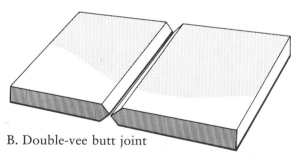

B. Double-vee butt joint

Courtesy MECO St. Louis, U.S.A.

Figure 9-9 Edge preparation for braze welding a butt joint

9-6 BRAZE WELDING JOINTS

Braze welding is used often on lap, tee, and corner joints. Although butt and edge joints can be braze welded, this process is not recommended unless some sort of edge preparation on the metal has been carried out.

BRAZE WELDING A VEED BUTT JOINT

A veed butt joint is a basic butt joint in which the edges to be joined are prepared in a special way. The edges are prepared in this way to allow the molten weld metal to penetrate the full thickness of the base metal. The edges are prepared in a single vee (Figure 9-9A) or a double vee (Figure 9-9B), depending on the thickness of the base metal.

EXERCISE #3
STEPS IN BRAZE WELDING A SINGLE-VEE BUTT JOINT

1. Obtain two pieces of metal each about 50 mm × 150 mm × 6 mm (or 2 in. × 6 in. × 1/4 in.)
2. Obtain braze-welding rods and prepare the welding equipment.

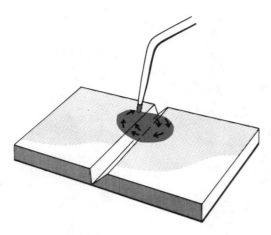

A. Movement of torch

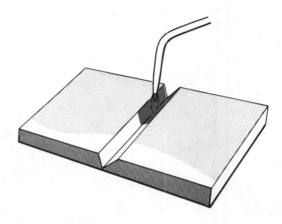

B. Concentrating the heat

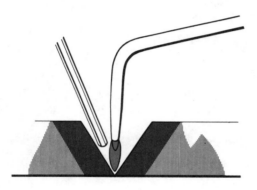

C. Applying the welding rod

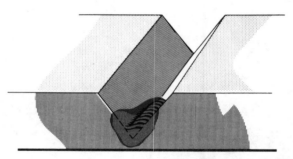

Courtesy MECO St. Louis, U.S.A.

D. Filling the bottom of the vee

Figure 9-10   Welding a single-vee butt joint

3. Prepare the edges to be joined by bevelling each one so that when they are placed together they form a vee.

4. Place the two pieces flat on the welding bench. Make sure that they are properly aligned and cleaned.

5. After preheating the metal, tack weld each end with the braze welding rod.

6. Start at one end and heat the metal by moving the torch in a circular motion (Figure 9-10A).

7. When the base metal has become a dull, red colour, move the torch to the bottom of the vee and heat along the entire length of the vee. This pro-

cess is shown in Figure 9-10B.

8. Apply the welding rod, and proceed to braze weld along the joint (Figure 9-10C).

9. In the case of a 6 mm (1/4 in.) thick piece of metal, two or three layers of braze weld should be sufficient.

10. Do not attempt to fill the vee in one pass of welding. Complete one bead of welding, joining the two pieces at the bottom of the vee. Then start over again, and weld layer on top of layer until the vee has been filled (Figure 9-10D).

11. Remember to observe all the rules of braze welding given earlier.

TEST YOUR KNOWLEDGE

1. What is the appearance of a good braze-welded bead?
2. What precautions must be remembered with regard to the base metal in braze welding?
3. What is meant by preheating?
4. Of the five basic joints, which ones are not recommended for braze welding?
5. Why must certain joints be veed before they can be braze welded?

BUILDING UP A GEAR TOOTH WITH BRAZE WELDING

Braze welding is often used to repair broken parts or to build up surfaces that have become worn by usage. Let us consider a tooth that has been broken off a large gear wheel.

The broken area is first cleaned and made ready for repair (Figure 9-11A). The area is then built up with braze welding as shown in figures 9-11B and 9-11C. The smooth shape was made by using only the flame and a

A. The first stage of repair

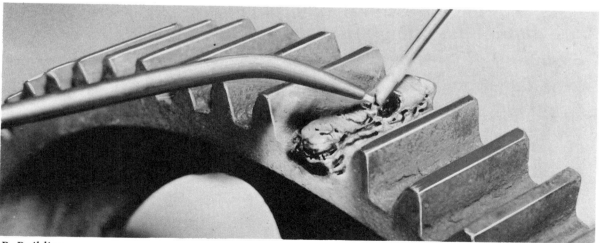

B. Building up

Figure 9-11   Braze welding a gear tooth

Courtesy of Union Carbide Canada Limited

C. Finished weld

D. Finished tooth

Figure 9-11   (cont'd)

welding rod. The tooth is then machined to a proper size and is ready for use again (Figure 9-11D).

The tooth can also be formed and shaped by using carbon blocks during the braze-welding operation (Figure 9-12). A skilful welder can finish the tooth so that further machining is not necessary.

OTHER BRAZE WELDING APPLICATIONS

Braze welding is also an excellent method of joining galvanized iron. (The galvanized coating on iron protects the metal from rusting.) Although this coating will be burned off during any welding operation, the braze weld actually spreads and covers most of the area where the burning off occurred. Since braze welding also prevents iron from rusting, it takes the place of the galvanized protective coating. This, and another braze-welding application are shown in figures 9-13 and 9-14.

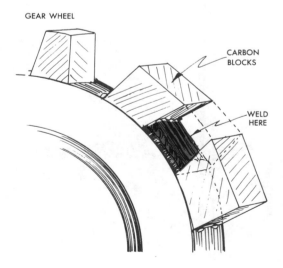

Figure 9-12   Another method of building a gear tooth

Courtesy of Union Carbide Canada Limited

Figure 9-13 Braze welding galvanized pipe

Courtesy of Union Carbide Canada Limited

Figure 9-14 Ornamental railing joined with braze welding

ADVANTAGES OF BRAZE WELDING

Braze welding requires less heat than fusion welding because it is not necessary to wait until the base metal is molten. This also allows the joint to be completed quickly. Therefore, braze welding is faster than fusion welding. By using less heat and moving faster, less distortion is produced in the base metal.

DISADVANTAGES OF BRAZE WELDING

When braze welding ferrous metals, the weld area will be a different colour from the base metal. Braze welding also deteriorates at temperatures over 260°C (500°F). It should not be used on parts that would be subjected to high temperatures while in use. Figure 9-15 shows a suitable application for braze welding.

A. Tack welding a new section in place

Courtesy of Union Carbide Canada Limited

B. Braze welding a new section

Figure 9-15 Braze welding an automobile

9-7 BRONZE WELDING (SURFACING)

Bronze welding, or **surfacing**, is a term applied to the method of building up, by braze welding, parts that have become worn by friction. Pistons are a good example of this type of part. When a piston becomes worn, it must be scrapped or built up by adding cylinder liners. However, with bronze surfacing the piston can be easily and economically rebuilt before the wear has gone far enough to affect the efficiency of the machine.

REBUILDING A PISTON WITH BRONZE WELDING

The piston is prepared for bronze welding. Then grooves are cut in the piston at the points where the most wear exists (Figure 9-16). The grooves are filled in with bronze metal, and a layer is welded all around the outside of the piston and over the grooves to build up its diameter. Figure 9-17 shows the actual welding operation. The piston is surrounded by fire bricks (to keep the heat in) and is being rotated while the welder applies the bronze weld metal. A completely welded and rebuilt piston is

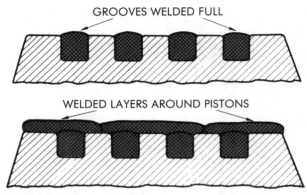

GROOVES WELDED FULL

WELDED LAYERS AROUND PISTONS

A. Welding procedure

A. Piston ready for welding

Courtesy of Union Carbide Canada Limited

B. Weld in progress

Figure 9-17   Filling in the grooves with bronze metal

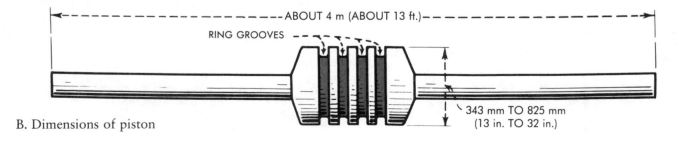

ABOUT 4 m (ABOUT 13 ft.)

RING GROOVES

343 mm TO 825 mm
(13 in. TO 32 in.)

B. Dimensions of piston

Figure 9-16   Preparing a piston for bronze welding

Courtesy of Union Carbide Canada Limited

shown in Figure 9-18. Now the piston is machined down to the correct size. The piston shown in Figure 9-19 was rebuilt for approximately half the cost of a new piston.

Courtesy of Union Carbide Canada Limited

Figure 9-18 Completed weld

Courtesy of Union Carbide Canada Limited

Figure 9-19 Final machining in progress

ADVANTAGES AND DISADVANTAGES OF BRONZE WELDING (SURFACING)

Since this is a braze-welding process, the same advantages and disadvantages apply. There is one more important disadvantage that should be mentioned, however. Where the piston (or parts) are subject to a push-pull type of wear and have been rebuilt by bronze welding at least once, there is a possibility of the base metal cracking. This occurs only with steel. Worn steel should be bronze welded only once. Cast iron, however, may be bronze welded over and over again.

TEST YOUR KNOWLEDGE

1. Name two industries that use braze welding.
2. What is the purpose of cleaning the base metal?
3. What is the purpose of tinning the metal?
4. What is the most common type of braze-welding rod used?
5. What is the purpose of using a flux for braze welding?
6. What is the proper temperature for braze welding?
7. What happens if the metal is overheated?
8. What happens if the base metal is too cold?
9. What is the proper flame for braze welding?

POINTS TO REMEMBER

- Soldering uses filler metals with melting points below 425°C (800°F); brazing and braze welding use filler metals with melting points above.
- Braze welding does not use capillary action; soldering and brazing do.
- Before soldering, brazing, or braze welding, the metal must be perfectly cleaned, using flux.
- Extreme caution should be used, since fumes can be toxic.
- The base metal must not be melted.
- Lap joints are best for soldering and brazing.
- In soldering and brazing, the gap or clearance is critical.
- Braze welding can be used on almost any joint properly prepared, and to build up surfaces.
- All flux residue must be removed.

WORDS TO REMEMBER

solder	flux	zinc
braze	silver	bronze
capillary action	corrosive	galvanized
alloy	residue	tinning

Bronze Welding (Surfacing)   **93**

REVIEW QUESTIONS

1. What is the main difference between soldering and silver brazing?
2. What is the main difference between silver brazing and braze welding?
3. What alloys are used in soft solder?
4. Describe one type of flux used in soft soldering.
5. Give one example of capillary action that can be found in most homes.
6. Why are you cautioned to use the flux sparingly?
7. How does the amount of spacing in the joint affect the strength of the completed joint?
8. Name three advantages of braze welding.
9. Name one disadvantage of braze welding.
10. What is the greatest danger in braze welding?
11. What causes this danger?
12. Describe how the metal is preheated before the actual braze-welding operation is carried out.
13. Why must ventilation be excellent?
14. Why would the lap, tee, and corner joints be most suitable for braze welding?
15. Why is braze welding considered an excellent method of joining galvanized iron?
16. Why would the colour difference be considered a disadvantage?
17. What is the main difference between fusion and nonfusion welding?

10

METAL CUTTING PROCESSES

Although some workers are employed as full-time "burners," most welders will do some cutting or severing (also known as "burning") of metal during their normal day's work. In this chapter you will learn various non-mechanical methods of cutting or severing metal used in the welding industry. (Mechanical methods, such as shearing or nibbling, will not be covered.) After learning the basic principles and methods of cutting or severing metals, you will be able to develop skills in the practical applications of metal cutting and removal by doing the exercises.

10-1 BACKGROUND

Many fuel gases, some of which were described in Chapter 4, are used in oxyfuel cutting. The cutting procedure with these gases is basically the same as with the oxy-acetylene process. In this chapter, the flame exercises will apply to oxy-acetylene, since oxy-acetylene is still the most widely used oxyfuel combination in schools. However, there should be no difficulty in adapting the techniques discussed to any other oxyfuel gas combination. With different oxyfuel gas combinations, the same equipment may be used. Only a different type of cutting tip is required.

Before the oxy-acetylene process was introduced in industry around 1900, most metal had to be cut with a mechanical or manual saw. If the metal had to conform to a certain shape, the cutting had to be done with a milling machine, planer, or lathe. If the design was very complicated, the metal was usually cast in a foundry and then machined to the correct size.

All of these methods were slow and required a great number of people to produce a finished part. With the introduction of oxy-acetylene cutting, however, it was found that many of the complicated shapes that were previously cast could be formed much more quickly and at a lower cost. Today it is possible to cut very complicated shapes and maintain tolerances of a few hundredths of a millimetre by using the oxy-acetylene process (Figure 10-1).

Courtesy of Union Carbide Canada

Figure 10-1   Cutting

The first oxy-acetylene cutting torches had a copper tube clamped to the outside of the welding torch. This tube carried an independent supply of oxygen. The procedure for cutting was to heat the metal with the welding flame, shut off the flame, turn on the oxygen in the extra tube, and direct the stream of oxygen onto the preheated metal. This heating and application of oxygen to the heated spot continued until the metal was cut through. Although crude, this method worked and was the forerunner of today's cutting torch.

10-2 PRINCIPLE OF OXY-ACETYLENE CUTTING

Oxy-acetylene cutting, or, as it is sometimes called, oxy-acetylene burning, is used only to sever ferrous metals (metals containing iron). The melting of the metal plays a very small part in oxy-acetylene cutting. The most important part of the process is the **oxidation** of the metal.

When a ferrous metal is heated until it is red hot and then exposed to pure oxygen, a chemical reaction takes place between the heated metal and the oxygen. This is the oxidation reaction, and it produces a great amount of heat.

Figure 10-2 illustrates this reaction. When the piece

Courtesy of Union Carbide Canada Limited

Figure 10-2   Oxidation

of wire with a red-hot tip is placed in the container of pure oxygen, it bursts into flame immediately and is completely consumed. Similarly, in oxy-acetylene cutting, the combination of red-hot metal and pure oxygen causes rapid burning and oxidation of the metal. By this continuous process of oxidation, the metal can be cut through very rapidly.

Figure 10-3A shows an operator cutting through a steel shaft. This shaft was 450 mm (or 18 in.) thick and weighed more than 9 t (or 10 tons). It was cut through in 16 minutes.

A. Cutting through a steel shaft

B. Cutting through a reinforced concrete wall

Courtesy of Union Carbide Canada Limited

Figure 10-3   Oxy-acetylene cutting

Another use for the oxy-acetylene cutting torch is shown in Figure 10-3B. An operator is cutting through a 355 mm (or 14 in.) thick, reinforced concrete wall. This method is most effective because there is no noise or vibration as there would be if heavy jackhammers were used.

SAFETY RULES FOR OXY-ACETYLENE CUTTING

Since this process uses oxy-acetylene equipment, the rules that have been learned so far will apply. Goggles, gloves, and protective clothing must be worn. There are, however, some additional rules that must be observed.

1. The work area should be clear of unnecessary items.
2. Care must be taken to protect yourself and others from flying sparks (Figure 10-4).
3. Be certain that the metal being cut is properly supported and balanced so that it will not fall on feet or hose.
4. Be sure that there is a clear space underneath the cut in order to allow the slag from the cut to run free of the metal.
5. Particular attention should be paid to the location of the hose and any inflammable material.
6. Care must be taken when starting a cut. If the wrong method is used, the hot metal may be blown back in the operator's face.

10-3 OXY-ACETYLENE CUTTING EQUIPMENT

The basic equipment for cutting is similar to that required for welding, that is, a supply of gas, hose, regulators, and a torch. The same cylinders that are used for welding can be also used for cutting. Since this process uses more oxygen, a manifold system would be best. The same hose can be used as in welding, but where heavy or continuous cutting is to be carried out, a hose

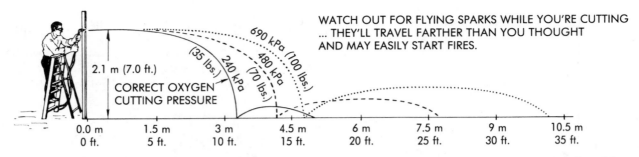

WATCH OUT FOR FLYING SPARKS WHILE YOU'RE CUTTING ... THEY'LL TRAVEL FARTHER THAN YOU THOUGHT AND MAY EASILY START FIRES.

OXYGEN PRESSURE THAT IS TOO HIGH CAN BLOW SPARKS TWICE AS FAR AS NEED BE; OXYGEN IS WASTED ALSO.

Courtesy MECO St. Louis, U.S.A.

Figure 10-4   Cutting hazard

with a larger bore is required. (This ensures an adequate supply of gas.) The same type of regulators are used, as well. However, if heavy cutting is to be carried out, regulators capable of producing much higher pressures are required. The cutting torch, however, is quite different from the welding torch.

THE OXY-ACETYLENE CUTTING TORCH

The purpose of the cutting torch is to supply the flame to preheat the metal and to supply the stream of pure oxygen for cutting. In the cutting torch (Figure 10-5), the oxygen and acetylene valves at the rear of the torch control the preheat flames. The lever controls the high-

pressure oxygen jet for making the cut.

The method of mixing the gases in a cutting torch is the same as the method used in welding torches. They are mixed at equal pressures, or they are mixed using the injector principle. Figure 10-5 shows the internal construction that allows for this mixing, in one type of torch. Note the cutting oxygen tube which allows the pure oxygen to reach the tip without being mixed.

CUTTING ATTACHMENTS

Sometimes, instead of using a cutting torch, a cutting attachment is added to a welding torch handle (Figure 10-6). This will perform the same function as the cutting torch. With the cutting attachment, however, there will

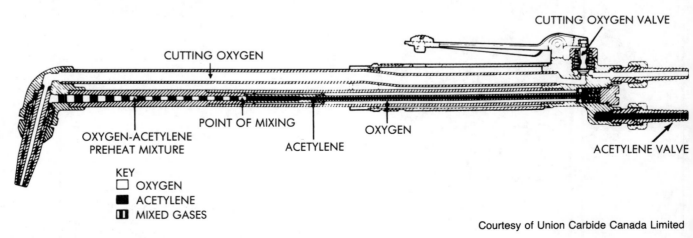

KEY
☐ OXYGEN
■ ACETYLENE
▥ MIXED GASES

Courtesy of Union Carbide Canada Limited

Figure 10-5   Mixture of gases in the torch

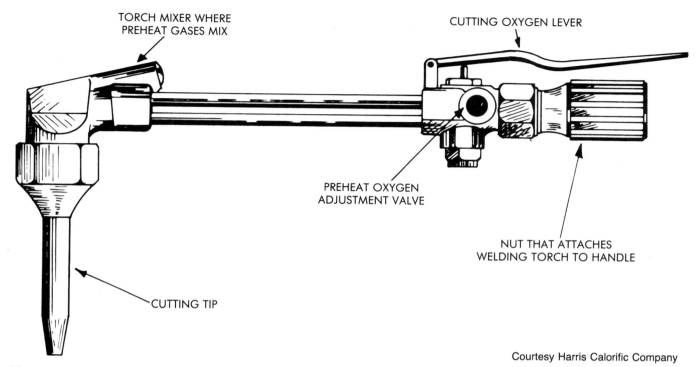

TORCH MIXER WHERE
PREHEAT GASES MIX

CUTTING OXYGEN LEVER

PREHEAT OXYGEN
ADJUSTMENT VALVE

NUT THAT ATTACHES
WELDING TORCH TO HANDLE

CUTTING TIP

Courtesy Harris Calorific Company

Figure 10-6   Cutting attachment

be three valves (two oxygen and one acetylene) and a cutting lever.

> It must be clearly understood that, when using a cutting attachment, the regular oxygen valve on the torch handle does not control the oxygen supply. The oxygen supply should be controlled by the valve on the cutting attachment. For this reason, the welding torch oxygen valve must be wide open at all times when using the cutting attachment. If this valve is not left open, backfiring could easily occur, causing damage to the torch. People who use oxy-acetylene equipment and are unfamiliar with the basic rules place themselves and others in danger. There is one rule that must always be followed when using a cutting attachment. Always be sure when changing from a cutting to a welding operation that the pressures are reduced at the regulators, not at the welding torch valves.

Let us say that you are using 140 kPa (20 psi) oxygen and 20 kPa (3 psi) acetylene for cutting, and you change to a Number 2 welding tip. You should now be using 15 kPa (2 psi) oxygen and 15 kPa (2 psi) acetylene in an equal-pressure torch. If you try to adjust the pressures at the torch valves instead of at the regulators, the higher oxygen pressure will cause the oxygen to back up the acetylene hose and immediately a mixed, highly explosive gas will collect in the acetylene hose. When this happens, the acetylene regulator gauge will show an increase in pressure, although no adjustment has been made to the pressure-adjusting screw.

There are many types and designs of cutting torches available today. Figures 10-7 to 10-10 illustrate some of these.

TEST YOUR KNOWLEDGE

1. What is another name for oxy-acetylene cutting?
2. What metals are cut by this process?

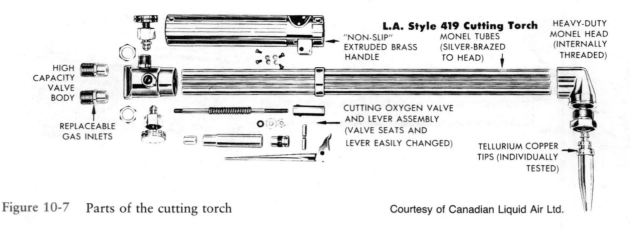

L.A. Style 419 Cutting Torch

HIGH CAPACITY VALVE BODY

REPLACEABLE GAS INLETS

"NON-SLIP" EXTRUDED BRASS HANDLE

MONEL TUBES (SILVER-BRAZED TO HEAD)

CUTTING OXYGEN VALVE AND LEVER ASSEMBLY (VALVE SEATS AND LEVER EASILY CHANGED)

HEAVY-DUTY MONEL HEAD (INTERNALLY THREADED)

TELLURIUM COPPER TIPS (INDIVIDUALLY TESTED)

Figure 10-7   Parts of the cutting torch   Courtesy of Canadian Liquid Air Ltd.

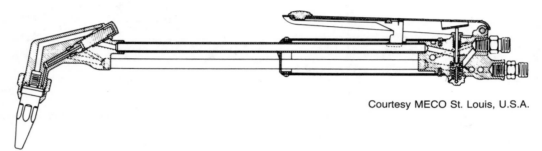

Courtesy MECO St. Louis, U.S.A.

Figure 10-8   Cutting torch

3. What has the oxidation process to do with cutting?
4. Why must the pressures at the regulators always be changed when changing from a cutting to a welding operation?
5. What is the main difference between a cutting torch and a cutting attachment?
6. What is the main safety precaution to be observed when using a cutting attachment?
7. Describe briefly the construction of a cutting torch.

CUTTING TIPS

Cutting tips are made with a ring of openings surrounding the cutting oxygen hole (see Figure 10-11). Each of these openings supplies a preheat flame, giving an even distribution of heat all around the oxygen jet and making it possible to change the direction of the cut at any time. By changing the tip to match the thickness of the metal, any thickness of metal may be cut.

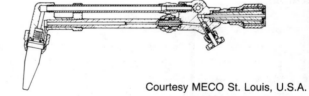

Courtesy MECO St. Louis, U.S.A.

Figure 10-9   Cutting attachment

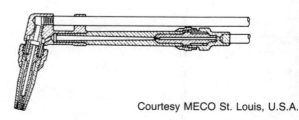

Courtesy MECO St. Louis, U.S.A.

Figure 10-10   Cutting torch

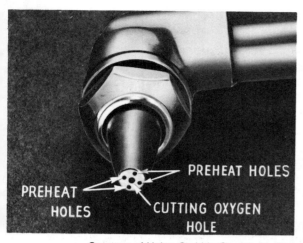

PREHEAT HOLES
PREHEAT HOLES
CUTTING OXYGEN HOLE

Courtesy of Union Carbide Canada Limited

Figure 10-11   Cutting tip

To change a cutting tip, simply unscrew the cutting head nut and remove the tip. The new tip is inserted, and the head nut is retightened (Figure 10-12). The torch is again ready for use.

Most trouble in cutting is caused by the tip holes becoming blocked by small particles of hot metal that stick to the end of the tip. A clear, cylindrical jet of oxygen will always produce a smooth cut. Any obstruction either in the hole or at the end of the tip will slow down the speed and produce a rough cut.

CUTTING PRESSURES

As with the welding torch, it is impossible to list all the different makes and corresponding pressures for each cutting tip. A partial list is shown in the cutting chart shown in Table 10-1, but it is always safer to use the manufacturer's recommendations for the particular torch being used. As in welding, the thicker the metal, the larger the size of tip required.

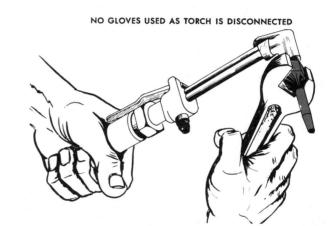

NO GLOVES USED AS TORCH IS DISCONNECTED

Figure 10-12   Installing the tip

TEST YOUR KNOWLEDGE

1. Describe the construction of a cutting tip.
2. What would be the result of the tip becoming partly blocked?

TABLE 10-1 CUTTING CHART

Tip Size		Metal Thickness													
	(inch)	$1/8$	$1/4$	$3/8$	$1/2$	$3/4$	1	$1^{1}/_2$	2	3	4	5	6	8	10
	(mm)	3	6	9.5	12.5	19	25	38	50	75	100	125	150	200	255
L.A.			0	1	1	2	2	3	4	5	5	6	6	7	7
Meco		L00	L0	L1	L1	L2	L2	L2	L2	L3	L3	L3	L4	L5	L6
Linde (#33)		0	0	1	1	1	1								
Linde (CW202)		3	3	4	4	5	5	7	7	7	9	11	11	11	
Linde (type E)		3	3	4	4	5	5	5	7	7	7	9	9	11	

EXERCISE #1
STEPS IN LIGHTING THE CUTTING TORCH

1. Check that the equipment is properly assembled.
2. Be sure to wear the proper protective clothing.
3. Make sure the torch valves are closed and then set the gauges to the correct pressure.
4. Open the acetylene torch valve a 1/4 turn, and light the gas with a friction lighter.
5. Open the acetylene torch valve all the way.
6. Open the oxygen torch valve slowly until a neutral flame is obtained.
7. With the torch lit and adjusted to a neutral flame, press the lever, and check the flame for neutral as in Figure 10-13.
8. To extinguish the flame, release the cutting lever, and shut off first the acetylene torch valve, then the oxygen torch valve.

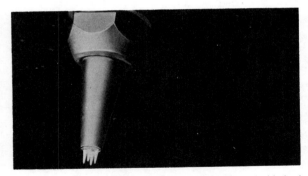

Courtesy of Union Carbide Canada Limited

Figure 10-13   Checking the flame

10-4 CUTTING A STRAIGHT LINE

EXERCISE #2

1. Make sure that the area is clear and that the equipment is properly assembled.
2. Wear the proper protective clothing.
3. Select a piece of metal and place it on the cutting table. Remember that it must be supported.

4. Make sure that the tip corresponds to the metal thickness.
5. With a straight edge and soapstone, draw a line on the metal where the cut is to be made.
6. Mark the line at 5 mm (or 1/4 in.) intervals using a centre punch and hammer. Thus if the chalk line is rubbed out, there will be no need to stop, because the punch mark will show.
7. Light the torch and start at one end of the metal. The torch should be held at a 90° angle to the metal and inclined 5° in the direction of travel (figures 10-14 and 10-15).

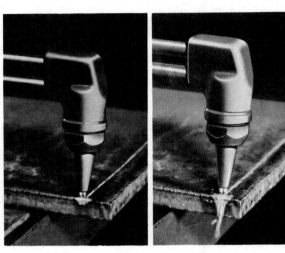

Courtesy of Union Carbide Canada Limited

Figure 10-14   Starting the cut

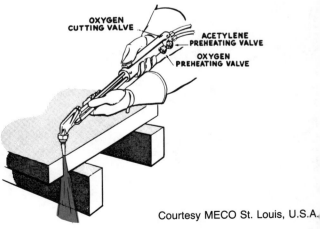

OXYGEN CUTTING VALVE

ACETYLENE PREHEATING VALVE

OXYGEN PREHEATING VALVE

Courtesy MECO St. Louis, U.S.A.

Figure 10-15   Correct position for starting cut

8. The inner cone of flame must be held 3 mm (or 1/8 in.) to 6 mm (or 1/4 in.) away from the metal at all times. If the tip is allowed to touch the metal, it can result in backfire and the hot metal may be blown back into the operator's face.

9. Having lighted the torch and assumed the correct position, proceed to heat a spot at the edge of the metal to a red heat.

10. When the metal has reached a red heat, press the cutting lever and wait until the metal at that spot has been cut through. Proceed to cut along the line at a steady speed (Figure 10-16).

11. If the cut is being made correctly, slag and a fine spray of sparks will appear under the metal. The sparks should be blowing slightly forward in the direction of the cut. Droplets of molten slag should fall slowly from the cut. Also, the correct cutting speed is accompanied by a sputtering sound.

If the metal is cut at the proper speed, the kerf (the space left when the metal is cut) will be clean and free of slag, and the top and bottom edges of the cut will also be square. If the movement is too slow, the kerf will have a rounded top edge, and slag will adhere to the bottom of the cut. However, if the movement is too fast, there will not be enough time for the oxygen jet to go all the way through the metal, and the piece will not be severed (Figure 10-17).

If the metal is not cut through at some parts, it will be necessary to turn off the cutting oxygen (by releasing the lever) and to restart at the part where the cut did not penetrate (Figure 10-18).

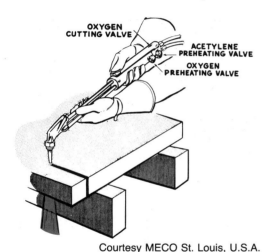

Courtesy MECO St. Louis, U.S.A.

Figure 10-16   Cut in progress

Courtesy of Union Carbide Canada Limited

Figure 10-18   Restarting at a point where the metal was not cut through

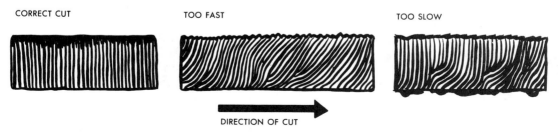

Figure 10-17   Effects of speed

> Care must be taken here to reheat the metal properly so that there is no danger of the metal splashing back in the operator's face.

COMMON FAULTS IN CUTTING

One incorrect method of cutting is shown in Figure 10-19. The reason that the sparks are being projected at an angle, instead of downwards, is that the cut is not going all the way through the metal. This error will cause a part of the molten metal to be blown back against the torch, which might result in backfiring. This problem is caused by the torch being moved too quickly or else by insufficient oxygen pressure.

Figure 10-20A shows a good cut. The others have various defects caused by different cutting faults.

CUTTING HINTS

An easier method of ensuring a straight cut is shown in Figure 10-21. A heavy bar or angle iron is clamped beside the line and used as a guide for the torch. This is beneficial if the cut is a long one.

When cutting round objects, such as bars or shafts, make a small gouge with a cold chisel at the point where the cut is to be started.

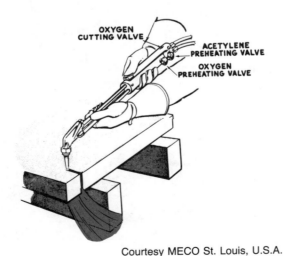

Courtesy MECO St. Louis, U.S.A.

Figure 10-19 Incorrect cutting procedure

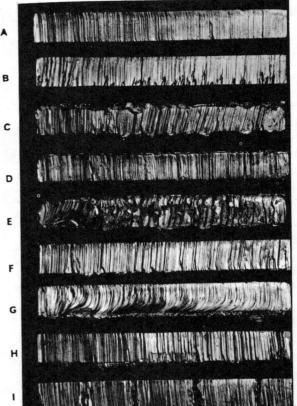

Courtesy of Union Carbide Limited

Figure 10-20   A comparison of cuts
A. A good cut. Edges are square, and lines of cut are vertical.
B. Preheat flames were too small, and speed was too slow.
C. Preheat flames were too long; top edge is melted over.
D. Oxygen pressure was too low, and speed of travel was too slow.
E. Oxygen pressure was too high, and tip size was too small.
F. Cutting speed was too slow; tip size and pressures were correct.
G. Cutting was done too quickly; tip size and pressures were correct.
H. Torch was moved along the cut with an unsteady hand.
I. Cut was lost and not carefully restarted at four places.

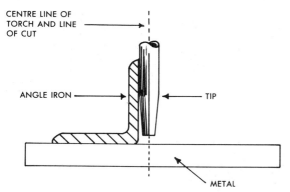

Figure 10-21   A straight line cutting aid

TEST YOUR KNOWLEDGE

1. How can you tell if a good cut has been made?
2. Describe the results of cutting too slowly and too quickly.
3. What does kerf mean?
4. Why should the material be properly supported?
5. Why should particular attention be paid to the location of the hose and inflammable material?
6. What type of flame is used for oxy-acetylene cutting?
7. Why is the line marked with a centre punch?

10-5 PIERCING A HOLE/ CUTTING A CIRCLE

PIERCING A HOLE

Wherever possible all cuts should be started at the edge of the metal. However, sometimes it is necessary to start

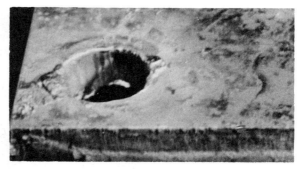

Courtesy of Union Carbide Canada Limited

Figure 10-22   Piercing a hole

a cut at a location other than at the edge. For example, it may be necessary to cut a hole in the centre of a piece of metal (Figure 10-22).

EXERCISE #3 STEPS IN PIERCING A HOLE

1. Light the torch. Adjust to a neutral flame with the cutting lever depressed. Release the lever.
2. Hold the torch at the spot where the hole is to be pierced (Figure 10-23A).
3. When the spot begins to melt, raise the torch approximately 12 mm (or 1/2 in.) above the metal (Figure 10-23B).
4. At the same time, the cutting lever should be slowly depressed, and the torch moved slightly from side to side (Figure 10-23C).
5. When the metal has been pierced, lower the torch to the correct cutting distance, and proceed with the cut (Figure 10-23D).

Figure 10-24 shows the entire process.

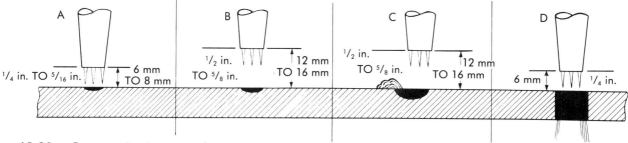

Figure 10-23   Correct piercing procedure

Courtesy of Union Carbide Canada Limited

Figure 10-24
Piercing a hole

Courtesy of Union Carbide Canada Limited

TEST YOUR KNOWLEDGE

1. Why is the torch raised when the metal begins to melt?
2. Why should the lever be depressed slowly?
3. Why is the torch lowered after the metal has been pierced?

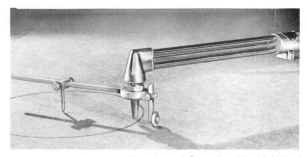

Courtesy of Canadian Liquid Air Ltd.

Figure 10-25   Flash circle burner

CUTTING A CIRCLE

Small circles may be cut by piercing a hole and rotating the torch in a circular manner until the hole has the required diameter. Cutting a large hole and keeping it round is quite difficult, and requires a great deal of practice.

An aid which is often employed in cutting large circles is the **flash circle burner** shown in Figure 10-25. This device works on the same principle as a compass, allowing a perfect circle to be cut with ease.

EXERCISE #4
STEPS IN CUTTING A CIRCLE WITH A FLASH CIRCLE BURNER

1. With a pair of dividers, lay out a circle on a piece of metal.
2. With a centre punch and hammer, mark the circle, and make a deep mark at its exact centre.
3. Attach the flash circle burner to the torch. The distance between the pointer of the circle burner and the centre of the torch nozzle orifice should be equal to the radius of the circle.
4. To check this, place the pointer in the deep centre punch mark. If the measurement is correct, the centre of the tip hole will be in line with the layout line of the circle.
5. Light the torch, and pierce a hole in the metal close to the layout line. Now move the torch in a straight line until the pointer can be put in the deep centre mark.

6. Proceed to cut the circle, keeping the pointer in the mark and moving at a uniform speed.
7. Do not allow the pointer to leave the deep mark until the cut is completed.

In cutting very large circles or arcs, the cut can best be made in sections, using the hands or elbows as a pivot point (Figure 10-26). Before the actual cut is made, one or two practice tries should be made (with an unlit torch) to get the best and most comfortable position possible.

Figure 10-26   Cutting large circles

There does not seem to be any limit to the thickness of the metal that can be cut. Metal as thick as 2.4 m (or 8 ft.) has been cut successfully using the oxy-acetylene process. This, of course, requires special cutting equipment, but thicknesses between 750 mm and 1000 mm (or 30 in. × 40 in.) have been cut manually. Although more skill is required to cut thicker pieces, the same basic techniques are used. (See Figures 10-27 and 10-28.)

TEST YOUR KNOWLEDGE

1. If the inside of the circle is to be saved, on which side of the line should the starting hole be pierced?
2. While the circle is being cut, where should the pointer be located?
3. In cutting large circles, what is the purpose of making one or two tries with an unlit torch?

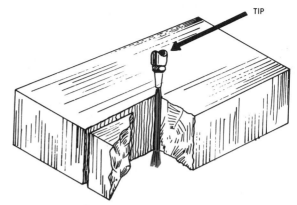

Courtesy of Union Carbide Canada Limited

Figure 10-27   Cutting thick metal

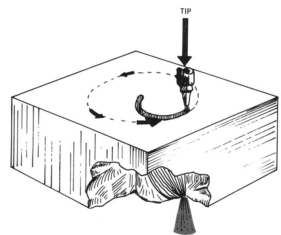

Courtesy of Union Carbide Canada Limited

Figure 10-28   Cutting circles in thick metal

BEVELLING METAL

Bevelling is cutting the metal at an angle rather than square. To bevel a piece of metal, the torch is inclined at an angle, as shown in Figure 10-29.

The important point to remember is that, when selecting the tip size, the thickness of the bevel should be considered, not the thickness of the metal (Figure 10-30). Also, if the position of the cutting nozzle is changed, as shown in Figure 10-31, more heat will be supplied to the cutting area.

Piercing a Hole/Cutting a Circle   **107**

Courtesy of Union Carbide Canada Limited

Figure 10-29   Cutting a bevel

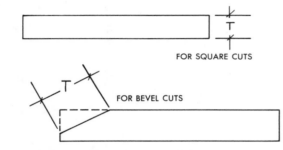

Figure 10-30   Thickness of metal in a bevel

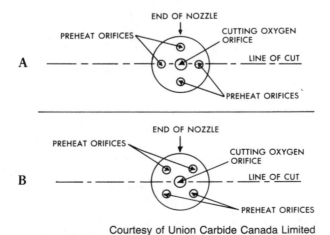

Courtesy of Union Carbide Canada Limited

Figure 10-31   Nozzle setting for square cuts (A) and bevel cuts (B)

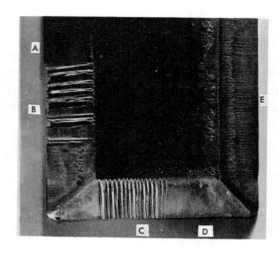

Courtesy of The Lincoln Electric Company

Figure 10-32   Faults in bevel cutting

A. This section is slightly cupped just below the top edge because of excess oxygen pressure.
B. This section is very bad. The deep grooves were caused by frequent stopping and starting.
C. Not enough preheat was used in this section.
D. This is a good cut. Edges are uniform and smooth.
E. Slight beading along top edge indicates a little too much preheating was used. Otherwise, it is a fair cut.

10-6 CUTTING CAST IRON

Some faults common to bevel cutting are shown in Figure 10-32.

The oxy-acetylene process is greatly used in severing heavy scrap metal sections because it is less costly and more portable than other methods. Removal of large cast iron gears and pulleys from shafts is another common use of this process. It also lends itself to edge preparation of large cast iron welds. Cutting cast iron is more expensive than cutting steel, however, due to the composition of cast iron. Since cast iron cutting is also a slower process, more gas is used.

The ease of cutting depends on the composition of the metal. The better grades of cast iron (those that are machinable) are easier to cut than those used for items such as counterbalances, and floor gratings. These poorer types of cast iron require more gas and result in a wider kerf and a slower cutting speed.

> Considerably more heat, sparks, and slag will be generated in cast iron cutting than in steel cutting. It is therefore essential that strict attention be paid to correct clothing, protective equipment, and safety practices.

For cutting the better grades of cast iron, set the regulators to deliver the proper pressures as indicated in Table 10-2. The regulator adjustments are made, of course, with the cutting valve open. Next, light the torch and adjust the preheating flame so that it will show an excess of acetylene. This adjustment should also be made with the cutting valve open to avoid any change in the characteristic of the flame during the actual cutting operation.

The excess of acetylene is indicated by the length of the white inner cone, as in welding, and must be varied to suit the grade and thickness of the metal being cut. This will vary from very little or no excess of acetylene for extremely thin sections, to an excess of 25 mm to 50 mm (or 1 in. to 2 in.) for very heavy or thick sections. Since cast iron cutting is expensive, plan the work carefully. For example, do not start the cut unless you are certain that you can complete it without stopping. If the cut is stopped on a heavy section it will be difficult to restart and will increase gas consumption and cost. As the cutting of cast iron requires a higher ignition temperature, it would be wise to preheat the heavier sections along the line of cutting. Having preheated the metal, bring the tip of the torch to the starting point. Hold the torch on an angle of approximately 40° to 50° and heat a spot about 12 mm (or 1/2 in.) in diameter to a molten condition (Figure 10-33). With the end of the preheat flame about 5 mm (or 1/4 in.) from the metal, start to move the torch with a swinging motion (side to side) as shown in Figure 10-34 and open the high-pressure cutting valve. Gradually bring the torch along the line of cut, continuing the swinging motion. As the cut progresses, straighten the torch angle to approximately 65° to 75°, as shown in Figure 10-35, increasing the penetration of the cut.

If the first attempt is a failure, keep trying. Additional

TABLE 10-2 CAST IRON CUTTING PRESSURE TABLE (STANDARD OR SUPER CUTMASTER CUTTING TORCH)

Size of Tip	Thickness of Metal mm (in.)	Oxygen Pressure kPa (lb./in.²)	Acetylene Pressure kPa (lb./in.²)
L3 Style C	12 (1/2) 19 (3/4) 25 (1) 38 (1 1/2) 50 (2)	280 (42) 310 (44) 350 (50) 420 (62) 490 (70)	48 to 55 (7 to 8)
L-4 Style C	75 (3) 100 (4) 150 (6) 200 (8) 250 (10) 300 (11 3/4-12)	550 (80) 620 (86) 760 (120) 920 (130) 1040 (150) 1170 (160)	55 to 70 (8 to 11)

Courtesy *MECO* St. Louis, U.S.A.

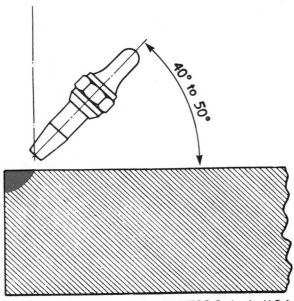

Courtesy MECO St. Louis, U.S.A.

Figure 10-33   Starting a cast iron cut

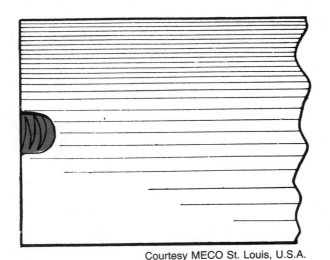

Courtesy MECO St. Louis, U.S.A.

Figure 10-34   The torch is moved in a swinging motion

heat is favourable to cast iron cutting and success should follow. The width of the cut will vary with the thickness and grade of cast iron. Cuts will be wider for the heavier sections or poorer grades. The same swinging movement

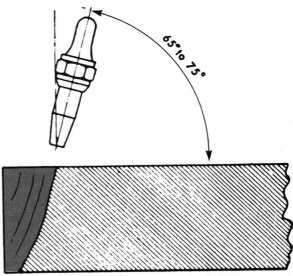

Courtesy MECO St. Louis, U.S.A.

Figure 10-35   Straightening the torch to 65° to 75°

is carried throughout the entire length of the cut. As experience and confidence develops, the length of the swinging action may be reduced. This will result in a narrower kerf and less gas consumption. On heavy sections, sufficient heat is usually generated to allow the cut to proceed without interruption. On the lighter sections, however, more difficulty is experienced. On lighter or thinner sections quite often the top edge will become dark. This indicates that the section is too cold for further progress. If this occurs, start over again by heating a small circle as before. This time, however, gradually raise the torch and incline it so as to cut away the lower portion of the section. Then proceed as before. As long as the top of the cutting edge appears bright, continue the cut until it is completed. In cast iron cutting, the lag of the cut is always more pronounced than in steel, and even with the torch held straight, it cannot be entirely eliminated.

Proceed at a slow steady pace. Do not try to hurry the cutting action.

STACK CUTTING

The operation in Figure 10-36 is called stack cutting. A number of pieces of metal are piled one on top of the

Courtesy of Union Carbide Canada Limited

Figure 10-36   Stack cutting

other and held tightly by means of clamps or tack welds. The pieces are then cut as one single unit and will produce a number of identical parts. The torch in this case is operated mechanically.

Figure 10-37 shows the scope of the oxy-acetylene cutting process. The equipment is a powder lance, and it is being used to cut a 1.2 m (or 4 ft.) section from a

Courtesy of Union Carbide Canada Limited

Figure 10-37   Cutting a concrete wall

reinforced concrete wall. This wall is part of an underground turbine test pit.

10-7 METAL POWDER CUTTING (POC)

In this process, **iron powder** is injected into the oxygen stream before it leaves the cutting tip, creating extra heat and a flux to oxidize the base metal. Powder cutting is gradually being replaced by newer processes such as plasma arc cutting. However, for many years it was the only successful method of cutting stainless steel, high-nickel steel, and aluminum.

When these metals are cut, they form an oxide which actually has a higher melting point than the parent metal. The formation of these oxides prevented further oxidation of the base metal. This caused the cutting action to cease, since cutting is based on the continual formation and removal of oxidized metal. When iron powder was introduced to the cutting area, it burned, and the temperature at the cut increased. Then the oxides with higher melting points did melt. This allowed the cut to continue. The first torch used for powder cutting was a basic oxy-acetylene cutting torch with an extra tube fastened to the side of the torch to supply the iron powder. Over the years, improvements were made until special torches designed specifically for powder cutting were developed. However, the process is basically the same as cutting with an ordinary oxy-acetylene torch. It may be carried out mechanically or manually. It may also be done with single or multiple torches as in any other cutting process currently in use.

Powder cutting has sometimes been referred to as flux injection. However, this is a slightly different process. With **flux injection**, a chemical flux is added to the oxygen stream, but it does not burn like the iron powder. Instead, it forms a more fluid slag with the oxides. The slag is then blown away by the oxygen jet.

10-8 SHIELDED METAL ARC CUTTING (SMAC)

A primitive but effective cut can be made with an ordinary arc welding electrode or a carbon electrode and a regular welding machine. The cut will have a rough appearance. This is because it is a melting process, which produces the same effect as holding the electrode too long in one spot. Any arc welding electrode may be used, but an (E41010-11) E6010-11 will work best. If using carbon electrodes, graphite or hard carbon are most suitable.

The amperage used in SMAC is 30% higher than would normally be used for the same electrode when welding in the flat position. With the higher amperage, small electrodes will heat up more quickly. This means that electrodes smaller than 0.4 mm (5/32 in.) should not be used. If possible, you should start at the top edge of the metal. When the arc is struck, you then move the electrode away to form a long arc. When the metal starts to melt, you shorten the arc. This long arc/short arc technique is continued until a kerf has been formed. Then you gradually move along the line of cut, continuing to use this same technique. Some electrodes are specially designed for cutting metal with the arc. They are **hollow**, which allows the oxygen a direct passage through to the area being cut.

10-9 AIR CARBON ARC CUTTING (AAC)

This process, called air carbon arc cutting by the AWS, is also commonly referred to as arc air gouging. Widely used for gouging out defects in welds or flaws in castings, AAC is also used for preparing the edges of plates for welding. AAC makes use of the fact that when an arc is struck, the base metal immediately under the electrode starts to melt. If a jet of air is directed at this molten metal, the molten metal is blown away. AAC does not depend on oxidizing metal as oxy-acetylene cutting does. It can therefore be used with all metals.

Although this is a relatively simple process, the following safety precautions should be noted. Considerable quantities of sparks are generated because of the high air pressure used to blow the molten metal away. Fire precautions must therefore be strictly enforced. Because AAC can be used on a wide variety of metals (with attendant fumes)

there must be adequate ventilation. Finally, since the compressed air used in AAC produces a loud noise, ear protection must be worn. Of course, the usual protective clothing for welding and cutting must also be worn.

POWER SOURCE

Any standard welding power source can be used with AC, as long as it has an open circuit voltage (OCV) of at least 60 V. Alternating current (AC) should be used only with an electrode designed for AC. If a rectifier is used, it must be three-phase. Generators are often used. However, they will increase the noise level. Because of the high surges of power during the process, any power source used should have overload protection.

ELECTRODES

There are several types of electrodes available for AAC. Some of these are the round, semi-round, and flat. Among the round electrodes available are ones that screw into the other electrodes, to form one continuous electrode. Direct current (DC) electrodes can be plain or copper-coated. AC electrodes are copper-coated only. The most commonly used electrode is the carbon graphite copper-coated electrode, similar to the ones used in carbon arc welding (CAW). The size of the electrode will determine the maximum width of the groove. The electrodes range in size from 0.4 mm (5/32 in.) to 25 mm (1 in.) and are used at amperages from 90 A to 2200 A. As a rule of thumb, the groove should be about 3 mm (1/8 in.) wider than the electrode.

AIR SUPPLY

Ordinary compressed air from a pipeline, compressor, or cylinder is used in the AAC process. The correct pressure will depend on the size of the electrode used. However, pressure should not be less than 275 kPa (40 psi) or more than 700 kPa (100 psi). The volume of the compressed air must be sufficient to blow away the molten metal, of course.

ELECTRODE HOLDERS

The most common type of manual holder is shown in Figure 10-38. The electrode is held in the jaws of the holder, which can be rotated to any angle. The jaws are also equipped with air passages which allow the compressed air to be directed along the electrode path to the molten metal. Each holder has a button or lever which, when depressed, operates the high-pressure air supply. The power and air are supplied to the holder through a specially designed cable.

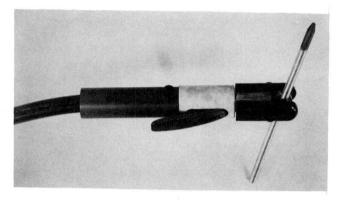

Courtesy The Lincoln Electric Co.

Figure 10-38   Electrode holder used in air carbon arc cutting (AAC)

EXERCISE #5
CUTTING (GOUGING) WITH AIR CARBON ARC CUTTING (AAC)

1. Obtain a piece of mild steel 12 mm (or 1/2 in.) thick.
2. Position electrode in holder with 150 mm (or 6 in.) sticking out.
3. Set amperage for electrode chosen.
4. Make sure air jets on torch are pointing towards arc strike area.
5. Turn the air on and turn welding machine on.
6. Strike the arc (remember to observe all safety precautions).
7. Establish angle (remember that the higher the angle, the more the arc will penetrate).

8. When arc, angle, and air stream are established, proceed to move along the cutting or gouging line.
9. If possible, keep your arm on an arm rest. The steadier the movement of your hand, the smoother the cut or gouge will be.

Figures 10-39 and 10-40 show the air carbon arc cutting process.

Courtesy The Lincoln Electric Co.

Figure 10-39   A gouge being made by air carbon arc cutting (AAC)

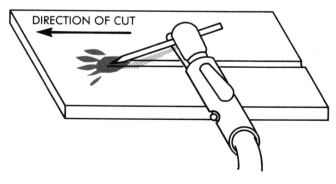

DIRECTION OF CUT

Figure 10-40   Positioning for air carbon arc cutting (AAC)

10-10 PLASMA ARC CUTTING (PAC)

Plasma arc cutting is much faster than oxy-acetylene cutting. At the same time, it uses less heat and can be done on all metals. By forcing a high-pressure gas over the arc inside a specially designed holder and through a very small orifice (hole), the gas is heated to the temperature of the plasma (see Figure 10-41). The gas is then forced by the high pressure through the orifice. (This process is similar to the one that occurs in the engine of a supersonic jet plane.) It is not uncommon for the gas to reach temperatures of 110 800°C (20 000°F). The usual power source is DCSP with a minimum open circuit voltage (OCV) of 100 V.

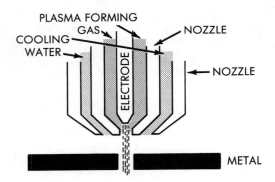

Figure 10-41   Plasma arc cutting (PAC)

The electrode used is a standard thoriated tungsten electrode. (This is the same electrode that would be used in GTAW.) The gas used to form the plasma is selected according to the type of metal being cut. Nonferrous and carbon steels use a nitrogen or nitrogen mix as a plasma former. The newer, more exotic metals such as titanium use an argon gas. Because of the high temperatures generated, a cooling system is necessary to keep the torch handle cool. Under ideal conditions, using a 19 mm (3/4 in.) plate, a plasma arc cutting will cut 5 times faster than the oxy-acetylene process. With PAC it is possible to cut 38 mm (1 1/2 in.) of metal at speeds of up to 11 mm/s (25 in./min.).

10-11 UNDERWATER CUTTING

Underwater cutting is simply normal cutting that is done underwater. Both arc and oxyfuel cutting processes may be used. It requires specially designed equipment. And with oxyfuel processes, only some of the gases can be used underwater. These are propane, hydrogen, acetylene, and some mixtures of fuel gases. One of the problems that had to be solved before underwater cutting could be used was the **back pressure on hoses** as the depth increased.

Propane is unsuitable for use in shallow depths. Acetylene can be used up to depths of approximately 6 m (20 ft.). In depths greater than this the back pressure increases quite rapidly. The pressure of the acetylene would have to be raised to offset this back pressure. However, as you learned in Chapter 4, acetylene cannot be used at pressures over 100 kPa (15 psi). The newer gases such as MAPP are being tried out, but even MAPP cannot be used at depths greater than 30 m (100 ft.) because of the back pressure. To date, the only gas that can be used successfully at any depth is hydrogen. (Hydrogen is the only gas that does not liquefy below a certain depth.)

It is possible to cut underwater using ordinary cutting methods. These work only in very shallow water, however. With the arc process, special equipment must be used, including insulated holders and hollow electrodes coated with ceramic. With this process, it is also preferable to use DC, rather than AC. A jet of high-pressure oxygen is passed through the hollow electrode, similar to the oxygen lance method. This process can be used at any depth. Because of the high amperage and the presence of water, special precautions are taken to protect the diver.

10-12 MECHANIZED CUTTING

The first cutting machine was a regular cutting torch mounted on a motorized carriage. It was used just for cutting straight lines. Although not much faster, it was more accurate than a hand-held torch. Further development led to the addition of a trammel bar or radius rod (see Figure 10-25) with a fixed centre point for cutting circles. The first template machines were then developed. A metal template was suspended above the metal to be cut and a magnetic tracer followed the simple shape. At the same time, the torch cut the pattern on the metal below. A further development came with the introduction of multiple-cutting torches, all cutting the same pattern at the same time. Then automatic machines began to be used. They were controlled by tracing devices, such as a motorized tracing wheel, which followed a drawn outline. With the introduction of the photo-electric cell, mechanized cutting came into the electronic age. This electronic eye simply follows a black and white silhouette to trace the cutting line. This, with some refinement, is the process most commonly used today.

Regardless of the type of machine being used, the same principles apply to cutting today as when the first hand-held torch was developed. Anyone with a good background knowledge of oxyfuel cutting can easily understand the mechanics of the present-day machines.

POINTS TO REMEMBER

- Oxy-acetylene cutting is also called oxy-acetylene burning.
- It is not the flame that cuts the metal. It is the chemical reaction between the hot metal and the oxygen.
- The quality of the cut can be judged by observing the slag and sparks on the underside of the metal.
- The lever controls the cutting oxygen.
- Always use a clean tip.
- When using a cutting attachment, the welding torch oxygen valve must be opened all the way.
- Check the flame with the cutting lever depressed.
- Check that all metal to be cut is properly supported.
- The thickness of the metal determines the size of the tip to be used.
- The size of the tip determines the pressures to be used.
- Observe all safety precautions.

WORDS TO REMEMBER

oxidation	slag	alternating
severing	cutting lever	current (AC)

chemical reaction	centre punch	direct current (DC)
cutting attachment	jackhammer	gouge
flash circle	stack cutting	plasma
burner	cutting nozzle	back pressure
kerf	powder cutting	photo-electric
bevelling	electrode	cell
	open circuit voltage (OCV)	

REVIEW QUESTIONS

1. What defects are caused by cutting at too slow a speed?
2. What defects are caused by cutting too quickly?
3. What happens if the torch oxygen valve is not opened all the way when a cutting attachment is being used?
4. Why is it necessary to follow safety rules when cutting metal with the oxy-acetylene process?
5. What defects are produced when the cutting orifice in the tip is obstructed?
6. Why should the tip never be allowed to touch the metal?
7. List three rules that must be observed when using the oxy-acetylene cutting process.
8. Describe all the characteristics that indicate a good cut has been made.
9. What is the correct position of the torch when cutting a straight line?
10. What precautions should be observed when piercing a hole?
11. How does bevelling differ from ordinary cutting?
12. What is meant by stack cutting?
13. To cut a 355 mm (14 in.) circle, how much distance should there be between the pointer and the centre of the cutting nozzle?
14. Is it easier to cut a 50 mm (2 in.) piece of metal than to cut a 6 mm (1/4 in.) piece of metal? Give reasons for your answer.
15. With the torch you are now using, what size of tip is required to cut the following:

a. a piece of metal 12 mm (1/2 in.) thick?
b. a piece of metal 19 mm (3/4 in.) thick?
c. a piece of metal 38 mm (1 1/2 in.) thick?
d. a piece of metal 50 mm (2 in.) thick?

16. With the torch you are now using, what size tip would be required to cut and bevel a piece of metal 65 mm (2 1/2 in.) thick?

17. Why is a ring of preheat holes preferable to a single preheat hole in the cutting tip?

18. After completing a cutting operation on a 6 mm (1/4 in.) piece of metal, what changes would be required to cut a 40 mm (1 1/2 in.) piece of metal?

19. What is the purpose of using a heavy bar to make a straight line cut?

20. Why is a round bar first marked with a cold chisel before the cut is started?

21. Why is it more expensive to cut cast iron than it is to cut steel of the same thickness?

22. When cutting cast iron, what determines the ease of cut?

23. Correct safety practices should always be observed in any cutting operation. What are the extra hazards in cutting cast iron that make it even more essential that all safety practices are followed?

24. Why is it wise to plan the work carefully?

25. If the top edge becomes dark when cutting thin sections of cast iron, what does this indicate?

26. What other fuel gases can be used for cutting?

27. What is powder cutting?

28. Why is hydrogen gas the most useful gas in underwater cutting?

29. Describe the air carbon arc cutting (AAC) process.

30. What is meant by the term **arc gouging**?

31. Why is a shielding gas used in plasma arc cutting?

ELECTRICAL PROCESSES

11

ARC WELDING SAFETY

The welders shown in Figure 11-1 are wearing the clothing and equipment that will protect them from the sparks, heat, and light given off during the arc welding process. In arc welding, only a few common sense precautions need to be taken.

11-1 SAFETY RULES FOR ARC WELDING

1. Always wear a helmet with the correct grade of filter lens.
2. Check lens for cracks before starting to weld.
3. Wear fire-resistant clothing at all times.
4. Before you start welding, make sure that others are protected from the rays that will be given off by the arc.
5. Use a nonreflecting screen to protect others working near you.
6. Never strike an arc near an unprotected person.
7. Wear dark-coloured clothing. Light-coloured clothing will reflect the arc.
8. Keep sleeves rolled down, and the collar buttoned up.

Courtesy of Ontario Hydro

Figure 11-1 Protective clothing for arc welding

Courtesy of Canadian Liquid Air Ltd.

Figure 11-1 (cont'd)

9. Switch machine off when work is completed.
10. Do not leave electrode in holder.
11. Never work in a damp or wet area.
12. Wear flash goggles with side shields at all times.
13. Make sure that the workpiece and/or bench is properly grounded.
14. Do not use pipelines for grounding purposes.
15. Do not overload cables.
16. Never strike an arc on a compressed gas cylinder.
17. Report eye flash immediately.
18. Put electrode stubs in a separate, metal container. Do not throw them on floor.
19. Do not change polarity if machine is being used.
20. Do not operate a fuel-powered welding machine without ensuring proper exhausting of engine fumes.

11-2 ELECTRIC SHOCK

When a person comes in contact with an electric current he or she receives an electric shock which can cause violent reaction and even death.

> To avoid electric shock, observe the following rules:
> 1. Turn off machines when they are not in use.
> 2. Wear gloves when handling equipment.
> 3. Keep all equipment dry. Do not stand in water when welding, as water is an excellent conductor of electricity.
> 4. Be careful of dampness of any kind. Even perspiration inside gloves on a very hot day can cause electric shock.

Fortunately, the law enforces strict regulations with regard to welding machines. Under normal circumstances, it is unlikely that anyone would die from a shock received from a welding machine.

11-3 EYE FLASH

The brilliant light given off in arc welding contains **ultraviolet** and **infra-red rays**. These rays are similar to those of the sun and can cause similar effects. Eye flash is caused by looking at an unscreened arc without proper protection. Unfortunately, it is difficult to tell whether or not eye flash has occurred until approximately six to eight hours later. The symptoms include a burning sensation and an irritation similar to that caused by sand in the eyes. It is painful whether the eyes are open or closed.

The sensible thing to do, of course, is to avoid looking at an arc unless you are wearing the proper equipment. Sometimes, however, you may receive a flash by accident, no matter how careful you are. There are medi-

> As a rule, accidental eye flashes do not permanently harm the eyes, but repeated flashes can cause cataracts and even permanent blindness. Students should report all eye flashes to the instructor at once.

cations available to relieve the irritation, but if it is severe or if it persists, a doctor should be consulted.

11-4 ARC BURN

Ultraviolet and infra-red rays can also cause a severe case of arc burn. Normal suntan lotions will relieve a mild case of arc burn. However, if the burn is severe, a doctor should be consulted.

> To avoid arc burn:
> 1. Wear long-sleeved shirts, and keep the sleeves rolled down.
> 2. Keep shirt front buttoned.
> 3. Wear protective equipment.
> 4. Always check helmet before starting to weld to make sure the coloured glass is not cracked or broken.

TEST YOUR KNOWLEDGE

1. Describe how a person can receive an electric shock.
2. List four rules for avoiding electric shock.
3. What steps should be taken by a person who thinks he or she has received an eye flash?
4. What rays are given off during arc welding?
5. State the four rules for avoiding arc burn.

ELECTRODE STUBS

Electrode stubs are the short ends of used electrodes that are to be thrown away. They should be disposed of very carefully. To prevent waste they should be no more than 50 mm (2 in.) long when discarded. Keep a metal container in the welding area for disposal of these stubs.

SLAG

The coating which forms on top of an arc weld is called slag. When first deposited, it is very hot. When cool, it becomes solid and hard. Take care when chipping off slag to make sure that it does not strike you or some other person nearby.

11-5 PROTECTIVE CLOTHING AND EQUIPMENT

To protect a welder from sparks during the welding operation, jackets, aprons and sleeves made of leather must be worn (Figure 11-2). This type of clothing is flame-resistant and therefore provides excellent protection for arc welding. The amount of protective clothing necessary depends on how much welding is being done and in what position the welding is being performed. A skull cap to protect the hair, and leggings and anklets to protect the feet are necessary for some welding jobs.

This clothing will protect the welder not only from sparks, but also from the ultraviolet rays of arc welding.

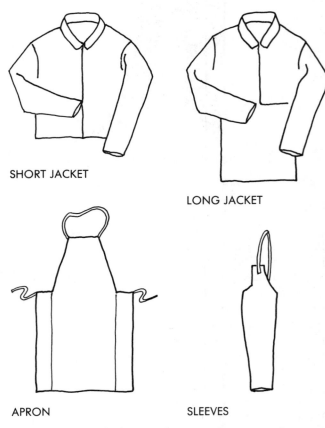

SHORT JACKET

LONG JACKET

APRON

SLEEVES

Figure 11-2 Clothing to be worn for protection from sparks

Some clothing material, such as cotton, will not keep out the rays. In fact, the clothing itself may deteriorate with prolonged exposure.

During any arc welding operation, all parts of the body should be completely covered.

FACE SHIELDS

To protect oneself from the rays of the arc and hot sparks, face shields (a helmet or hand shield) are used. The helmet is safer for beginners, but the hand shield is used frequently in industry (Figure 11-3).

Courtesy of The Lincoln Electric Company

Figure 11-3   Helmets, hand shields, and chipping goggles

Face shields should be made of a tough insulating material, such as fibre, with side pieces at least 50 mm (or 2 in.) deep. They should be lightweight. The most suitable helmet is the one with a flip front which allows you to lift the coloured glass or lens when you are not welding (Figure 11-4). Then you can see what you are doing without removing the complete shield and still be protected from the hot slag when chipping the weld. If this type is not used, special safety goggles must be worn for chipping.

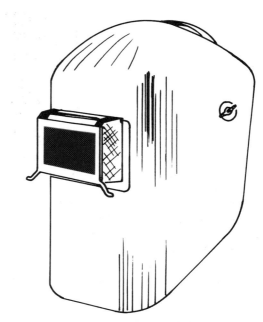

Figure 11-4   Flip-front helmet

All helmets are fitted with adjustable headbands (Figure 11-5). Sweat bands can also be purchased for these helmets by each welder. If the helmet is too tight or too loose (in the downward movement), it can be adjusted easily by turning the screws on the outside of the helmet with a screwdriver.

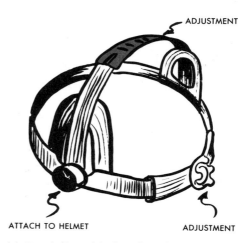

ADJUSTMENT

ATTACH TO HELMET   ADJUSTMENT

Figure 11-5   Adjustable headband for helmets

TEST YOUR KNOWLEDGE

1. Why is it necessary to wear a face shield?
2. Name the two types of face shields.
3. Why is the helmet most suitable for beginners?

LENSES

To enable the welder to see while welding and to filter out the harmful rays of arc welding, a coloured lens is used in the helmet. These lenses are usually green and graded by number. They are offered in standard sizes. For example, a Number 6 is a light-coloured lens, and a Number 12 is a dark-coloured lens. The most popular grade used is a Number 10 (Figure 11-6). Since lenses are expensive, they are protected by a clear glass or a plastic plate. Magnifying lenses and special bifocal lenses are also available for anyone who requires eye correction.

---

1. Replace any cracked or chipped lenses immediately.
2. Always protect the coloured lens with a clear plate.
3. Be sure to use the correct grade of lens.

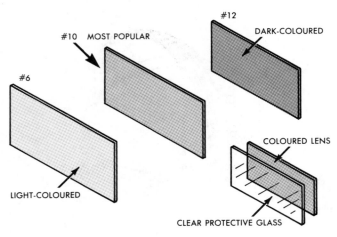

Figure 11-6   Lenses

TABLE 11-1 RECOMMENDED LENS SHADE NUMBERS FOR USE IN VARIOUS WELDING OPERATIONS

Welding or Cutting Operation	Size (mm)	Electrode (in.)	Shade Number
Shielded Metal Arc Welding	1.5-3.9	1/16-5/32	10
	4.7-6.5	3/16-1/4	12
	7.9-9.5	5/16-3/8	14
Gas Tungsten Arc Welding			
Ferrous	—	—	12
Nonferrous	—	—	11
Gas Metal Arc Welding			
Ferrous	1.5-3.9	1/16-5/32	12
Nonferrous	1.5-3.9	1/16-5/32	11
Atomic Hydrogen Welding	—	—	10-14
Carbon Arc Welding	—	—	14
Oxygen Cutting			
Light - to 25 mm (1 in.)	—	—	3-4
Medium - 25 mm-150 mm (1 in.-6 in.)	—	—	4-5
Heavy - over 150 mm (over 6 in.)	—	—	5-6

Data from AWS A6.2-68 and ANSI Z49. 1-67.
Courtesy of The Lincoln Electric Company

GLOVES

Gloves with long gauntlets protect the hands and wrists from arc rays. They are usually made of chrome leather and are available in glove or mitt form. Reinforcement between thumb and forefinger is important to prevent excessive wear and to catch hot sparks when welding is done out of position (Figure 11-7).

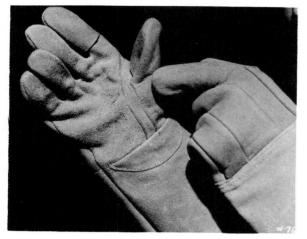

Courtesy of The Lincoln Electric Company

Figure 11-7   Area of reinforcement on gloves

> Gloves must be worn when arc welding, but the gloves must not be used to pick up hot metal. Heat makes the gloves stiff, hard, and awkward to use.

CURTAINS

All welding booths should be equipped with curtains of fire-resistant canvas. These curtains should be closed by the welder using the booth to eliminate the danger of eye flash to anyone passing by or working in the area. In industry, it is not always possible to surround the welding area with a curtain. Portable shields like the one shown in Figure 11-8 are used for this situation. The welder is responsible for ensuring that they are in place before welding.

FIRE-RESISTANT BLANKETS

Another piece of equipment that is desirable is the fire-resistant blanket. It is used to **wrap** around anyone whose

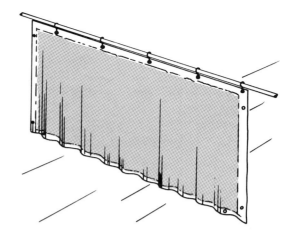

Figure 11-8   Portable, fire-resistant shield

clothing has caught fire or to throw over burning equipment or material. The blanket can also be used to protect material from burning sparks. These blankets are supplied complete with a metal container that can be hung on the wall (Figure 11-9). A tug on the tape quickly releases the blanket for use.

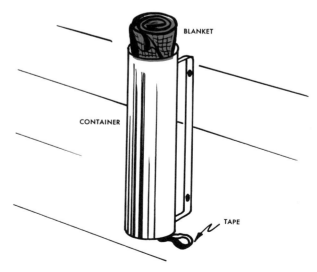

Figure 11-9   Fire-resistant blanket and container

CHIPPING HAMMER AND WIRE BRUSH

Although not safety equipment, the chipping hammer and wire brush are essential parts of the welder's equipment (Figure 11-10). All welds should be chipped and brushed on completion.

These tools come in a wide variety of shapes and sizes. They should be used frequently and always kept in good condition.

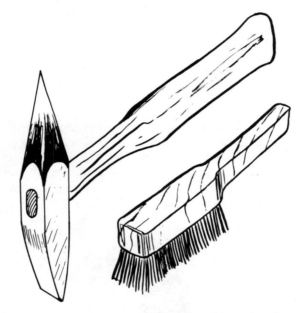

Figure 11-10   Chipping hammer and wire brush

POINTS TO REMEMBER

- Observe the rules for avoiding electric shock.
- Be careful to avoid eye flash.
- Report all eye flashes at once.
- Long sleeves should be worn when welding.
- Stubs and slag are sources of danger.
- Always wear gloves while welding.
- Check the helmet for cracks in the lens before using it.
- Use the correct grade of lens, and see that it is properly protected.

WORDS TO REMEMBER

electric shock	infra-red rays	lens
eye flash	electrode stubs	asbestos
ultraviolet rays	face shield	slag

REVIEW QUESTIONS

1. Why is it necessary to wear a helmet with special glass?
2. Why is it necessary to wear gloves?
3. What causes eye flash?
4. Describe the effects of eye flash.
5. How can arc burn be prevented?
6. What are the four rules to help prevent electric shock?
7. What is an electrode stub?
8. When should an electrode stub be discarded?
9. What is slag?
10. What hazards are associated with slag?

12

BASIC ARC WELDING EQUIPMENT

Volta, Ampere, Oersted, Ohm, and Faraday were all early experimenters in electricity and magnetism. Approximately 20 years after Volta developed the voltaic cell, Oersted established a connection between electricity and magnetism. This, in turn, led to the discovery of magnetic lines of force and magnetic fields. Ten years later, Faraday carried this research even further by discovering how to obtain electricity from magnetism by induction. He had laid the foundation for the development of electrical instruments and machinery, which depend on both electricity and magnetism. "Electricity from magnetism and magnetism from electricity" is the principle that lies behind the operation of electrical machines. These experiments, together with the development of electrodes (Chapter 13), led to the introduction of the many arc welding processes we know today.

In any arc welding process, the intense heat required to melt the base metal is produced by an electric arc. A skilled welder must have some knowledge of electricity for safety and to understand the operation of arc welding equipment. Although arc welding is no more dangerous than other welding processes, certain precautions must be observed because of the high amperages used and the radiation given off by the arc, among other things. These will be discussed in detail throughout the chapter as will the relationship between electricity and the various pieces of equipment used in the processes described.

12-1 ELECTRICITY

We know of electricity by its effects. It is an invisible force of attraction that creates an electric charge. If a pathway is provided between charged objects that attract each other, an electric current will result. This electric current is really a flow of electrons from the object that has more electrons to the object that has fewer electrons. When the electrons in a current move in the same direction at all times, they cause a **direct current**. When the electrons reverse their direction at regular intervals they cause an **alternating current**.

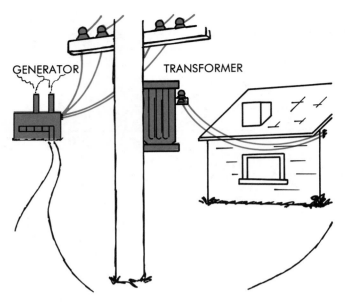

Figure 12-1 The electric current that is sent along the wires is really a flow of electrons

The chief sources of electrical energy at the present time are:

1. Water power
2. Fuels—Liquid (gasoline, diesel, etc.)
   —Solid (coal)
3. Atomic reactors

Many methods are used to produce electricity. Whatever the method, it is most important that the current generated should be quickly and cheaply transmitted from one place to another. Nearly all the electricity used in our homes and industry is in the form of alternating current (AC). It is produced by alternating current generators called **alternators.**

For lighting and heating, both AC and DC are equally useful. However, AC is used most where demand for electricity is great. Where distribution of large amounts of electric power is necessary, high voltages (pressure) are required. Power is measured by the product of volt-age and amperage. So if the voltage was low, that is, 230 V, the current output from a large generating station would have to be many hundreds of thousands of amperes to supply the heat and light for a large city. With AC the voltage can be raised or stepped up to a still higher value by means of a device called a **transformer.** This makes it possible to use cables of reasonably small diameter at the receiving end of the line. The voltage can just as readily be stepped down again by another transformer to the low level required by the consumer. This is not possible with DC.

Electric current (the flow of electrons) is measured in **amperes (A).** The number or quantity of electrons that pass in a given period of time determines the current strength. (It is similar to the flow of water in a pipe being expressed in litres per minute.) The pressure in an electric circuit is measured in **volts (V).** It is similar to the pressure in a water pipe and moves the current along the wire or conductor. Amperage, then, is the amount of electric current. Voltage is the pressure required to move the current.

From experiments you may have done in other years, you may know that there is a connection between electricity and **magnetism.** A magnetic force is formed around any current-carrying conductor. The force around a single wire carrying a current is rather weak, but if the wire is wound into a coil, the force is much stronger. Years ago, Michael Faraday and other scientists found that an electric current could be transferred to another metal conductor if it was placed beside the first current-carrying conductor without actually touching it. This was called **magnetic induction.** This principle forms the basis of transformers and most electric equipment today.

INDUCED CURRENTS

If a coil is rotated between the poles of a magnet as in Figure 12-2A, an electric current is induced in the coil. This is an alternating current and the combination of coil and magnet is an alternating generator. If the magnet is rotated instead of the coil, the results are the same. In DC generators, it is the coil that is usually rotated, while in alternators, the magnet is rotated. To produce DC from the AC generated, a commutator is used with the alternator. This, of course, is only a very basic explanation. Today's generators are much more sophisticated.

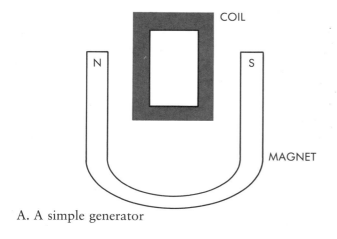

A. A simple generator

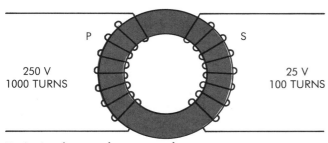

B. A simple step-down transformer

Figure 12-2 Induced currents

TRANSFORMERS

You can create a simple transformer by wrapping two, separate insulated wire coils around an iron ring. One coil can be called P and the other, S. If coil P is connected to an electric source, a current will be induced in coil S. Coil P is called the **primary** and coil S is called the **secondary** current. If the coils are properly insulated, they can be wound directly on top of each other. The current that is transmitted from P to S will be in a ratio approximately equal to the number of turns in the two coils. So if P has 100 turns and S has 1000 turns then the current in S will be 10 times greater than the current in P. If P had 250 V and the same number of turns in the coils as stated above, then S would have 2500 V and would be called a **step-up transformer**.

If P had 1000 turns and 250 V and S had 100 turns,

S would have 25 V and would be called a **step-down transformer** (Figure 12-2B).

GENERATORS

The simplest kind of generator is a coil of wire which rotates between the poles of a permanent magnet. The terminals of the coil are attached to two metal insulated rings called slip rings. As the coil turns, an electric current is generated. This turning coil is called an alternator. The assembly containing the coils is called an armature and the magnet is called a field magnet. Modern generators have a device called a commutator instead of the slip rings. They also contain more than one coil which, in turn, results in more poles. Thus they are called **multi** or **bipolar** generators. Machines which supply current for their own field magnets are called **self-exciting** generators. (Figure 12-3 shows one kind of generator.)

Courtesy of Hobart Brothers Company

Figure 12-3 Hobart mode D-412 DC-AC welder generator combined with diesel engine

HEAT

Electric current has been described as a flow of electrons. The number of electrons that flow in a minute or second is called amperage. The pressure that moves the electron is called voltage. An electric current generator or alternator is simply a means of setting the electrons in motion. A current of electricity produces not only a magnetic field but also heat. This heat results from the electrical resistance encountered. It is this combination that is made use of in welding. In welding this heat is created when the welder first establishes the arc by touching the electrode to the metal or superimposing a starting current on the electrode. When the gap or space is established between the electrode and the work, resistance is created and heat is produced. The rate at which the heat is produced depends on the resistance and the quantity of electricity flowing.

ELECTRICITY IN WELDING MACHINES

In welding, the relationship between voltage (the pressure) and amperage (the amount of electricity flowing), is most important. In arc welding, there are two voltages to be considered: (1) open circuit voltage (OCV) and (2) arc voltage (AV). OCV is the voltage that exists between the terminals of the welding machine when there is no welding being performed. It is approximately 70 V to 80 V. AV is the voltage between the electrode and the base metal during the actual welding operation (15 V to 40 V). When the arc is struck and welding is in progress, the OCV drops down to the level of the AV (from about 80 V to 40 V). At the same time, the arc voltage increases. Then as the arc lengthens, the arc voltage rises further and the amperage falls. As the arc is shortened, the AV drops and the amperage rises.

The first welding machines were constant current (CC) machines with a drooping volt/amp relationship (Figure 12-4A). They were and still are used for SMAW and GTAW because a steady current (amperage) is very important in these processes. With GMAW, constant voltage is more important (Figure 12-4B). About 30 years ago, another machine was developed to be used with this process. It is the constant voltage or constant potential (CV or CP) machine which has a constant and much lower OCV. The output voltage of a CV machine remains constant over a range of amperages. This is desirable for GMAW, for which a steady voltage is essential. This lower OCV used in the GMAW process allows the arc to be started more quickly, without the sudden surge of power that is familiar in SMAW. This

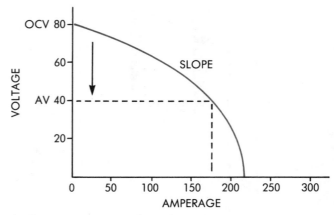

A. Constant current (drooping arc)

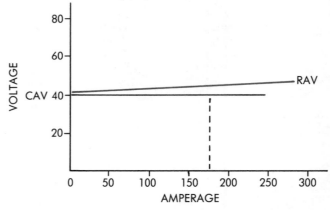

B. Constant voltage

Figure 12-4   The volt/amp relationship

prevents the wire in GMAW from burning back into the tube. More improvements were later made, which allowed for control of the slope or shape of the volt/amp curve, variable voltage, variable slope, pulsed arc, and rising arc voltage.

Each of these improvements was designed to overcome obstacles as they arose during the development of new welding techniques and processes. For example, some GMAW processes use a much lower voltage and amperage than SMAW processes. Although the drooping volt/amp machine with constant current was used for GMAW, it was extremely difficult to start the arc and control the arc length. By using CV it was possible to adjust the arc length by varying the speed of the wire feed unit.

The ability to control the voltage and change it (variable voltage) and the ability to control the slope (the shape of the volt/amp curve) allows welding conditions to be changed drastically. It has led to the development of different types of metal transfer, such as spray, short-circuit, and globular. (These are discussed later in this book.)

Rising arc voltage (RAV) is the power source most suitable for spray. It is admirably suitable for semi-automatic and automatic welding processes because, as the name implies, the voltage is automatically increased when the amperage is increased. In this way, a constant arc gap is maintained between the welding wire and the base metal. The drooping arc/volt machine normally used for SMAW can be used for GMAW processes, but because of the sharp slope from OCV to AV, the amount of amperage or current available will cause poor arc starting.

However, a CV power source is not suitable for SMAW because the low volt/amp relationship can cause damage to the machine through overload. Table 12-1 shows the types of power sources to be used in each process.

TABLE 12-1 PROCESSES AND POWER SOURCES

For These Processes	Use This Type of Power Source	
SMAW	CC	AC/DC
GMAW	CV	DC
GTAW	CC	AC/DC

12-2 ARC WELDING MACHINES

To weld successfully with electricity the welding machine must be able to control the force of the electricity, increase or decrease the power as required, and be safe for handling. Three main types of machines are used in arc welding:
1. an AC (alternating current) machine
2. a DC (direct current) machine
3. an AC/DC machine (a combination of the two).
Figure 12-5 shows types of power sources provided by different welding machines.

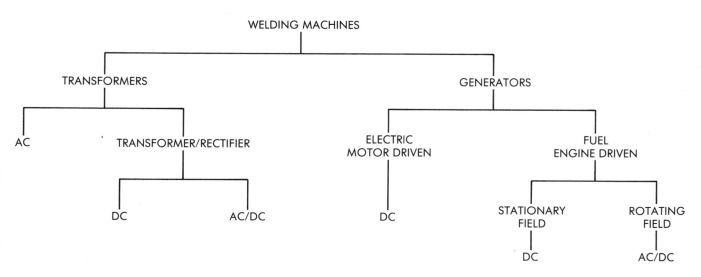

Figure 12-5   Types of power sources

ALTERNATING CURRENT MACHINES

AC machines are usually called **transformers** (Figure 12-6). They transform the electric current from the main line (which has high voltage/low amperage) to a safe but usable welding current (which has low voltage/high amperage). This is done inside the machine by an arrangement of a primary and secondary coil and a movable reactor.

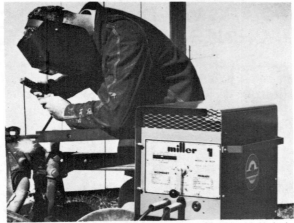

Courtesy of Canadian Liquid Air Ltd.

Figure 12-6   A transformer (AC) in use

Courtesy of The Lincoln Electric Company

A generator (DC)

DIRECT CURRENT MACHINES

DC machines fall into two basic types: **generators** (Figures 12-7 and 12-8) and **rectifiers** (Figures 12-9A and B). In a DC generator, the current is generated by the rotation of an armature in an electrical field. This generated alternating current is picked up by an arrangement of carbon brushes and a commutator and is changed to a direct current. Rectifiers are basically AC transformers to which a rectifier stack (Figure 12-9A) has been added. The alternating current supplied by the transformer (Figure 12-9B) is fed into the rectifier stack, which changes it to direct current.

AC/DC MACHINES

AC/DC machines supply either alternating or direct current. Figure 12-10 on page 132 shows an AC/DC machine used in GTAW.

DEFINITIONS

Before using welding machines in electrical welding processes, it is helpful to be familiar with the following terms. (Some of them have already been discussed in the preceding sections.)

Alternating current (AC) is an electric current in which electrons flow in one direction but then reverse their direction at regular intervals.

Direct current (DC) is an electric current in which electrons flow in one direction at all times.

Voltage (V) is the pressure required to move the electric current.

Arc voltage (AV) is the voltage across the arc (between the electrode and the base metal) during the actual welding operation.

Open circuit voltage (OCV) is the voltage that exists between the terminals of the welding machine when no welding is being performed.

Volt/amp curves are graphs showing the voltage and amperage output of a welding machine and the maximum short-circuit current for a particular machine setting.

Constant voltage indicates a steady voltage regardless of the amperage output of the welding machine.

Variable voltage is used to control the OCV within very fine limits.

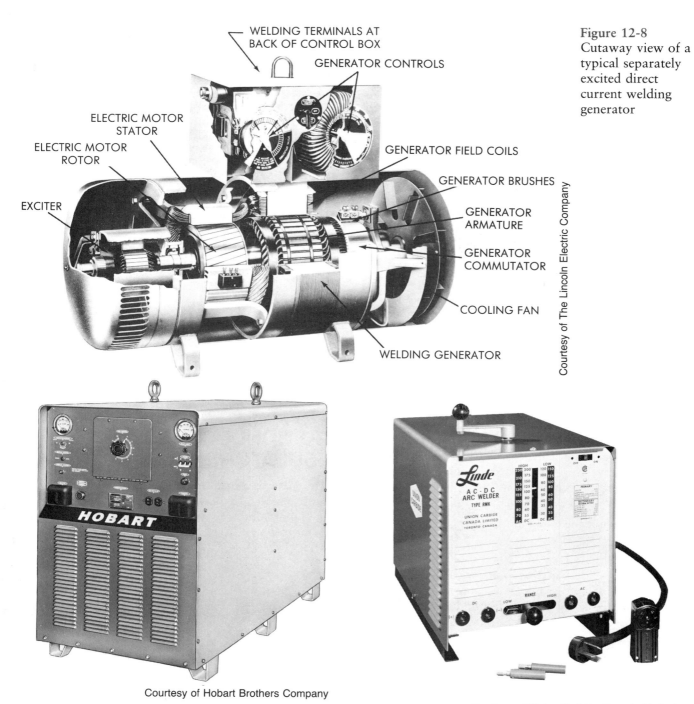

WELDING TERMINALS AT BACK OF CONTROL BOX

GENERATOR CONTROLS

ELECTRIC MOTOR STATOR

ELECTRIC MOTOR ROTOR

EXCITER

GENERATOR FIELD COILS

GENERATOR BRUSHES

GENERATOR ARMATURE

GENERATOR COMMUTATOR

COOLING FAN

WELDING GENERATOR

Figure 12-8
Cutaway view of a typical separately excited direct current welding generator

Courtesy of The Lincoln Electric Company

Courtesy of Hobart Brothers Company

Figure 12-9A A Hobart RC-750 rectifier constant-voltage 3-phase DC power source

Courtesy of Union Carbide Canada Limited

Figure 12-9B An AC/DC welding machine

Figure 12-10   Miller model 250 AC/DC-HF GTAW
welder

Courtesy of Canadian Liquid Air Ltd.

Variable slope is used to control the shape of the volt/amp curve. This controls the voltage.

Amperage (A) is the amount of electricity flowing. It also represents the power or heat of an arc welding machine. Welding with a small-diameter electrode requires fewer amperes than welding with a large-diameter electrode. The amperage indicator and control are usually located on the front of the welding machine.

Machine output is the maximum amperage at which the machine will work. It may vary from 100 A to 1200 A, depending on the size of the machine.

Duty cycle. A welding machine rated at 20% duty cycle is designed to operate at maximum amperage for a period of two minutes of every ten. In industry the usual duty cycle rating is 60%, or six minutes of every ten. This rating was established to prevent damage to welding machines. Using a machine above the rated capacity will cause it to fail.

Power supply. If welding is required at several different locations, a welding machine powered by gasoline or diesel fuel is often used because it is portable and independent of power lines.

Welding current comparison. DC welding permits the widest choice of electrodes and current range and the best arc stability. It is usually used for out-of-position work, sheet metal welding, pipe welding, hard surfacing, and stainless steel welding. AC welding produces less weld spatter, uses less electrical power, and requires less maintenance. It is ideal for downhand welding of heavy plate using large electrodes. An AC/DC machine, of course, offers the advantages of both.

WELDER PROBLEMS

The list of possible problems, causes, and remedies shown in Table 12-2 has been provided so that the student will have a better understanding of these machines. It is in no way intended as a repair guide for students.

Maintenance of all machines should only be carried out by qualified maintenance personnel because of the danger of shock or burn.

12-3 CONDUCTORS AND INSULATORS

A conductor is a material or substance which allows an electric current to flow through it. An insulator is a material or substance which does not allow the electric current to flow through it.

CONDUCTORS ⟷ INSULATORS		
GOOD	MEDIUM CONDUCTORS	POOR
Silver	Human body	Air
Copper	Wood (dry)	Glass
Other metals	Marble	Ebonite
Charcoal	Paper	Oil
Water		Rubber

TABLE 12-2 TYPICAL TROUBLE SHOOTING GUIDE FOR AN ARC WELDER

Trouble	Cause	Remedy
Welder will not start	Line switch not turned "ON" Supply line fuse blown Power circuit dead Overload relay tripped Loose or broken power, electrode, or ground lead Wrong voltage Polarity switch not centred (AC-DC units only)	Place line switch in "ON" position Replace (check reason for blown fuse first) Check input voltage Let cool, remove cause of overloading Replace lead or tighten and repair connection Check input voltage against instructions Centre switch handle on +, −, or AC
Welder starts but blows fuse after welding begins	Open circuit to starter button Short circuit in motor or other connection Fuse too small	Repair Check connections and lead for correct size of fuse Check instruction manual for correct size
Welder starts but stops soon after welding begins	Proper ventilation hindered Overloading—welding in excess of rating Fan inoperative Motor Generator Sets— wrong direction of rotation brushes worn or missing wrong driving speed Excessive dust accumulation in welder	Make sure all case openings are free for proper circulation of air Operate welder at rated load and duty cycle Check leads and connections Check connection diagram Check brushes for pressure on commutator Check nameplate for correct motor speed Clean thermostat, coils, and other components
Variable or sluggish welding arc	Current too low Low line voltage Welding leads too small Poor ground, electrode, or control-circuit connections Motor Generator Sets—Brushes improper, weak springs, not properly fitted Rough or dirty commutator	Check recommended currents for rod type and size being used Check with power company Check instruction manual for recommended cable sizes Check all connections. Clean, repair or replace as required Check and repair Turn down or clean commutator

TABLE 12-2 (cont'd)

Trouble	Cause	Remedy
Welding arc is loud and spatters excessively	Current setting is too high Polarity wrong	Check setting and output with ammeter Check polarity; try reversing or an electrode of opposite polarity
Polarity switch won't turn	Contacts rough and pitted from improper turning under load	Replace switch
Welder won't shut off	Line switch has failed mechanically	Replace switch
Arcing at ground clamp	Loose connection or weak spring	Tighten connection or replace clamp
Electrode holder becomes hot	Loose connection, loose jaw, inadequate duty cycle	Tighten connection or replace holder
Touching welder gives shock	Frame not grounded	See instruction manual for proper grounding procedure

Courtesy of The Lincoln Electric Company

WELDING CABLES

The cable used in welding (Figure 12-11) is a **conductor covered by an insulator**. It must be capable of carrying the electric current to and from the welding operation without overheating, yet be as light and flexible as possible. The conductor part of the cable is made up of many fine strands of wire woven together. Aluminum or copper wire is used. The aluminum wire has much less mass than the copper wire but cannot carry as much current as the copper. The greater the number of strands in a cable the greater its flexibility. The strands are wrapped in heavy brown paper which is encased in a neophrene or rubber cover.

As the **length** of the cable increases, there will be a drop in the voltage. Therefore, the distance from the welding machine to the work area should be as short as possible. Cables should not be coiled, but should always be straightened out to avoid the possibility of generating a magnetic field which could have a negative effect on

Courtesy of The Lincoln Electric Company

Figure 12-11   Welding cables

the performance of the welding machine. The **size** of welding cable used is also important. A cable too small

TABLE 12-3 CABLE SIZE

Cable Size (metres/feet)

Amperage (DC)	33.5 m/100 ft.	45.7 m/150 ft.	61 m/200 ft.	76.2 m/250 ft.	91.4 m/300 ft.
Below 100	6	4	3	2	1
100	4	3	3	2	1
150	3	2	1	1/0	2/0
200	2	1	1/0	2/0	3/0
250	1	1/0	2/0	3/0	4/0
300	1/0	2/0	3/0	—	—

Note

1. As the number of the cable becomes smaller, the size of the cable is larger. For example, a #1/0 (one/ought) cable is larger and will carry more current than a #6 cable.
2. Table 12-3 shows cable size for DC welding. If working with AC, use the next largest size of cable for the same amperage. For example, if you are using DC at 200 A and a total cable length of 33.5 m (100 ft.), a #2 cable would be correct, but if you are using AC at 200 A and 33.5 m (100 ft.) cable length, a #1 cable would be the correct one to use.
3. Use Table 12-3 as a guide only. A local welding supply company or manufacturer will be able to provide you with more specific information.

for the amperage will cause the cable to overheat. Table 12-3 shows the size of cable and total length necessary for a particular amperage.

> An overloaded cable is one that is continually used at higher amperages than its rated capacity. This can cause overheating and breakdown of the insulation. Cables should be inspected frequently for wear or bare sections. Apart from the danger of shock, a bare live cable could cause accidental eye flash and/or fire.

Courtesy of Canadian Liquid Air Ltd.

Courtesy of The Lincoln Electric Company

Figure 12-12   Electrode holders

ELECTRODE HOLDERS

Electrode holders are used to grip the electrode and to provide an insulated handle. Holders come in a variety of shapes and sizes. Figure 12-12 shows two of the more common types used. The size of the holder required depends on the maximum amperage to be used. The important point is that the holder should be lightweight, yet capable of carrying sufficient current to avoid overheating.

CONNECTORS

It is very important to use the proper method of attaching the holder to the welding cable. Connectors of the type shown in Figure 12-13 make it easy to connect and disconnect cables and fit new cables when required.

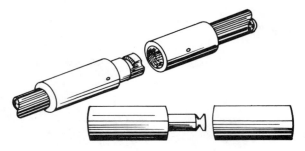

Figure 12-13   Cable connectors

Check holders for loose connections or broken insulation, and report any defects immediately. Remember that if the insulation is broken or gone, there is no protection against electric shock.

GROUND CLAMPS

The ground clamp is fastened to the piece of metal that is to be welded. This completes the welding circuit when the electrode is touched to the metal. Ground clamps that are hand sprung are most convenient and provide the easiest method of securing the ground clamp to the base metal (Figure 12-14).

Remember that if the metal to be welded is not grounded, the circuit is not complete, and there is a definite danger of electric shock.

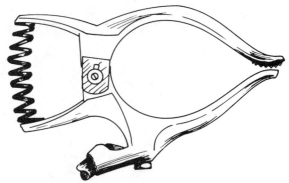

Figure 12-14   Hand-sprung ground clamp

TEST YOUR KNOWLEDGE
1. What is a conductor of electricity?
2. What is an insulator?
3. Give one good example of each.

12-4 SHIELDED METAL ARC WELDING (SMAW)

Shielded metal arc welding (SMAW) is widely used today. As you learned in Chapter 2, it is a fusion process because it melts the base metals being joined. SMAW is used, for example, in shipbuilding, locomotive and boilermaking, in structural work, and in other branches of engineering (Figures 12-15 to 12-17).

The welder using SMAW has a special holder which grips the electrode. As the welder brings the electrode close to the base metal, an arc is created by an electric current that flows between the electrode and the base metal. The arc, which is very hot, causes the base metal and the electrode to melt. The molten metal from the electrode then flows into the joint.

Courtesy of The Lincoln Electric Company

Figure 12-15   Rebuilding lugs for chain drive sprockets with SMAW

Courtesy of The Lincoln Electric Company

Figure 12-16   An all-welded ship

Courtesy of The Lincoln Electric Company

Figure 12-17   Landing gear of welded construction

12-5 THE WELDING CIRCUIT

Figure 12-18 illustrates the arc welding circuit. The circuit begins at A, where the electrode cable is attached

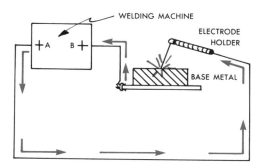

Figure 12-18   The arc welding circuit

to one terminal of the welding machine, and ends at B, where the ground cable is attached to the other terminal of the welding machine. The welding current flows through the electrode cable to the electrode holder. From the holder it flows to the electrode and across the gap between the end of the electrode and the base metal, forming the arc. From the base metal, it goes back through the ground cable to the welding machine, as indicated by the arrows. Power in this circuit may be lost for any one of several reasons. Figure 12-19 shows points at which power may be lost.

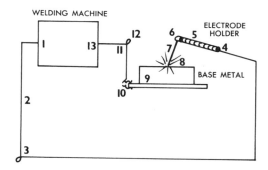

Figure 12-19   Points of possible power loss

LOSSES OF POWER IN THE WELDING CIRCUIT

1. Faults in connecting the electrode cable to the machine.
2. Cable too small (resulting in overheating of the cable).
3. Faults in the cable (breaks or partial breaks).

4. Faulty connection of the cable to the holder.
5. Defects in the holder.
6. Poor contact between the electrode and the holder.
7. Overheating of the electrode.
8. Incorrect arc length.
9. Poor contact between the base metal parts.
10. Poor connection between the ground clamp and the base metal.
11. Ground cable too small (resulting in overheating).
12. Breaks in the ground cable.
13. Poor connection between the ground clamp and the machine.

12-6 POLARITY

An electric current causes a magnetic force around a current-carrying conductor. Because the lines of magnetic force end at the negative and positive terminals of an electric current, the terminals may be called the negative pole and the positive pole. The polarity of a machine refers to the direction of the current flow. Polarity can be obtained only on a DC machine. It cannot be obtained on an AC machine because of the current reversal.

When the electrode cable is connected to the positive terminal of the welding machine, the machine is on positive polarity. When the electrode cable is connected to the negative terminal of the machine, the machine is on negative polarity.

In industry, positive and negative polarity are referred to as **reverse** and **straight** polarity, respectively (Figure 12-20). Most welding machines are marked with a plus and minus sign to show whether they have reverse or straight polarity.

TERM	COMMON NAME	SIGN
Positive	Reverse	+ (plus)
Negative	Straight	- (minus)

It is not necessary to change the cables in order to change polarity. On most machines, this is accomplished by moving a lever or dial on the front of the welding machine.

With some arc welding processes the polarity to be used is determined by the metal being welded (see chap-

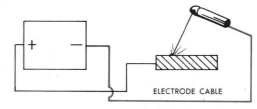

A. Straight (positive) polarity

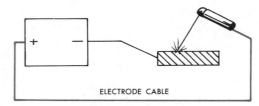

B. Reverse (negative) polarity

Figure 12-20   Polarity of welding machines

ters 16 and 17). However, in the SMAW process the polarity to be used is determined by the coating of the electrode used (see Chapter 13). For example, when an E41010 (E610) electrode is used it operates best on DCRP (Direct Current Reverse Polarity). When using DCRP, the electrode is positive and the base metal is negative. (DC is a continuous current which is positive or negative depending upon which is selected.) With DCRP, two-thirds or 70% of the heat is concentrated at the electrode. The electrode therefore burns at a faster rate and the penetration of the base metal is shallower than if DCSP (direct current straight polarity) were being used. In DCSP only 70% of the heat is concentrated at the base metal and only 30% at the electrode. In this case, the base metal is hotter, resulting in deeper penetration of the base metal when welding with AC. As the name AC implies, the current reverses itself. That is, it continually changes back and forth from positive to negative. For example, with a 60-cycle current, AC reverses direction 120 times per second.

12-7 ARC BLOW

Arc blow is a condition caused by magnetic deflections of the arc. These deflections result from the electric current creating a magnetic flux or force around a current-carrying conductor. Arc blow can often be experienced when welding in a corner using DC. The magnetic lines of force tend to travel in circles around the electrode (the current-carrying conductor) like ripples in water when a stone is dropped into it. If one can picture these ripples moving along the metal as welding progresses, imagine their meeting circles of force coming from the ground clamp (also a current-carrying conductor). The disturbance occurs at the point where the two sets of circles or ripples meet (Figure 12-21). The arc becomes very erratic and the molten metal from the electrode wavers and is difficult to direct.

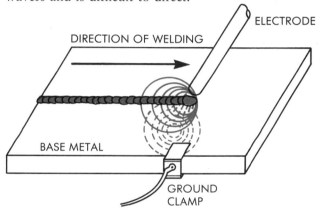

Figure 12-21   Arc blow

To eliminate or minimize arc blow:

a. Change to AC.
b. Move the ground clamp to a new location on the work.
c. Change the direction of welding.
d. Use a magnetic ground clamp.

The constant reversal of AC does not allow the flux or force to build up.

Note
To avoid possible damage to the welding machine do not change the polarity switch while welding is in progress. If the switch is moved during welding, arcing of the contact surfaces of the switch can occur. This results in damage to the machine and possible burn to the person moving the switch.

TEST YOUR KNOWLEDGE

1. What is SMAW?
2. What creates the heat required to melt the electrode?
3. Name two industries that use SMAW.
4. Describe the welding circuit.
5. Name the three types of arc welding machines.
6. Define polarity.

POINTS TO REMEMBER

- The difference between AC and DC.
- Check all connections before starting. Turn the machine off first.
- The difference between straight polarity and reverse polarity.
- The polarity to be used depends on either the metal being welded or, with SMAW, the electrode being used.
- The workpiece must be grounded properly.

WORDS TO REMEMBER

alternating current	generator	conductor
	rectifier	connector
direct current	reactor	circuit
amperage	commutator	reverse polarity
voltage	poles	straight polarity
transformer	insulation	
alternator		

REVIEW QUESTIONS

1. What are the chief sources of energy used at present to produce electricity?
2. What is amperage?
3. What is voltage?
4. Define AC and DC.
5. Is alternating current (AC) better than direct current (DC) for heating and lighting?
6. Why are step-up and step-down transformers used?
7. What is magnetic induction?

8. Explain the relationship between the number of turns in a primary coil and the number of turns in a secondary coil.

9. In a generator, how is the alternating current changed to direct current?

10. What is another name for an AC machine?

11. What are the two basic types of machines that produce direct current?

12. What is an AC/DC machine?

13. What comparisons can be made between AC and DC machines with regard to performance?

14. Explain what is meant by the following duty cycles:
    a. 10%
    b. 40%
    c. 100%

15. What is the difference between a conductor and an insulator?

16. Why should holders and cables be checked frequently for breaks?

17. Describe the arc welding circuit.

18. List five points that can cause loss of welding power.

19. What is meant by machine output?

20. On which type of machine is polarity obtained?

21. What is the meaning of straight and reverse polarity?

22. What danger exists if the base metal is not grounded?

23. What is arc blow?

24. How is arc blow caused?

25. What steps can be taken to eliminate or minimize arc blow?

13

ELECTRODES

The electrode is the most important part of the welding circuit, and in this chapter a brief look at its history and development will lead into a thorough explanation of present-day electrodes (Figure 13-1). Students will find the information in this chapter invaluable in furthering their careers. The research, manufacture, testing, and matching of electrodes to new metals is an industry in itself.

13-1 HISTORY

In the late 1800s experiments were done with a carbon electrode and the intense heat of the electric arc to join metals. A few years later, a bare iron wire was substituted for the carbon electrode, thus eliminating the need for a separate filler rod. In the early 1900s, it was discovered that the physical, mechanical, and chemical properties of the weld improved if a coating was applied to the bare iron wire.

Some early experiments also included wrapping the

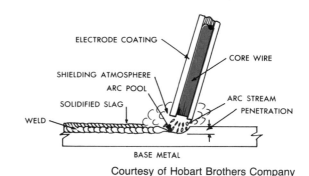

Courtesy of Hobart Brothers Company

Figure 13-1   Present-day electrodes

bare electrode with asbestos and cotton cloth soaked in sodium silicate (water glass). Asbestos and sodium silicate are both fire-resistant materials. They were used to prevent the coating from burning too quickly. From these early experiments the present-day electrodes were developed. These consist of a metal core wire to which has been added a coating of carefully selected chemicals. In fact, although the early attempts were rather crude, present-day electrodes contain, among other things, cotton, and sodium silicate.

13-2 ELECTRODE PRODUCTION

Bare electrodes (Figure 13-2) are still used by experienced operators in situations where any flux entrapment would be detrimental. However, they are used only on rare occasions. With bare electrodes, the weld loses some desirable characteristics, such as strength. Although electrodes are manufactured today with coatings that range from bare to medium to heavy coated, the most frequently used are the heavy coated.

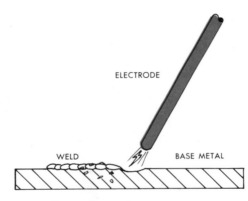

Figure 13-2   Bare electrode

Coatings on electrodes are usually applied by dipping or extrusion. The most popular is the extrusion method where the bare wire is covered with coating in a paste form. The paste-covered wire is then forced through a small circular die which reduces the coating to the correct size for the particular type of electrode. The length of wire is then brought into contact with a small high-powered wire brush, which scrapes off the paste and leaves approximately 25 mm (or 1 in.) of the electrode bare. This bare end is the part that is normally gripped in the electrode holder. The electrodes are cut by a small guillotine to the correct length and are then dried in baking ovens. From here they are sent to the packing house for packing, shipping, and distribution.

The dies used in the extrusion process are carefully and frequently inspected for wear or damage because any die that is slightly out of round will produce an electrode that has a heavier coating on one side. This results in an uneven burning of the electrode during welding. (One side would burn more quickly than the other.) This could have serious consequences on high-quality work that is continually checked by X-ray. Uneven burning rarely happens, though, since all electrodes are produced under strictly controlled conditions and high quality inspection.

13-3 ELECTRODE CHARACTERISTICS

THE CORE WIRE

The core wire of an electrode (Figure 13-3) will be made of the same metal as the assembly being welded, in most cases. For example, mild steel would be welded with an electrode made of a mild steel core wire. The core wire would be aluminum for an electrode used on an aluminum base metal. Similarly, a copper core wire would be used for welding copper. The combination of elements used in the coating produce the special characteristics of each electrode type.

> The main purpose of the core wire is to carry the electrical energy to the arc and to supply suitable added metal for deposit.

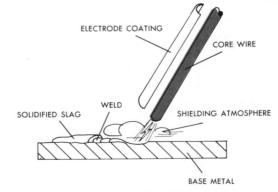

Figure 13-3   Bare electrode with coating

COATINGS

The coating has many functions. Without a shield, molten metal will combine with the oxygen and nitrogen in the air. It is therefore necessary to shield both the metal being added from the electrode and the molten weld metal. (Molten weld metal is the mixture of molten base metal and the molten metal from the electrode, which, when it solidifies, forms the actual weld.) An arc may be shielded by enveloping it in an inert gas. This gas will not enter into a chemical reaction with the molten metal. The coating of the electrode provides the shielding gas. This is the shielded metal arc welding (SMAW) process.

> The coating minimizes contamination from the atmosphere by providing a shield.

Some of the elements used in coatings are magnesium, aluminum silicates, and talc, which are all **slag formers**. Calcium fluorides, calcium carbonates, ferro manganese, ferro silicon, and ferro titanium are **fluxing agents**. Sodium silicate, commonly called water glass, is used as a **binding agent**. Cellulose, which forms a gas, protects the weld area.

> **Function of Coatings**
> The main function of an electrode coating is to:
> a. minimize contamination of the weld metal by oxygen and nitrogen from the surrounding atmosphere;
> b. compensate for losses of certain elements during the transfer of metal across the arc by including alloys in the coating;
> c. concentrate the arc on a specific area by forming a cup at the end of the electrode (a result of the slower melting of the coating).

SLAG

The coating also forms a slag on top of the molten weld metal. The slag protects the molten metal during cooling and also helps shape the weld. It is removed after the weld has cooled. Besides forming a protective layer over the weld, the slag must possess the following characteristics:

> a. have a melting point lower than that of the weld metal. Otherwise there would be a danger of the slag solidifying before the deposited metal does;
> b. have a density in the molten state which is less than that of the weld metal, so that it may float to the surface;
> c. must be viscous (thick) enough that it does not flow over too large an area. It serves to prevent contamination to the weld metal from the surrounding atmosphere;
> d. contain no elements which will react undesirably with the weld metal;
> e. expand, but in a different way from the weld metal, so that it will break away from the weld metal when cold;
> f. have a surface tension that will prevent large globules from forming.

TEST YOUR KNOWLEDGE

1. What is the main purpose of the core wire?
2. What is a characteristic of inert gas that is important for SMAW?
3. What is the purpose of the coating?
4. What does slag do?

In addition to the above characteristics welding electrodes may be grouped according to the following points.

The Method of Manufacture:
a. Solid extrusion
b. Extrusion with reinforcement
c. Dipping

Type of Coating and Slag:
a. A cellulose coating produces a thin slag.
b. A rutile coating produces a fluid and or sticky slag.

c. An oxide silicate coating produces a heavy solid or inflated slag.

d. A lime fluoride coating will produce a glassy slag.

Welding Position in Which the Electrode May Be Used:

a. A #1 indicates the electrode may be used in all positions (flat (downhand), vertical, horizontal, and overhead).

b. A #2 indicates that the electrode should be used only in the flat or downhand position.

c. A #3 indicates that the electrode can be used only in the flat position.

d. A #4 indicates that the electrode should be used in the vertical down position only.

Welding Current:

a. alternating current (AC)

b. direct current reverse polarity (DCRP)

c. direct current straight polarity (DCSP)

Type of Penetration:

a. light

b. medium

c. deep

13-4 ELECTRODE IDENTIFICATION

Because there are so many different types of electrodes on the market, it can be very confusing to choose the correct one for the work to be done. As a result, the AWS (American Welding Society) has established a numbering system which is used by the welding industry. The AWS A-5.1 specification for mild and low alloy steel uses codes such as E6014, E10014, E6011.

This is how the numbers are read:

1. The letter E indicates that the rod is for arc welding.

2. The next two numbers (if four digits are used) or three numbers (if five digits are used) multiplied by 1000 indicate the tensile strength of the weld metal in psi.

3. The next to last number indicates the position in which the electrode can be used. The position may be **flat, vertical,** or **overhead.** The flat position is further divided into horizontal and downhand. A number 1 here

would indicate that the electrode could be used in all of the positions. A number 2 would indicate that the electrode can only be used in the flat position (horizontal or downhand).

4. The last number indicates the electrical characteristics of the electrode, for example, AC, DC, and DC straight or reverse. This last number, however, has become somewhat unreliable because of the type of electrodes used today.

An E7024 electrode, for instance, will have the following characteristics:

E	• electrode (arc welding)
70	• multiplied by 1000 means 70 000 psi tensile strength
2	• flat position (horizontal or downhand)
4	• AC and DC (straight and reverse)
E7024	

Therefore an E7024 electrode is an electrode for arc welding. It has a tensile strength of 70 000 psi, and it should be used only in the horizontal and/or downhand positions. It may be used on AC or DC. When used on DC, it can be used on straight or reverse polarity, although some manufacturers recommend DC reverse only when using direct current.

THE CSA NUMBERING CODE

The CSA (Canadian Standards Association) standard for mild and low alloy steel electrodes is W48-1M 1980, which has almost identical characteristics with the AWS A5.1 standard (see Table 13-1). The difference lies in the fact that the CSA uses SI metric and the AWS still uses the inch-pound system to indicate tensile strength of an electrode. The AWS measures tensile strength in pounds per square inch. The CSA uses megapascals (MPa). In the case of the E7024 electrode, 70 000 pounds per square inch translates into 480 000 MPa. Under the CSA specification, E7024 becomes E48024 but the requirements the electrode must meet are the same in both cases (Figure 13-4).

TABLE 13-1 AWS AND CSA CODING

AWS A-5.1	CSA W48-1M 1980			
Class	Old Code		Metric Code	
E6010	E6010	W48.1	E41010	W48.1-M
E6011	E6011	W48.1	E41011	W48.1-M
E6011	E6011	W48.1	E41011	W48.1-M
E6012	E6012	W48.1	E41012	W48.1-M
E6012	E6012	W48.1	E41012	W48.1-M
E6013	E6013	W48.1	E41013	W48.1-M
E6013	E6013	W48.1	E41013	W48.1-M
E7014	E7014	W48.1	E48014	W48.1-M
E7024	E7024	W48.1	E48024	W48.1-M

Note
Under the CSA code, the letter "M" stands for metric.

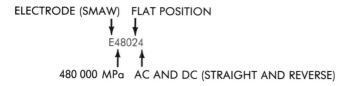

Figure 13-4   The CSA numbering code for electrodes

While all metric standards have not been finalized, the following conversions will probably apply in determining electrode measurements.
Length of electrode: millimetres instead of inches.

inches	9	12	14	18	28	36
mm	225	300	350	450	700	1000

Diameter of electrode: millimetres instead of inches:

inches	1/16	5/64	3/32	1/8	5/32	3/16	1/4	5/16
mm	1.6	2.0	2.5	3.2	4.0	5.0	6.0	8.0

Many manufacturers use trade names and numbers for their own particular brand of electrodes **but all containers and each electrode must have the appropriate AWS/CSA number stamped on them.** For example, the electrode E7024 (E48024) described above is named Rocket 24, Easyarc 12, L.A. 7024 by various companies but all of them must meet the specifications of AWS A5.1 and CSA W48.1 and this must be indicated on the container and electrode (Figure 13-5). Table 13-2 shows the AWS and CSA classification for SMAW electrodes.

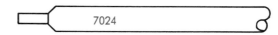

Figure 13-5   Electrode stamped with AWS number

13-5 ELECTRODE SIZE AND AMPERAGE

The size of the electrode to be used will depend on a number of factors:
1. the thickness of the metal,
2. how the edges of the joint are prepared,

TABLE 13-2 AWS/CSA CLASSIFICATION FOR SMAW ELECTRODES

CSA W48-1M 1984	AWS A5.1	Current/ polarity	Coating type	Application characteristics	Welding position
E41010	E6010	DCRP	cellulose	For X-ray quality welds. Deep penetration, light slag	all
E41011	E6011	DCRP/DCSP AC	cellulose	Same as for E41010/E6010 but can also be used with AC	all
E41012	E6012	AC or DCSP	rutile	For general purpose work with poor fit up. Medium penetration and slag.	all
E41013	E6013	DCRP/DCSP AC	rutile	For good-quality general purpose work. Heavy slag, mild penetration.	all
E41014	E6014	DCRP/DCSP AC	rutile, iron powder	Similar to E41013/E6013. Mild penetration, heavy slag, smooth weld appearance. Can be dragged.	all
E41015	E6015	DCRP	low hydrogen	For low alloy and mild steels. Medium penetration. Glassy slag.	all
E41016	E6016	DCRP/DCSP AC	low hydrogen	As above for E41015/E6015 but can be used on AC.	all
E41018	E6018	DCRP or AC	low hydrogen	Excellent for low alloy and mild steel. Medium glassy slag, excellent penetration.	all
E41024	E6024	DCRP/DCSP AC	rutile, 50% iron powder	For extra weld metal deposition. Mild penetration, smooth weld appearance. Can be dragged.	flat welds, horizontal fillets
E41028	E6028	DCRP or AC	low hydrogen, 50% iron powder	Combination of low hydrogen and iron powder. Extra weld metal deposit. Can be dragged. Very smooth appearance in weld, heavy glassy slag.	horizontal fillets, flat welds

The above table is only a sample. Check with your local electrode manufacturer or distributor who will supply complete information on all welding rods, usually in a pocket booklet.

3. the position of the joint (flat, vertical, overhead),
4. the skill of the welder.

Figure 13-6 shows how electrode size is determined.

The amperage to be used will depend on:
1. the size of electrode chosen,
2. the type of coating on the electrode,
3. the power source (AC, DCRP, DCSP).

Table 13-3 can be used as a guide when selecting the electrode size and the amperage for a particular welding operation.

Courtesy of Canadian Liquid Air Ltd.

Figure 13-7   Electrode containers

ELECTRODE CONTAINERS

The maximum and minimum amperage to be used with an electrode is usually printed on the manufacturer's carton or container (Figure 13-7). Using this information, one should set the welding machine at a point midway between the two amperages given. Strike the arc, listen to the sound, and watch the molten puddle.

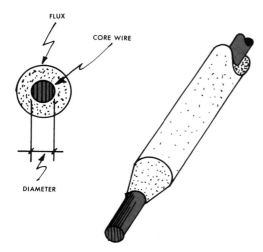

Figure 13-6   Electrode size

TABLE 13-3 SELECTING ELECTRODE SIZE AND AMPERAGE

Metal Thickness		Electrode Size		Amperage
Metric	Inch-pound	Metric	Inch-pound	
1.3 mm	18 gauge	1.6 mm	1/16 in.	50-80
1.6	16	2.5	3/32	50-80
1.9	14	3.2	1/8	90-135
2.7	12	3.2	1/8	90-135
3.4	10	4.0	5/32	120-175
4.8	3/16	4.0	5/32	120-175
6.4	1/4	4.0	5/32	120-175
7.9	5/16	5.0	3/16	200-275
12.7	1/2	6.0	1/4	250-350
19.0	3/4	6.0	1/4	250-350
25.4	1	6.0	1/4	325-400

Certain factors will indicate whether the amperage should be raised or lowered. If a correct amperage is used there is a steady crackling sound and a quiet puddle. When welding out of position (vertical or overhead), reduce the amperage by 10% to 15%.

13-6 IRON POWDER ELECTRODES

Many electrodes today contain iron powder in the coating. The amount of iron powder added to the coating may vary from a very small amount to as much as 60%. When welding with an alternating current using ordinary electrodes, arc stability is a problem. With a 60% duty cycle machine and the reversal of the alternating current, the arc tries to cut out 120 times per second. This causes the arc to go out or the electrode to stick. The addition of iron powder eliminates this.

The addition of iron powder has many other advantages. The first advantage is easy slag removal. In many cases, the slag will curl away from the weld (Figure 13-8). Even if the slag does not curl up, it may be removed with very little effort.

Courtesy of The Lincoln Electric Company

Figure 13-8   Slag removal

The second advantage is speed. Note the difference between Figure 13-9 and Figure 13-10. The weld in Figure 13-9 was made with an E41012 (E6012) electrode, while the weld in Figure 13-10 was made with an iron powder electrode. The iron powder electrode was 30% faster and resulted in a better appearance.

Note the difference in the coatings shown in Figure 13-11. Both electrodes are the same size, but the one on the right is an iron powder electrode and has a much heavier coating. Because of the deep cup at the end of the electrode, these electrodes can be operated at a much higher amperage than non-iron powder electrodes.

The excellent ductility of the metal in these electrodes is shown in Figure 13-12. A bead was run on top of a

Courtesy of The Lincoln Electric Company

Figure 13-9   Fillet weld made with an ordinary electrode

Figure 13-10   Fillet weld made with an iron powder electrode

Courtesy of The Lincoln Electric Company

Figure 13-11   A comparison of coatings

piece of metal, and the metal was then bent into the shape shown. Another advantage of iron powder electrodes is the ease with which they can be used. But because of the higher amperage, faster speed, and the larger puddle produced, slight difficulty may be experienced in following curved shapes, such as the one shown in Figure 13-13.

Welds made with iron powder electrodes tend to leave the face of the weld slightly concave, as shown in Figure 13-14. However, as can be seen, there is still complete fusion at the root of the joint. Iron powder electrodes are usually used on AC because of the higher amperage required. They have a softer arc than non-iron powder electrodes.

Figure 13-12   Ductility

Courtesy of The Lincoln Electric Company

Figure 13-13   Curved welds

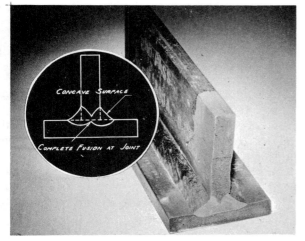

Figure 13-14   Penetration and concave surface of weld made with an iron powder electrode

Courtesy of The Lincoln Electric Company

TEST YOUR KNOWLEDGE

1. How is the size of an electrode determined?
2. Describe one method for finding the amperage for a certain size of electrode.
3. List two advantages of adding iron powder to an electrode.
4. Why can iron powder electrodes be used at a higher amperage?

13-7 LOW HYDROGEN ELECTRODES

Another electrode which has become popular in industry is the low hydrogen electrode. The presence of hydrogen in molten metal means that porosity will more likely be formed during solidification of the weld metal. It also increases the possibility of underbead cracking. The low hydrogen coating was designed to have a low moisture content, thus preventing the introduction of hydrogen into the weld from the electrode. Too much emphasis cannot be placed on keeping this type of electrode dry. In industry they are usually kept in heated ovens until required. These electrodes are used for high quality work or for welding alloy steels.

The technique for using low hydrogen electrodes, although not difficult, differs in some ways from that used for other electrodes. For this reason some practical hints on their use may be advantageous.

Angle of electrode. The angle is similar to that used for other electrodes. However, if the angle is varied too much, it can cause an unstable arc, poor finish, and porosity.

Arc length. As long as the arc is kept very short, as in Figure 13-15, it will be stable and provide complete shielding. A long arc will cause porosity.

Weaving. Weaving should be done as little as possible. Single beads are preferable for keeping a short arc. Wide weaves should be avoided (Figure 13-16).

Excellent-quality welds are the main advantage in using low hydrogen electrodes. However, failure to observe a few simple precautions can result in porosity.

Courtesy of The Lincoln Electric Company

Low Hydrogen Electrodes   **149**

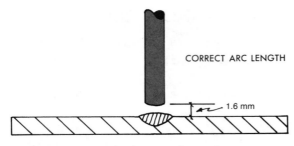

CORRECT ARC LENGTH

1.6 mm

Figure 13-15   Low hydrogen electrodes

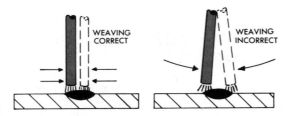

WEAVING CORRECT

WEAVING INCORRECT

Figure 13-16   Weaving with low hydrogen electrodes

The following faults will not necessarily result in a porous weld, but they will most certainly increase the possibility of porosity.

1. Damp electrodes will cause porosity at the beginning of the weld. This disappears, however, after about 25 mm (or 1 in.) of the electrode has been used.
2. A long arc or trapped slag will cause porosity.
3. If the amperage is too low, the arc will not heat the metal. The weld will then freeze (stick to the base metal) too quickly, trapping gases in the weld.
4. Welding on metal with a thick scale or rust will cause porosity. The porosity may not be apparent on first runs, but will show up in multiple layers.
5. Porosity in fillet welds can be caused by using too large an iron powder electrode. The thick coating will touch the sides of the tee joint, preventing a short arc from being held. A root pass with a smaller electrode will eliminate this and ensure good penetration.
6. The wrong polarity can lead to porosity in the weld. DC reverse is recommended.

> **Note**
> On CSA-coded electrodes the letters CH indicate controlled hydrogen.

13-8 ELECTRODE COST DATA

It is sometimes necessary or desirable to estimate the cost of electrodes on work being performed. Tables 13-4 and 13-5 will help you estimate electrode quantity and cost for a variety of joints. (To understand the tables, read the information below, first.)

Electrode requirements have been calculated as follows:

$$M1 = \frac{M2}{1 - L}$$

Where M1 = mass of electrodes required
M2 = mass of steel deposited
L = total electrode losses

To find out the mass of steel deposited, it is necessary to calculate first the volume of deposited metal (area of the groove multiplied by the length). This volumetric value is then converted to mass by the factor 7.8 g/cm³ for steel. Where weld reinforcement is involved, it is added to the requirements for net, unreinforced welds.

Should you encounter a variation in conditions or joint preparation that is not shown in the tables, substitute appropriate figures in the $M1 = \frac{M2}{1 - L}$ formula and calculate it.

In Figure 13-17, for example, with a 25 mm (1 in.) fillet weld, it would require 1375 g (3.033 lbs.) of electrodes per 300 mm (per linear foot) of weld but actually only 770 g (1.698 lbs.) of steel are deposited per 300 mm (linear foot) calculated from Table 13-4.

Figure 13-18 is a square edge groove butt joint with a gap "G". The joint is welded from one side only. From Table 13-5, if the thickness "T" is 8 mm (5/16 in.) and the bead "B" is 12 mm (1/2 in.) with a gap of 2.4 mm (3/32 in.), it would require 136 g (0.30 lbs.) per 300 mm (linear foot) of electrode with the actual deposit of 77 g (0.170 lbs.) of weld metal.

As can be seen from the two examples above, if one is involved in estimating costs, one must have a thorough understanding of all factors pertinent to welding.

TABLE 13-4 ELECTRODE CONSUMPTION ON HORIZONTAL FILLET WELDS

Size of Fillet L (millimetres)	Grams of Electrodes Required per 300 mm of Weld* (Approx.)	Steel Deposited per 300 mm of Weld-Grams
3.0	22	12
4.5	50	29
6.5	85	48
8.0	135	75
9.5	195	108
12.5	345	193
16.0	538	300
19.0	773	433
25.0	1375	770

* Includes scrap and spatter loss
Courtesy of Hobart Brothers Company

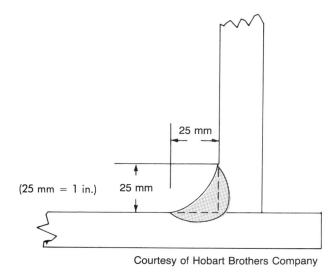

25 mm

(25 mm = 1 in.)   25 mm

Courtesy of Hobart Brothers Company

Figure 13-17   Horizontal fillet weld

TABLE 13-5 ELECTRODE CONSUMPTION OF SQUARE GROOVE BUTT JOINT WELDED ONE SIDE

Joint Dimensions (millimetres)			Grams of Electrodes Required per 300 mm of Weld* (Approx.)		Grams of Steel Deposited per 300 mm of Weld	
T	B	G	Without Reinforcement	With Reinforcement**	Without Reinforcement	With Reinforcement**
4.5	9.5	0	—	73	—	40
		1.6	18	91	9	50
6.5	11.0	1.6	23	104	12	59
		2.4	32	118	18	65
8.0	12.5	1.6	27	122	15	70
		2.4	41	136	23	77

* Includes scrap end and spatter loss
** r = height of reinforcement
Courtesy of Hobart Brothers Company

TABLE 13-6 ELECTRODE CONSUMPTION OF SQUARE GROOVE BUTT JOINT WELDED TWO SIDES

Joint Dimensions (millimetres)			Grams of Electrodes Required per 300 mm of Weld* (Approx.)		Grams of Steel Deposited per 300 mm of Weld	
T	B	G	Without Reinforcement	With Reinforcement**	Without Reinforcement	With Reinforcement**
3.0	6.5	0	—	95	—	54
		0.8	14	109	6	60
4.5	9.5	0.8	18	163	9	90
		1.6	32	177	18	99
6.5	11.0	1.6	45	213	24	118
		2.4	64	240	36	131

* Includes scrap end and spatter loss
** r = height of reinforcement
Courtesy of Hobart Brothers Company

TABLE 13-7 ELECTRODE CONSUMPTION OF "V" GROOVE BUTT JOINT

Joint Dimensions (millimetres)			Grams of Electrodes Required per 300 mm of Weld* (Approx.)		Grams of Steel Deposited per 300 mm of Weld	
T	B	G	Without Reinforcement	With Reinforcement**	Without Reinforcement	With Reinforcement**
6.5	5.5	1.6	68	114	39	65
8.0	8.0	2.4	141	209	78	117
9.5	10.5	3.0	226	318	128	179
12.5	14.0	3.0	395	622	222	291
16.0	18.0	3.0	612	762	342	437
19.0	21.5	3.0	880	1066	494	699
25.0	29.0	3.0	1565	1815	875	1015

* Includes scrap end and spatter loss
** r = height of reinforcement
Courtesy of Hobart Brothers Company

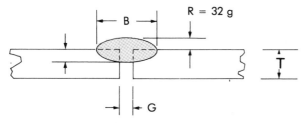

Courtesy of Hobart Brothers Company

Figure 13-18 Square edge groove butt joint welded one side

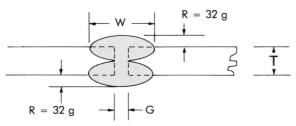

Courtesy of Hobart Brothers Company

Figure 13-19 Square edge groove butt joint welded two sides

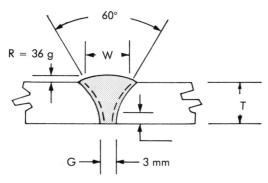

Courtesy of Hobart Brothers Company

Figure 13-20 Vee groove butt joint

If root of top weld is chipped or flame gouged and welded, add 32 g to steel deposited (equivalent to approximately 60 g of electrodes).

POINTS TO REMEMBER

- The core wire carries the electrical energy to the arc and supplies filler metal for the weld area.
- The coating minimizes contamination, compensates for metal loss, and concentrates the arc.
- Numbering and amperage are among the factors to be considered when selecting an electrode.
- Set the amperage halfway between the maximum and minimum amperage recommended by the manufacturer of the electrode. Then adjust after observing the arc.
- All electrodes must conform to the AWS/CSA standards.
- Most electrodes today contain some iron powder in the coating.
- Iron powder electrodes have a much heavier coating than other electrodes.
- A close or short arc is necessary when using low hydrogen electrodes.

WORDS TO REMEMBER

core wire	tension	midpoint
coating	globules	diameter
function	viscous	porosity
element	numbering	ductility
density	system	hydrogen
	classification	reinforcement

REVIEW QUESTIONS

1. Name the three methods of manufacturing electrodes.
2. List four functions of the coating on an electrode.
3. What is meant by shielded arc?
4. What is the advantage of having the coating form a cup at the end of the electrode?
5. What is the purpose of the slag?
6. Name the six characteristics a slag should possess.
7. Why should the slag have a lower melting point than the weld metal?
8. Name the five characteristics used to group electrodes.

9. What factors should be considered when selecting an electrode for SMAW?

10. A cellulosic coating produces what type of slag?

11. What is the main difference between the AWS and the CSA numbering system?

12. Pick one electrode code using the CSA numbering system, and describe the characteristics of that electrode.

13. What factors determine the size of electrode to be used?

14. What factors decide the amperage that should be used?

15. How is the manufacturer's recommended amperage followed?

16. Name two advantages of adding iron powder to electrodes.

17. Why can iron powder electrodes be used at much higher amperages than non-iron powder electrodes?

18. Why has the low hydrogen electrode become popular in industry?

19. What is the best method of storing low hydrogen electrodes?

20. What is the main advantage in using low hydrogen electrodes?

21. On which polarity should low hydrogen electrodes be used?

22. Why is it necessary to use a short arc with low hydrogen electrodes?

23. Calculate the amount of weld metal required for the joints shown in figures 13-19 and 13-20.

24. Name three incorrect procedures that can cause porosity when using low hydrogen electrodes.

14

SHIELDED METAL ARC WELDING FUNDAMENTALS (SMAW)

14-1 Skill and Practice
14-2 Basic Rules
14-3 Striking the Arc
14-4 Running a Bead
14-5 Weaving Motions
14-6 Padding or Buildup

Shielded metal arc welding as shown in Figure 14-1 is a widely used process. It is not difficult, but requires patience and practice to acquire the necessary skills. In this chapter, you will learn the fundamentals necessary to produce a good weld with SMAW. SMAW is a process of joining metals by the heat created by an electric arc, and much of the success of this type of welding will depend on the welder's ability to control and direct the welding process.

Courtesy of Hobart Brothers Company

Figure 14-1 SMAW

14-1 SKILL AND PRACTICE

The quality of an arc weld depends upon the knowledge and skill of the welder. Skill comes with practice. There are six basic factors a beginning welder should keep in mind. The first two concern body position and protection. The remaining four have to do with the welding process itself.

1. Correct position
2. Face protection

155

3. Arc length
4. Electrode angle
5. Speed of travel
6. Amperage

Correct Position. Welding is easier to do if the welder is in a comfortable position (Figure 14-2). The following is good practice.
1. With the machine off, insert an electrode in the holder.
2. Grasp the electrode holder comfortably in the right hand.
3. Grasp the right wrist with the left hand.
4. Place the left elbow on the welding bench.
5. Line the electrode up with the base metal.
6. Practise moving the electrode along the metal, using the left elbow as a pivot.

Left-handed students should reverse the positions described above.

> The machine must be turned off while practising is underway.

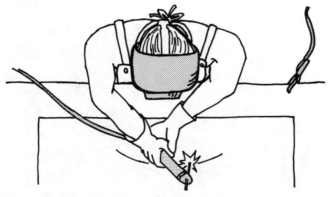

Figure 14-2   Correct welding position

Face protection.
1. Place the helmet on your head. Make sure that it fits properly.
2. Assume the position outlined above.
3. Make sure that the machine is off.
4. Keep the position and gently nod your head.
5. Continue to nod your head until the helmet comes down over your face (Figure 14-3).

6. Lift the helmet up again, and repeat this practice until it becomes easy.

This procedure allows you to adjust your helmet without disturbing your original position.

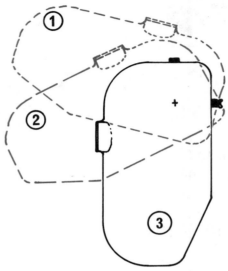

Figure 14-3   Helmet positions

14-2 BASIC RULES

Arc length. Arc length is the distance between the tip of the electrode and the base metal being welded. The correct distance must be maintained.

Angle of electrode. During welding, the electrode must be held at the correct angle.

Speed of travel. If a good weld is to be obtained, the correct speed must be maintained.

Amperage. Incorrect amperage (heat) will result in a poor weld.

Some welders use the word LASH to remind them of these last four points. Each letter in LASH stands for a point to be remembered (see Figure 14-4.)

> L—arc length
> A—angle of electrode
> S—speed of travel
> H—heat (incorrect amperage)

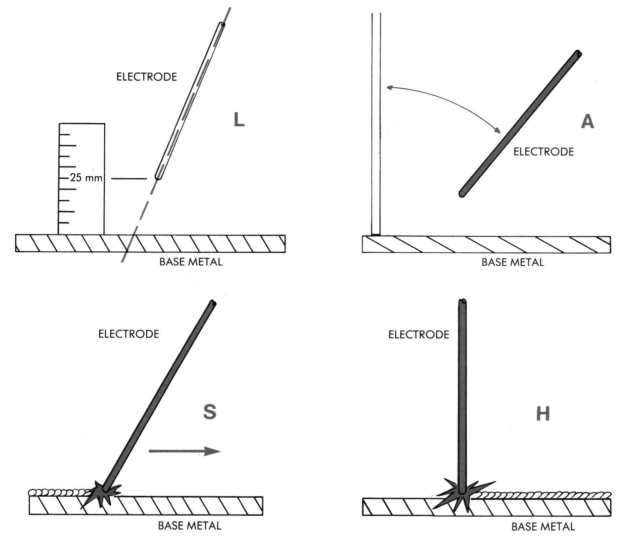

Figure 14-4 LASH Length of arc **L** Angle of electrode **A** Speed of travel **S** Heat (amperage) **H**

TEST YOUR KNOWLEDGE

1. On what factors does the quality of the weld depend?
2. List the six basic factors that should be kept in mind in doing a weld.
3. What does each letter in the word LASH stand for?

14-3 STRIKING THE ARC

Striking the arc involves touching the electrode to the base metal to make an arc. Two methods are used: **scratching** and **tapping**.

The scratch method is similar to striking a large match. The tap method is a straight up and down tapping motion as the name implies. In both cases the welding current forms an arc as soon as the electrode touches the base metal. If it were held in this position, the electrode would freeze (stick) to the metal. To avoid this, the electrode is raised as soon as it comes into contact with the metal and the metal is transferred across the arc in globules. However, the arc will go out if the electrode is raised too far from the metal, and the whole procedure will have to be repeated.

EXERCISE #1
STEPS IN USING THE
SCRATCH METHOD

1. Check that the ground clamp is attached properly.
2. Wear protective clothing.
3. Obtain a piece of metal about 50 mm × 150 mm × 6 mm (or 2 in. × 6 in. × 1/4 in.). If the metal is dirty, brush it clean before setting it on the welding bench. Dirt or rust make a poor connection.
4. Obtain welding rods and set the machine to the correct amperage.
5. Placing the bare end of the electrode in the holder, grasp the holder comfortably, and assume the correct welding position.
6. Turn the machine on.
7. Hold the electrode about 25 mm (or 1 in.) above the base metal. It should be perpendicular to the metal and inclined 20° to 30° in the direction of travel (Figure 14-5).
8. Lower the helmet in front of your eyes.

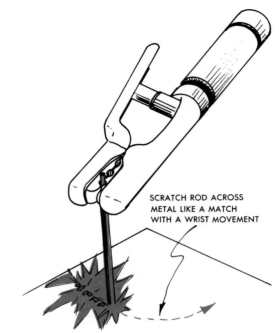

Figure 14-6   The scratch method

9. Strike the arc by quickly and gently dragging the electrode across the base metal, using a wrist movement only (Figure 14-6).
10. If the arc has been properly struck, a burst of light will be produced.
11. Withdraw the electrode approximately 6 mm (or 1/4 in.). Hold this length for a second or two, then lower the electrode until it is 3 mm (or 1/8 in.) away from the metal (Figure 14-7).
12. Repeat this exercise until the arc can be struck every time without the electrode freezing.

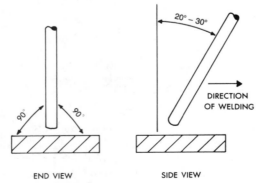

Figure 14-5   Electrode angle

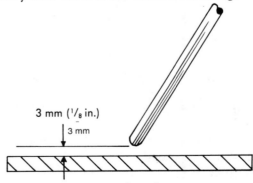

Figure 14-7   Correct arc length

EXERCISE #2
STEPS IN USING THE TAP METHOD

The steps in striking the arc by the tap method are exactly the same as those for the scratch method, except for step 9. Instead of scratching or dragging the electrode on the metal, a tapping motion is used. Therefore step 9 will read as follows:

> 9. Strike the arc by moving the electrode down until it touches the metal. When a burst of light appears, move the electrode up 6 mm (or 1/4 in.), hold for a few seconds, then lower the electrode until it is 3 mm (or 1/8 in.) away from the metal (Figure 14-8).

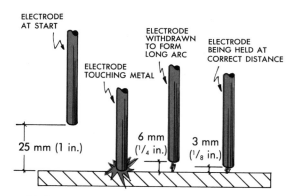

Figure 14-8   The tap method

The distance of 3 mm (or 1/8 in.) is approximate and must be judged, of course. This is the correct arc length for most electrodes. However, the sound of the arc can also be used as an aid. If the electrode is held too far away from the metal, a hissing sound will be heard and eventually the arc will go out. If the electrode is held too close to the metal, it will stick. With the correct distance, however, a steady crackling sound will be heard.

Both of these methods should be practised and strict attention paid to distinguishing between the different sounds. An experienced welder should be able to strike the arc using either the scratch method or the tap method. Though the scratch method is easier for the beginner, pit marks are left on the metal. When marking the metal is not permitted for certain types of work, such as stainless steel vessels, **the tap method is then best.**

TEST YOUR KNOWLEDGE

1. Name the two methods used to strike the arc.
2. Which method is easier for beginners?
3. Describe one situation when the tap method should be used.
4. What is meant by the term "freezing"?
5. If the electrode is held the correct distance from the base metal, what sound should be heard?

14-4 RUNNING A BEAD

Before assembling and welding the various joints, skill must be developed in running a bead because the bead is basic to most welding operations (Figure 14-9).

EXERCISE #3
STEPS IN RUNNING A BEAD

1. Obtain a piece of metal about 50 mm × 150 mm × 6 mm (or 2 in. × 6 in. × 1/4 in.).
2. Obtain some welding electrodes. Insert one in the holder.
3. Make sure that the proper equipment is worn.
4. Set the machine to the correct amperage, and turn the machine on.
5. Assume the correct position, and strike the arc.
6. Move the electrode in one direction, keeping the correct arc length and angles discussed previously.
7. As the weld is progressing, you will notice that the electrode is being burned up and is becoming shorter in length. To compensate for this shortening of the electrode, keep lowering the hand that is holding the holder. The correct distance must be maintained.

Figure 14-9   Running a bead

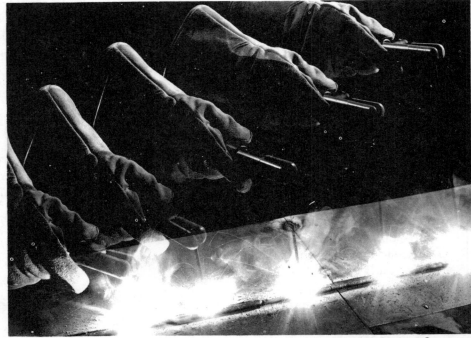

Courtesy of Hobart Brothers Company

8. Try to maintain an even speed. Travelling too fast will result in a narrow, stringy weld; travelling too slowly will result in the weld metal piling up.

Figure 14-10 shows various qualities of beads. The descriptions below indicate how each bead was produced. Use these as a guide in running your own beads.

A. A good bead with the correct amperage and speed.

B. A fair bead, but the amperage was too low.

C. A poor bead: the amperage was too high.

D. A fair bead: the amperage was too low, causing weld metal to pile up on the base metal.

E. A poor bead: again the wrong current was used.

F. A good bead, but the speed of travel was too slow. Note how high and wide the bead is.

G. A poor bead: the amperage was correct, but the speed of travel was too fast.

TEST YOUR KNOWLEDGE

1. Why must skill be developed in running a bead?
2. Why does the electrode become shorter as the weld progresses?
3. What causes the arc to become too long and go out?
4. What happens when the electrode is held too close to the base metal?

EXERCISE #4
RUNNING PARALLEL BEADS

Parallel beads are two single beads placed side by side.

1. Check the welding machine and protective clothing.
2. Obtain a piece of metal about 50 mm × 150 mm × 6 mm (or 2 in. × 6 in. × 1/4 in.).
3. Obtain some electrodes, set the welding machine, insert an electrode in the holder, and turn the machine on.

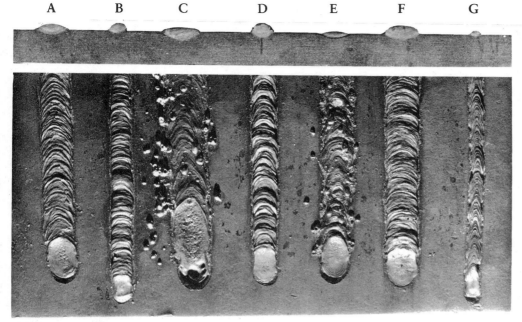

A   B   C   D   E   F   G

Figure 14-10
Examples of beads

Courtesy of The Lincoln Electric Company

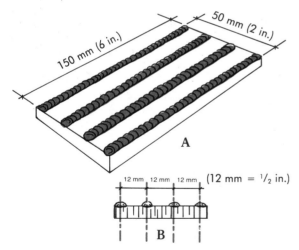

Figure 14-11   Parallel beads

4. Strike the arc and run a bead on the surface of the metal along the 150 mm (or 6 in.) length, as close to the edge as possible.

5. Make another bead approximately 16 mm (or 5/8 in.) away from the first bead in exactly the same manner.

6. Repeat this until there are four equidistant beads, each one approximately 150 mm (6 in.) long with 16 mm (5/8 in.) between the centres of the beads (Figure 14-11).

7. Chip and wire brush the beads, and examine them for flaws.

8. Repeat on the other side of the metal and on some new metal until skill is developed.

If difficulty is experienced in the beginning, lines may be drawn on the metal using a ruler and chalk or soapstone. These lines can be seen with the helmet down after the arc has been struck and can be used as a guide at first.

TEST YOUR KNOWLEDGE

1. Why should the beads be run along the 150 mm (6 in.) length?

2. What is meant by parallel beads?

14-5 WEAVING MOTIONS

When depositing weld metal, it is often desirable to make the weld wider than a single bead. To do this the elec-

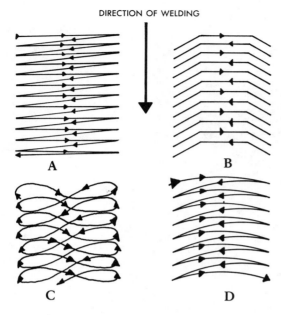

DIRECTION OF WELDING

A   B

C   D

Figure 14-12   Weaving motions

2. Obtain a piece of metal about 50 mm × 150 mm × 6 mm (2 in. × 6 in. × 1/4 in.).
3. Obtain some electrodes, set the welding machine, insert an electrode in the holder, and turn the machine on.
4. Run four beads 12 mm (1/2 in.) apart on the surface of the metal as in Figure 14-13A.
5. Chip and wire brush each bead.
6. With the weaving motion shown in Figure 14-13B, run a weave between the two beads on the left, overlapping half on each bead (Figure 14-13C).
7. Chip, wire brush, and inspect for flaws.
8. Repeat this exercise on the other two parallel beads.

trode is moved forward in a weaving motion (from side to side) along the line of weld. By weaving in this manner, more metal can be deposited over a wider area. There are a number of weave motions that can be used in welding. Of the four shown in Figure 14-12, A is the most popular.

Whichever motion is used, it must be uniform. If the weave motion is not uniform or close enough, the result will be poor fusion and slag will be trapped between the welds.

TEST YOUR KNOWLEDGE

1. Why must the weave motion be uniform?
2. What is the most important point to be remembered when making a weave motion?
3. In weaving, how is the electrode manipulated?

EXERCISE #5
STEPS IN WEAVING

1. Check the welding machine and protective clothing.

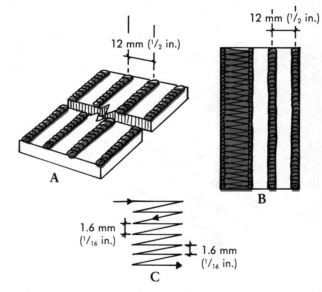

12 mm (1/2 in.)

12 mm (1/2 in.)

A

B

1.6 mm (1/16 in.)

1.6 mm (1/16 in.)

C

Figure 14-13   Parallel beads and weaves

14-6 PADDING OR BUILDUP

Another exercise that will rapidly improve welding skill is padding, or buildup. It is used to build up worn areas on shafts, shovels, grader blades, railway frogs, and other areas where metal has been worn away. Padding is a most useful exercise and has saved many thousands of dollars in industry. Both single beads and weaves are used in building up or padding. The beads or weaves are laid side by side so that each new weld overlaps the one preceding it (Figure 14-14A).

If the welds do not overlap, slag will be trapped in the hollows between the welds, resulting in porosity, or holes (Figure 14-14B). All welds **must** overlap, and all welds **must** be cleaned before the next weld is applied. If required, more weld metal may be applied to build up the thickness of the part (Figure 14-14C).

The second layer of the weld metal should be applied at right angles to the first layer. If necessary, a third layer should be applied at right angles to the second layer, etc., until the metal is built up to the required height (Figures 14-14D and E). By applying the welds at right angles to each other in a crisscross fashion, a smoother weld will be obtained. There will also be less chance of holes appearing in the weld metal.

When welding is done close to the edge of the base metal, the weld has a tendency to spill over. To prevent this, clamp a carbon plate or piece of heavy copper along the edge to keep the weld metal in place. The carbon or copper will not fuse to the weld metal. If the carbon or copper plate appears to be stuck to the weld metal, a sharp blow with a hammer will dislodge it. This is an excellent method of keeping an edge straight and will save unnecessary grinding or filing (Figures 14-15 and 14-16).

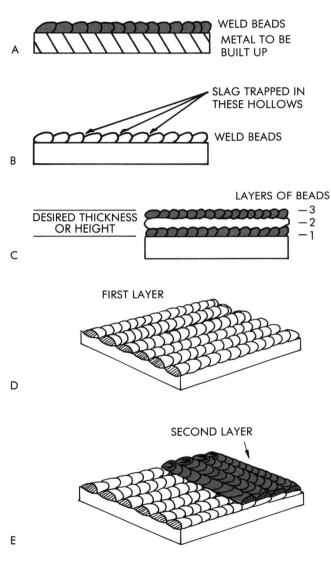

Figure 14-14   Buildup
A. The first layer
B. Faults in first layer
C. Multilayers
D. Building up
E. More buildup

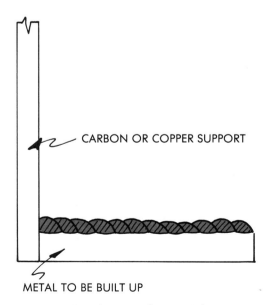

Figure 14-15   Keeping an edge straight

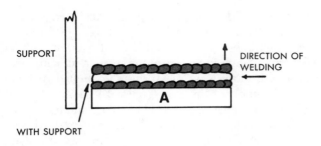

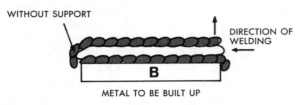

Figure 14-16   Buildup with and without support

TEST YOUR KNOWLEDGE

1. Why is padding useful to industry?
2. How many layers of weld can be applied?
3. What are two important points to be remembered when padding?

POINTS TO REMEMBER

- The quality of the weld depends on the knowledge and skill of the welder.
- There are six basic factors to be remembered: position, protection, arc length, angle of electrode, speed of travel, and amperage.
- Scratch and tap methods are used to strike the arc.
- If the electrode is held too close to the metal, it will stick; if held too far away, it will go out.
- The correct sound is a steady, crackling sound.
- The electrode is being consumed as welding progresses.
- A good bead will be uniform in height and width.
- Weaving covers a larger area than a single bead.
- In padding, run the layers at right angles to each other.

WORDS TO REMEMBER

arc length
protection
position
scratching
tapping

freezing
hissing
crackling
stringy

parallel beads
weaving
overlap
padding
buildup

REVIEW QUESTIONS

1. What is meant by arc length?
2. Why is it necessary each time to check that the ground clamp is properly attached?
3. Why should both the tap and scratch methods be practised?
4. When running a bead, at what angles should the electrode be held?
5. What is the main difference between the two methods of striking the arc?
6. Why must running a bead be practised until skill is developed?
7. When running a bead, why must the hand holding the holder be continually lowered?
8. What are parallel beads?
9. What is the difference between a single bead and a weave?
10. Why must the layers in padding overlap?
11. What effect is accomplished by running the welds at right angles to each other?
12. Why is it not advisable to use the scratch method when welding stainless steel?
13. What is the advantage in using a carbon plate or piece of copper over a steel plate when building up a piece of metal?
14. Explain why it is necessary to assume a comfortable position when arc welding.
15. Why does the arc go out if the electrode is held too far away from the metal?
16. What effect does speed have on the finished weld?

15

BASIC SMAW JOINTS

Now that you have learned how to run a bead with SMAW, you can apply this operation to an area of welding with which you are already familiar. Each of the five basic joints that you read about in Chapter 8 can be joined with a single arc welding bead. These five joints (Figure 15-1) are the

> butt joint
> tee joint
> lap joint
> corner joint
> edge joint

Arc welding is best suited to heavy metal. (Heavy metal is thicker than the metal used for oxy-acetylene welding.) One advantage of arc welding is that thick metals can be welded more quickly. There is also less distortion because the metal starts to melt as soon as the arc is struck. Therefore, it is not necessary to preheat the metal as you would have to do in oxy-acetylene welding.

This chapter will discuss only welding metals that are 6 mm (or 1/4 in.) and thicker, although any thickness of metal can be arc welded if the welder has adequate expertise.

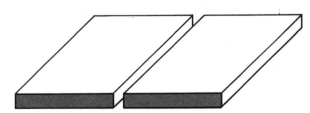

A. The butt joint is a joint between members lying in the same plane.

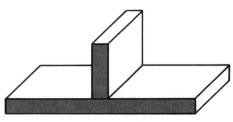

B. The tee joint is a joint between members located at right angles to each other.

Figure 15-1   Basic joints

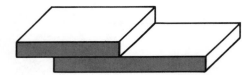

C. The lap joint is a joint between overlapping members.

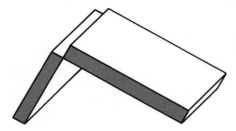

D. The corner joint is a joint between members located at right angles to each other.

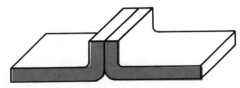

E. The edge joint is a joint between the edges of parallel members.

Figure 15-1 (**cont'd**)

Courtesy of Hobart Brothers Company

Figure 15-2   SMAW

15-1 MAKING FILLET WELDS

The weld that is deposited on a tee joint or lap joint is called a fillet weld. (Quite often the tee joint is called a fillet joint.) There are two kinds of fillet welds: the horizontal (Figure 15-3) and the downhand (Figure 15-4). Both are used frequently in industry.

Whenever possible, the assembly is placed so that the joint will be welded in the downhand position. In the downhand position, the joint can be welded more quickly because it is possible to use larger electrodes and higher amperages than can be used in the horizontal position.

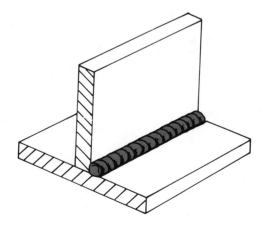

Figure 15-3   Horizontal fillet weld

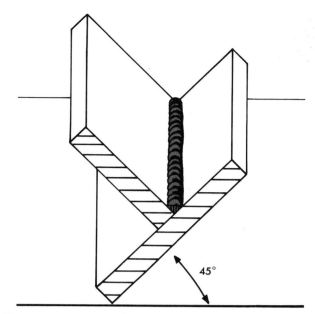

Figure 15-4 Downhand fillet weld

TEST YOUR KNOWLEDGE

1. What is another name for a tee joint?
2. Name the two types of joints that use fillet welds.
3. Why are the joints welded in the downhand position?

EXERCISE #1
STEPS IN MAKING A HORIZONTAL FILLET WELD

1. Assemble a tee joint or a lap joint.
2. Obtain a welding rod, and set the amperage on the machine.
3. Turn on the machine.
4. Hold the electrode so that it is pointing into the corner of the joint at an angle of 45° to the horizontal plate (Figure 15-5A).
5. The electrode should be inclined 15° to 20° in the direction of travel (Figure 15-5B).
6. Lower the helmet in front of your eyes and strike the arc.

7. Proceed to weld along the joint.
8. Watch the bead carefully for excessive buildup or undercut. Increase the speed or change the angle of the electrode to correct these faults if they appear.

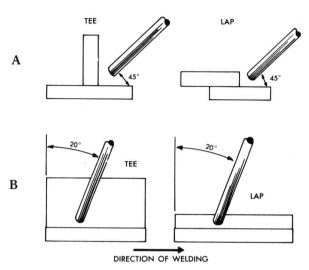

Figure 15-5 Electrode angle

EXERCISE #2
MAKING A DOWNHAND FILLET WELD

This exercise is similar to making a horizontal fillet weld, except that the position of the joint and the angle of the electrode are changed.

To make a downhand fillet weld, follow the steps for the horizontal fillet weld, but place the joint on the welding bench at a 45° angle, as shown in Figure 15-6, rather than flat on the bench. Also, when you start to weld, hold the electrode in a vertical position inclined 15° to 20° in the direction of travel. Figure 15-7 shows good fillet welds on both a tee and a lap joint.

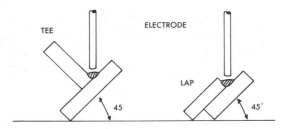

Figure 15-6 Downhand fillet weld

MAKING A THREE-PASS HORIZONTAL FILLET WELD

This weld can be applied to a tee or lap joint. It is used for very heavy metal. In order to obtain full strength, the weld must be larger than one fillet weld pass.

EXERCISE #3
STEPS IN MAKING A THREE-PASS HORIZONTAL FILLET WELD

1. Prepare a tee or lap joint.
2. Obtain a number of welding electrodes.
3. Set the welding machine on the proper amperage, and turn it on.
4. Run the first bead on the corner as a single-pass fillet weld (Figure 15-8A).
5. Chip, clean, and check the bead.
6. Run a second bead, half on the first bead and half on the plate, with the electrode at an angle of 70° to 80° to the horizontal plate (Figure 15-8B).
7. Chip, clean, and check.
8. Run a third bead, half on the second bead and half

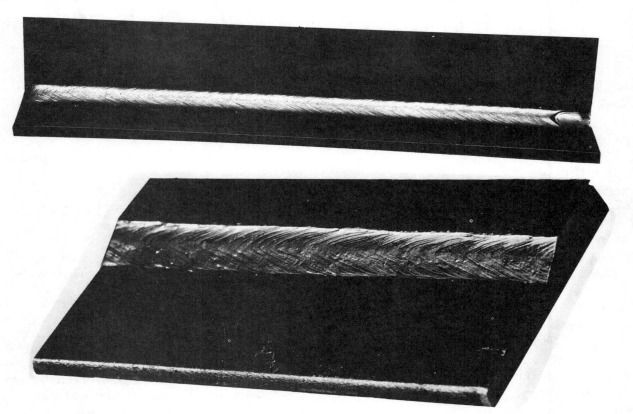

Figure 15-7 Good fillet welds

Courtesy of The Lincoln Electric Company

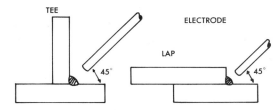

Figure 15-8A   First pass

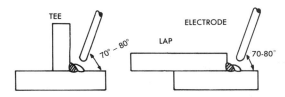

Figure 15-8B   Second pass

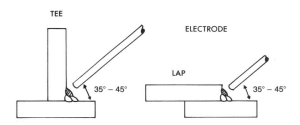

Figure 15-8C   Third pass

on the vertical plate, with the electrode at an angle of 35° to 45° to the vertical plate (Figure 15-8C).

9. Chip, clean, and check.

Any number of passes may be deposited. However, the above pattern should always be followed. That is, all beads on the horizontal leg should be run at a 70° to 80° angle to the horizontal plate. All beads on the vertical leg should be run at a 35° to 45° angle to the vertical plate (figures 15-9 and 15-10).

EXERCISE #4
STEPS IN MAKING A THREE-PASS DOWNHAND FILLET WELD

1. Assemble a tee joint.
2. Set the tee joint at a 45° angle to the welding

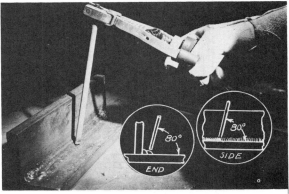

Courtesy of The Lincoln Electric Company

Figure 15-9   All passes laid on horizontal plate

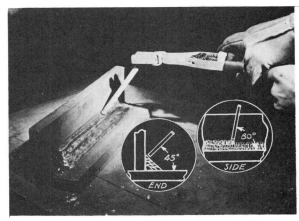

Courtesy of The Lincoln Electric Company

Figure 15-10   All passes laid on vertical plate

bench (Figure 15-11A). Figure 15-12 shows how to support the tee joint.

3. Obtain a welding rod. Remember the higher amperage.
4. Set the amperage on the machine. Turn the machine on.
5. Strike an arc, and proceed to run a single fillet weld in the corner of the joint.
6. Hold the electrode in a vertical position at an angle of 15° to 20° in the direction of travel.
7. Complete the weld. Chip, clean, and check.

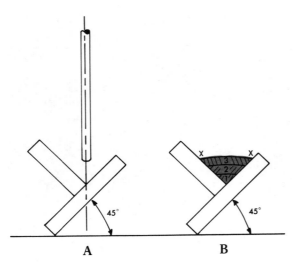

Figure 15-11 Making a three-pass downhand filled weld

8. Proceed to weld a second layer on top of the first weld with a slight weaving motion.
9. Again, after completing the weld, stop, chip, clean, and check.
10. Weld the third and last layer with a slightly wider weaving motion (Figure 15-11B).

On weaving motions, hesitate at the sides (x) to eliminate undercut.

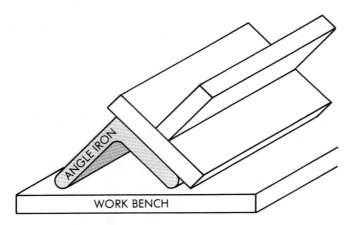

Figure 15-12 One method of supporting the joint for welding in a downhand position

Fillet welds are among the most important welds because 70% of all joints welded in industry are tee or lap joints.

TEST YOUR KNOWLEDGE

1. Why is a weaving motion used for second and third pass?
2. Why is it necessary to hesitate at the sides when weaving?
3. Why can higher amperages be used on a downhand fillet?
4. Why is a wider weaving motion necessary with the third pass?

Figure 15-13 shows a 16-pass fillet weld made on a plate that is 32 mm (or 1 in.) thick. Figure 15-14 shows the ideal shape and typical faults in horizontal fillet welds. For good weld examples look again at Figure 15-7.

Courtesy of The Lincoln Electric Company

Figure 15-13 Sixteen-pass fillet weld on a 32 mm (1 in.) thick plate

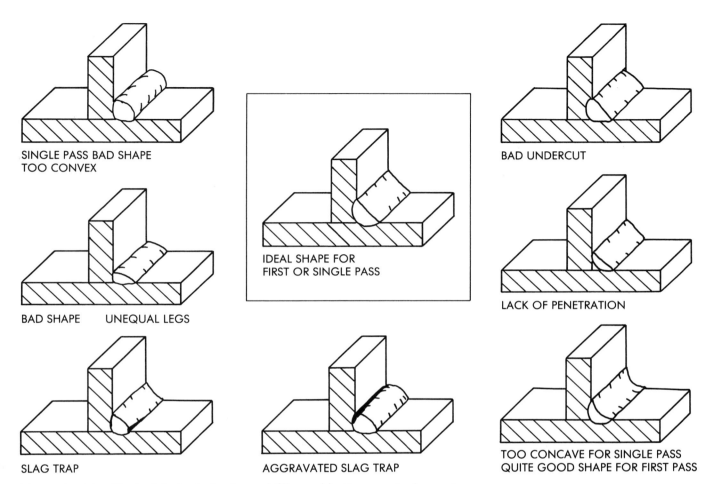

SINGLE PASS BAD SHAPE
TOO CONVEX

BAD SHAPE UNEQUAL LEGS

SLAG TRAP

IDEAL SHAPE FOR
FIRST OR SINGLE PASS

AGGRAVATED SLAG TRAP

BAD UNDERCUT

LACK OF PENETRATION

TOO CONCAVE FOR SINGLE PASS
QUITE GOOD SHAPE FOR FIRST PASS

Figure 15-14 Typical faults in horizontal fillet welds (first or single pass)

TEST YOUR KNOWLEDGE

1. List the angles used for first, second, and third pass.
2. Why is it important to clean each pass?
3. What precaution must be observed when running a number of passes?

EXERCISE #5
ALTERNATE ASSEMBLY OF METAL FOR DOWNHAND FILLET WELDS

Assemblies other than the usual tee joint design may be used for practising fillet welds (Figure 15-15).

1. Obtain three pieces of metal instead of two. Four welds can now be made instead of two.
2. Assemble as shown and proceed to weld as in Exercise #4.

This assembly has the following advantages:

1. If the pieces of metal are properly set up, the assembly will support itself.
2. One piece of metal is saved on each assembly.
3. Less time is required to assemble tee joints, giving more time for practice.
4. Distortion of the metal is prevented if the welds are placed on alternate sides.

Since cost of materials and salvaging are important areas that cannot be neglected in any welding shop, it

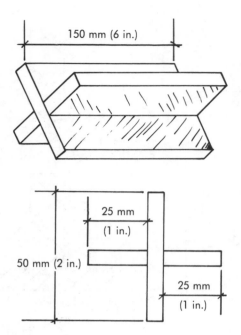

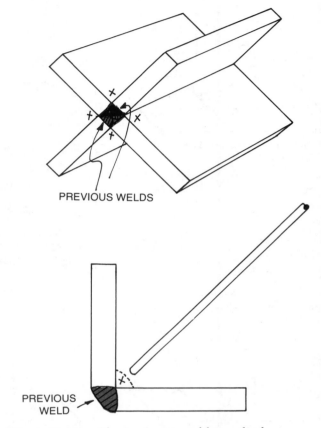

PREVIOUS WELDS

Figure 15-15 Alternative assembly for downhand fillet welds

PREVIOUS WELD

Figure 15-16 Alternative assembly methods

is possible (with a little care) to achieve an alternate assembly for fillet welds by using pieces of metal that have previously been assembled and welded in corner joint exercises (Figure 15-16). It is also possible to use an angle iron for this exercise. Usually, an iron 150 mm × 150 mm × 6 mm (or 6 in. × 6 in. × 1/4 in.) is sufficient (Figure 15-17).

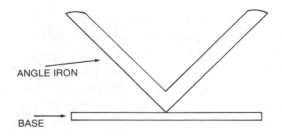

ANGLE IRON

BASE

Figure 15-17 Using an angle iron for fillet weld exercise

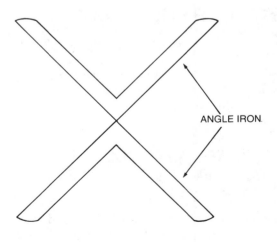

ANGLE IRON

15-2 FILLET WELD CHARACTERISTICS

There are three general types or shapes of fillet welds. Figure 15-18 shows the shape of an **ideal** fillet weld. Every fillet weld should look like this. But since the shape can be obtained only by mechanical means, such as machining and grinding, it would be very expensive to produce.

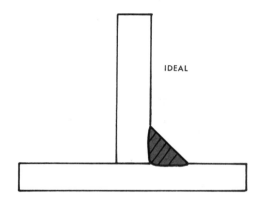

Figure 15-18   Ideal fillet weld shape

A **convex** fillet weld is shown in Figure 15-19. Most fillet welds look like this, especially when made with conventional electrodes, such as E41012 or E41013 (E6012 or E6013). The amount of buildup is usually 4 mm to 3 mm (1/8 in. to 3/16 in.). Any more than this is unnecessary and will result in wasted electrode metal, wasted time, and greater distortion.

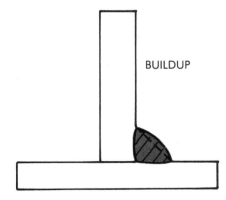

Figure 15-19   Convex fillet weld

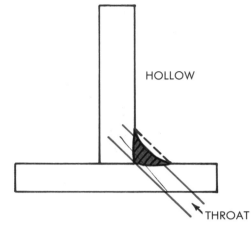

Figure 15-20   Concave fillet weld

Most fillet welds made using the newer, heavily coated iron powder electrodes look like the **concave** fillet weld in Figure 15-20. The depression or hollow should be between 1.5 mm and 3 mm (1/16 in. and 1/8 in.). Any more than this will result in a weak weld and possible cracking.

FILLET WELD GAUGES

The size of a fillet weld is determined by the **leg length**. In a properly made fillet weld, the leg lengths should be equal (Figures 15-21 and 15-22). There are different designs of fillet gauges, but they are all designed to measure the leg length and the throat (Figure 15-23).

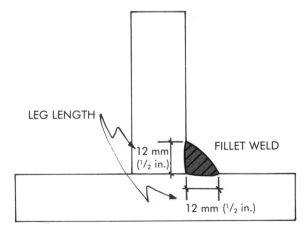

Figure 15-21   Leg length measurements

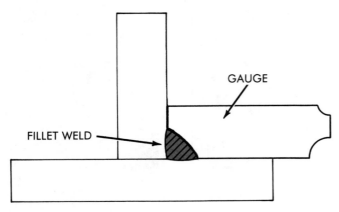

Figure 15-22   Measuring the leg length

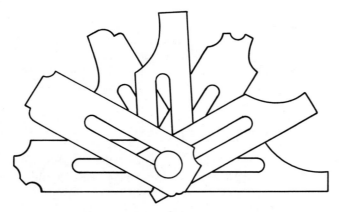

Figure 15-23   Fillet weld gauge

TEST YOUR KNOWLEDGE

1. Name the three types or shapes of fillet welds.
2. What methods are used to produce an ideal fillet weld?
3. What is the difference between a convex and a concave fillet weld?
4. What are the results of too much buildup on a convex fillet weld?
5. What would be the result of too great a hollow in a concave fillet weld?
6. How is the size of a fillet weld measured?
7. What is the purpose of a fillet-weld gauge?
8. What is meant by the leg length of a fillet weld?

15-3 THE CORNER JOINT

Arc welding a corner joint is not difficult because the natural vee formed by the plates helps to guide the electrode and hold the weld metal in place (Figure 15-24A).

EXERCISE #6
STEPS IN WELDING A CORNER JOINT

1. Obtain two pieces of metal about 50 mm × 150 mm × 6 mm (or 2 in. × 6 in. × 1/4 in.).
2. Prepare a corner joint.
3. Set the machine, lower your helmet, and tack the joint.
4. Take the position as when running a bead.
5. Point the electrode into the vee, and incline it at an angle of 20° in the direction of travel (Figure 15-24B). Remember to keep the electrode at a 90° angle to the joint.
6. Strike an arc, and proceed to run a bead along the joint.

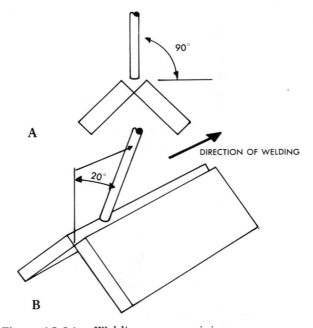

Figure 15-24   Welding a corner joint

7. Keep the arc short, and do not allow the weld metal to spill over the edges of the vee.
8. If the metal tends to spill over, increase the speed of travel.
9. Stop, chip, clean, and inspect the weld.

An alternative corner joint can be made from salvaged pieces used for running beads and weaves (Figure 15-25).

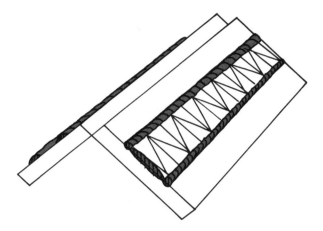

Figure 15-25   Corner joint made from salvaged pieces

TEST YOUR KNOWLEDGE

1. What makes the corner joint an easy joint to weld?
2. What angles are used to weld this joint?
3. How can the metal be prevented from spilling over?

MAKING A MULTIPLE-PASS WELD ON A CORNER JOINT

The multiple-pass weld is used to fill large vee shapes formed by corner joints that are made of very heavy plate. These joints cannot be filled with only one bead of welding. Since corner joints like these are similar to single-vee butt joints, they may be used as such for practice in welding a single-vee butt joint (Figure 15-26).

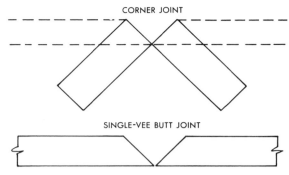

Figure 15-26   Similarity of joints

EXERCISE #7
STEPS IN MAKING A MULTIPLE-PASS CORNER JOINT

1. Prepare a corner joint.
2. Obtain a welding rod, and set the machine.
3. Lower your helmet after you have turned the machine on.
4. Run the first bead into the corner as when welding a single-pass corner weld.
5. Chip, clean, and check.
6. The remaining passes may be filled in as single beads or as weaves (Figure 15-27).

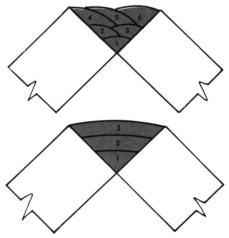

Figure 15-27   Single beads and weaves on a corner joint

7. Be sure to chip each pass before applying the next one.
8. The electrode should always be held at a 90° angle to the joint and inclined 20° in the direction of travel.

TEST YOUR KNOWLEDGE

1. What is the purpose of the multiple-pass weld?
2. Can beads or weaves be used to fill this joint?
3. At what angles should the electrode be held at all times?
4. The corner joint is similar to what other joint?

15-4 THE BUTT JOINT

The butt joint is the most difficult joint to master. It requires practice, and it is widely used in industry. The following points must be observed carefully.

Amperage. As with any other weld, an amperage that is too high will cause burn-through. An amperage that is too low will cause poor or no penetration (Figure 15-28).

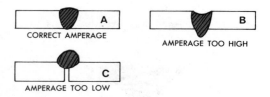

Figure 15-28   Effects of amperage on welded joints

Alignment. In any joint, proper alignment is important, but in a butt joint, it is essential. Figure 15-29 shows the correct and incorrect methods of alignment in a butt joint.

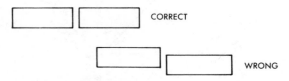

Figure 15-29   Alignment

Joint setup. To be strong, the weld must penetrate the joint completely. Too many welders neglect this important point, and a poor weld or joint results. If the gap or space is too narrow, penetration of the joint will be impossible (Figure 15-30). If however, the gap or space between the plates is too large, burn-through will cause holes and too much penetration (Figure 15-31).

Figure 15-30   Gap too small

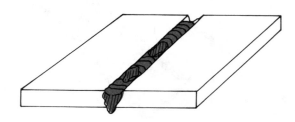

Figure 15-31   Gap too large

Up to a certain thickness of metal (approximately 6 mm or 1/4 in.), it is possible to obtain complete penetration by welding both sides of the joint (Figure 15-32). At other times, it will not be possible to obtain complete penetration without some form of edge preparation.

Figure 15-32   Joint welded both sides for complete penetration

EDGE PREPARATION

As the thickness of the metal increases, it will become impossible to obtain complete penetration unless the edges of the metal are specially prepared. The edges of

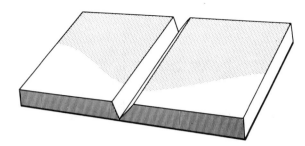

Figure 15-33   Single-vee joint

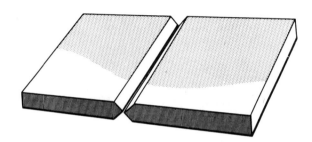

Figure 15-34   Double-vee butt joint

the metal are, therefore, transformed into shapes which will allow the weld to be made with good penetration.

1. On metal between 1.5 mm and 6 mm (or 1/16 in. and 1/4 in.) a butt may be formed without any special preparation of the edges, and good penetration will be possible.
2. On metal that is 6 mm and 19 mm (or 1/4 in. and 3/4 in.) thick, a single vee is formed (Figure 15-33).
3. On metals that are over 19 mm (or 3/4 in.) thick, a double-vee edge preparation is best (Figure 15-34).

TEST YOUR KNOWLEDGE

1. Why is special edge preparation necessary on some metal thicknesses?
2. Is it possible to obtain complete penetration on 19 mm (or 3/4 in.) thick metal without edge preparation?
3. Which type of edge preparation should you use on 12 mm (or 1/2 in.) thick metal to obtain good penetration?

WELDING A BUTT JOINT

Welding a butt joint is similar to running a bead. The only difference is that two pieces of metal are being joined by the weld and, therefore, more care must be taken.

EXERCISE #8
STEPS IN WELDING A BUTT JOINT

1. Obtain two pieces of metal about 50 mm × 150 mm × 6 mm (or 2 in. × 6 in. × 1/4 in.).
2. Assemble and tack weld the butt joint as shown in Figure 15-35A.
3. Strike the arc, and weld along the line of the joint where the edges of the metal are tack welded.
4. Proceed to weld as in running a bead. See Figure 15-35A and B for correct electrode angles.
5. Make certain that the weld metal or pool spreads so that it covers both pieces of metal.
6. After completing the weld, stop, chip, clean, and check. The centre of the weld should be in line

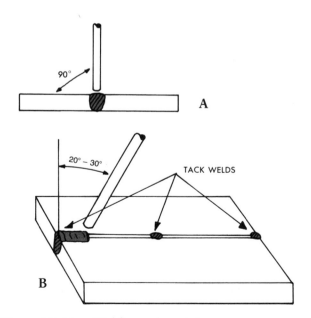

Figure 15-35   Welding a butt joint

with the centre of the joint. The weld metal should be spread evenly on both sides of the joint. The appearance of the weld should be the same as a single bead (smooth, even ripples, etc.) with complete penetration. (Figure 15-36 shows a gauge being used to check buildup.)

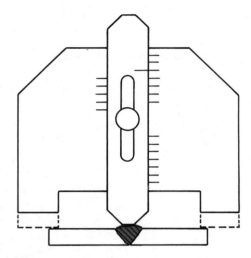

Figure 15-36   Checking buildup on a butt joint

TEST YOUR KNOWLEDGE

1. Why is it important to learn to weld a butt joint?
2. Why is correct amperage important?
3. Why is the correct alignment important?
4. Is it necessary to have complete penetration?
5. What happens if the space between the two pieces of metal is too narrow?
6. What happens if the space is too large?
7. When is it impossible to obtain complete penetration without preparing the edges?
8. What are the three important points that should be remembered when assembling a butt joint?

DEFECTS

TABLE 15-1 COMMON DEFECTS IN SMAW JOINTS — AND THEIR REMEDIES

Poor Fusion	Remedy
Not enough heat	Increase amperage
Welding too quickly	Decrease speed

Porosity	Remedy
Dirty metal	Clean the metal before starting
Arc too short	Hold longer arc
Wrong electrode	Check electrode

Lack of Penetration	Remedy
Wrong edge preparation	Check edge preparation
Not enough heat	Increase amperage
Welding too quickly	Decrease speed
Wrong angle of electrode	Change angle of electrode
Wrong size of electrode	Check and correct size of electrode

Undercut	Remedy
Wrong electrode angle	Correct angle of electrode
Current too high	Decrease amperage

POINTS TO REMEMBER

- A fillet weld can be applied to a tee joint and a lap joint.
- The angle of the electrode is always important when welding.
- The size of a fillet weld is determined by the leg length.
- A corner joint may be used instead of a single-vee butt joint, for practice.

- Alignment and gap are most important when assembling a butt joint for welding.

WORDS TO REMEMBER

fillet	convex	penetration
horizontal	concave	burn-through
downhand	alignment	leg length
		undercut

REVIEW QUESTIONS

1. Name the two kinds of fillet welds.
2. How many passes may be run on a fillet weld?
3. Why must all beads be chipped and cleaned?
4. At what angles are the electrodes held when making a horizontal fillet weld?
5. How can excessive buildup or undercut be corrected in a horizontal weld?
6. What exercise is similar to making a horizontal fillet weld?
7. The three-pass horizontal fillet weld applies to which of the following?
   a. a tee joint
   b. a lap joint
   c. both joints
8. Describe the procedure to be used when running a three-pass horizontal fillet weld.
9. What are the advantages of using the assembly shown in Figure 15-16?
10. What are the main differences between the types of fillet welds?
11. What method is used to determine the size of a fillet weld?
12. How is the leg length of a fillet weld determined?
13. What would be the result of underwelding a concave fillet weld?
14. Why is welding a corner joint not difficult?
15. When welding a corner joint, what steps should be taken to prevent the metal from spilling over?
16. Why is it faster to weld in the downhand position?
17. Why are multipass welds used?
18. Describe, using drawings and labels, the three types or shapes of fillet welds.
19. Why is double-vee preparation used in preference to single-vee, on metals over a certain thickness?
20. Why is arc welding best suited for heavy metals?

16

GAS TUNGSTEN ARC WELDING (GTAW)

As early as 1900, a patent was granted on the idea of an electrode surrounded by an inert gas. Experiments with this type of welding carried on through the 1920s and 1930s. However, it was not until the 1940s that the GTAW process was given full attention. Until the beginning of World War II, these experiments were limited because inert gases were so expensive. However, during the war, the aircraft industry urgently needed a faster and easier method of welding aluminum and magnesium to speed up production.

Because of the benefits derived in production, the extra expense of using inert gas on a large scale was justifiable. Although gas production has been streamlined now, inert gas still represents an extra, but justifiable, expense.

16-1 THE GTAW PROCESS

GTAW is a fusion process that generates heat by establishing an arc between a nonconsumable tungsten elec-

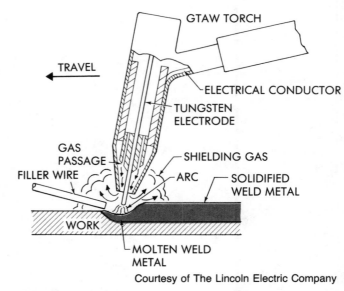

Courtesy of The Lincoln Electric Company

Figure 16-1   Gas tungsten arc welding

trode and the base metal. In this process, the electrode is not melted and used as a filler metal. Instead, a welding rod is fed into the weld area as in oxyfuel welding and in brazing.

Any welder with a background in oxyfuel welding and brazing will quickly adapt to the GTAW process because the techniques used are similar. The equipment, however, is the same type as the equipment used in arc welding. In GTAW, an inert gas shields the weld. The advantage of this process is that fluxes do not need to be used. Also, because there is no slag there is virtually no cleaning of weld areas.

After World War II, with nonferrous metals more in demand, many GTAW processes were developed under different names such as TIG (tungsten inert gas), heliarc, and argon arc. With GTAW, manufacturers did find one disadvantage. Metals over 6 mm (1/4 in.) had to be preheated before welding could be carried out. This led to the development of another process, GMAW (gas metal arc welding), which will be discussed in Chapter 17.

16-2 BASIC EQUIPMENT FOR GTAW

This is the basic equipment for GTAW:
1. An arc welding machine complete with cables.
2. A supply of inert gas complete with hose, regulators, etc.
3. A supply of water (for some types of torches).
4. A torch to which all of the above are connected and which also acts as a holder and handle. A switch for controlling all of the above may be incorporated in the torch handle.

Figures 16-2 and 16-3 show the basic GTAW equipment.

THE WELDING MACHINE

In SMAW, the type of current or polarity to be used depends on the electrode coating. In GTAW the **metal** being welded determines the current or polarity. AC, DCSP, or DCRP can be used. The welding machines used in the GTAW process have some unique features (although they may be used for other arc welding pro-

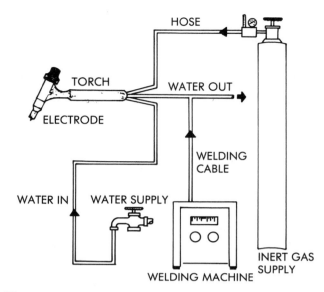

Figure 16-2   Basic GTAW equipment

cesses such as SMAW). For GTAW, they are equipped with:
1. a high-frequency (HF) unit which causes a spark to jump from the electrode to the base metal. Using this unit, the arc may be started without touching the electrode to the base metal.
2. a control system for operating the gas and water valves incorporated into the machine.
3. remote controls operated by a foot lever or a hand switch. (Only some machines have this feature.)
4. a contact switch which will close the gas and water valves at a certain time after the weld has been completed. (This is also an optional feature.)

In a direct welding current, although 70% of the heat is at the positive terminal and 30% at the negative terminal, the results shown in Figure 16-4 were observed. Using the same amperage (125 A) for both DCRP and DCSP, the electrons flowed to the base metal, concentrating 70% of the heat there. In DCRP, 70% of the heat is concentrated at the electrode. This means that a smaller electrode can be used on DCSP for the same amperage. This produced deeper penetration and a more stable arc for welding (Figure 16-5). But DCSP did not have the ability to penetrate the oxide film that forms on metals such as aluminum. Alternating current (AC) has the ability to penetrate the oxide film, but

A. Left view

Figure 16-3　The internal design of a GTAW machine

Courtesy of Hobart Brothers Company

B. Right view

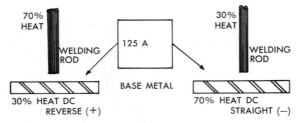

Figure 16-4　Influence of polarity on electrode size

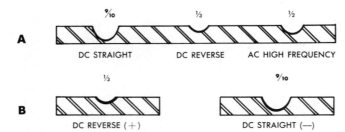

Figure 16-5　Penetration

because the arc extinguishes every half cycle (between the positive and negative halves of the current's cycle), it was considered unsuitable. However, this problem was overcome by superimposing a high-frequency current across the arc. This superimposed current was called alternating current high frequency (ACHF). It maintained the arc during the zero point in the AC cycle and provided a path for the alternating current to follow.

The ACHF is used when welding metals that have an oxide film on the surface. DC straight polarity is used for metals that do not require cleaning of the oxide film (steel, copper, and stainless steel, for example). The HF unit also prevents contamination of the tungsten electrode because the spark jumping across the arc allows the welding arc to be struck without the electrode touching the base metal.

Table 16-1 shows different metals and the power sources that should be used when welding them using GTAW.

TABLE 16-1 METALS AND POWER SOURCES FOR GTAW

Metal	Power Source	
Aluminum	ACHF	(DCRP)
Brass/alloys	DCSP	(ACHF)
Copper/alloys	DCSP	
Low carbon steel	DCSP	(ACHF)
Stainless steel	DCSP	(ACHF)

The current shown in brackets is an alternative choice for that metal.

16-3 SHIELDING GASES

The two most frequently used gases for GTAW are **argon** and **helium**, which are inert gases. Inert simply means that the gas will not react or combine with other elements. The main purpose of the gas is to shield the weld and the welding electrode from contamination by the atmosphere. Argon is recommended for manual GTAW because it will produce the same effects as 2.5 times as much helium. However, helium is preferred for automatic and semi-automatic GTAW because it produces a hotter arc and deeper penetration.

Some manufacturers have been experimenting with a mixture of argon and helium with excellent results. In welding aluminum and its alloys, a mixture of argon and helium will produce higher welding speeds and deeper penetration than argon gas alone. The better features of argon such as easier arc starting, good cleaning action, and lower gas consumption are still retained. Recently, additions of hydrogen and nitrogen to argon and helium have proved successful in the welding of stainless steels. Adding these gases has prevented bead discoloration of the metal. Argon, a much denser gas than helium, provides a better shield when welding in the downhand position. Helium will supply better shielding for out of position welding (particularly in the overhead position) because it is not as dense a gas. Although helium will provide a hotter arc and deeper penetration, this can result in distortion of the base metal if thin metal sections are used. Therefore, in industries, argon gas is used on thin metal sections. There are always exceptions to the rule, but in general the recommended gases for GTAW are as noted in Table 16-2.

TABLE 16-2 METALS AND GASES FOR GTAW

Metal	Gas
Aluminum	Argon
Brass/alloys	Helium or Argon
Copper/alloys under 3 mm (1/8 in.)	Argon
Copper/alloys over 3 mm (1/8 in.)	Helium
Low carbon steel	Argon
Stainless steel	Argon

TEST YOUR KNOWLEDGE

1. What does inert mean? What is the purpose of the inert gas shield?
2. Name the four basic pieces of equipment used in GTAW.
3. What type of welding machines are used for GTAW?
4. What is the purpose of the HF unit?
5. How is the polarity determined in the GTAW process?

16-4 REGULATORS, FLOWMETERS, TORCHES, AND COOLING SYSTEMS

Regulators and Flowmeters

The accurate control of the flow of gas is most important in GTAW. The combination argon-helium regulators are calibrated in litres per hour. Where it is desirable to check the gas flow during welding, a flowmeter is used with a regulator. A flowmeter consists of a glass tube marked in litres per hour and a small ball inside the glass tube (see Figure 16-6). When the gas pressure is adjusted at the regulator, a stream of gas passes through the

FLOWMETER

Courtesy of Union Carbide Canada Limited

Figure 16-6   Flowmeter

flowmeter and lifts the ball to the exact pressure being delivered to the torch.

The metering/regulator is similar to the type used for oxy-acetylene welding. One gauge registers cylinder pressure. The other registers the flow of gas at a constant rate in litres per hour. A calibrated dial and a needle are used, rather than the ball arrangement in the flowmeter (Figure 16-7).

Courtesy of Union Carbide Canada Limited

Figure 16-7   Metering/regulator

THE GTAW TORCH

Since GTAW is basically an arc welding process, it is not surprising that the first GTAW torch was an ordinary electrode holder with a tungsten electrode and a copper tube which supplied the inert gas. The GTAW torch now consists of a handle and a collet assembly for the electrode and a nozzle (Figure 16-8).

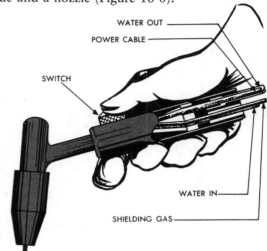

WATER OUT
POWER CABLE
SWITCH
WATER IN
SHIELDING GAS

Figure 16-8   The gas tungsten arc torch

Collets

The collet is available in diameters to suit the electrode diameter. Its main purpose is to locate and secure the electrode and to provide a passage for the welding current. The collet cap protects the electrode from damage or contamination and is made in sizes to suit the length of the electrode (Figure 16-9).

Nozzles

The nozzles for GTAW are of two general types: ceramic and metal. The ceramic nozzles are used with air-cooled torches and the metal nozzles with water-cooled torches. The main purpose of the nozzle is to protect the electrode and direct the shielding gas (Figure 16-10).

COOLING SYSTEMS

Two types of cooling systems are used with GTAW torches:

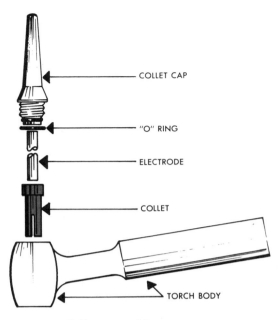

Figure 16-9   Collet assembly

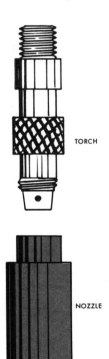

Figure 16-10   Nozzle

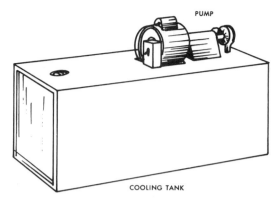

Figure 16-11   Cooling system

1. When using amperages below 150 A, air-cooled torches are used. They depend on the surrounding air in the atmosphere for cooling.
2. When amperages in excess of 150 A are being used in GTAW, the torch is water-cooled. Where a water-cooled torch is used, the water lines may be hooked up to a water tap and the return fed into a floor drain. If this is not possible, a cooling tank may be used, in which the water is recirculated (Figure 16-11).

16-5 ELECTRODES FOR GTAW

Tungsten electrodes now have a classification like other electrodes. The AWS and CSA use the codes shown in Table 16-3.

When electrodes come from the manufacturer, they have blunt ends, as shown in Figure 16-12. Before being used, however, the ends have to be prepared by being ground to a point or melted to form a ball, depending on the type of welding current being used (see Figure 16-13). For AC, a ball-shaped end should be used. For DCSP, the end should be ground to a point, and for DCRP, a ball-shaped end should be used, but with a smaller ball end than the one used for AC. To achieve this, the electrode should be ground to a point first, and then melted to form a ball.

TABLE 16-3 TUNGSTEN ELECTRODE CLASSIFICATIONS

AWS code	Tip colour	Designation
EWP	Green	Pure tungsten
EWth-1	Yellow	Tungsten + 1% thorium
EWth-2	Red	Tungsten + 2% thorium
EWzr	Brown	Tungsten + Zirconium

E means electrode
W means tungsten
th means thorium
zr means zirconium

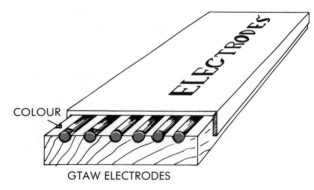

Figure 16-12   Electrodes as manufactured

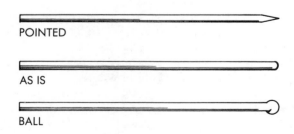

Electrode ends

Care must be taken in grinding electrodes. An electrode that is not properly ground can cause improper gas shielding and contamination of the weld. These electrodes are also brittle and expensive. Therefore, when snapping off the end to regrind, care must be taken to remove only the contaminated portion.

TEST YOUR KNOWLEDGE

1. What is the purpose of the collet?
2. When is a cooling system used?
3. What colour is used to identify a pure tungsten electrode?
4. What is the purpose of the nozzle?
5. What do the letters EWP mean?

16-6 GTAW PRACTICE

Although GTAW is an arc welding process, in some ways it resembles the oxyfuel process. For example, a filler may be used at times to supply additional weld metal. Before starting to weld, remember these few basic points:

1. Always check that the gas (and water if it is being used) are turned on and set correctly.
2. If the torch is equipped with a starting switch on the handle, make sure that it is kept depressed during the entire welding operation.
3. If ACHF is being used, it is not necessary to touch the metal with the electrode when starting the arc.
4. Check the polarity before starting. DCRP is much hotter than DCSP at the same amperage.
5. Check the electrode extension (the length it sticks out from the nozzle). The electrode should extend approximately 3 mm (1/8 in.) beyond the nozzle for beads. The extension will vary from 3 mm (1/8 in.) to 6 mm (1/4 in.) for the welding of different joints.
6. If using an HF unit, set for the type of current being used. For example, when AC is being used, the unit would be set for continuous use. When DC is being used, however, the unit would be set for start only and then cut out as soon as the welding arc was established.

EXERCISE #1
STRIKING THE ARC

1. Position the hands as shown in Figure 16-14. Then move the torch downwards with a slight swinging motion.
2. With AC the arc will commence when the electrode is approximately 3 mm (1/8 in.) above the base metal.

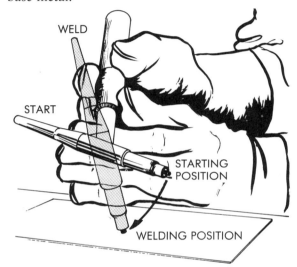

Figure 16-14 Starting technique

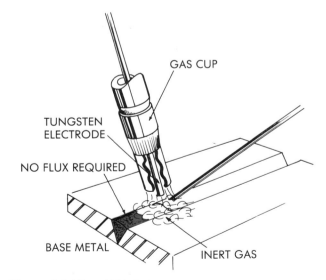

Figure 16-15 GTAW in progress

3. With DC (*unless* an HF unit is used), it is necessary first to touch the electrode to the base metal or to a starting block made of copper or carbon. This prevents contamination of the tungsten electrode. Then the arc length will be increased to 3 mm (1/8 in.) by withdrawing the electrode after it has been struck.
4. When the arc has been struck, the torch should be rotated in a small circular motion to establish a puddle.

Figure 16-15 shows the GTAW process.

> Observe all arc welding safety precautions.
> Before doing the following exercises, practise striking the arc and study Table 16-4 carefully. Practice and observation at this point will eliminate many problems that can occur when welding actually begins.

ADVANTAGES OF GTAW

- With GTAW, the molten weld metal has maximum protection from atmospheric contamination.
- Since no flux is being used, there is no danger of slag inclusions in the weld. Also, there will be no need to remove flux residue.
- Properly executed GTAW makes very smooth welds, which makes this process suitable for food or medical containers where entrapped decaying organic material could have serious consequences.
- Because there is no weld splatter, cleaning time is reduced considerably.
- GTAW can be used at higher speeds with less distortion than oxyfuel welding.

GTAW PROBLEMS

Two of the common problems that beginners will encounter with GTAW are porosity and cracking in the deposited weld metal. Study the list of possible causes of and remedies for these two problems, as outlined in Table 16-5.

TABLE 16-4 CHARACTERISTICS OF GTAW ARCS

Arc Characteristic	Power Sources for GTAW		
	ACHF	DCSP	DCRP
Arc starting and operation	With high frequency, arc starts without touching work. Strike on starting block; when electrode is thoroughly heated, re-ignite arc in the joint. This reduces tungsten inclusions at start of weld. Hold at starting point until weld pool is established. Add filler at leading edge of pool, but to one side of centreline.	Hot arc forms puddle immediately. Strike arc on work within weld width to avoid marking work. Runout tabs or striking plates are often desirable. Use of high frequency to strike arc is recommended.	Same as AC, but touch electrode to work.
Stability	Smooth arcing; no snapping or cracking sounds (argon).	Stable in helium.	Stable (argon).
Instability: electrode contamination	Oxides resulting from contact of hot electrode with air or from contact with oxides or metal in weld pool cause arc instability. Dress or cut off tip or replace electrode.	Same as AC.	Same as AC.
Electrode too large	May result in unstable arc and excessive bead width. Use smallest electrode that will carry current.	Same as AC.	Same as AC.
Excessive arc length	Unstable arc results; shorten arc length.	Same as AC.	Same as AC.
Narrow joints	May cause arc to jump from side to side. Widen groove where possible or bring electrode closer to work.	—	—
Length	Maintain short arc (about equal to electrode diameter; approximately 3 mm or $1/8$ in.). If arc is too long, root penetration will not be complete, particularly in fillet welding; possible undercutting,	Short, about 1.5 mm.	Long, 5 mm to 6 mm ($3/16$ in. to $1/4$ in.).

TABLE 16-4 (cont'd)

Arc Characteristic	Power Sources for GTAW		
	ACHF	**DCSP**	**DCRP**
	excessive bead width, and poor weld contour may also result.		
Breaking the arc	Gradually reduce arc length or current to minimize weld craters. Continue adding filler at the same time where applicable. Snap torch to horizontal position to break arc.	Same as AC.	Same as AC.

Courtesy of The Lincoln Electric Company

TABLE 16-5 CAUSES OF AND REMEDIES FOR POROSITY AND CRACKING IN GTAW WELDS

Cause	Contributing Factors	Corrective Measures
Hydrogen	Dirt containing oils or other hydrocarbons; moisture in atmosphere or on metal, or a hydrated oxide film on metal; moisture in gas or gas lines. Base metal may be source of entrapped hydrogen (the thicker the metal, the greater the possibility of entrapped hydrogen). Spatter.	Degrease and mechanically or chemically remove oxide from weld area. Avoid humidity; use dry metal or wipe dry. Reduce moisture content of gas. Check gas and water lines for leaks. Increase gas flow to compensate for increased hydrogen in thicker sections. To minimize spatter, adjust welding conditions.
Impurities	Cleaning or other compounds, especially those containing calcium.	Use recommended cleaning compounds; keep work free of contaminants.
Incomplete root penetration	Incomplete penetration in heavy sections increases porosity in the weld.	Preheat; use higher welding current, or redesign joint geometry.
Temperature	Running too cool tends to increase porosity due to premature solidification of molten metal.	Maintain proper current, arc length and torch travel speed relationship.
Welding speed	Too great a welding speed may increase porosity.	Decrease welding speed and establish and maintain proper arc length and current relationship.

TABLE 16-5 (cont'd)

Cause	Contributing Factors	Corrective Measures
Solidification time	Quick freezing of weld pool entraps any gases present, causing porosity.	Establish correct welding current and speed. If work is appreciably below room temperature, use supplemental heating.
Chemical composition of weld metal	Pure aluminum weld metal is more susceptible to porosity than is an aluminum alloy.	If porosity is excessive, try an alloy filler material.
Cracking	Such causes of porosity as temperature, welding time, and solidification may also be contributing causes of cracking. Other causes may be discontinuous welds, welds that intersect, repair welds, cold-working either before or after welding, and weld-metal composition. In general, crack-sensitive alloys include those containing 0.4% to 0.6% Si, or 1.5% to 3.0% Mg, or 1.0% Cu.	Lower current and faster speeds often prevent cracking. However, a change to a filler alloy that brings weld-metal composition out of cracking range is recommended where possible.

Courtesy of The Lincoln Electric Company

Careful observation of GTAW procedures during all practice welds will eliminate many problems and produce good, clean, sound welds.

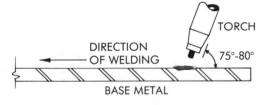

Figure 16-16   Running a bead without a welding rod

EXERCISE #2
RUNNING A BEAD WITHOUT A WELDING ROD (GTAW)

1. Strike the arc, and obtain a molten puddle.
2. When the puddle becomes bright and fluid, move the torch along the base metal at a slow and steady speed.
3. Hold the torch at approximately 75° to 80° as shown in Figures 16-16 and 16-17.
4. This is similar to running a bead in oxy-acetylene welding, and the same type of flaws will appear. That is, travelling slowly will cause a hole, etc.

EXERCISE #3
RUNNING A BEAD WITH A WELDING ROD (GTAW)

1. Strike the arc, and obtain a molten puddle.
2. When the puddle is established, move the torch to the rear of the puddle, and add the welding rod.
3. Remove the welding rod a short distance (6 mm or 1/4 in.) and bring the torch over to the front of the puddle. Reheat the metal and when it again becomes bright and fluid, add more welding rod.

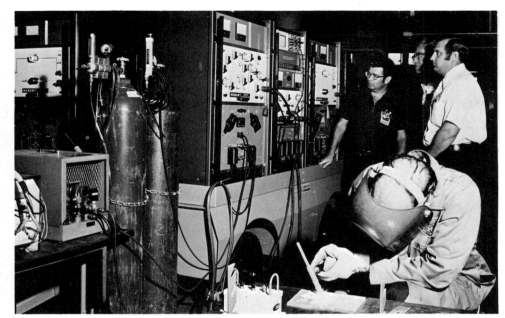

Courtesy of Hobart Brothers Company

Figure 16-17
Correct position for
application of the Hobart
Cyber-tig: welding without
a rod in GTAW

4. The angle of the rod should be approximately 15°
   from the base metal, and the angle of the torch
   should be approximately 75° to 80° at all times
   (Figure 16-18).
5. Repeat these movements along the entire length of
   the metal. As in oxy-acetylene welding, the height
   and width of the bead will depend on the speed
   and amount of welding rod that is added.

   Once exercises #2 and #3 (running a bead with

and without a welding rod) have been mastered, the
basic joints should be assembled and practised.

TEST YOUR KNOWLEDGE

1. What is a copper starting block used for?
2. What is the proper arc length in GTAW?
3. After the arc has been struck, what is the purpose
   of moving the torch in a circular motion?
4. What will determine the height and width of the
   bead in GTAW?

EXERCISE #4
WELDING A BUTT JOINT WITH
THE GTAW PROCESS

1. Obtain two pieces of 1100 series aluminum
   150 mm × 75 mm × 5 mm (6 in. × 3 in. ×
   3/16 in.) thick.
2. Obtain welding rod, 1100 or 4043 series, 2.4 mm
   (3/32 in.).
3. Set AC transformer at 55 A.
4. Set HF unit on continuous.

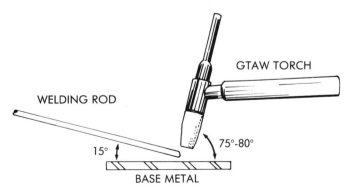

Figure 16-18   Running a bead with a welding rod

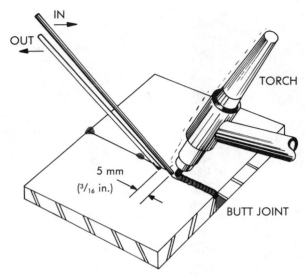

Figure 16-19 Welding a butt joint

5. Set gas flow argon at 10 cfh (283 L/h). Use a 9.5 mm (3/8 in.) nozzle.
6. Set metal up in a butt joint with no gap. Remember to support the metal.
7. Turn on the power and gas, and strike an arc.
8. Tack weld each end and centre.
9. Establish puddle at right end of joint (if you are right-handed).
10. Proceed to weld along the joint as in running bead with a rod in oxyfuel welding (Figure 16-19). Make sure that complete penetration is taking place.
11. When finished, shut off the power and gas and clean the weld.

The same process can be carried out on other joints. Figure 16-20 shows the correct torch and rod angles for these joints.

A. shows the angles of the rod and torch for a lap joint.
B. shows the shape of the weld in a lap joint.
C. shows the angle of the torch when welding a corner joint.
D. shows the angles of the rod and torch for a tee joint.
E. shows the torch angle for welding butt joints.
F. reviews the angles used for running a bead.

POINTS TO REMEMBER

- GTAW is in some ways similar to oxyfuel welding.
- The inert gas acts as a shield for the molten metal.
- The GTAW machine can also be used for SMAW.
- A high-frequency unit should be used with AC for best results.
- An HF unit is used with DC for starting only.
- Inert gases are expensive and should not be wasted.
- Make sure that the gas (and water if it is being used) are turned on and set properly before starting to weld.
- If AC is used, it is not necessary to touch the base metal to start the arc.
- If DC is used, it is necessary to touch the base metal or starting block to start the arc.
- The correct angle of torch must be maintained for proper gas shielding.

WORDS TO REMEMBER

tungsten	calibrated	thorium
frequency	collet	characteristics
inert	ceramic	superimpose
flowmeter	zirconium	extension
		contamination

REVIEW QUESTIONS

1. What do the letters GTAW stand for?
2. For which industry was this process originally developed?
3. What did the first GTAW torch look like?
4. What is the purpose of the HF unit?
5. Give one example each of the AWS and CSA codes for electrodes.
6. What is the purpose of the collet cap?
7. What is the purpose of a flowmeter?
8. Why is AC used for welding aluminum?

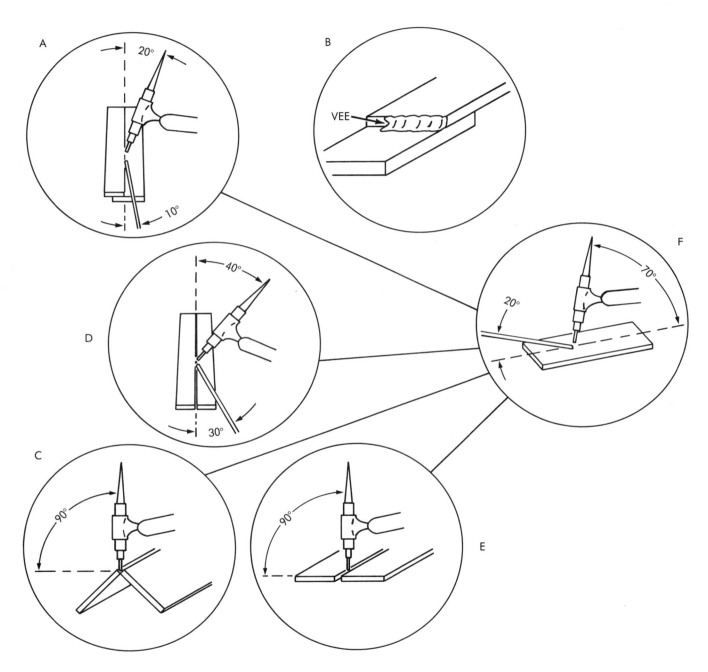

Figure 16-20   Using the correct angle

9. Why is argon recommended for GTAW?

10. Why is DCRP not recommended for GTAW?

11. Why is it necessary to remove the oxide film that appears on the surface of some metals?

12. Why is the GTAW process considered suitable for welding food and medical containers?

13. Name two advantages of GTAW.

14. What are two common problems for beginning welders in GTAW?

15. Why must care be taken when grinding electrodes?

16. When using AC, what shape should the end of the electrode be?

17. Which gas is recommended for the following metals: aluminum, low carbon steel, and stainless steel?

18. When welding stainless steel, what advantage does the addition of hydrogen and/or nitrogen have on the weld bead?

19. Describe the advantages and disadvantages of argon and helium as shielding gases.

20. Which type of current is recommended for welding aluminum, copper, and brass?

21. What factor decides the type of current to be used in GTAW?

22. Name the four basic pieces of equipment required for GTAW.

17

GAS METAL ARC WELDING (GMAW)

In the 1940s a patent was taken out for a process which involved feeding a wire electrode continuously through a gas-shielded arc. This was the beginning of the MIG process (metallic inert gas welding) which is now officially listed by the AWS and CSA as gas metal arc welding (GMAW). This type of arc welding has been refined and streamlined since the early days and many related processes have been developed. Some processes use a bare wire electrode shielded with an inert gas. Others use a flux-coated electrode similar to the ordinary arc welding electrode. Still others use a hollow electrode which has a flux inside the electrode. Some processes use a combination of fluxed electrode and shielding gas.

Different methods of transferring the molten metal across the arc are also used. The process may be manual, semi-automatic, or automatic. GMAW is now one of the **major processes** used in the welding industry Figures 17-1 and 17-2 show GMAW in progress.

17-1 BASIC EQUIPMENT FOR GMAW

This is the basic equipment for GMAW:
1. an arc welding machine complete with cables,
2. a supply of inert (shielding) gas complete with hose, regulators, etc.,
3. wire feed mechanism,
4. electrode (reel or spool),
5. welding gun complete with hose and cables (determined by the type of process to be used).

Figure 17-3 shows this basic equipment.

Courtesy of The Lincoln Electric Company

Figure 17-1 Operator using the GMAW process

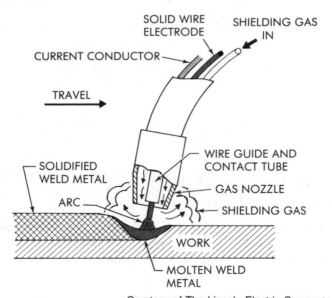

SOLID WIRE ELECTRODE

SHIELDING GAS IN

CURRENT CONDUCTOR

TRAVEL

SOLIDIFIED WELD METAL

ARC

WIRE GUIDE AND CONTACT TUBE

GAS NOZZLE

SHIELDING GAS

WORK

MOLTEN WELD METAL

Courtesy of The Lincoln Electric Company

Figure 17-2 Principle of the gas metal arc welding process (GMAW)

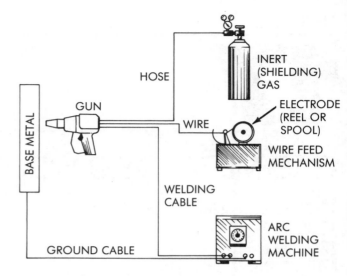

HOSE

INERT (SHIELDING) GAS

GUN

BASE METAL

WIRE

ELECTRODE (REEL OR SPOOL)

WIRE FEED MECHANISM

WELDING CABLE

ARC WELDING MACHINE

GROUND CABLE

Figure 17-3 Basic GMAW equipment

THE WELDING MACHINE

A specially designed welding machine is necessary for GMAW. Instead of the usual 60% duty cycle associated with regular welding machines, the GMAW machine requires a 100% duty cycle. A DC rectifier or generator is used and it is operated on direct current reverse polarity (DCRP). These machines are also constant voltage machines (Figure 17-4), which means that the voltage will change very little, even with a great change in the amperage. In using the GMAW process with a constant voltage machine, the amperage is controlled by the rate of wire feed speed. The greater the wire feed speed, the higher the amperage will be. This makes the arc self-adjusting.

THE WIRE FEED MECHANISM

The wire feed mechanism is made up of a system of rollers and gears run by a motor. If the dial on the wire feeder is turned to increase the amount of welding wire being fed into the weld area, it automatically increases the amperage. This increased current is used to melt the extra welding wire. The simplified wire feed unit in Figure 17-5 shows how the wire is fed through the mechanism. Today's units are more sophisticated than this. They control not only the amperage, but also the gas

Courtesy of Hobart Brothers Company

Figure 17-4 Constant voltage rectifier

and water flow (among other functions). There are three methods of moving the welding wire: "push", "pull", and a combination "push/pull". The push method is used with hard wires such as steel. The pull method is used with softer wires such as aluminum. The push/pull combination is used sometimes on construction sites where it is not possible to take the whole unit to work and where long cables are required. The drive rolls that actually feed the wire must be changed to suit the type and size of wire being used.

WELDING GUNS

The GMAW gun is used in conjunction with the wire feed unit. In the case of the push method, the gun would simply receive the wire being pushed from the wire feed unit. The pull gun contains drive units in the handle of the gun which are used to pull the wire to the gun. Figure 17-6 shows a special type of gun which is light and portable. The wire feed is contained in the handle of the gun. This makes the wire feed unit an integral part of the welding gun. Besides receiving the wire, the gun must also provide the gas shield, the power, and the cooling

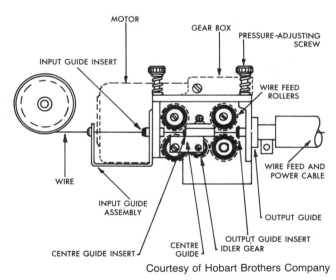

Courtesy of Hobart Brothers Company

Figure 17-5 A simplified wire feed mechanism for GMAW

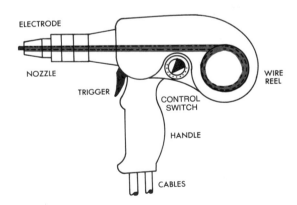

Figure 17-6 Light, portable GMAW gun

water (if necessary). It also needs a switch which will activate all the controls. Figures 17-7 to 17-9 show various types of guns used in GMAW. Figure 17-9 also shows wire feeders and cables.

Basic Equipment for GMAW   **197**

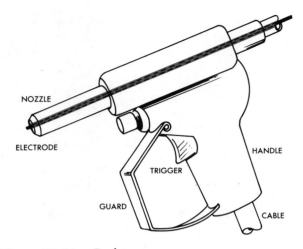

Figure 17-7A   Push gun

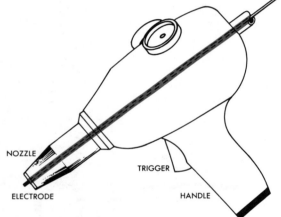

Figure 17-7B   Pull gun

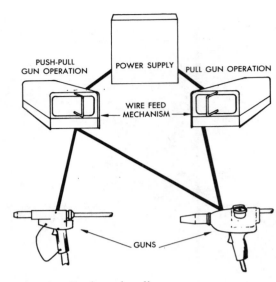

Figure 17-8   Push and pull guns

WELDING WIRE

As with ordinary arc welding electrodes in SMAW, the wire used in GMAW is designed to match the type of base metal being welded. Depending on the process being used, the wire may be solid, bare, fluxed, or flux-cored (hollow wire with a flux inside). Welding wires are identified under the CSA W48-4 M1980 and the AWS A5-18 specifications.

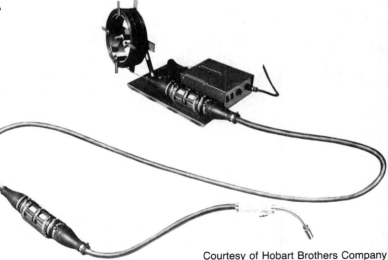

Courtesy of Hobart Brothers Company

Figure 17-9
Wire feeder, cable, and gun for GMAW
A. Wire feeder and cable

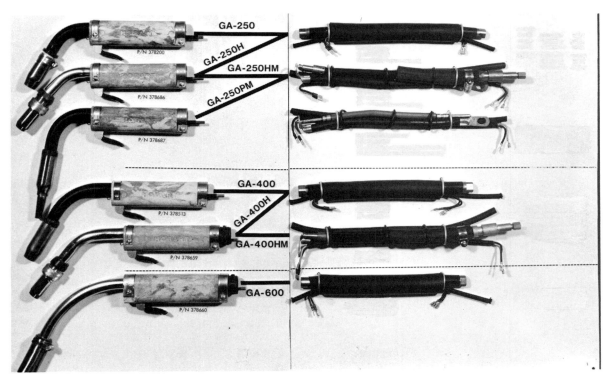

B. Guns and Cable assemblies

Figure 17-9 (cont'd)

Courtesy of Hobart Brothers Company

The CSA/AWS Specifications for GMAW Wires	
ER	stands for GMAW electrode
* 480	multiplied by 100 means 480 000 MPa tensile strength
S	stands for solid wire
** 3	designates the chemical composition of the wire and the mechanical properties of the deposited metal

* The AWS code for this electrode would be ER70S3 which differs from the CSA code only in that the number "70" stands for 70 000 psi (equivalent to 480 000 MPa).

** The last number "3" stands for the chemical composition as follows:
0.07-12 C   1.0-1.3 Mn   0.50-0.70 Si   0.017 S   0.010 P
The balance would be made of iron (Fe).

In the preceding example, whether the electrode is coded according to CSA or AWS, its characteristics remain the same. It is a solid wire, which will produce a high-strength weld. This particular example is widely used for welding carbon and high-strength low alloy steels. For flux-cored welding wires, the letter "T" would be substituted for the letter "S" in the last example. If you associate the letter "T" with "tube" you will remember that this wire is hollow.

SHIELDING GASES

As in other kinds of arc welding, the main purpose of the shielding gases is to prevent contamination of the weld metal. Shielding gases also influence the welding arc and affect the depth of penetration and the amount of welding spatter produced. The three main gases used in GMAW are argon, helium, and carbon dioxide (or a

Basic Equipment for GMAW   **199**

TABLE 17-1 SHIELDING GASES AND GAS MIXTURES FOR GMAW

Shielding Gas	Chemical Behaviour	Uses, Remarks
Argon	Inert	For welding most metals, except steel
Helium	Inert	Al and Cu alloys, for greater heat and to minimize porosity
A and He (20%-80% to 50%-50%)	Inert	Al and Cu alloys, for greater heat input and to minimize porosity. Quieter, more stable arc than with He alone
A and Cl (trace Cl)	Essentially Inert	Al alloys, to minimize porosity
N_2	Reducing	On Cu, permits very powerful arc; used mostly in Europe
A + 25%-30% N_2	Reducing	On Cu, powerful but smoother operating, more readily controlled arc than N_2 alone; used mostly in Europe
A + 1%-2% O_2	Oxidizing	Stainless and alloy steels, also for some deoxidized copper alloys
A + 3%-5% O_2	Oxidizing	Plain carbon, alloy, and stainless steels; requires deoxidized electrode
A + 20%-30% CO_2	Oxidizing	Various steels; used principally with short-circuiting arc
A + 5% O_2 + 15% CO_2	Oxidizing	Various steels; requires deoxidized wire; used chiefly in Europe
CO_2	Oxidizing	Plain-carbon and low alloy steels; deoxidized electrode is essential

Note

Courtesy of The Lincoln Electric Company

Al = aluminum; Cu = copper; Ar = argon; Cl = chlorine; N_2 = nitrogen; He = helium; CO_2 = carbon dioxide; O_2 = oxygen.

mixture of these gases), which produce the best and least expensive gas possible. Helium is the most expensive gas, followed by argon and then carbon dioxide. However, cost is not the only factor to be considered. Argon produces a very narrow bead, while helium produces a wide bead. Carbon dioxide produces a thicker bead than argon and a thinner one than helium. When used by itself, carbon dioxide has a tendency to produce a harsh arc with a lot of spatter. (A small addition of argon, however, will stabilize the arc and eliminate much of the spatter.) The shielding gas used will depend on the welding process, the type of base metal, and the results desired. Table 17-1 lists some suggested shielding gases for various metals.

REGULATION OF THE SHIELDING GAS

The regulators and flowmeters used for GMAW are the same as those used in GTAW. (See Chapter 16.)

17-2 GMAW FUNDAMENTALS

GMAW is similar to SMAW with the difference that the GMAW electrode is one continuous roll of wire. This eliminates much of the starting and stopping to change electrodes that is necessary in SMAW. A person who has been arc welding with ordinary electrodes should not find it difficult to learn GMAW. Once the arc has been struck, many of the skills learned in SMAW will apply to this process. For instance, moving the rod at a faster speed will produce a smaller puddle, prevent burn-through and decrease penetration. As in SMAW, listening to the sound of the arc will provide information that affects the quality of the weld. As with SMAW, a "soft" arc is best. (Figure 17-10 shows a GMAW operation.)

17-3 ARC METAL TRANSFER

As researchers studied the transfer of metal across the arc in GMAW, they discovered that under certain conditions the metal would spray across the arc. (In SMAW, the metal was transferred across the arc in globules.) It was also discovered that, by manipulating the amperage and voltage, a short-circuit condition could be attained. Therefore, with basically the same equipment, a number of different processes are possible. In GMAW, there are three methods of transferring metal across the arc: **dip** (or short-circuit), **globular**, and **spray transfer** (Figure 17-11).

DIP (OR SHORT-CIRCUIT) TRANSFER

When the amperage and the voltage are at the lowest range for a small-diameter wire and the machine is activated, the electrode touches the base metal and freezes.

Figure 17-10   GMAW in progress

At this point, as in SMAW, there is no arc and the amperage and voltage increase. This causes the wire to melt. As the wire melts, the amperage and voltage return to their original level, and the whole process starts again. Each time, a small piece of wire melts onto the base metal.

GLOBULAR TRANSFER

In globular transfer, the drops of molten metal are transferred across the arc by their own weight. That is, the wire melts and the globules drop into the weld puddle because a certain arc length is maintained. Unfortunately, because the molten metal is fluid, it tends always to drop straight down, making it very difficult to weld

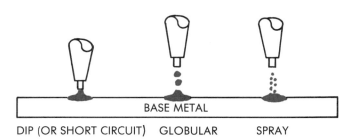

DIP (OR SHORT CIRCUIT)   GLOBULAR   SPRAY

Figure 17-11   Metal transfer across the arc

out of position. (This is similar to using a heavy iron powder electrode in the SMAW process.)

SPRAY TRANSFER

As the amperage increases, the metal transfer changes from globular to spray. The globules are much smaller, more frequent, and are actually propelled across the arc. In spray transfer, an inert gas or an inert gas with a small amount of oxygen acts as the shielding gas. Because of the high amperages required for spray transfer, the weld metal is very fluid and difficult to control in out-of-position welding. This has led to the development of pulsed arc, in which a current is superimposed on the regular welding current. This automatically controls the high current by lowering the heat input. (At the same time, the high current necessary for spray conditions is retained.)

17-4 GMAW PRACTICE

EXERCISE #1
STRIKING THE ARC

1. Check that you have the proper safety equipment.
2. Check that cable connections are tight, and start the welding machine.
3. Turn on the cooling system.
4. Set the wire feed mechanism to desired speed, and turn the switch to the on position.
5. Press the trigger on the gun, and allow the wire to feed through until it projects about 6 mm (1/4 in.) beyond the nozzle (Figure 17-12). Stop by releasing the trigger or giving another pull on the trigger, depending on the type of gun used.
6. Check the gas cylinder connections, and open the cylinder valve slowly.

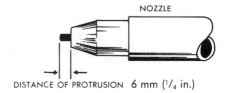

NOZZLE

DISTANCE OF PROTRUSION 6 mm ($^1/_4$ in.)

Figure 17-12   Electrode extension (stick out)

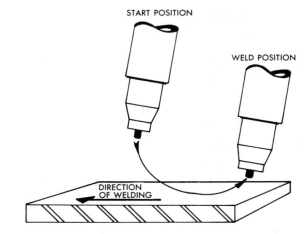

START POSITION

WELD POSITION

DIRECTION OF WELDING

Figure 17-13   Striking the arc

7. Press the gun trigger to activate the gas, and adjust the regulator or flowmeter to the desired pressure. Release or re-pull the trigger to stop.
8. Cut off the wire that has protruded more than 6 mm (1/4 in.) beyond the nozzle with a pair of wire-cutting pliers.
9. Set the voltage to meet the job requirements.
10. The amount the electrode (wire) should protrude beyond the nozzle will depend on the actual process being used, but this can be corrected by means of an inching button, or control, on most guns.
11. Obtain a piece of metal, and place it on the welding bench.
12. Set the welding machine and gas flow, etc., according to the thickness of metal and previous instructions.
13. Hold the gun above the metal and put helmet in place.
14. Pull the trigger on the gun to start gas flow and wire feed.
15. Use the scratch method of starting (Figure 17-13).
16. The arc can be extinguished by raising the gun away from the metal or releasing or re-pulling the trigger.
17. If the electrode freezes to the metal, activate the trigger to stop the welding current, and cut the wire with pliers.

18. Practise until the arc can be struck successfully each time.

Running a Bead

> Check equipment and clothing for safety.
> Obtain a piece of metal, and place it on the welding bench.
> Set the welding machine, gas flow, etc.

1. Pull the trigger, strike the arc, and form a puddle on the base metal.
2. Once the puddle is established, move the gun along the metal at a uniform speed to produce a smooth, even weld (Figure 17-14).

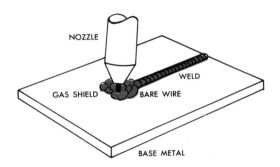

Figure 17-14   Running a bead

3. Keep the wire at the front, or leading edge of the puddle as welding progresses.
4. The angle at which the gun is held is most important. The gun should be inclined about 5° to 10° from the vertical (Figure 17-15). Too much of an angle on the gun will give a poor gas coverage to the weld.

Having practised striking the arc and running beads, the next step is to assemble and weld the various joints.

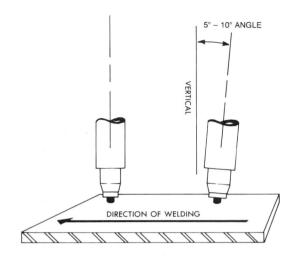

Figure 17-15   Electrode angle

WELDING JOINTS WITH GMAW

When welding fillet welds on tee and lap joints in the horizontal position, the gun should be positioned approximately 45° to 60° from the horizontal and the lead angle should be 5° to 15° (Figure 17-16). For groove and butt joints, the gun should be held at a right angle to the joint and inclined 10° to 15° in the direction of travel (Figure 17-17).

17-5 FLUX-CORED ARC WELDING (FCAW)

Flux-cored arc welding is a GMAW process. However, the wire used is a hollow tube and contains a flux which is used with or without a shielding gas. The flux inside the tubular wire contains the same elements as the coating on an SMAW electrode. These elements also perform in the same manner as those in an ordinary coating. They act as deoxidizers, slag formers, and arc stabilizers. The shielding gas performs the same function as any other shielding gas. Plates up to 19 mm (or 3/4 in.) can be welded with full penetration and no edge preparation. Even when groove joint preparation is necessary for full penetration, the grooves will be much smaller than in normal preparation. The equipment is basically the same as that used for GMAW (see Figure 17-18). The power, or welding current, is controlled by the electrode exten-

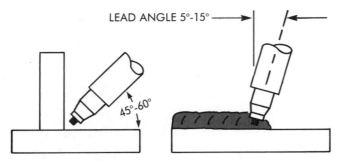

Figure 17-16 Gun position for tee and lap joints in GMAW

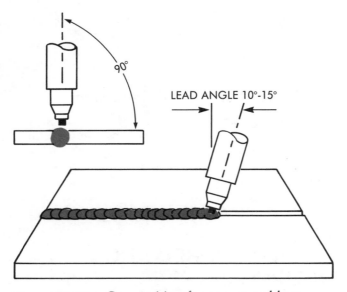

Figure 17-17 Gun position for groove and butt joints in GMAW

sion (stick out). A general rule of thumb by which stick out can be set is by multiplying the wire diameter by 15.

Example:

Diameter of Wire		Electrode Extension approximate	
(in.)	(mm)	(approx. in.)	(mm)
0.030	0.75	7/16	12
0.350	0.90	1/2	13
0.045	1.15	5/8	16

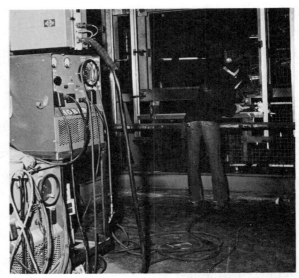

Courtesy of Hobart Brothers Company

Figure 17-18   GMAW machines

Carbon dioxide or an argon/carbon dioxide mixture (25/75) is used for the shielding gas. The welding technique is the same as GMAW. Use a forehand or rightward movement with the gun inclined approximately 10° in the direction of travel.

Welding wires are classified under CSA as W48.5M 1982 and AWS as A5.20. However, instead of the letter "S" for solid wire, the letter "T" is used to represent flux-cored wire.

17-6 SUBMERGED ARC WELDING (SAW)

This process was developed to help protect deposited weld metal from atmospheric contamination. It can also be adapted to automatic welding.

Early experiments using ordinary coated electrodes and an ordinary electrode holder with a power-driven carriage were unsuccessful for a number of reasons. Two problems became apparent: (1) the electrode coatings were susceptible to damage; (2) the length of electrode allowed only short welds to be made before the electrode required changing.

The submerged arc process eliminated both these

problems. A granular flux was used instead of the coating, and a continuous reel of bare wire replaced the electrode. This allowed better control of the chemical composition of the flux. The quality of the deposited weld metal was therefore improved considerably.

In this process, an arc is formed between the parent or base metal and the electrode. However, the arc is completely buried under the flux. None of the high-intensity light rays normally associated with arc welding are visible (Figure 17-19).

The process may be semi-automatic. In this case, the welder guides the welding gun manually, but the electrode is fed mechanically into the weld area. It is also possible to move either the welding head of the machine or the parent metal by means of a mechanical fixture. This makes the process fully automatic (Figures 17-20 and 17-21). The electrode performs the same function as any other arc welding electrode. It conveys current to the joint, supplies filler metal, etc. The flux performs the same function as a coating. It protects the weld from atmospheric contamination, forms a protective slag over the weld, and can add alloys to the weld. Any extra but unused flux in the weld area is collected by a vacuum system and recycled into the flux container for re-use.

The submerged arc process used today is a very sophisticated process. It depends on electronic controls which maintain or adjust automatically the arc voltage, arc length, and wire (electrode) speed and feed. Two,

Courtesy of The Lincoln Electric Company

Figure 17-20   Splicing or joining deck plates of a ship using the submerged arc process (SAW)

three, and sometimes more wires are used simultaneously instead of a single electrode. The submerged arc process is usually used on thick metal plates. Extremely high amperages (over 500 A) can also be used with this process. Because of these high amperages, welding speeds are increased considerably. This results in less distortion, less shrinkage, and almost no spatter in the weld area. At the same time, deep penetration is still possible. This process is sometimes referred to as the **hidden arc, union-melt,** or **buried arc process.**

The submerged arc process is used in the flat or horizontal position. Usually, little edge preparation is required. A square edge butt preparation is sufficient for many operations.

This is the basic equipment necessary for SAW:
- a power source
- electrode reel
- flux hopper
- control panel
- cables.

AC or DC may be used. The capacity of the machine will depend on the application. It is possible to use an ordinary arc welding generator or heavy-duty transformer for the submerged arc process. If extremely high

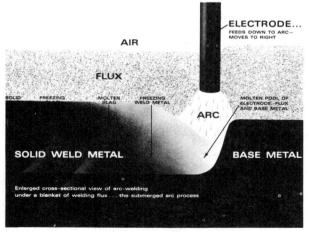

Courtesy of The Lincoln Electric Company

Figure 17-19   Mechanics of SAW

Figure 17-21

Schematics of various wire feeder arrangements for fully automatic SAW

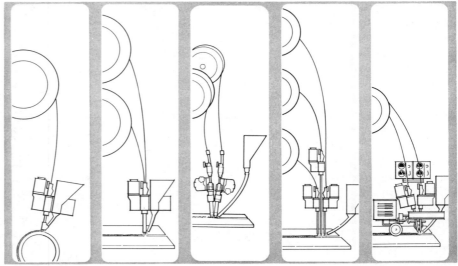

Courtesy of The Lincoln Electric Company

currents are to be used, two or more machines may be hooked up in parallel, as long as the same types of machines are used.

In this process, metal is deposited at an extremely high rate (over 5m/min or 16 ft./min on some operations), so a reel of wire and an automatic feed system and control are necessary. A flux hopper or container dispenses the flux at the welding area in the required amount as the weld is being made. The composition of this flux is carefully controlled. As a basic arc welding process, the same faults occur with much the same results. For example, amperage may be too high or too low and speed of travel too fast or too slow. In addition, however, too much or too little flux can result in a rough uneven weld and/or porosity.

In addition to being an excellent process for welding thick metals, SMAW is versatile. The following chart will perhaps demonstrate the range and adaptability of

Although the arc is hidden or submerged and a face shield is unnecessary during the welding operation, care should be taken just as in arc welding to avoid accidental striking of the arc. Because of the high amperages, this could result in extreme eye flash. Usually the end of the electrode is completely covered with the flux before the arc is struck. Because the flux is nonconductive, a popular method of starting the arc is to place a piece of steel wool between the tip of the electrode and the work piece. This eliminates the need for touching the electrode to the work. **SPECIAL CAUTION:** Because of the extremely high amperages (1000 A in some operations), care should be taken when working with the equipment to avoid deadly electric shock.

Plate Thickness	Amperage	Voltage	Electrode	Speed
1.5 mm (16 gauge)	450 A	24 V	3.0 mm (1/8 in.)	2800 mm/min
12.5 mm (1/2 in.)	1000 A	35 V	4.17 mm (3/16 in.)	430 mm/min

Both the 16 gauge and the 1/2 in. metal were prepared in a square edge butt joint with a gap and a backing bar, and a single electrode was used.

Courtesy of The Lincoln Electric Company

Figure 17-22   Making circular welds with SAW

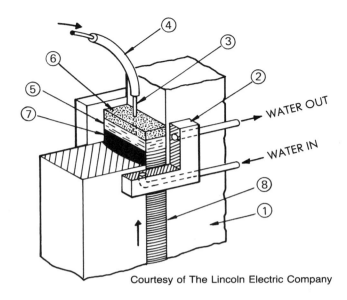

Courtesy of The Lincoln Electric Company

Figure 17-23   Schematic of electroslag welding (ESW): (1) base metal; (2) water-cooled copper plates (shoes); (3) electrode; (4) electrode guide tube; (5) molten weld metal; (6) molten slag; (7) solidified weld metal; (8) finished weld

this process. Figure 17-22 shows just one application of SAW.

17-7 ELECTROSLAG AND ELECTROGAS WELDING (ESW/EGW)

Electroslag welding is a process developed from the submerged arc process. It is used mainly in the vertical position for the welding of thick metal. The joint on which it is usually used is a square edge butt joint. As with the submerged arc process, the electroslag process has been improved so that more than one electrode can be used at the same time. The electrodes can also be moved from side to side as they progress up the joint. Electroslag welding has been further improved by the addition of an inert gas shield while welding is in progress. When the inert gas shield is being used the process is called electrogas welding.

The principle behind ESW and EGW is similar to SAW in that welding takes place beneath a flux. The joint is enclosed in copper plates commonly called "shoes" (see Figure 17-23). Powdered flux is then introduced into the box formed by the shoes and the edges of the joint. When the electrode is struck under the flux inside this box, it quickly melts the flux underneath which the electrode melts to form the filler metal for the joint. The process is completely automatic with wire feed, current, and flux feed constantly adjusting. The welding head (Figure 17-24) is either suspended above the joint or mounted on a vertical track which is motor driven. Whichever method is used, the head is usually self-adjusting and the rate of travel controlled. Usually, a solid wire is used for electroslag, while a flux-cored wire is used for the electrogas welding process. These are a few of the advantages of electrogas and electroslag welding:

1. No edge preparation is necessary.
2. In electrogas, no slag needs to be cleaned up.
3. The process is very fast.
4. Very heavy metals can be welded in one pass.

Electroslag and Electrogas Welding   **207**

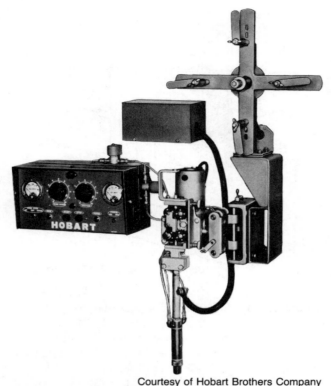

Courtesy of Hobart Brothers Company

Figure 17-24   SAW

TROUBLESHOOTING WIRE AND FLUX FEEDING EQUIPMENT

Although electrogas and electroslag welding have many advantages, their wire and flux feeding equipment can sometimes pose problems. Some of the more common problems associated with wire and flux feeding units are outlined in Table 17-2. Study them until you are familiar with them all.

17-8 PLASMA ARC WELDING AND CUTTING (PAW/PAC)

Plasma arc welding is not a new process. Experiments were carried out with the plasma arc 100 years ago. It

is only in recent years, however, that a method of utilizing it for welding and cutting was developed. PAW is more like GTAW than GMAW because a tungsten electrode and a filler rod with the same gases is used for both PAW and GTAW. The main difference between PAW and GTAW is in the design of the nozzle (see Figure 17-25).

Most PAW processes are performed with a DC constant current (drooping) type machine, with DCSP. If AC is used, it must have an HF unit. A gas such as argon is passed over an electric arc which heats the gas to a plasma stage. At the same time, the gas is forced through a small orifice in the nozzle at a high velocity (similiar to that of the engine in a supersonic jet plane). Temperatures of 10 800°C (20 000°F) are commonly reached. This, of course, creates a highly concentrated arc. A cooling system is necessary to keep the torch handle and the nozzle cool. Just as in GTAW and GMAW, a shielding gas is used to protect the molten metal. Argon, helium, or a suitable mix of gases is used for this purpose.

The PAW process can be used to weld metals with foil thickness. Two types of arc can be formed in this process: (1) a nontransferred arc in which the arc is created between the tungsten electrode and the nozzle (the base metal is not part of this electrical circuit) and

Courtesy of Union Carbide Canada Limited

Figure 17-25   The PAW nozzle

TABLE 17-2 TYPICAL TROUBLESHOOTING GUIDE FOR WIRE AND FLUX FEEDING EQUIPMENT

Trouble	Causes	What to Do

Wire Feeding
Wire feeding rough or jerky or wire feeding stops completely.
	Cable liner may be dirty.
	Electrode may be dirty or rusty.
	
	Nozzle contact tip may have been burned or partly melted causing hole to be undersized.
		Clean cable.
		Replace with clean electrode.
		If conditions are extremely dirty or electrode is old (solid wire only), put a wiper on the wire before it enters the guide tubes. Use a piece of cloth or felt saturated with "Pyroil B" held around the wire with a light clamp.
		Replace with new tip.
		Drill contact tip:
		   1/8 (3.2 mm) wire—No. 28 drill
		   .120 (3.5 mm) wire—No. 29 drill
		   3/32 (2.4 mm) wire—No. 36 drill
		   5/64 (2 mm) wire—No. 40 drill

Flux Feeding (Submerged Arc) Flux flow stops while welding. If there is flux in the hose right behind the gun (test by squeezing), the stoppage is in the gun.	Flux tube in the gun may be blocked. Magnetic particles may cause bridging at the nozzle tip. Bridging occurs only when welding.	Remove the gun from the cable. Check the tube in the gun and the cable handle. Pass flux over a magnetic separator when filling the flux tank.
Flux stoppage not in the gun. (Be certain there are no kinks or collapsing of the hose.)	There may be a piece of slag in the hose.	Work back along the hose squeezing it until flux can be felt. Shake the hose and feel for slag at this point. Blow out hose with air if necessary.
Flux stoppage not in the gun. (Be certain there are no kinks or	Flux tank outlet may be clogged. Pressure in the tank may be set	If there is no flux in the hose, check the tank outlet for large pieces of slag or paper. Set pressure regulator for 180-205 kPa.

TABLE 17-2 cont'd

Trouble	Causes	What to Do
collapsing of the hose.)	improperly	Set pressure for 380-415 kPa. when using a gun-cable extension assembly.
Excessive air blow and uneven flux flow from the gun.	Tank may be almost empty. (May look as if the tank is full at the sides but it will be down to the bottom in the centre.) Flux may be falling away from the weld faster than it is being fed. Pressure in the tank may be too high.	Refill the tank. Alter procedure or make a flux dam. Set pressure regulator for 180-205 kPa. Set pressure for 380-415 kPa when using a gun-cable extension assembly.
Flux in tank gets wet.	There may be water in the air line. The copper bleeder may be clogged.	It is possible to get water from air lines when first starting in the morning. Blow out air lines before connecting them to the tank. Be certain that a slight amount of air is escaping from the crimped end of the copper tube below the flux tank.

Courtesy of The Lincoln Electric Company

(2) a transferred arc where the arc is between the base metal and the electrode.

PAW uses essentially the same equipment as GTAW, but the PAW machine has a much higher OCV. The gas used to form the plasma is selected according to the type of metal being cut. With nonferrous and carbon steels, a nitrogen or nitrogen mix is used as a plasma former. Under ideal conditions, a plasma arc will cut a 19 mm (or 3/4 in.) plate 5 times as quickly as the oxyfuel process.

17-9 LASER BEAM WELDING AND CUTTING (LBW/LBC)

The word **laser** stands for Light Amplification by the Stimulated Emission of Radiation and refers to the concentration and frequency of light waves. Lasers can be used for welding or cutting. By concentrating a brilliant light beam through a ruby laser rod with mirrors, a highly intense energy beam may be directed to a specific area. This beam generates so much heat in a tiny area for such a short time that although the assembly is actually fused, it is possible to touch the area with the bare hand immediately after the weld has been made.

> **Note**
> Although the above point was made for emphasis, one should never touch a freshly welded area with the bare hand without first testing the area for heat.

This process has limited application at present and is used only in the electronic and aero industries. However, experiments are being carried out at present to make the process more usable. For example, researchers are looking for a replacement for ruby as the lasing agent. Sapphire and different gases and gas mixes are now being tested as replacements.

17-10 ROBOTIC WELDING

The newest field in welding is that of robot arc welding introduced in the 1970s. Today there are thousands of robot arc welding stations in use. The forerunners of the welding robot station include automatic and semi-automatic welding machines (Figure 17-26) and welding positioners, used to position welds (usually in the down-hand position), for faster welding. These have all been used for many years. With the electronic age, however, these familiar pieces of equipment have been developed into the welding robot station. This station controls, positions, and welds a product to precise specifications, drawn from a computer memory. With this technology, tomorrow's welder will be relieved of some of the repetitious operations common on assembly lines. Robotic welding will increase productivity and improve quality, but it will not replace the knowledgeable skilled welder working on skyscrapers, in mines, underwater or in any area where problem solving for welding projects is required right on the job. However, it is notable that technology has progressed in only 80 years from using crude equipment to strike an arc with a bare electrode to welding "by computer". Today's new welding technology, however, still consists of refinements of that first weld.

Courtesy of Ontario Hydro

Figure 17-26   The Pickering G.S. "B" automatic welding machine

POINTS TO REMEMBER

- GMAW could be considered an extension of SMAW.
- The inert gas acts as a shield for the weld area.
- A GMAW machine cannot be used for ordinary arc welding.
- GMAW machines are rated at 100% duty cycle.
- Check that gas and water are turned on before starting to weld.
- In GMAW the amperage is controlled by the speed of the wire feed.
- The two basic types of welding guns are push and pull.
- If done properly, the GMAW process is cleaner and faster than SMAW.
- The usual method of welding is from right to left, if you are right-handed.
- When running a bead, the electrode is usually kept at the leading edge of the puddle. This enables you to see the puddle more clearly.
- These processes may be manual, semi-automatic, or fully automatic.
- In SAW care must be taken to avoid severe eye flash.
- Electroslag is a process developed from SAW.
- Robotic welding is currently the most used new technology in welding.

WORDS TO REMEMBER

inert   trigger   schematic
welding gun   drive rollers   granular
reels   flux-cored   buried
constant voltage   deoxidizers
wire feeder   carbon dioxide

REVIEW QUESTIONS

1. What do the letters GMAW stand for?
2. What is the duty cycle of a GMAW machine?
3. Why is it important to hold the welding gun at the correct angle?
4. What is the purpose of the inert gas?
5. How is the amperage controlled in GMAW?
6. What are the types of metal transfer in this process?
7. What does a drooping volt/amperage relationship mean?
8. What types of wire are available for GMAW?
9. What is another name for SAW?
10. Why was the SAW process developed?
11. What precaution should be taken with regard to eye flash in the SAW process?
12. From which process was the electroslag process developed?
13. In which position are the two processes most used?
14. Name a likely future development in welding.

P A R T

FURTHER SKILLS

18

METALS OTHER THAN LOW CARBON STEEL

All metals that are used commercially can be welded by any of the basic arc and oxyfuel welding processes described in this book and, of course, by the newer processes such as GTAW and GMAW. Industry is turning more and more to the newer processes. However, quite often only the basic arc and oxyfuel equipment are available on a job site for welding metals other than low carbon steel. This chapter will be devoted to a general discussion of welding metals other than low carbon steel, and the basic arc and oxyfuel processes suitable for each type of metal. Technique and practical tips will be emphasized.

18-1 WELDING METALS OTHER THAN LOW CARBON STEEL

The following basic points should be kept in mind when welding metals other than low carbon steel.

1. The metal must be clean.
2. Preheating is usually necessary.
3. Expansion and contraction will play an important part, so study the assembly to be welded carefully before welding.
4. Be sure that all parts are supported. Nonferrous metals tend to collapse during welding if they are not properly supported.
5. If possible, allow enough time to complete the weld in one operation. Try to avoid leaving the weld unfinished.
6. Choose a filler metal appropriate to the base metal.
7. Be careful when using a flux. Too much or too little flux can ruin an otherwise successful weld.

18-2 CAST IRON

Cast iron is not difficult to weld. It presents only two main problems:

1. The amount of expansion and contraction that occur when the metal is welded.
2. The effects of heat on the properties of the cast iron.

Failure to understand and apply the law of expansion and contraction is almost always responsible for unsatisfactory repairs. Each job should be fully understood before the welding itself is attempted. Chapter 22, Expansion and Contraction, should be studied carefully before any cast iron assembly is welded.

If possible, it is best to preheat cast iron to a dull red colour before welding. The entire casting must be heated, not just the part to be welded. The heating and cooling of cast iron during manufacture, and in any welding operation, will greatly influence the composition of the metal and the final outcome of any welding operation. During the manufacture of cast iron, the cooling speed will affect cast iron as follows:

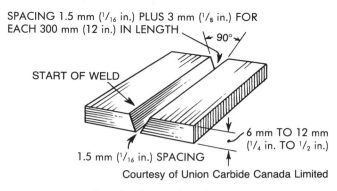

SPACING 1.5 mm (1/16 in.) PLUS 3 mm (1/8 in.) FOR EACH 300 mm (12 in.) IN LENGTH

90°

START OF WELD

6 mm TO 12 mm (1/4 in. TO 1/2 in.)

1.5 mm (1/16 in.) SPACING

Courtesy of Union Carbide Canada Limited

Figure 18-1 Standard practice pieces

EXERCISE #1
FUSION WELDING CAST IRON (OF)

The pieces shown in Figure 18-1 are standard practice pieces for cast iron welding. They may be prepared in the welding shop or purchased from a local foundry.

Speed of Cooling	Characteristics of Metal	Type of Cast Iron Produced
slow	low strength but machinable	gray
medium	high strength but machinable	gray (refined)
fast	hard, brittle; not machinable	white

PREHEATING TEMPERATURES

If using SMAW, preheat to 260°C-600°C (500°F-1200°F). If using oxyfuel (OF), preheat to 490°C-600°C (900°F-1200°F).

Note
Never preheat to more than 760°C (1400°F). Above that temperature, changes in the properties of the cast iron will occur, causing excessive cracking.

1. Prepare or obtain two pieces of cast iron as shown in the figure.
2. Prepare the welding equipment, and obtain welding rod and flux.
3. Place the pieces in position for welding. The edges should be slightly separated to allow for contraction. About 1.5 mm (1/16 in.) should be enough.
4. Heat and tack weld each end of the metal.
5. Preheat the assembly along its full length. Use the motion shown in Figure 18-2.
6. When the metal has reached a dull, red colour, bring the welding flame down to the metal at one

Cast Iron   **215**

end until the inner cone of the flame is almost touching the edges (Figure 18-3).

7. Heat the welding rod slightly, near the flame, then dip the rod in the flux and place it in the weld area.

8. Melt the sides of the vee, and make them flow towards the bottom. Now add metal from the welding rod until a single molten puddle is formed. Proceed to weld along the vee. Do not attempt to fill the vee in one pass. Dip the welding rod in the flux and then the weld area with a uniform movement.

9. Avoid the habit of pulling the torch away from the weld. Rather, use a slow circular movement which ensures fusion and does not cause a loss of heat.

10. At times it may be necessary to break up oxide that has formed by stirring the molten puddle with the welding rod. If the metal is very dirty, pull the oxides out of the weld area with the welding rod. Tapping the welding rod on the bench will remove the oxides from the rod.

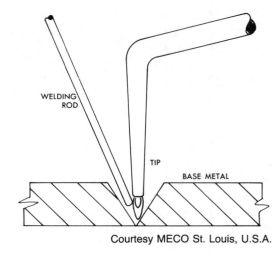

Courtesy MECO St. Louis, U.S.A.

Figure 18-3   Concentrating the head

Handling Problems

Cast iron does not solidify immediately when the flame is removed. It remains liquid for some time. This condition presents two problems: (1) the fluid cast iron weld metal may flow without bonding to the base metal; (2) the weld may collapse. The first problem can be avoided by watching the molten puddle carefully and bringing all parts up to the fusion temperature. The second problem is usually experienced by beginners and is caused only by lack of experience or knowledge of the metal. The force or velocity of the flame, with the metal in liquid condition, sometimes results in the metal collapsing. To avoid this, there must be a solid base in the metal at all times. This can be accomplished by moving the torch in a circular manner, in much the same way as shown in Figure 18-2, and not allowing the flame to rest in any one spot too long.

A frequent cast iron welding application is filling holes in castings. To do this, preheat the metal to fusion temperature. Move the flame and weld slowly down the sides of the hole. At the same time, change the angle of the torch so that the flame is moving around the inside of the hole without being concentrated in one area too long. This will also help to keep the molten puddle fluid and divert the force of the flame. This method should also be used where small sections may be missing (Figure 18-4).

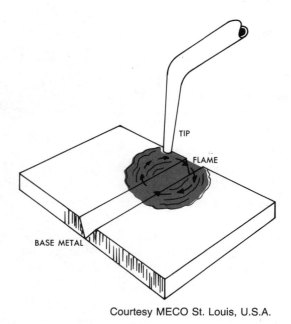

Courtesy MECO St. Louis, U.S.A.

Figure 18-2   Torch movement during heating

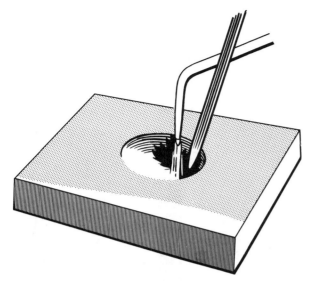

Courtesy MECO St. Louis, U.S.A.

Figure 18-4   Filling holes in castings

BRAZE WELDING CAST IRON

Cast iron will lend itself to braze welding unless a colour match is desired. Special care must be taken to ensure that the metal is clean and properly prepared. If the edges of the vee are prepared by grinding or machining, graphite flakes will spread over the area. These must be removed by filing and preheating before braze welding. (The graphite interferes with proper tinning action.)

The weld metal made by braze welding, if done properly, is usually stronger and has more ductility than the cast iron. Braze welding is carried out in the manner discussed previously in Chapter 9. Again, do not try to fill the vee in one pass if the same type of test pieces as those in Exercise #1 are being used. Study Figure 18-5. The correct appearance of the first bead is shown in A, and the incorrect shape is shown in B. The second and third passes are also shown in Figure 18-5. Note that the second layer is concave, and the third is convex and built up above the surface of the metal. A good bead is shown in Figure 18-6. The chisel is being used to remove the glassy slag formed by the flux during the welding operation.

The piece of cast iron shown in Figure 18-7 has been

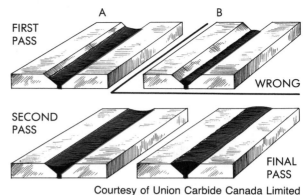

Courtesy of Union Carbide Canada Limited

Figure 18-5   Braze welding a butt joint

Courtesy of Union Carbide Canada Limited

Figure 18-6   Cleaning the braze weld

broken through the weld to show the uniformity of the weld metal. Note the absence of holes and the even appearance. A cast iron gear wheel is shown in Figure 18-8. The broken arm has been prepared for braze welding. Note the clean appearance of the metal at either

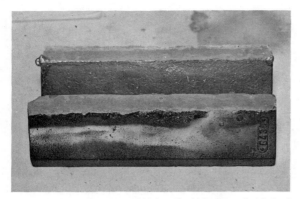

Courtesy of Union Carbide Canada Limited

Figure 18-7 Appearance of a good braze bead on a cast iron joint

Courtesy of Union Carbide Canada Limited

Figure 18-8 Preparation for braze welding

side of the crack. The special type of joint shown in Figure 18-9 is known as a shear-vee joint. It is used frequently in braze welding cast iron pipe.

FUSION WELDING CAST IRON BY THE SHIELDED ARC WELDING PROCESS (SMAW)

Cast iron may also be welded with the SMAW process (Figure 18-10). Three types of electrodes may be used for cast iron welding:

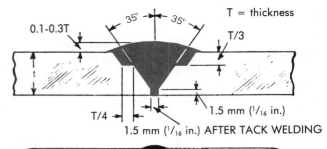

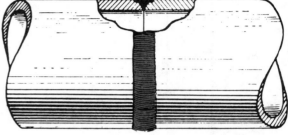

Courtesy of Union Carbide Canada Limited

Figure 18-9 Shear-vee joint

1. an electrode with a mild steel core wire (E St),
2. an electrode with a nickel core wire (E Ni),
3. an electrode with a 55% nickel and a 45% iron core wire (E Ni Fe).

An electrode with a mild-steel core wire is used if the part being repaired will not require machining when the welding is completed. This electrode is best used with DCRP but may be used with AC. It should be used at the lowest possible amperage.

An electrode with a nickel core wire is used if the part will require machining after welding. This electrode is best used with DCRP but can also be used with AC and DCSP. An electrode with a nickel/iron core provides a balance. That is, the deposited weld metal will be machinable but it will not be as soft as the deposit made with the nickel core wire. AC or DCRP is recommended for these electrodes.

With SMAW, the assembly does not need to be preheated before the cast iron can be welded. This makes SMAW valuable for this welding process in that it saves time and expense. However, the weld must be made slowly and carefully if there is no preheating. In addition, the amperage should always be as low as possible while still producing a good weld.

Figure 18-10
SMAW repair on
cast iron

Courtesy of Canadian Liquid Air Ltd.

TABLE 18-1 SUGGESTED ELECTRODE SIZES AND AMPERAGE FOR CAST IRON (SMAW)

Electrode Size		Suggested Amperage	
(mm)	**(inch)**	**(AC)**	**(DC)**
2.4	3/32	50- 90	45- 75
3.0	1/8	90-120	80-110
4.0	5/32	100-140	100-130
4.8	3/16	135-175	120-160

EXERCISE #2
WELDING CAST IRON USING SMAW (WITH PREHEAT)

1. If possible, the casting to be repaired should be preheated to 600°C (1110°F).
2. The entire casting should be preheated, not just the area to be welded.
3. The joint should be clean and edges prepared (if necessary).
4. A normal to short arc length should be maintained.
5. When restarting a bead, strike the arc at the leading edge of the crater, move the electrode back to fill the crater, and then continue in the direction of welding.

Cast Iron   **219**

6. Be sure to clean the crater each time before starting.

7. Allow the casting to cool slowly and uniformly.

EXERCISE #3
WELDING CAST IRON USING SMAW (WITHOUT PREHEAT)

1. Clean and prepare the casting in the usual manner.
2. Run short beads about 40 mm (1 1/2 in.) in length.
3. Stagger these beads along the crack or joint.
4. The casting should never be allowed to become hot, except where the actual weld metal is deposited.
5. After each short bead is deposited, time must be allowed for it to cool before depositing the next bead.
6. Continue in this manner until the weld is completed.
7. Obviously this will be a slow process. (It is sometimes referred to as **cold welding**.)
8. Light peening is beneficial but should be carried out as soon as the arc is broken. (Peening is the term used to describe gentle taps with a manual or mechanical hammer.)

STUDDING A CAST IRON JOINT

Studding a joint means screwing small metal studs into the cast iron and then welding over them. This provides additional strength when needed. Studding is usually done when the piece cannot be preheated or when the cast iron pieces are very heavy and there is limited room for the metal to expand and contract.

EXERCISE #4
STEPS IN STUDDING A CAST IRON JOINT

1. Prepare a vee along the crack of the surface to be welded.
2. Obtain the correct type of welding rod.

3. Drill and tap holes along the vee to suit the size of the stud.
4. Screw the studs into the tapped holes. They are usually inserted to a depth equal to their diameter. The studs should project about 6 mm (or 1/4 in.) above the surface of the metal (Figure 18-11).
5. One or two beads are deposited around each stud first. They provide fusion of the steel stud and the iron casting.
6. The complete groove is then filled with weld.

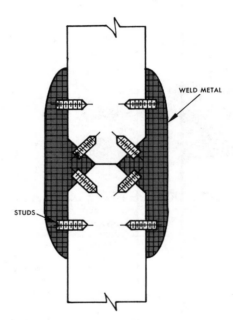

Figure 18-11   Studding a cast iron joint

18-3 MALLEABLE IRON

When first cast, this particular metal becomes a hard, brittle, white cast iron. By annealing the white cast iron slowly, it is changed into a casting which is much softer and more ductile. If malleable iron is reheated as in fusion welding, it will become white cast iron again (Figure 18-12). Therefore, the best way to weld malleable iron is to braze weld it. In braze welding the malleable iron is not heated to a temperature high enough to cause it to change back to a white cast iron.

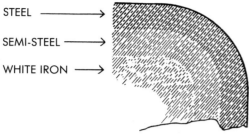

STEEL ⟶

SEMI-STEEL ⟶

WHITE IRON ⟶

Courtesy MECO St. Louis, U.S.A.

Figure 18-12   Malleable iron

Braze welding of malleable iron is carried out in exactly the same manner as braze welding of steel. Malleable iron can be fusion welded in the same way as any other cast iron, but it must first be reheated and annealed in a furnace. If arc welding is to be used on malleable iron, the same electrode that is used to weld copper (E Cu Sn C) should be used.

TEST YOUR KNOWLEDGE

1. What is the main problem in welding cast iron?
2. Why is a flux used in cast iron welding?
3. How is the flux applied to the weld area?
4. What is the procedure to be used if the puddle is very dirty?
5. What precautions must be taken with regard to braze welding cast iron?
6. Describe the correct appearance of the first, second, and third passes in a three-pass braze weld.
7. Describe the appearance of a good braze weld.
8. What are the two types of electrodes used for welding cast iron by the arc welding process?
9. What is the main difference between these electrodes?
10. What is meant by studding a cast iron joint?

18-4 ALUMINUM

Aluminum is a soft, ductile metal of high tensile strength. It is widely used for parts that require both lightness and strength. When molten, it oxidizes very readily, creating a problem in aluminum welding. Aluminum melts at approximately 650°C (1200°F), almost half the temperature required to melt iron. It conducts heat almost three times as quickly as iron, and it has a 50% greater shrinkage than iron.

Table 18-2 gives the heat conductivity of aluminum in relation to various common metals.

TABLE 18-2 HEAT CONDUCTIVITY OF METALS

Silver	100.00
Copper	73.6
Gold	53.2
Aluminum	31.3
Brass	23.1
Zinc	19.0
Tin	14.5
Iron	11.9
Steel	11.6
Lead	8.5
Platinum	8.4

HANDLING PROBLEMS

Aluminum is softer and more ductile than cast iron and can stand considerably more expansion and contraction before breaking. However, it has very little strength when hot, and when brought to the melting temperature it will collapse unless properly supported. Also, it does not change colour in the way that steel does during welding. The beginning welder may therefore encounter some difficulties with aluminum.

In addition, since aluminum has a lower melting point than steel, it would seem that a smaller-size welding tip than the one required for welding the same thickness of steel should be used. But because aluminum conducts heat so quickly, the same size of welding tip is used for the same thickness of both metals.

WELDING ALUMINUM (OF)

When first heated and melted, an aluminum joint does not run or fuse readily, especially if dirt or oxides are present. A puddling rod should be made from a 6 mm (or 1/4 in.) mild steel welding rod by flattening one end with a hammer (Figure 18-13). These rods are used to add the flux and stir the metal in the weld area, bringing the welding rod metal and the base metal together.

Do not attempt to weld the entire joint at one time. Weld approximately 50 mm (or 2 in.) at a time, puddling the weld through to the root and adding sufficient filler rod to complete that portion of the weld. This is done because each time a new surface of aluminum is exposed, a surface of oxide is formed.

Wherever possible, use sheet steel or carbon to support the welded portion. Carbon can be purchased in a paste or solid form, and the paste can be moulded to suit any irregular shape.

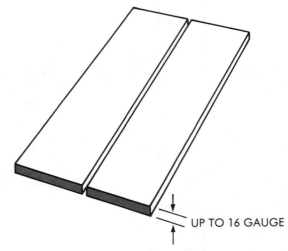

Courtesy of Union Carbide Canada Limited

Figure 18-15   Butt joint

ALUMINUM JOINT DESIGNS

The flange type joint is used for welding aluminum sheet which is 16 gauge or less (Figure 18-14). The simple butt joint may also be used on 16 gauge or less, but the flange joint is preferable. Figure 18-15 shows a typical butt joint.

A notched butt joint is used for sheet aluminum from 15 to 5 gauge in thickness (Figure 18-16). The notches

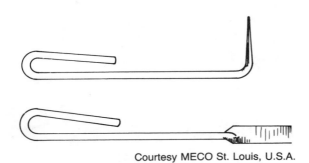

Courtesy MECO St. Louis, U.S.A.

Figure 18-13   Puddling rods

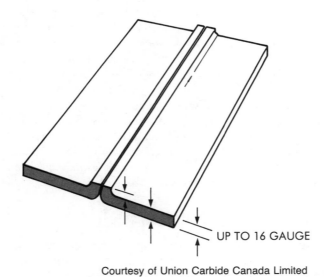

Courtesy of Union Carbide Canada Limited

Figure 18-14   Flange joint

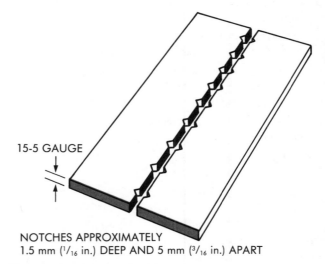

NOTCHES APPROXIMATELY
1.5 mm ($^1/_{16}$ in.) DEEP AND 5 mm ($^3/_{16}$ in.) APART

Figure 18-16   Notched butt joint

are made with an ordinary cold chisel and should be about 5 mm (or 3/16 in.) apart and 1.5 mm (or 1/16 in.) deep. A single-vee joint with a notched straight nose is used for heavy metal up to 11 mm (or 7/16 in.) thick (Figure 18-17). For metal thicker than 11 mm (or 7/16 in.), a double-vee butt joint should be used (Figure 18-18).

Aluminum is weak when hot, so to avoid the possibility of buckling and distorting from welding, the pieces are sometimes supported in special fixtures in industry.

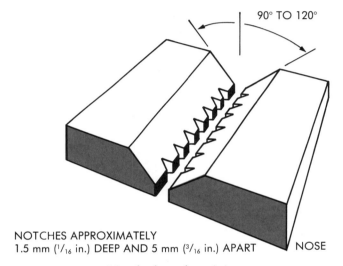

NOTCHES APPROXIMATELY
1.5 mm (¹/₁₆ in.) DEEP AND 5 mm (³/₁₆ in.) APART   NOSE

Figure 18-17   Notched vee butt joint

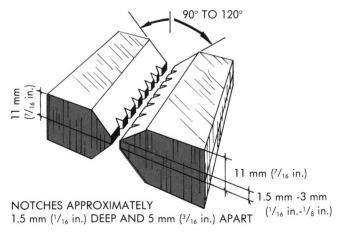

NOTCHES APPROXIMATELY
1.5 mm (¹/₁₆ in.) DEEP AND 5 mm (³/₁₆ in.) APART

Figure 18-18   Double-vee notched butt joint

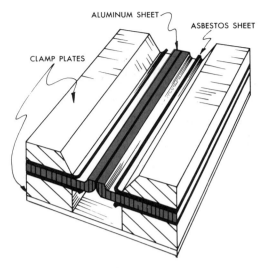

Figure 18-19   Welding fixture

Note that the support sheets do not come right up to the weld in Figure 18-19.

In any lap joint, the flux will be trapped between the two pieces of metal, making removal of the flux almost impossible. Thus a lap joint should be avoided, but if a lap joint has to be welded, it should be sealed along the edges as shown in Figure 18-20. The trapped flux will eventually corrode both pieces from the inside out.

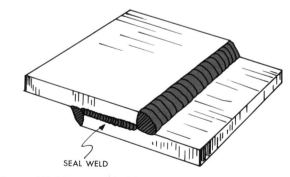

Figure 18-20   Welded lap joint

ARC WELDING ALUMINUM

Aluminum can be welded with an electrode of the AL-43 classification, and DC reverse polarity should be used. These electrodes have silicon in the coating, which

Figure 18-21   Arc welding aluminum

prevents excessive oxidation and helps dissolve any aluminum oxides that may be formed during welding. When using these electrodes, a very short arc must be held. In fact, the coating should be lightly touching the molten puddle (Figure 18-21). In restarting the weld, the scratch method should be used to break the heavy flux coating at the tip of the electrode.

18-5 WHITE OR DIE-CAST METAL

Some white metal castings cannot be welded. The average melting point of these castings is 427°C (800°F). Aluminum and magnesium castings melt at temperatures between 537°C (1000°F) and 593°C (1100°F), while the zinc base die-castings melt at a temperature as low as 370°C (700°F).

Since the melting point is so low, great care must be taken when welding to ensure that the parts will not collapse. It is often possible to support the parts by using a mixture of powdered heat-absorbing material and water. This mixture, in the form of a paste, is applied to the underside of the joint. As welding progresses, the paste hardens to give a firm support to the joint.

All protective coatings, such as the chrome plating used in auto parts, should be removed from the area to be welded. Unless the parts are very thick, it will not be necessary to vee them out. A special white metal welding rod should be used, and a puddling rod such as the one described under aluminum welding will be helpful. However, it is not necessary to use a flux.

EXERCISE #5
STEPS IN WELDING WHITE METAL

1. The entire part should be preheated before welding begins. If the assembly is small, place it on a piece of sheet metal and heat the underside of the sheet metal.
2. A very small welding tip should be used, regardless of the thickness of the metal.
3. The flame should always be carburizing, and the inner cone of the flame should be held about 25 mm to 50 mm (1 in. to 2 in.) away from the metal at all times.
4. When the base metal and the welding rod start to melt, dip the rod into the molten puddle, using a stirring action to ensure complete penetration. The puddling rod may be used to stir the puddle and to smooth the finished weld.

White metal has become very popular in recent years in the automobile industry for grilles, door handles, carburetors, and many other parts. It is also used in trophies, ornaments, and hardware.

18-6 COPPER

Copper conducts heat much more rapidly than any other commercial metal (Figure 18-22). The melting point of copper is less than that of iron and steel, but copper conducts heat much more quickly (almost 7 times faster). Because the heat is conducted so rapidly, the metal expands and contracts quickly, and a crack is likely to occur at or near the weld. The high rate of heat conductivity also makes necessary a larger oxy-acetylene tip than needed for the same thickness of iron or steel.

Cold copper is very ductile but hot copper is very brittle. Therefore, special care must be taken when welding this metal.

OXY-ACETYLENE WELDING OF COPPER

Copper should be prepared for welding in the same manner as other metals. That is, the vee should be properly prepared and the metal cleaned. To prevent contraction and cracks or internal strains, the metal should be preheated.

It is quite difficult to maintain ductility in copper during welding. A special welding rod and flux are necessary, each containing an element which will oppose the action of the oxygen on the copper. A neutral flame should be used, but the cone of the flame should not come into contact with the metal at any time.

For repair purposes, copper may be braze welded using silver or bronze alloys. Follow the general procedures for braze welding.

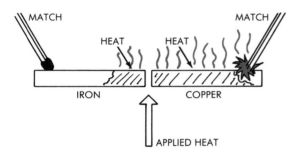

Figure 18-22 Heat conduction of copper and iron

ARC WELDING COPPER

Copper may be arc welded using an electrode of the AWS classification. The E Cu Sn C electrode should be used on DC reverse polarity. On thin metal it is not necessary to preheat, but as the weld progresses it may be necessary to reduce the amperage. At all times, a fairly short arc should be held, but the coating should not touch the molten metal.

18-7 BRASS AND BRONZE

Brass and bronze are the result of combining copper with other metals, such as zinc and tin. Since these metals have different melting points, care must be taken in welding the alloy to prevent changing the characteristics.

OXY-ACETYLENE WELDING OF BRASS AND BRONZE

Brass and bronze should be prepared with particular care to prevent the heated area from collapsing. Use the same joint designs as those used for steel. The flame should not be allowed to touch the molten metal at any time. The welding rod should be of the same composition as the base metal, and a flux should be used. The adjustment of the flame is most important. An oxidizing flame will prevent the alloying elements in the base metal and the welding rod from boiling out. However, the amount of excess oxygen required varies with each alloy and can be determined only by practice. The alloys can be braze welded, of course.

ARC WELDING BRASS AND BRONZE

These metals can be arc welded using the same electrode (E Cu Sn C) and technique as those used for copper.

> Take great care when welding brass and bronze because their fumes are highly toxic. Wear a respirator and perform the work in a well-ventilated area.

POINTS TO REMEMBER

- Make certain that you know the type of metal that is to be welded.
- Metals melt at different temperatures. Make sure that you know the melting point of the metal to be welded.
- The cleaner the metal is, the more chance you have of success.
- Most thin sections require support during welding.
- Do not overlook the effects of expansion and contraction.
- Try to estimate these effects and take steps to prevent or correct them.
- Match the welding rod to the job.
- Use a flux sparingly.
- Be careful of toxic fumes.
- Study the job well before starting to weld. Try to think of obstacles ahead of time.

WORDS TO REMEMBER

preheat   malleable   toxic
cold welding   brittle   ductility
studding   support

REVIEW QUESTIONS

1. What is the purpose of preheating the metal?
2. What precaution should be observed with regard to the use of flux?
3. To what colour must cast iron be preheated?
4. Is the whole casting or just part of the casting preheated?
5. If a vee is prepared on a cast iron piece, what further steps should be taken before welding?
6. What are the characteristics of a good braze weld.
7. What is the best procedure to use on malleable iron?
8. What are the seven points that generally apply to nonferrous metals?
9. What is the purpose of the puddling rod in welding aluminum?
10. What is the procedure for arc welding aluminum?
11. What precautions must be observed when welding white metal?
12. What type of flame is used for welding white metal?
13. What effect could expansion and contraction have on copper?
14. What is the safety hazard when welding brass or bronze?
15. What type of electrode is used for welding brass and bronze?
16. Why should the metal be cleaned before welding?
17. Why is it necessary to support the metal, especially if the pieces of metal are very thin?
18. Why is it necessary to use a larger size welding tip for copper welding than for steel welding, even if the metals are the same thickness?
19. Under what condition would cast iron not be braze welded?
20. Aluminum conducts heat more quickly than iron or steel. What effect does this have on choosing a tip size for welding?
21. Why should a lap joint be avoided in aluminum welding?
22. In arc welding a thin piece of copper, why is it necessary to reduce the amperage as the weld progresses?
23. Obtain several pieces of nonferrous metals of approximately the same size and thickness. Apply the welding flame to them and note the following points of comparison.
    a. speed at which they melt,
    b. time required to melt,
    c. colour change while heating,
    d. fumes given off, if any.
24. Why does cast iron lend itself to braze welding?

19

POSITIONAL WELDING

The welder who can weld out of position or perform positional welding is well on the way to becoming a skilled craftsman. The same equipment is used as in other welding processes. The joints will also be the same ones on which you have already practised in previous exercises. However, you will find them in positions other than flat. Because of the effects of gravity, the weld metal will tend to flow downwards. In this and subsequent chapters, you will be able to develop skill in directing the weld metal where you want it to go.

19-1 WELDING POSITIONS

Welding out of position simply means that the joint to be welded is not placed in the flat position as in previous exercises. There are four basic welding positions: **flat, vertical, horizontal,** and **overhead** (figures 19-1 and 19-2). These positions are used for all welding processes, and they remain the same regardless of which process

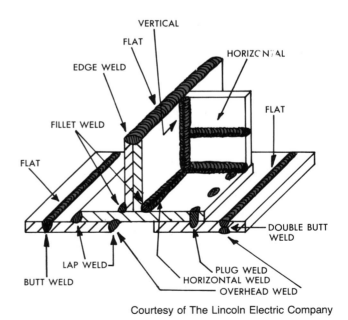

Courtesy of The Lincoln Electric Company

Figure 19-1   Welds and positions

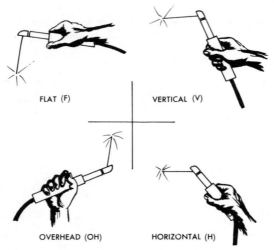

FLAT (F)   VERTICAL (V)

OVERHEAD (OH)   HORIZONTAL (H)

Courtesy of The Lincoln Electric Company

Figure 19-2   Basic welding positions

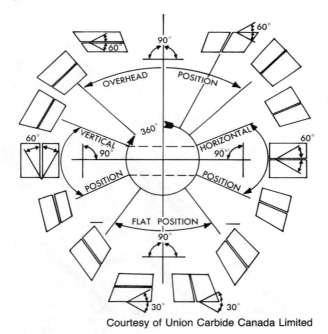

Courtesy of Union Carbide Canada Limited

Figure 19-3   Welding positions

is used. The welding itself is not changed by the position. That is, a corner joint is still a corner joint whether it is done in the flat, vertical, or overhead position. The bead and the weave also remain the same. The only

difference is the position in which the weld metal is deposited.

The angles at which the joint may be tilted before it is considered to have changed position are shown in Figure 19-3.

All of the previous exercises can be practised in these different positions. The remarks regarding flaws, that is, porosity, undercut, and buildup, remain the same no matter what the position of the joint being welded. After learning a few basic fundamentals peculiar to out-of-position welding, you will find that it is no more difficult than welding in the flat position.

TIME ECONOMY

Welding out of position is performed only when necessary. It is time-consuming and should be avoided whenever possible. However, a lot of out-of-position welding is still done in industry, and the skilled welder should be able to weld in any of the positions discussed above.

Figure 19-4 shows how time-consuming welding out of position is. In Figure 19-4A a fillet weld is being made in the vertical position from the bottom up. Every minute 115 mm (or 5 in.) of joint are welded. In Figure 19-4B the same joint is welded in the flat position. The speed has been increased to 300 mm (or 12 in.) of joint every minute. In Figure 19-4C the same joint has been tilted at a 10° angle, and the welding speed has been increased to 490 mm (or 20 in.) every minute. At an angle of 10°, the joint is still considered to be in the flat position.

BASICS

When welding out of position, the following points must be remembered.

Flat welding. The weld metal is laid on top of the base metal. The base metal acts as a support.

Vertical welding. The base metal acts as only a partial support, and the weld metal that has already been deposited must be used as an aid (Figure 19-5).

Horizontal welding. As in vertical welding, the base metal gives only partial support, and the deposited weld metal must be used as an aid.

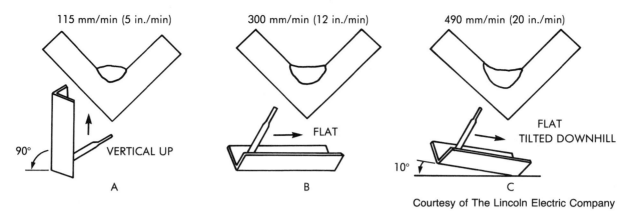

Figure 19-4   Position versus speed

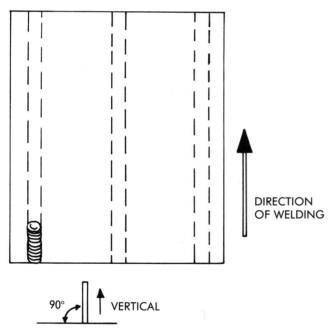

Figure 19-5   A vertical bead

Overhead welding. The base metal supports the molten weld metal only slightly.

Little difficulty will be experienced in vertical or overhead welding if the puddle is kept flat or shallow and not allowed to form a large drop. The flat puddle will adhere (stick) to the base metal more easily than a large drop.

In vertical, horizontal, and overhead welding, there is little support from the base metal. The molten puddle is liquid and will fall or run down the base metal unless it is prevented. The welder is able to keep the molten puddle flat and place it where desired by skilful manipulation of both the welding rod and the torch in oxyfuel welding and of the welding rod in arc welding.

TEST YOUR KNOWLEDGE

1. What does welding out of position mean?
2. Name the four basic welding positions.
3. What effect does welding out of position have on the type of weld or joint design?
4. How does welding out of position compare to welding in the flat position with regard to porosity and other flaws?
5. What is the difference between welding in the flat position and welding in the vertical position with regard to speed?
6. Name three points that must be remembered when welding out of position.
7. In which position does the base metal provide the least support for the weld metal?
8. Why should the puddle be kept flat or shallow in vertical or overhead welding?

9. How is the welder able to keep the puddle shallow?

10. What would happen to the molten puddle if it were not kept shallow in the vertical position?

11. In which direction is the torch pointed when welding a butt joint in the overhead position?

19-2 OXY-ACETYLENE WELDING: VERTICAL POSITION

Vertical welding is performed in one of two ways, from the bottom of the joint to the top (**vertical up**) or from the top of the joint to the bottom (**vertical down**). Most vertical oxy-acetylene welding is done vertical up. Welding in the vertical position with oxy-acetylene is not difficult if the points already mentioned are kept in mind, that is, metal support, keeping the puddle flat, and correct manipulation of the welding rod and torch.

Since either single beads or weaves are the two fundamental operations in welding, the following exercises will be devoted to giving you practice in performing these welds in different positions.

EXERCISE #1
STEPS IN RUNNING A BEAD

1. Obtain a piece of metal, and place in position as shown in Figure 19-6. The metal must be secured to prevent it from falling.

2. It will be easier if the metal is placed at a 45° angle, then raised to 90° as skill is developed.

3. Obtain a welding rod, and set the torch pressures.

4. Light the torch, and adjust to a neutral flame.

5. Start a small puddle at the bottom of the metal (Figure 19-7).

6. Add welding rod (from the top) to the puddle in a rhythmic motion (Figure 19-8). The movement is similar to that used when welding in the flat position.

7. Watch the puddle carefully. If it starts to run down, flick the torch to the side and allow the

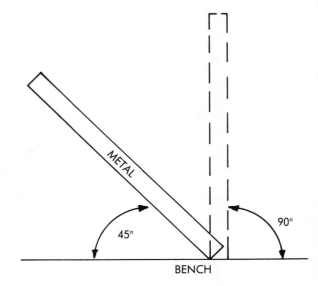

Figure 19-6   Beginning position

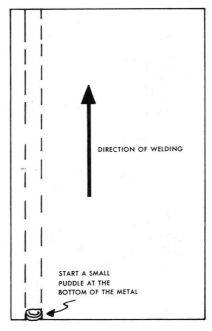

Figure 19-7   Starting puddle

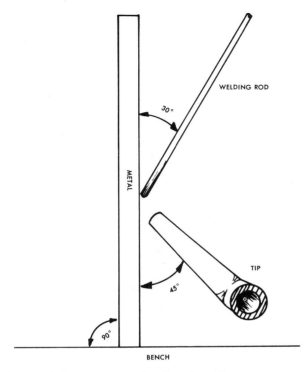

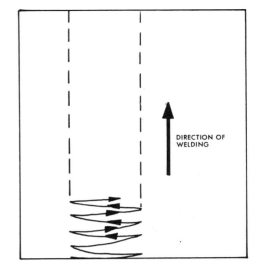

Figure 19-9   Weaving

Figure 19-8   Position of rod and torch

puddle to cool. Then start over again from the point where you stopped.

8. The torch should be held so that the flame is pointing upwards to help control the molten puddle.

WEAVING

As you learned in previous chapters, weaving is a steady movement from side to side that is required to deposit a wider bead (Figure 19-9). No difficulty occurs in doing this weld in the vertical up position if the puddle is kept flat.

The torch and the welding rod are kept at approximately the same angles as when running a single bead (Figure 19-10). In the case of weaving, however, the torch and the welding rod are moved in a zigzag manner and are kept on opposite sides of the weld, that is, when

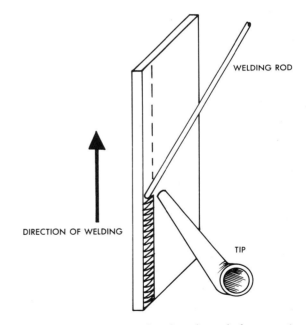

Figure 19-10   Position of rod and torch for weaving

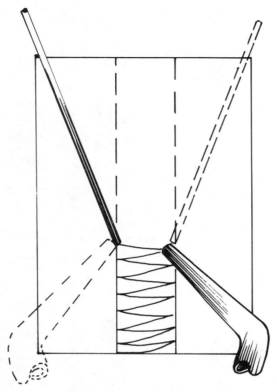

Figure 19-11   Proper torch and rod manipulation in weaving

the torch is at the right of the puddle, the welding rod is at the left (Figure 19-11). The welding rod is kept in the molten puddle during welding. Note that it is not dipped in and out as when running a single bead.

EXERCISE #2
WELDING A BUTT JOINT: VERTICAL UP POSITION

1. Obtain two pieces of mild steel 75 mm × 150 mm × 1.5 mm (or 3 in. × 6 in. × 1/16 in.).
2. Obtain a welding rod of copper coated mild steel (1.5 mm or 1/16 in.).
3. Set torch pressures for tip selected.
4. Tack weld pieces of metal in a butt joint with a gap of 1.5 mm (1/16 in.). (This can be done in the flat position.)

5. Secure the butt joint in the vertical position.
6. Light the torch and concentrate flame on the tack weld at the bottom of joint.
7. Hold torch at the angle shown in figures 19-8, 19-12, and 19-13.

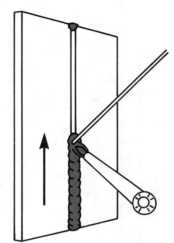

Figure 19-12   Welding a butt joint in the vertical up position

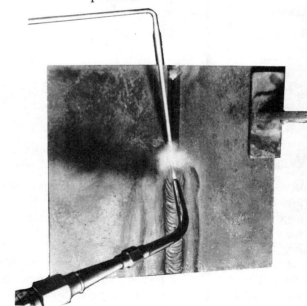

Courtesy of Union Carbide Canada Limited

Figure 19-13   Correct position of rod and torch for vertical welding

232   Positional Welding

8. Keep the welding rod in the outer flame to reheat.
9. As soon as the tack weld begins to melt, add more welding rod.
10. Continue slowly up the joint, adding rod as the puddle melts.
11. Be sure to keep the puddle flat.
12. Remember that if the puddle becomes too fluid it will run down.
13. When the top tack weld is reached, a gradual withdrawal of the torch and extra addition of welding rod will prevent the top of the joint from burning away.

19-3 OXY-ACETYLENE WELDING: HORIZONTAL AND OVERHEAD POSITIONS

As can be seen from Figure 19-14, a butt joint welded in the vertical position is not very different in appearance from a butt joint welded in the flat position. Welding a butt joint in the horizontal position is perhaps the most difficult procedure to master. Figure 19-15 shows a horizontal butt joint.

Courtesy of Union Carbide Canada Limited

Figure 19-14   Vertical butt joint

Courtesy of Union Carbide Canada Limited

Figure 19-15   Horizontal butt joint

EXERCISE #3 WELDING A BUTT JOINT: HORIZONTAL POSITION

1. Obtain two pieces of metal 75 mm × 150 mm × 1.5 mm (or 3 in. × 6 in. × 1/16 in.).
2. Obtain a welding rod of copper-coated mild steel (1.5 mm or 1/16 in.).
3. Set torch pressures for the tip selected.
4. Tack weld in a butt joint with a gap of 1.5 mm (1/16 in.).
5. Secure the butt joint in the horizontal position as shown in Figure 19-16.

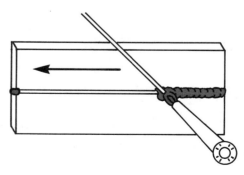

Figure 19-16   Welding a butt joint in the horizontal position

6. Light the torch and concentrate the flame at the tack weld at the end of plate.

7. Point torch slightly upwards at a 10° to 15° angle.

8. Keep the welding rod in the outer flame to preheat.

9. As soon as the tack weld begins to melt, add the welding rod.

10. Continue slowly across the joint from right to left (if you are left-handed, you should reverse direction).

11. Feed the welding rod from the top in order to keep top plate from burning away.

12. Manipulate the torch in a crescent shape motion from top to bottom in order to spread heat and to control the puddle.

OVERHEAD POSITION

In overhead welding with the oxy-acetylene process, the flame must be carefully controlled and the welding rod properly manipulated to prevent the molten metal from forming too large a puddle and dropping out of the joint.

In Figure 19-17 note how the torch points straight into the weld when welding a butt joint in the overhead position.

EXERCISE #4
WELDING A BUTT JOINT: OVERHEAD POSITION

1. Obtain two pieces of metal 75 mm × 150 mm × 1.5 mm (3 in. × 6 in. × 1/16 in.).

2. Obtain a copper-coated mild-steel welding rod, 1.5 mm (1/16 in.).

3. Set torch pressure for the tip selected.

4. Tack weld in a butt joint with a gap of 1.5 mm (1/16 in.) between the two pieces of metal.

5. Secure the butt joint in the overhead position, as shown in Figure 19-17A.

6. Light the torch and concentrate the flame at the tack weld at the right-hand end of the joint (for welders who are right-handed).

7. Point the torch upward at a 10° to 15° angle from the metal.

8. Keep the welding rod in the outer flame to preheat.

9. As soon as the tack weld begins to melt, add the welding rod.

10. Continue slowly across the joint from right to left. (If you are left-handed, you should reverse direction.)

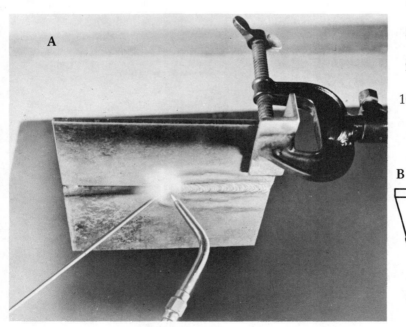

A

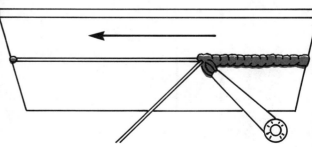

B

Courtesy of Union Carbide Canada Limited

Figure 19-17   Welding a butt joint in the overhead position

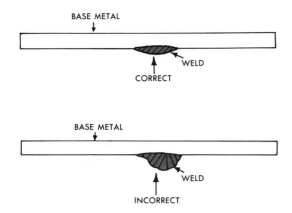

Figure 19-18   Overhead welding

11. Add the welding rod to the puddle in front of the torch (as shown in Figure 19-17B).
12. Practise keeping the molten puddle small. Remember that gravity will tend to pull the molten metal down, as shown in Figure 19-18.

19-4 WELDING HEAVIER METALS

After mastering the fundamentals of positional welding on light-gauge metals, the next step is to prepare joints

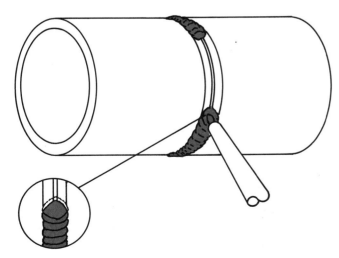

Figure 19-19   The keyhole method

in heavier metal and to practise welding them. Techniques are similar with welding light and heavy gauge metal. However, larger tips and welding rods are required for heavier metal. To obtain full strength when welding groove or butt joints, complete penetration is necessary. To achieve this penetration in heavy metals, many experienced welders use what is commonly referred to as the **keyhole method**.

When the joint has been properly assembled and set up, a hole is punched (melted) through the groove at the beginning of the weld. Since a weld is simply a series of layers placed one on top of the other, the welder only needs to move the torch or electrode ahead, enlarge the hole, then come back and deposit a layer of weld metal (Figure 19-19). This technique is carried out on the full length of the joint, but the hole remains the same size throughout the entire operation. This technique gives a smooth, uniform, even weld and good penetration. Patience and practice is required to do this, but it is well worthwhile. It is the technique used by highly skilled welders who, among other things, can earn top wages.

19-5 ARC WELDING: VERTICAL POSITION

Welding in the vertical position may be performed up or down. Each has a certain advantage. Welding up deposits more weld metal and will require fewer passes to fill large areas. It also results in more penetration (if done properly) and gives the beginner more control over the molten puddle. Welding down (starting at the top of the metal) is used mostly on light-gauge metal. It is very easy, if the slag is not allowed to run ahead of the weld metal. Welding down is faster and causes less distortion, but it does not deposit as much weld metal as in welding vertical up.

EXERCISE #5 STEPS IN RUNNING A BEAD DOWN

1. Obtain a piece of metal, and place it in position for vertical welding.
2. Obtain an electrode, set the machine, and turn it on.

3. The electrode should be held at an angle of 50° to 60° as shown in Figure 19-20.
4. Strike the arc, and make a puddle at the top of the metal.
5. Move the electrode down in a straight line, keeping a short arc.
6. Watch the puddle carefully. The slag should not be allowed to run ahead of the weld metal.
7. If the slag does run ahead of the weld metal, stop, chip, and restart the weld where you stopped.

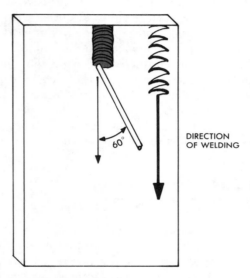

Figure 19-20   Running a bead vertical down

EXERCISE #6
STEPS IN RUNNING A BEAD UP

1. Place a piece of metal in position for vertical welding (Figure 19-6).
2. Obtain an electrode, and set the machine.
3. The electrode should be held so that it is pointing upwards 5° to 10°.
4. Turn on the machine, strike the arc, and make a puddle at the bottom of the metal.
5. Deposit a small amount of metal, and stop.
6. Immediately restrike the arc, and deposit more metal. Stop again.

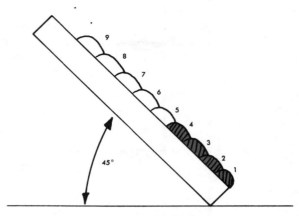

Figure 19-21   Building up a bead

7. The second deposit should be partly on top of and partly above the first deposit (Figure 19-21). The deposits are placed like building blocks, one on top of the other.
8. Continue these steps until the top of the metal has been reached.
9. Chip, clean, and check the weld.

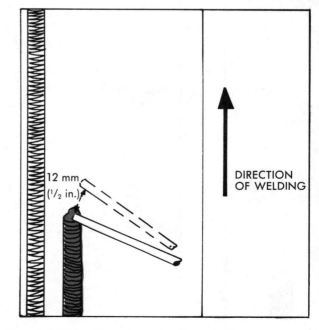

Figure 19-22   Running a bead vertical up

This is the method used in welding vertical up. However, the experienced welder does not stop between each deposit. He or she merely flicks the electrode away, allowing the weld to solidify as shown in Figure 19-22.

As you become more skilled, you will find that you can quicken the pace until you no longer stop between deposits, but merely move the electrode away from the weld about 12 mm (or 1/2 in.) by holding a long arc and then return to deposit more metal.

WEAVING UP AND DOWN

The same procedures and techniques are used for weaving vertical as are used for weaving in the flat position. The only difference is in the position of the metal (figures 19-23 and 19-24). As was mentioned earlier, the puddle must be kept flat or shallow and must not be allowed to form a large drop. In weaving vertical (up or down), particular attention must be paid to the sides of the weld. Moving away from the sides too rapidly will cause undercut. To avoid undercut, hesitate at the sides (marked x in Figure 19-25). This hesitation allows the metal to build up there.

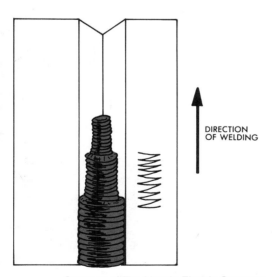

Courtesy of The Lincoln Electric Company

Figure 19-23   Weaving vertical up

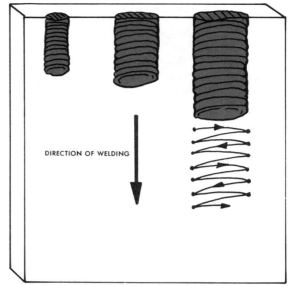

Courtesy of The Lincoln Electric Company

Figure 19-24   Weaving vertical down

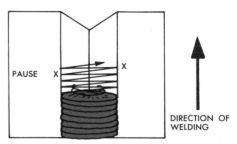

Courtesy of The Lincoln Electric Company

Figure 19-25   Preventing undercut

EXERCISE #7
WELDING A SINGLE VEE BUTT JOINT: VERTICAL UP POSITION (WITH DCRP)

1. Obtain two pieces of mild steel 75 mm × 250 mm × 6 mm (or 3 in. × 10 in. × 1/4 in.).
2. Obtain a welding rod: E41010 (E6010); 3 mm (or 1/8 in.).
3. Prepare the edges of the metal in a 30° bevel with a 1.5 mm (or 1/16 in.) land (see Chapter 23) or

Arc Welding: Vertical   **237**

use the plates to form a corner joint for expediency.

4. Assemble the joint with a 1.5 mm (or 1/16 in.) gap, tack welding at each end.

5. Secure the joint in the vertical position (Figure 19-26).

6. Position the electrode so that it is pointing upwards at 10° to 20° and is facing directly into the centre of the joint (see Figure 19-27).

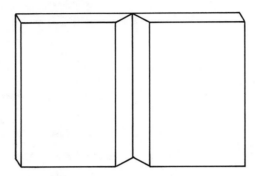

Figure 19-26   A single-vee butt joint in vertical position

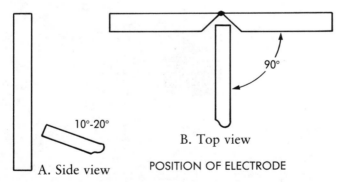

Figure 19-27   Position of the electrode in arc welding a single-vee butt joint vertical up

7. Start at the bottom of the joint and form a small ledge. Proceed upwards using a short whipping motion.

8. Continue until the top of the joint has been reached. Remember to maintain a short arc and a

whipping motion, and do not let the arc extinguish. If possible, establish a keyhole at the start.

9. Clean the weld and examine the back or root side of the joint. Complete penetration should be observed and the face pass should be smooth and flat.

10. Commence the second pass using a slight weaving motion as shown in Figure 19-25 to prevent undercut.

11. Continue to the top; then chip and clean the weld.

EXERCISE #8
WELDING A TEE JOINT: VERTICAL UP POSITION (WITH DCRP)

1. Obtain two pieces of mild steel 75 mm × 250 mm × 6 mm (or 3 in. × 10 in. × 1/4 in.).

2. Obtain a welding rod: E41010 (E6010); 3 mm (or 1/8 in.).

3. Assemble the joint and tack weld at each end. Clean tack welds.

4. Secure the joint in the vertical position.

5. Position the electrode so that it is pointing upwards at a 10° to 20° angle and facing directly into the centre of the joint (Figure 19-28).

6. Start at the bottom of the joint and proceed to weld upwards, using a short whipping motion.

7. Continue until the top of the joint has been reached.

8. Chip and clean the first pass. Check for irregularities.

9. For each succeeding pass, use a slight weaving motion pausing at the edges to avoid undercut.

10. Chip and clean each pass, checking for undercut and smoothness.

Do the same weld again, but this time, use a low hydrogen electrode E48018 CH (controlled hydrogen) (E7018). This electrode can be used with AC or DCRP. Try both. When using this electrode, do not

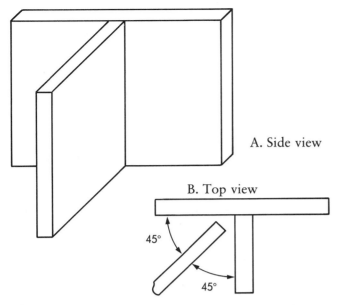

A. Side view

B. Top view

45°
45°

Figure 19-28   Fillet weld on a tee joint: vertical up

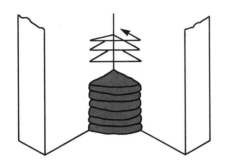

Figure 19-29   Block weaving

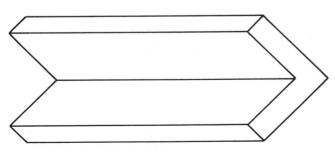

Figure 19-30   Angle iron

whip the electrode. Use a block movement as shown in Figure 19-29.

> **Note**
> To save time in preparation and to allow for more welding practice time, an angle iron (Figure 19-30) may be substituted for the tee joint. For testing purposes, however, a tee joint will be necessary.

19-6 ARC WELDING: OVERHEAD POSITION

Welding in the overhead position is not difficult if you remember to keep the puddle flat. Do not attempt to deposit too much weld metal at one time. Practise the same exercises as before (beads, butt, and fillet welds), but in the overhead position (Figure 19-31).

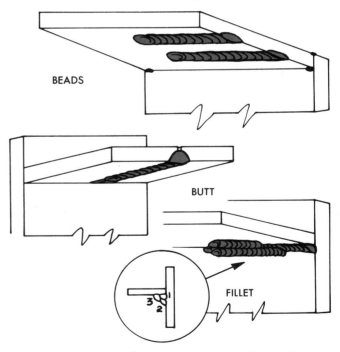

BEADS

BUTT

FILLET

Courtesy of The Lincoln Electric Company

Figure 19-31   Overhead welding

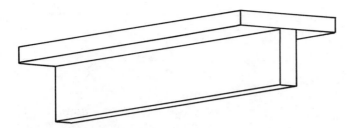

Figure 19-32   Overhead tee joint

EXERCISE #9
WELDING A TEE JOINT: OVERHEAD POSITION (WITH DCRP)

1. Obtain two pieces of mild steel 75 mm × 250 mm × 6 mm (or 3 in. × 10 in. × 1/4 in.).
2. Obtain a welding rod: E41010 (E6010); 3 mm (or 1/8 in.).
3. Assemble the tee joint (Figure 19-32), tack weld at each end and clean the tacks.
4. Secure the joint in the overhead position.
5. Position electrode so that it is 20° to 30° from the vertical plate and is leaning 5° to 15° in the direction of travel.

6. Start welding at the left-hand side of joint. Proceed to weld along the joint using a short back and forward whipping motion.
7. Hold a short arc all the time that the weld is in progress.
8. Continue until the weld is complete. Clean and check the weld.
9. If multiple passes are to be made, the second pass should be placed between the first pass and the vertical plate so that the second weld half overlaps the first pass.
10. Similarly, if a third pass is made, it should be directed between the first weld and the top or horizontal plate (Figure 19-33).

19-7 PIPE WELDING

Pipe welding is a highly skilled welding operation. Pipe welders are paid a good salary. Any of the welding processes can be used for pipe welding. However, specific aspects of pipe welding are mentioned here because the skills required are more a matter of position than of process. No matter which process is used, the technique is almost the same as welding a single-vee butt joint on plate (with or without a backing strip). The difference between welding pipe and plate is that, in pipe welding, continual adjustments must be made to the angle of the torch, gun, or electrode to ensure complete penetration. In order to ensure complete penetration, one should be

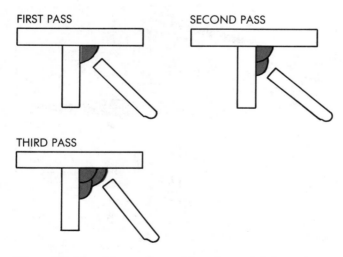

Figure 19-33   Electrode position for multiple passes

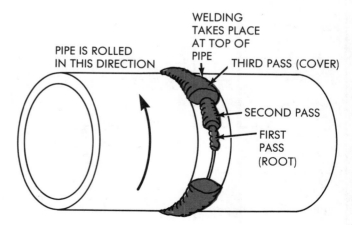

Figure 19-34   Pipe welding in the flat position

familiar with the **keyhole** technique described earlier. Also, the angle must constantly be adjusted for a circumferential (circular) weld. Pipes may be welded in all positions. They may be welded using stringer beads or weaves or a combination of both.

Figure 19-34 illustrates welding a pipe in the **flat position**. The pipe is rotated so that welding is always carried out at the top of the pipe. In this illustration three passes are being placed in the groove. Figure 19-35 shows how the groove is welded in the **horizontal position**. Usually the passes are placed in stringer beads.

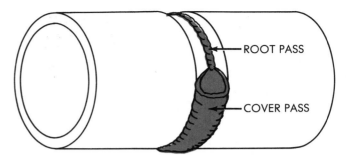
Figure 19-37 Fixed position

Sometimes a "cover" or "wash" pass is welded over the stringer passes as a final weld. This weld is applied in a circular motion with a quick sweep down and a little hesitation at the bottom of the sweep (Figure 19-36). Figure 19-37 shows a weld being made in the **fixed position**. This requires the welder to weld around the pipe without moving it. The welds are made in the flat, vertical and overhead positions. The normal practice is to start at the bottom of the pipe and weld up both sides. However, in certain circumstances, the weld will be started at the top and welded down on both sides as in vertical down welding (Figure 19-38).

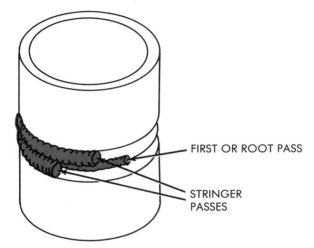
Figure 19-35 Pipe welding in the horizontal position

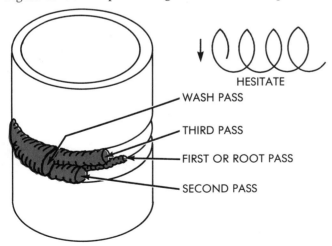
Figure 19-36 Pipe welding in the horizontal position with a wash pass

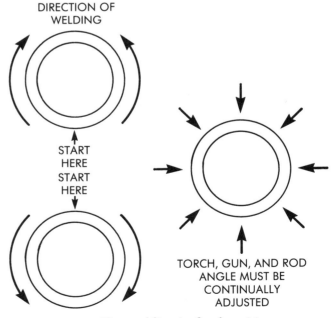
Figure 19-38 Pipe welding in fixed position

TEST YOUR KNOWLEDGE

1. In vertical welding, why is it easier to place the metal at a 45° angle when beginning?
2. What is the basic difference between running a bead vertical and weaving vertical?
3. What is the difference between welding vertical up and welding vertical down in arc welding?
4. What are the two main points to be observed when welding with the arc in the overhead position?

POINTS TO REMEMBER

- There are four basic welding positions.
- The same welding processes can be used in all of these positions.
- The type of joint does not change, only the position.
- Out-of-position welding is performed only when necessary.
- A skilled welder should be able to weld in any position.
- Out-of-position welding is time consuming.
- Metal support plays an important part in out-of-position welding as does the cohesiveness of the puddle.
- The puddle must be kept shallow.
- Hesitating at the sides of a weave will eliminate undercut.

WORDS TO REMEMBER

flat	overhead	undercut
horizontal	manipulation	whipping
vertical	control	flick
		downhand

REVIEW QUESTIONS

1. How many basic welding positions are there?
2. Give one example illustrating that welding out of position takes longer than welding in the flat position.
3. What is the reason for insisting that the puddle be kept flat in overhead welding?
4. Which welding position provides the most metal support for the weld metal? Explain why in your own words.
5. What are the advantages of welding "vertical up" as compared to welding "vertical down" in arc welding?
6. Why is the electrode flicked away in welding vertical up?
7. Based on the speeds shown in Figure 19-4 how long will it take to weld a joint 1.5 m (5 ft.) long in the vertical and the flat positions?
8. Using the same speeds assume that a joint 30 m (100 ft.) long has been welded in the flat position. How much faster could it have been welded if it had been tilted 10°?
9. If out-of-position welding is time consuming, why is it used at all?
10. What is meant by the fixed position in pipe welding?
11. What is the main difference between welding pipe and welding plate?
12. What is a "cover" or "wash" pass?
13. In order to ensure complete penetration, what technique is used?
14. In what positions are pipes welded?

CHAPTER

20

HARD SURFACING

Hard surfacing is an industry in itself. Many welded or fabricated assemblies are hard surfaced when new to meet the special applications for which the assembly will be used—for example, pipeline valves, gear teeth, and bulldozer blades and teeth. Many other items are repaired with the hard surfacing process because of wear, friction, and corrosion. These items are repaired and/or rebuilt to their original shape at a fraction of the cost of a new assembly.

Any welding process may be used for hard surfacing, and any one of a wide variety of welding rods, powders, and fluxes may be used. Students desiring positions in the hard surfacing industry would do well to study chemistry and metallurgy in addition to learning the necessary welding skills.

In this chapter, only two of the wide variety of hard surfacing processes will be discussed. These are the oxy-acetylene and the shielded arc welding processes, the first an oxyfuel process and the second an arc welding process.

20-1 BACKGROUND

As the name implies, hard surfacing is the application, to a piece of metal, of a coating or surface that is harder than the base or parent metal. This surface is applied for a number of reasons:
- to resist corrosion,
- for protection against high temperatures or sudden temperature changes,
- to resist wear caused by abrasion, erosion, friction, or impact.

The providing of a wear-resistant surface is probably the most important of these applications. Figure 20-1 shows one step in the hard surfacing operation.

The hardening process was probably first used when metal weapons were forged. The method would have involved heating the sword and quenching it in a liquid solution to obtain a hard surface with a soft centre. This method was no doubt replaced by the blacksmith actually applying a hard metal on top of a softer metal. This method was probably used in the making of farm implements. Today, of course, hard surfacing is an industry in itself. The process is used to rebuild worn parts, or is applied to a new part that will be subject to wear.

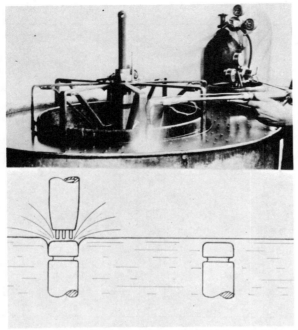

Courtesy of Union Carbide Canada Limited

Figure 20-1　Quenching in solution

Any or all of the welding processes may be used for hard surfacing. Carbon arc, oxy-acetylene, manual, semi-automatic, or automatic arc welding are all suitable. Sometimes the hard surface material may be sprayed on a piece of metal. This method is quite popular for re-building shafts which rotate in lathe type machines. There are many types of hard surfacing materials available, each one designed for a specific purpose. They may be applied in powder (Figure 20-2) or welding rod form. Some of the metals used in hard surfacing materials are iron, chromium, tungsten, manganese, silicon, carbon, cobalt, and nickel.

ADVANTAGES

Some of the advantages of hard surfacing are: (1) cheaper and softer metals can be used as a base metal with a harder surface applied; (2) due to the wear-resistant quality of the hard surface material, a piece of equipment will last longer; (3) many pieces of equipment can be salvaged.

In earlier years, hard surfacing was sometimes referred to as "Stelliting". Stellite is a trade name for a specific hard surfacing material. It is actually a class of hard cobalt alloys containing very small amounts of tungsten and chromium. In small work shops, hard surfacing is usually done with the oxy-acetylene or arc welding process.

20-2 HARD SURFACING WITH THE OXY-ACETYLENE PROCESS

For hard surfacing with oxy-acetylene, a standard oxy-acetylene torch is used. The selection of a tip size, however, is an important factor. The tip should have an orifice one size larger than would be used for steel welding of the same part. To prevent cracking, it is important that the part to be hard surfaced be preheated. (See Table 20-1 for more instructions on preheating.)

EXERCISE #1

1. Hold the torch so that excess acetylene flame is 30°-60° from the surface of the metal.
2. The tip of the inner cone should be approximately 3 mm (or 1/16 in.) from the metal.

Courtesy of The Lincoln Electric Company

Figure 20-2　Hard surfacing material

TABLE 20-1 PREHEATING INSTRUCTIONS

Base Metal	Preheat
Small steel parts containing up to 0.4% carbon	Preheat with torch and cool slowly away from draughts
Large steel parts containing up to 0.4% carbon and small parts of high-carbon and low alloy steels	Preheat 230°C–340°C (450°F–644°F) using auxiliary heat source and enclosing part in firebricks, etc. Cool slowly in sand, ashes, etc.
Large parts of mild steel that require a large area of hard surfacing, or large parts of high-carbon or low alloy steel	Preheat 400°C–490°C (752°F–914°F) using auxiliary heat source and enclosure. Cool slowly as above or in enclosure with controlled cooling
Air-hardening steel but not stainless steel	Preheat 593°C–648°C (1150°F–1198°F) using auxiliary heat source. Cool large parts slowly in a furnace. Small parts may be cooled in dry sand etc. *Note: a large area of deposit should be avoided on these metals*
Austenitic stainless steel (nonhardening) of welding quality	Preheat 593°C–648°C (1150°F-1198°F) using auxiliary heat source and cool slowly
12.14% Manganese (Austenitic) steel	Use arc welding process, keep cool by staggering welds, or weld on alternate jobs

3. Hold the flame in this position until the surface of the metal starts to show a glazed appearance. This is called "sweating".

4. Hold the welding rod so that it touches the surface of the metal and the inner cone is almost touching the welding rod.

> **Note**
> If the first drop of molten metal from the welding rod does not spread uniformly, or if it bubbles or foams, this is an indication that the base metal is too cold. It is not at the proper sweating temperature.

5. Spread the molten metal from the welding rod by withdrawing the rod and by manipulating the puddle with the flame. Do not spread the puddle with the welding rod.

6. Continue adding metal by dipping the welding rod into the molten puddle and by manipulating the torch until the desired area has been covered.

> **Note**
> If any dirt or scale appears in the puddle, float it to the surface with the flame manipulation. If it will not float to the surface, dislodge it with the welding rod. In extreme cases, it may be necessary to use a good cast iron welding flux.

7. Do not try to build up too much in one pass. If there is over a 3 mm (or 1/16 in.) deposit, use more than one pass.

8. If cracks or holes appear, preheat the part and re-melt the deposit in the immediate vicinity of the flaw. Flick any particles of slag or oxide from the puddle with the welding rod. Then add a little more deposit. If the flaw still appears, grind the flaw out. Then preheat and reweld.

20-3 STEPS FOR REPAIRING AUTOMOBILE VALVES WITH OXY-ACETYLENE

For this operation, you will need only oxy-acetylene equipment and old or used automobile valves. Your school's auto shop should be able to provide the valves. No special skills are required. If you can handle a torch, you should become proficient after practising on a few valves. Cracked valves present no great problem. The welding process of depositing the hard surfacing material actually welds the seating surface together. Valves too thin to be reground can be built up to their original

thickness by this method. It is claimed by one manufacturer that valves hard surfaced by their material will last up to six times longer than regular steel valves. Hard surfacing is a relatively simple and effective process. It is outlined in the following exercise.

EXERCISE #2

1. On a standard valve-grinding machine, clean off seating surface for welding.
2. Place the valve, with stem up, on a carbon fixture or carbon block.
3. Use an oxy-acetylene torch tip of approximately #50 drill size or its equivalent. Adjust the flame so that the acetylene feather is three times the length of the inner cone, 32 mm to 38 mm (or 1 1/4 in. to 1 1/2 in.) long.
4. Bring the seating surface up to sweating heat for approximately 12 mm (or 1/2 in.) in circumference (Figure 20-3). The carbon fixture will absorb some of the heat and prevent overmelting.
5. Deposit welds on the thin melted surface of the

Figure 20-3   Valve being heated to sweating

Courtesy of Deloro Stellite

Figure 20-4   Manipulating the puddle

Courtesy of Deloro Stellite

valve. The deposit need be no more than 1.5 mm (or 1/16 in.) thick. Always direct the inner cone of the flame on the molten pool. Keep melting drops of the welding rod into the molten pool on the valve face.

6. Continue to make the hard surfacing material flow around the circumference of the valve. Make sure that the valve is sweating just ahead of the molten pool at all times (Figure 20-4). On a 38 mm (1 1/2 in.) diameter valve, this should take approximately 1 1/2 minutes.

7. Complete the weld back to the starting point. Then remelt that place at the start and draw the torch away slowly from the deposit. This will prevent cracks caused by shrinkage at the start of the weld.

8. Rough-grind the deposit in a standard valve-grinding machine with a coarse grit.

9. Finish grinding the deposit to a mirror finish on a standard valve-grinding machine using a fine-grit grinding wheel.

As mentioned previously, the process you have just learned is an inexpensive one. The prices that follow are probably incorrect today because of inflation.

However, they show some of the savings that can be achieved by using hard surfacing instead of replacing parts. The following data was taken on a set of eight 38 mm (1 1/2 in.) diameter valves:

OPERATION	TIME (minutes)
Preparation by grinding: Less time than regular valve grinding because only the seating surface has to be cleaned	15 min
Depositing hard surfacing material: This includes time to preheat the valves up to welding temperature with the torch	12 min
Rough grinding deposit: Using a coarse standard stone in machine	12 min
Finish grinding: Using a fine grinding stone	8 min
Set-up time: Includes changing torch tip, changing wheels on grinding machine, trueing the stones, cleaning the valve grinder, buffing the valve stems	13 min
TOTAL TIME	60 min

Costs for Material and Time

Labour for one set of these valves at $12.00 per hour	$12.00
Cost of surfacing material (8 valves at $0.30 per valve)	2.40
Cost of welding gas	2.00
TOTAL COST	$16.40
Cost for 8 new steel valves at $10.00 each	$80.00
SAVINGS	$63.60

20-4 HARD SURFACING WITH SMAW

SMAW does not result in a pure deposit on the first pass or bead, as there is a certain amount of dilution by the base metal. This dilution produces a softer than normal surface. It has reduced resistance to wear, and will actually increase the toughness of the deposited metal.

EXERCISE #3

1. An AC or DC current may be used. As in steel welding, the choice will depend on the type of electrode. However, if AC is used, the machine should have an open circuit voltage (OCV) of at least 100 A. If DC is used, the electrode should be on reverse polarity. The amperage should be kept as low as possible, since only a surface weld is required.

2. Choose a flux-coated rod, rather than an uncoated rod. It will produce a smoother, flatter bead, which is less susceptible to cracking or blowholes. (There will also be less spatter or loss of deposited metal.)

3. For thin or narrow beads or when building up an edge, small-size electrodes should be used.

4. Hold the electrode almost vertical to the surface. Do not weave. Weaving can cause slag entrapment.

5. As in padding, straight beads should be applied. Keep penetration to a minimum.

6. If the bead requires a wider deposit, the beads should be applied side by side, with each bead overlapping the previous one by approximately one-third.

7. Each bead should be thoroughly cleaned before the next bead is deposited.

8. On large sections or parts (Figure 20-5), it is sometimes advantageous to use the skip method of welding. This means weld a piece, miss a piece, then weld another piece. In this way, you avoid concentrating the heat, which could cause overheating and make the base metal brittle.

Some modifications to this process may be made. If the part to be surfaced is badly worn, it may be built up to almost the correct height by ordinary arc welding electrodes. A layer of hard surfacing material is then applied. Sometimes, stainless steel electrodes or low hydrogen electrodes are used with a final deposit of hard surfacing material. As a temporary repair, an experienced welder may use an ordinary cast iron oxy-acetylene welding rod in an arc welding holder to create a hard surface.

POINTS TO REMEMBER

- Any or all of the welding processes may be used.
- There are many types of hard surfacing materials.
- To prevent cracking, it is important to preheat the part to be surfaced.
- The base metal must be brought to a "sweating" condition.
- The selection of tip size is important in the oxy-acetylene process.
- Do not try to build up too much in one pass.
- In arc welding, weaving should be avoided.
- Each bead should be thoroughly cleaned before depositing the next one.
- The choice of arc welding current will depend on the type of electrode.

WORDS TO REMEMBER

hard surfacing	friction	erosion
impact	corrosion	flaw
abrasion	sweating	

Figure 20-5
Hard surfacing a large auger using
an arc welding process

Courtesy of The Lincoln Electric Company

REVIEW QUESTIONS

1. Why are base metal parts coated with hard surfacing material?
2. When hard surfacing with SMAW and DC, which polarity is used?
3. What does the term "sweating" mean in the application of hard surfacing material?
4. Which type of oxy-acetylene flame is used for the hard surfacing process?

5. What are the characteristics of
   a. too much acetylene?
   b. too little acetylene?
6. Why is it advisable to preheat the base metal before applying the hard surfacing material?
7. What distance should the tip of the inner cone be from the base metal?
8. What torch angles are recommended when using the oxy-acetylene process for hard surfacing?
9. What defect can be caused by weaving with SMAW?

5

BASIC THEORY

21

METALLURGY

Very early in history, people discovered metal and realized how useful it could be. For centuries we have shaped and joined pieces of metal to make tools, utensils, weapons, and ornaments (Figure 21-1).

Weapons made of copper dating back to 4000 B.C. have been found in Egypt. Bronze pots and pans dating back to 2000 B.C. have also been found. Iron seems to have become popular around 1500 B.C. and at one time was considered more valuable than gold.

These metals were either used in their pure or original state or they were combined with other metals to make alloys. Today, most metals are alloys. A successful welder must be able to recognize various metals because different welding methods are used for different compositions of metals.

21-1 COMMON TYPES OF METALS

Metals are divided into two categories: ferrous metals, which contain iron, and nonferrous metals, which contain no iron. The table on the next page shows some of the metals in each category.

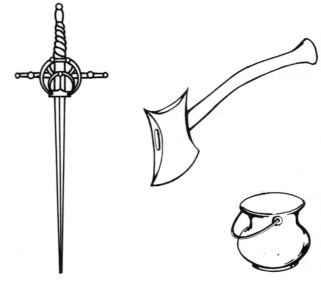

Figure 21-1   Ancient tools, weapons, and utensils

FERROUS METALS	NONFERROUS METALS	
Iron	Aluminum	Silver
Cast Iron	Copper	Brass
Steel	Lead	Bronze
Alloy Steels	Tin	Gold
Galvanized Iron	Nickel	Platinum
Tin Plate	Zinc	Pewter

ALLOYS

Making an alloy is similar to making a cake. When flour and water are mixed and baked, a plain cake is the result. Similarly, when a pure metal is processed and baked or cooked a **base metal** is the result. The plain cake can be varied by the addition of food colouring, flavouring, fruit, and other items. Similarly, the base metal can be varied by the addition of other elements and metals (Figure 21-2).

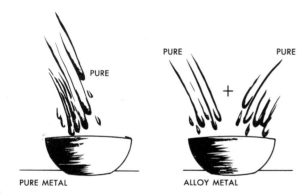

PURE

PURE   PURE

+

PURE METAL   ALLOY METAL

Figure 21-2   Metals and alloys

TEST YOUR KNOWLEDGE

1. Why must a welder be able to recognize certain metals?
2. What is meant by a pure metal?
3. What is meant by an alloy metal?
4. What is meant by nonferrous?
5. Is aluminum a ferrous or nonferrous metal?
6. Which of the following metals are ferrous: copper, lead, tin plate, silver, brass?

FERROUS METALS

Ferrous metal is a metal containing or made from iron and other elements. Iron is the most common and useful of all metals.

Pig iron is the iron obtained from the blast furnace. It is not used for manufacturing because it is brittle and still has many impurities.

Pure iron is made by removing the impurities in pig iron. Pure iron is of little use in manufacturing, except to make an alloy, because it is too soft. However, it is essential in the making of steel.

Wrought iron is made by adding scrap iron and ore to the pig iron, then heating the mixture in a special furnace. The mixture is worked into large balls of metal in the furnace. When they are removed, they are hammered and rolled so that some of the slag is trapped inside the metal. Wrought iron is soft and can be bent and worked into many shapes, such as horseshoes, chains, and ornamental railings. However, this metal has been largely replaced by mild steel in the manufacture of these products.

Cast iron is made by adding carbon and other ingredients to molten iron. The method of casting determines the type of cast iron produced. There are several different types of cast iron.

Steel, a hard strong ferrous metal, is made from refined iron to which other elements have been added to produce many different kinds of steel. Carbon is the main ingredient added to molten iron to produce steel. These are some of the different varieties of steels:

Low carbon steel (mild steel) contains small amounts of carbon. It is used in the manufacture of chains, nails, pipes, and structural shapes.

Medium carbon steel has a greater amount of carbon than mild steel and is used for axles and shafts.

High carbon steel has even higher carbon content. It is used for automobile springs, anvils, and saw blades.

Very high carbon steel has more carbon than the other three, but less than cast iron. It is used to make chisels, knives, and files.

Cast steels are steels which have been cast into shape rather than formed.

Alloy steels are produced by adding certain other elements. For example, nickel and chromium are added to produce stainless steel. Tungsten is added to produce sharp cutting edges. Manganese is added to produce hard cutting edges.

> **Note**
> The above ingredients can be added in different quantities and mixed to produce other kinds of metals. The actual control and manufacture of these metals is a complicated process.

NONFERROUS METALS

Aluminum in its pure state is like pure iron in that it is of little value in manufacturing. However, when other elements or metals are added, it can be used in thousands of items, ranging from aircraft and automobile parts to candy bar wrappers.

Copper is used in cooking utensils and electrical equipment. When it is mixed, or alloyed, with tin, a metal called **bronze** is produced. When it is alloyed with zinc, a metal called **brass** is produced.

Lead is one of the oldest metals known. It is used, among other things, to make type metal, solder, and paint pigments.

Zinc alloyed with copper produces brass. Die-cast parts for automobiles and the galvanized coating which protects metals are also made from zinc.

Nickel is used in the manufacture of stainless steels, monel metal (a nickel/copper alloy), and coins.

Tin is used to coat mild steel plate, to form tin cans, and is alloyed with copper to produce bronze.

Magnesium is similar in appearance to aluminum, but has much less mass. It is used mainly in the manufacture of aircraft parts.

Pure gold is too soft to be used alone, and for commercial use, it is alloyed with other metals. These alloying metals produce a variation in the characteristics of the gold, for example, in the colour. Gold is usually measured in carats. Pure gold is 24-carat gold.

Silver is rarely used in its pure form. Coins, table ware, and jewellery are always made of a silver alloy.

Sterling silver is required by law to contain at least 0.927 parts of silver.

As space exploration continues, so does the demand for metals that can be used in spacecraft. These metals have been produced because of the need for less mass, more strength, and higher resistance to heat, corrosion, and erosion. A number of new metals are being used successfully in spacecraft (Figure 21-3). Although these metals present certain problems in welding, solutions are being found. Some of the new metals are:

columbium	molybdenum	tantalum
titanium	vanadium	zirconium

Figure 21-3   Space-age metals

APPROXIMATE MELTING POINTS OF METALS

Metals melt at different temperatures. Table 21-1 shows the melting points of the more common metals.

TABLE 21-1 MELTING POINTS OF COMMON METALS

Metal	Melting Point	
	(°C)	(°F)
Tin	232°C	449°F
Lead	343°C	629°F
Zinc	419°C	786°F
Aluminum	621-648°C	1150-1198°F
Bronze	882-915°C	1620-1679°F
Brass	926-982°C	1699-1800°F
Silver	960°C	1760°F
Copper	1082°C	1980°F
Cast Iron	1232°C	2300°F
Monel Metal	1343°C	2440°F
High Carbon Steel	1371°C	2500°F
Medium Carbon Steel	1426°C	2600°F
Stainless Steel	1426°C	2600°F
Nickel	1449°C	2650°F
Low Carbon Steel	1510°C	2700°F
Wrought Iron	1593°C	2850°F
Tungsten	3410°C	6084°F

TEST YOUR KNOWLEDGE

1. What is the advantage of wrought iron?
2. What is the difference between very high carbon steel and cast iron?
3. What items can be made from medium carbon steel?
4. What is the difference between bronze and brass?
5. Name two new metals used in spacecraft.
6. Which has the higher melting point: lead or aluminum?
7. Which has the higher melting point: cast iron or wrought iron?
8. Which has the higher melting point: silver or nickel?

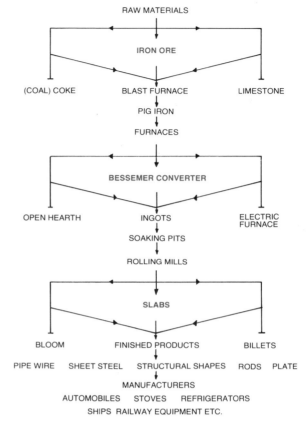

Figure 21-4   Manufacture of steel

21-2 IRON AND STEEL MAKING

Every day, people use hundreds of articles made of steel. Three basic materials, **iron ore**, **coal**, and **limestone** are needed to make this widely used product. In order to smelt the iron out of the ore, extremely high temperatures are necessary. **Coal**, the basic fuel, cannot produce this high temperature until it has been turned into **coke**. This is done in a coking oven (Figure 21-5).

MAKING STEEL

The first step in making steel is obtaining iron from the iron ore. This is done in a blast furnace. Alternate layers of iron ore, coke, and limestone are charged into the top

Courtesy Stelco

Figure 21-5   Pushing coke from an oven

of the furnace, a high cylindrical steel structure lined with heat-resistant brick. Superheated air is blown upwards in the furnace as the mixture of iron ore, coke, and limestone is coming down. The resultant heat separates the iron from the ore. Liquid iron accumulates at the bottom of the furnace, while a layer of slag forms above the iron. This is a continuous process and the slag and iron are drained off periodically (Figure 21-6). The iron is sent to the steel-making furnaces and the slag is converted to materials used in the construction industry.

There are various types of steel-making furnaces, including the Bessemer Converter, the Electric Furnace, the Open Hearth Furnace, and the Oxygen Furnace. Each has a different design and characteristic but they all produce steel. The mixture of molten iron, scrap metal, limestone, and other elements are very closely controlled to produce the type of steel required. When the steel is ready it is poured into **moulds** (this is sometimes called teeming), and allowed to cool. When cooled, the moulds are stripped off, leaving a solid piece of metal called an **ingot**. The ingots are then reheated to a uniform temperature in soaking pits before being sent to the shaping mills for processing.

In the shaping mills, rollers under extremely high pressure shape the reheated ingots into **blooms**, **billets**, and **slabs**. Blooms are usually square in cross-section as are billets, but billets are much smaller. Slabs have a rectangular shape. (Figures 21-7 and 21-8 show operations in the shaping mill.)

The next operation takes place at the rod and bar mill or the plate and strip mill. In the **rod mill**, the billets are reduced by the pressure of the rolls to small-diameter rods which will eventually become wire, nuts, bolts, nails, and screws. In the bar mill, such shapes as angle iron, tee bars, zee bars, and round and square bars are produced.

In the **plate mill** (see Figure 21-9), plates of varying widths and thicknesses are produced for ships, structural members, locomotives, large pipes, and tanks. Steel that has to be rolled thinner than plate is reduced in **hot strip mills**, and is used in truck bodies, railroad cars, line pipe and electrical appliances. The steel may also be sent to the **cold reduction mills**.

Extremely high pressures and speeds are used in some of these mills. In the cold reduction mill, for example, it is not unusual to use pressures of 20 685 MPa (2955 psi), speeds upon entering of 185 m/min (600 ft./min), and

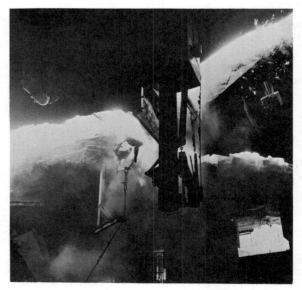

Courtesy Stelco

Figure 21-6   The blast furnace

speeds on leaving the mill of up to 1040 m/min (3400 ft./min).

Figure 21-10 shows the production of galvanized metal by the cold rolled method, where the zinc coating is

Courtesy Stelco

Figure 21-9   Plate leaves the finishing stand of a plate mill

Courtesy Stelco

Figure 21-7   Shaping an ingot in the shaping mill

Courtesy Stelco

Figure 21-8   A scarfer removes surface impurities from steel in the shaping mill

Courtesy Stelco

Figure 21-10   Galvanizing cold rolled sheet on the continuous galvanizing line applied in the same operation. These strips are coiled into huge rolls ready for transportation in one complete operation (Figure 21-11). The metal may also be annealed. This is the process of softening a metal by heating it and then cooling it at a slow rate. Figure 21-12 shows the annealing line at a steel plant.

Courtesy United States Steel Corporation

Figure 21-11   Finished metal rolled into coils

21-3 STEEL CLASSIFICATION

The terms low, medium, and high carbon in reference to steel indicate the amount of carbon in the steel in only a general way. Steel-making, however, is an exact science and a highly controlled manufacturing process. There are many more formal methods of identifying or classifying steels. Some of the agencies that establish these classifications are the S.A.E. (Society of Automotive Engineers), the A.S.T.M. (American Society for Testing Metals), and the A.I.S.I. (American Iron and Steel Institute). They all identify or classify metals. Since the method used by each is similar, let us look at just one method, the S.A.E. method. This system is based on the chemical analysis of the steel and uses a four-digit numbering system.

The **first digit** indicates the type of steel:

1 Carbon steel	6 Chromium vanadium steel
2 Nickel steel	
3 Nickel chromium steel	7 Tungsten steel
4 Molybdenum steel	8 No classification
5 Chromium steel	9 Silicon manganese steel

Courtesy United States Steel Corporation

Figure 21-12   An overall view of the continuous annealing line in the plant

TABLE 21-2 ELEMENTS USED IN STEEL, AND THEIR FUNCTIONS

Element	Purpose
Aluminum	deoxidizing, purifying
Boron	hardening
Carbon	hardening
Chromium	hardening, strengthening, antirust
Cobalt	hardening, strengthening
Copper	hardening, strengthening, antirust
Manganese	strengthening, toughening
Molybdenum	hardening, antirust, antishock
Nickel	toughening, strengthening, ductility
Phosphorus	This is not added to steel as it is already present as an impurity. However, a small amount improves strength, machinability, and antirust qualities
Silicon	strengthening, giving magnetic quality
Titanium	strengthening at high temperatures
Tungsten	hardening, toughening
Vanadium	hardening, toughening

The **second digit** indicates the percentage of alloy in the steel, for example, 10XX. The first "0" indicates there is no alloying element, that is, it is a plain carbon steel.

The **third** and **fourth digits** together indicate the carbon content of the steel. In 1010, for instance, the second 10 indicates that there are 10/100 of 1% carbon in the steel. 1010 would be classified as a low carbon steel. (It is the steel that is used as a core wire in most steel welding electrodes.) Table 21-2 outlines the main elements used in steel and the functions they perform.

THE MAIN ELEMENTS IN STEEL MAKING

Carbon. As stated previously, pure iron is soft and malleable. Having low tensile strength and hardness, it is of little commercial value. However, pure iron is the basic material for steels and cast irons. Significant changes in the mechanical properties of iron occur with the addition of small amounts of carbon. Iron with a carbon content of up to 0.3% is called mild steel. With 0.3% to 0.6% carbon, the metal is called plain carbon steel. At 0.6% to 1.7% it is called high carbon steel. Metal containing more than 1.7% carbon is called cast iron.

Manganese. Carbon is not the only element used in steel making. Manganese is an essential ingredient in steel because it promotes soundness and eliminates gas holes. Most important, it combines with sulphur to form manganese sulphide (MnS). A manganese content up to 1% is not unusual, although a 0.4% to 0.8% content is normal. Manganese will also give higher tensile strength and hardness to the metal without affecting ductility.

Chromium is added to steel to increase hardness and abrasion resistance.

Nickel is added for shock resistance and is used with chromium to form a wide variety of stainless steels.

Silicon does not directly affect the mechanical properties of metal but is generally present in small quantities up to 0.4% and combines with oxygen in the steel to form silicon dioxide. This floats to the top of the molten pool during production, thereby removing oxygen from the steel. If quantities greater than 0.4% are present, it has been added as an alloy for the purpose of giving magnetic properties to low carbon steel. This prevents the steel from scaling at high temperatures.

Oxygen forms iron oxides with the molten iron. This is undesirable because the oxides make the steel weak, brittle, and porous. For this reason, elements like silicon are added as deoxidizers.

Sulphur forms sulphide, which makes steel very brittle at high temperatures. This is called **hot shortness**, which means that the steel cannot be forged or worked without danger of cracking. One of the reasons for adding manganese in steel making is to eliminate or control the sulphur content.

Phosphorous. The presence of phosphorous in steel will greatly affect the ductility of the metal. This is known as **cold shortness**. Both the sulphur and the phosphorous limits are closely controlled in the manufacture of commercial steel.

BYPRODUCTS OF STEEL PRODUCTION

Steel can be manufactured into a vast range of products. In addition, however, many other familiar products depend on the byproducts of steel making for their basic ingredients.

During the coking process, gases in the form of heavy brown vapours are given off. These gases contain valuable chemicals that can be recovered.

One of the first products that can be obtained from these gases is **crude tar**. This coal tar is a heavy black viscous material that can be used for treating fish nets, or can be used as a rust inhibitor, or for roofing and sheathing materials.

Creosote can be extracted from the tar for use as a wood preservative. The tar can be separated into pitches of various consistency for road surfacing, roofing material, electrodes, metal coatings and masonry and pipeline protective materials.

Acids from the coal tar can be used as **resins** for making plastics, adhesives, and laminates as well as paint removers, metal cleaners, antiseptic solutions, and pharmaceuticals.

Napthalene, in its pure state, is used for insect repellants such as mothballs. It can also be used to make resins for paint and plastics.

Besides the tars and acids, light oil can also be recovered from the gases. This oil, when chemically treated and distilled, produces the following colourless liquids:

Benzol. This is used to make synthetic rubber, plastics, textiles, nylon, dyes, detergents, headache tablets, weed killers, and photographic chemicals.

Figure 21-13   A major steel company's research centre

Courtesy Stelco

Toluol. This is used for high-quality lacquers for auto finishes, food preservatives, perfumes, food flavours, certain dyes, drugs, bleaches, explosives, and aviation fuel.

Xylol. This is used as a diluting agent for plastic resins, paints, varnishes, and synthetic fibres like Dacron.

Ammonia from the gases, when converted to anhydrous ammonia, is used as a chemical fertilizer and a steel conditioner.

After all these byproducts have been extracted, the gas that is left can be reused as **a fuel gas** in the steel mill itself.

Even the **slag** that is formed in the iron-making furnaces is not discarded. It is crushed and graded for size and all iron particles removed. This slag is then used for home insulation, roofing gravel, ballast on railway tracks, and as an aggregate in concrete and asphalt mixes. Waste water is also recycled and acid and iron particles removed. The iron particles are used for magnetic tapes and for other purposes. Iron dust, scale, and even scrap steel are all recycled.

21-4 METAL IDENTIFICATION

To examine and identify all metals, industry has many well-equipped laboratories, expensive machinery, and trained technicians. Welders can use simple methods. By repeated practice one can become expert at spotting the differences among metal types. One test alone may determine the metal. However, several tests are usually required to be certain. The following are the more common tests.

Colour. Most of us are familiar with the colours of common metals:

METAL	COLOUR
Copper	Red
Brass	Yellow
Bronze	Gold
Cast iron	Gray
Stainless steel	Silver
Aluminum	White

Mass. By simply putting a piece of aluminum on one end of a scale and a piece of lead of the same dimension on the other, you can tell that the lead has more mass (Figure 21-14). The differences in masses of other metals are not always so obvious, however. These are some of the common metals, listed in order from least to greatest mass.

1. Aluminum	5. Nickel	9. Gold
2. Zinc	6. Copper	10. Platinum
3. Tin	7. Silver	
4. Iron	8. Lead	

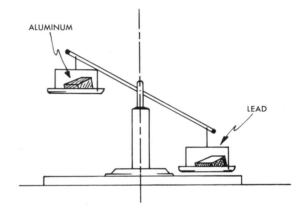

Figure 21-14 Mass or weight test

Flame test. Another test that may be used is the reaction of metals to heat. Different metals react differently under a source of heat. Compare a piece of aluminum and a piece of magnesium of the same size. Unless special equipment were used, the colour and mass of both pieces would be very similar. However, if some filings are shaved off each one and the flame of the torch applied to them, the aluminum filings will melt while the magnesium filings will burn with a white, brilliant light (Figure 21-15).

Magnet test. This is a very simple test which immediately separates the ferrous from the nonferrous metals. Apply a magnet to the metal. If the metal is attracted by the magnet, the metal is ferrous (Figure 21-16).

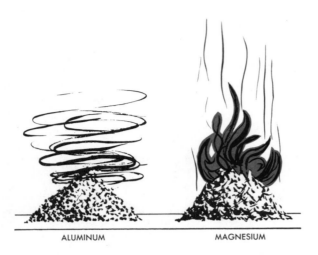

ALUMINUM   MAGNESIUM

Figure 21-15   Flame test

Spark test. Another method of identifying metals is to grind them on a grinding wheel and check the spark given off by the metal. Figure 21-17 shows different tests, including the spark test, which can help identify different kinds of steel and iron.

> Ferrous metals will be attracted to a magnet. Nonferrous metals will not be attracted to a magnet. Remember: NONferrous will be NONmagnetic.

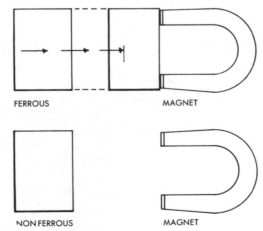

FERROUS   MAGNET

NON FERROUS   MAGNET

Figure 21-16   Magnet test

> Ferrous metals give off a spark. Nonferrous metals will not give off a spark. Remember: NONferrous will not spark.

Let us say that a piece has been broken off a casting and you want to know what kind of metal it is. Cast iron and cast steel are similar in colour, mass, and appearance. Both are also magnetic, but if you test them by grinding, the cast iron will give off a red spark, and the cast steel, a white-yellow spark.

POINTS TO REMEMBER

- An alloy is a mixture of metals.
- Metals can be divided into two categories: ferrous and nonferrous.
- Different metals melt at different temperatures.
- Different metals or elements are mixed to produce different alloys.
- New metals and alloys are still being produced.
- A welder must be able to identify at least all the common metals.
- Remember that one test may not be sufficient for complete identification of a metal.
- Nonferrous means nonmagnetic; nonferrous means no spark.
- The colour, mass, flame, magnet, and spark tests are the most common tests used.
- Three basic materials, iron ore, coal, limestone are required to make steel.
- The coal must first be turned into coke.
- Each steel-making furnace has a different characteristic.
- Extremely high pressure is used to shape the metal.
- Silicon does not directly affect the mechanical properties of the metal to which it is added, except in specific cases.
- As in welding operations, iron oxides are undesirable in the molten metal.
- Sulphur makes steel very brittle at high temperatures, creating a condition called hot shortness.
- Phosphorous will greatly affect the ductility of the metal, creating a condition called cold shortness.

TEST \ METAL	manganese steel	stainless steel	cast iron	wrought iron
appearance	DULL CAST SURFACE	BRIGHT, SILVERY SMOOTH	DULL GREY EVIDENCE OF SAND MOLD	LIGHT GREY SMOOTH
magnetic	NON MAGNETIC	DEPENDS ON EXACT ANALYSIS	STRONGLY MAGNETIC	STRONGLY MAGNETIC
chisel	EXTREMELY HARD TO CHISEL	CONTINUOUS CHIP SMOOTH BRIGHT COLOR	SMALL CHIPS ABOUT 3 mm NOT EASY TO CHIP, BRITTLE	CONTINUOUS CHIP SMOOTH EDGES SOFT AND EASILY CUT AND CHIPPED
fracture	COARSE GRAINED	DEPENDS ON TYPE BRIGHT	BRITTLE	BRIGHT GREY FIBROUS APPEARANCE
flame	MELTS FAST BECOMES BRIGHT RED BEFORE MELTING	MELTS FAST BECOMES BRIGHT RED BEFORE MELTING	MELTS SLOWLY BECOMES DULL RED BEFORE MELTING	MELTS FAST BECOMES BRIGHT RED BEFORE MELTING
 Spark *For best results, use at least 1500 m/min. on grinding equipment. (Cir. × r/min. 1000 = metres per minute)	 Bright White Fan-Shaped Burst	 1. Nickel-Black Shape close to wheel. 2. Moly-Short Arrow Shape Tongue (only). 3. Vanadium-Long Spearpoint Tongue (only).	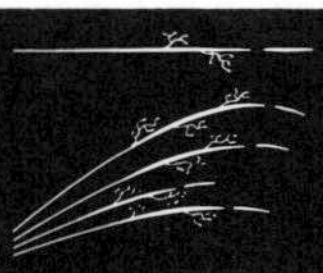 Red Carrier Lines (Very little carbon exists)	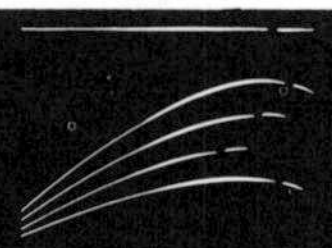 Long Straw Color Lines (Practically free of bursts or sprigs)

TEST \ METAL	low carbon steel	medium carbon steel	high carbon steel	high sulphur steel
appearance	DARK GREY	DARK GREY	DARK GREY	DARK GREY
magnetic	STRONGLY MAGNETIC	STRONGLY MAGNETIC	STRONGLY MAGNETIC	STRONGLY MAGNETIC
chisel	CONTINUOUS CHIP SMOOTH EDGES CHIPS EASILY	CONTINUOUS CHIP SMOOTH EDGES CHIPS EASILY	HARD TO CHIP CAN BE CONTINUOUS	CONTINUOUS CHIP SMOOTH EDGES CHIPS EASILY
fracture	BRIGHT GREY	VERY LIGHT GREY	VERY LIGHT GREY	BRIGHT GREY FINE GRAIN
flame	MELTS FAST BECOMES BRIGHT RED BEFORE MELTING	MELTS FAST BECOMES BRIGHT RED BEFORE MELTING	MELTS FAST BECOMES BRIGHT RED BEFORE MELTING	MELTS FAST BECOMES BRIGHT RED BEFORE MELTING
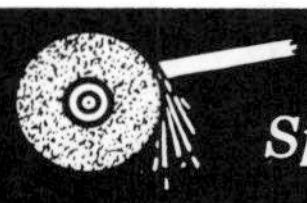 Spark* *For best results, use at least 1500 m/min. on grinding equipment. (Cir. × r/min. 1000 = metres per minute)	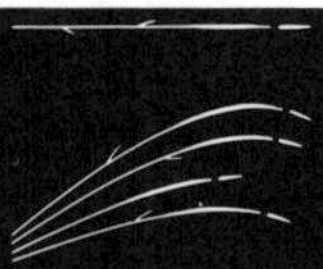 Long Yellow Carrier Lines (Approx. .20% carbon or below)	 Yellow Lines Sprigs Very Plain Now (Approx. .20% to .45% carbon)	 Yellow Lines Bright Burst Very Clear Numerous Star Burst (Approx. .45% carbon and above)	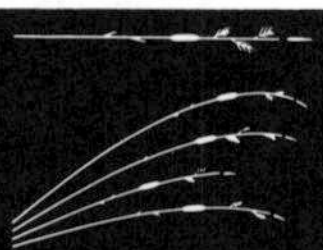 Swelling Carrier Lines Cigar Shape

Courtesy of Hobart Brothers Company

Figure 21-17 Tests for the identification of iron and steel

WORDS TO REMEMBER

alloy	limestone	silicon
ferrous	blast furnace	sulphur
colour	Bessemer	phosphorous
mass	converter	viscous
spark	open hearth	creosote
carbon	furnace	resins
corrosion	teeming	napthalene
base metal	ingot	benzol
nonferrous	moulds	toluol
pure metal	blooms	xylol
magnet	slabs	ammonia
iron ore	hot strip mills	anhydrous
coke	cold reduction mills	

REVIEW QUESTIONS

1. Name two metals used in ancient times.
2. Explain the difference between pure and alloy metals.
3. What are the two main categories into which metals are divided?
4. In which of these categories does steel belong?
5. What is the difference between the melting point of cast iron and that of low carbon steel?
6. What is pig iron used for?
7. How many types of cast iron are there?
8. Is tin or zinc added to copper to produce brass?
9. What is the purpose of adding tungsten to steel?
10. What are the three basic materials needed to make steel?
11. What is the purpose of a coking oven?
12. What is the purpose of a blast furnace?
13. Name four furnaces that are used in the steel-making operation.
14. What is meant by the term "teeming"?
15. What is an ingot?
16. What are the soaking pits used for?
17. List at least five byproducts of the steelmaking operation.
18. Explain how some of these byproducts are used in industry.
19. Explain the S.A.E. method of identifying metals.
20. List at least four elements used in steel making and state the purpose of each element.
21. Describe two tests used to identify metals.
22. Describe the colour difference between brass and bronze.
23. Do the following metals have greater or less mass than iron: tin, silver, copper, gold?
24. Describe one method of determining whether a piece of metal is aluminum or magnesium.
25. What information can be derived by applying a magnet to a piece of metal?
26. Of what advantage is the spark test for identifying metals?
27. Find out what type of metal is used mainly in aircraft manufacturing. Explain why this metal is preferred.
28. Find out what difference there is between the metal used in an automobile body and the metal used in automobile springs. Explain the reason for using different metals.
29. Explain in your own words why it is necessary for a welder to be able to identify metals.
30. Obtain pieces of various metals. Compare them under the following headings: metal, magnet, colour, mass, flame.

22

EXPANSION AND CONTRACTION

Any metal that is welded is subject to uneven heating and cooling. A welder should understand that this can affect the assembly that is being welded. It can cause distortion (in which the metal is bent out of shape), cracked welds, or welds that may be under such severe stress that they can crack when in service (Figure 22-1). This chapter outlines many of the methods used in industry to prevent or control distortion, as well as methods of relieving stress.

22-1 THE LAWS OF EXPANSION AND CONTRACTION

The art of welding will bring you into contact with the laws of expansion and contraction. To be a successful welder, you must understand these laws.

1. When a metal is heated, it expands (increases in size).
2. When a metal is cooled, it contracts (gets smaller).

To understand these laws, look at Figure 22-2. The bar is broken at X. If this assembly is welded, there will be no ill effects because the metal bar is free to expand and contract at the ends, Y and Z.

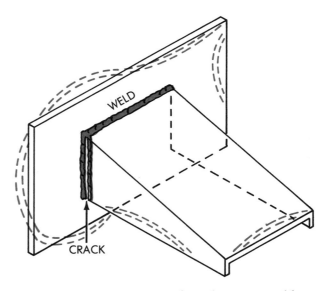

Figure 22-1   Distortion and cracking in a weld

In Figure 22-3, however, the broken bar has now become the middle member of a frame with the break at location A. If the weld is made in the same manner as the previous example, it will be found that, as the metal surrounding break A starts to cool, the ends D

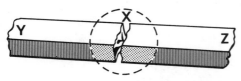

Figure 22-2　Cracked bar for repair

Courtesy MECO St. Louis, U.S.A.

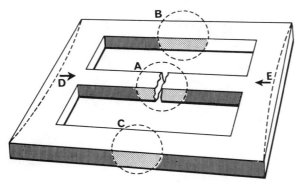

Courtesy MECO St. Louis, U.S.A.

Figure 22-3　Frame assembly

and E will not be free to contract because they are rigidly held by B and C. This would result in the metal bowing in, as shown by the arrows, or in the weld breaking again.

One method of offsetting the effects of expansion and contraction is to preheat certain areas of the assembly. For example, in Figure 22-3, if the parts B and C were heated at the spots indicated by the circles before welding, the break at A would open up. The weld could then be made; as the frame cooled, each part would contract the same amount.

There is nothing new or mysterious about expansion and contraction. All major or large assemblies are built with expansion joints included. These joints can be seen on such assemblies as bridges, railway lines, and piping systems. The forces of expansion and contraction cannot be prevented. However, they can be controlled.

TEST YOUR KNOWLEDGE

1. What happens to metal when it is heated?
2. What happens to metal as it cools?

3. Why were there no ill effects when the bar in Figure 22-2 was welded?
4. What could cause bowing or cracking in Figure 22-3?
5. Why are the members B and C heated prior to welding?
6. Give two examples of places where expansion joints are used.
7. Can the forces of expansion and contraction be prevented?
8. How can the above forces be controlled? Give an example.

The main reason for studying the forces of expansion and contraction is that they produce a condition known as **distortion**. There are three main types of distortion (see Figure 22-4).

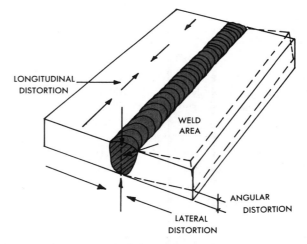

Figure 22-4　Types of distortion in butt joints

1. **Lateral distortion** is distortion across the weld.
2. **Longitudinal distortion** is distortion along the length of the weld.
3. **Angular distortion** is distortion where the metal pieces are pulled from the horizontal or vertical plane. Distortion in tee joints is usually angular (Figure 22-5).

Distortion can be controlled by carefully studying the assembly before welding and by using common sense. There are many methods of controlling distortion. A few are outlined in this chapter.

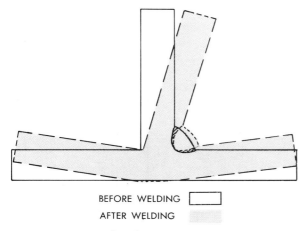

Figure 22-5   Angular distortion in tee joints

TEST YOUR KNOWLEDGE

1. What is the main reason for studying expansion and contraction?
2. What are the three main types of distortion?
3. What is the meaning of lateral distortion?
4. In which direction is longitudinal distortion caused?
5. What type of distortion is usually produced in tee joints?

22-2 CONTROLLING DISTORTION

The effect of heating the surface of steel may be readily demonstrated by placing a bar of steel in a vise (Figure 22-6). Use a piece about 25 mm wide, 12 mm thick, and about 200 mm long (or 1 in. × 1/2 in. × 8 in.). The 25 mm (or 1 in.) face, near the vise, is heated for a few seconds with a torch. The free end of the bar bends away from the heat source. When the flame is removed, the metal begins to cool, and the bar begins to straighten out.

As the metal cools even more, this process continues until there is a reverse and a permanent bend in the bar. Thus, when a metal is distorted by heat, it is not always possible to restore the original shape merely by reheating

the metal and allowing it to cool. Let us apply this idea to the two most common joints used in industry, the butt joint and the tee joint.

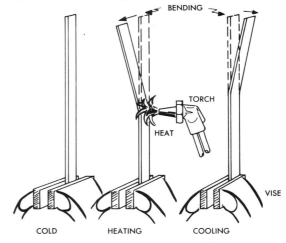

Figure 22-6   Heating and cooling effects

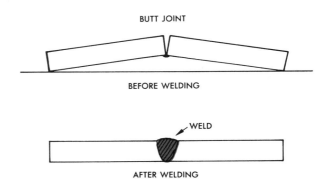

Figure 22-7   Presetting a butt joint

BUTT JOINTS

Figure 22-7 shows one method of controlling distortion. The amount of distortion is estimated, and the metal is set at an angle to allow for this. In other words the pieces are set out of alignment deliberately, so that the welding will pull them back to the proper alignment.

Butt joints may also be kept straight by using clamps and a backing material (Figure 22-8). Care must be taken to allow the pieces to move out and in, but not up and down.

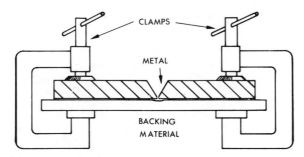

Figure 22-8 Clamping a butt joint

The use of heavy bars (**strongbacks**), or an arrangement as shown in Figure 22-9, will greatly assist in controlling distortion. This method is used frequently in the assembly of ships or large oil tankers where there are many butt joints. The welder applies the strongback just before starting to weld the joint.

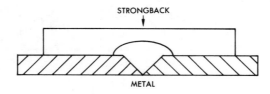

Figure 22-9 Strongback or retainer

The backstep method of welding is often employed on long seams or butt joints and is **most effective** in reducing distortion. Each weld is made in the direction of the arrow shown in Figure 22-10, so that each weld finishes where the previous weld was started.

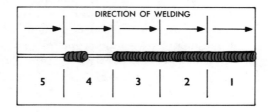

Figure 22-10 Backstep welding

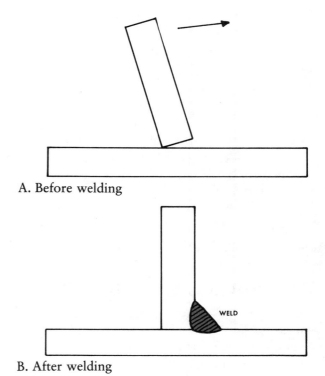

A. Before welding

B. After welding

Figure 22-11 Presetting a tee joint

TEE JOINTS

Figure 22-11 shows how to preset the pieces of metal so that the vertical piece is pulled into position by the contraction of the weld metal. This method is similar to the one shown in Figure 22-7.

The use of one member to keep the other straight is a procedure that lends itself well to the tee assemblies. Two pieces are placed back to back, as in Figure 22-12, and are joined temporarily by tack welds or clamps. After welding is completed, the pieces are separated.

As in Figure 22-10, the intelligent use of welding is sometimes all that is required to control distortion. Figure 22-13 shows how welding can control distortion of a tee joint. The welds are staggered by welding in the sequence shown.

Sometimes distortion can be made to work for us instead of against us. In auto body repair work, using heat to shrink the metal is quite a common practice

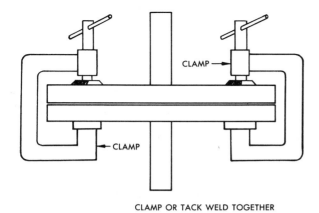

Figure 22-12   Back-to-back assembly

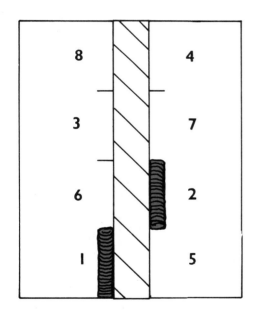

Figure 22-13   Staggered welding on a tee joint

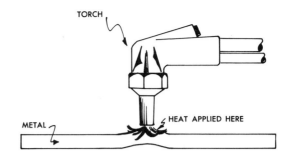

Figure 22-14   Removing a dent by heating and cooling

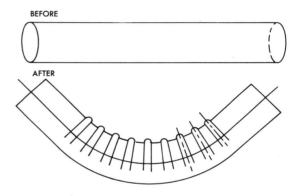

Figure 22-15   Wrinkle bending

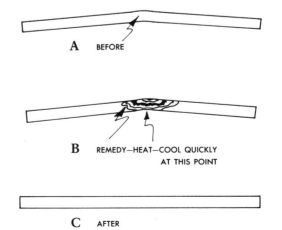

Figure 22-16   Straightening a bent piece of metal

(Figure 22-14). The metal is heated and then quickly cooled. In pipe work, heat is used to make bends in a pipe by a method known as **wrinkle bending** (Figure 22-15). A bent piece of metal may also be heated and cooled to bring it back to proper alignment (Figure 22-16).

The old-time blacksmith took advantage of the forces of expansion and contraction. Metal rims that were to be placed on wooden wagon wheels were heated and forced onto the wheel while they were still hot. When the rims contracted, they fitted snugly on the wheels. Today industry sometimes uses the same technique when assembling parts. This method is known as a **shrink fit**.

22-3 REPAIRING A FLYWHEEL OR PULLEY

Flywheels, pulleys, and similar circular parts are common items for repair. They also provide an excellent chance to study the problems of expansion and contraction.

Consider the flywheel with a broken spoke shown in Figure 22-17. Assuming that it is broken at point A, preheating the rim from W to X to a dull red heat will cause the rim to expand outwards. This will separate the edges of the broken spoke. While in this condition, the weld should be made as rapidly as possible and the whole wheel allowed to cool slowly. Thus, a good weld without the pressure of internal stresses will be produced. The expansion of the rim will offset or balance the contraction of the weld in the spoke. If the crack or break in the spoke is near the rim, it is only necessary to preheat the rim at M until it is red hot. This will expand the spoke and rim, separating the edges of the

break sufficiently to offset the contraction of the weld.

Sometimes proper allowances for expansion and contraction can be made without preheating. Let us look again at the spoke that is broken at point A. It is necessary in this case to lessen the rigidity of the rim. In order to do this, it is cut through at point P (close to the broken spoke). First, one side of the spoke is strongly "tacked" at the break. Then the other side is welded half through. The "tacked" side is then melted out and properly welded. If the weld was completed entirely from the one side, the contraction would probably cause the rim to be out of "round". Therefore, it is necessary that the original spacing be retained. The rim is now welded at the point P. If the edges at point P do not meet accurately, they may be made to do so by heating either at point M or point O according to which edge is low, and then welded.

If there are two broken spokes, as at A and B, the same general procedures as given above may be followed. In case it is necessary to preheat a large portion of the casting, the preheated area must always extend past the spokes adjacent to those fractured, as shown by Y-Z. If two diametrically opposed spokes, such as B and C, are broken, each spoke may be treated as independent of the other and welded by any of the methods previously described.

Figure 22-17 Expansion and contraction in a flywheel

Courtesy MECO St. Louis, U.S.A.

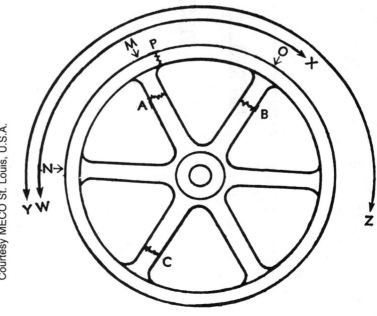

22-4 THERMAL CONDUCTIVITY

Many of the difficulties encountered in welding a joint are related to heating and cooling.

The transmission of heat in solids is by conduction, as opposed to convection or radiation. (You may learn about convection and radiation in science classes.) The measure of the rate of heat conducted in solids is called the thermal conductivity of the solid. The thermal conductivity of a material may be defined as the quantity of heat flowing through the unit cube of the material per second, measured by the difference between the temperatures of its opposite faces. The following table gives an idea of the thermal conductivity of some materials.

MATERIAL	THERMAL CONDUCTIVITY
Silver	1.00
Copper	0.918
Aluminum	0.500
Brass	0.200
Steel	0.1

Note
Silver is designated as 1 so that comparisons may be made among the materials.

When a source of heat is directed onto the surface of a piece of metal, heat is directed outward from the source through the metal. If the heat source is stationary, the heat spreads out in ever-widening concentric circles similar to the waves produced when a stone is dropped in water (Figure 22-18).

However, in welding, the heat source is not stationary but moving. The electrode or the torch and the heat waves (isotherms) become elongated. This makes them tend to bunch up in front of the heat source, and spread out behind it (see Figure 22-19).

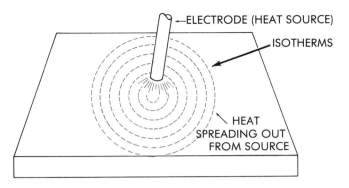

Figure 22-18   Heat spreading out from a stationary heat source

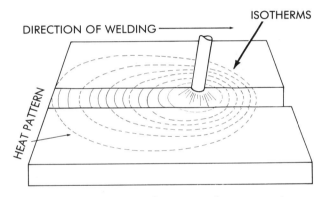

Figure 22-19   Heat wave formation from a moving heat source

TEMPERATURE GRADIENT

If a hot object comes into contact with a cold object, heat will be conducted from the hot to the cold object. The difference in temperature between the two objects is called the temperature gradient. Figure 22-20 shows how the temperature gradients change as heat is passed or transferred from the hot to the cold object. To create these gradients, the temperature of each object was measured every minute for six minutes (numbers 1 to 6 on the graph). The temperature of the hot object at the end of the first minute was marked on the vertical axis. The temperature of the cold object was marked on the horizontal axis. The two points were joined. This produced the gradient for the first minute. The same was

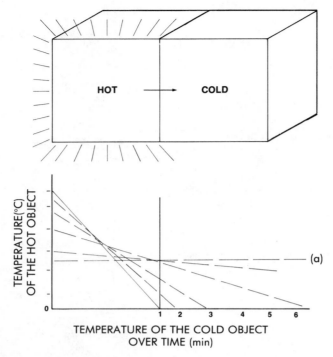

Figure 22-20   Temperature gradient

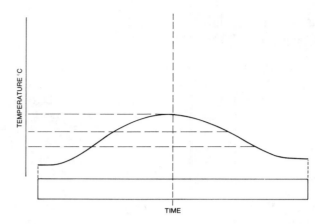

Figure 22-21   Heat distribution from a stationary heat source

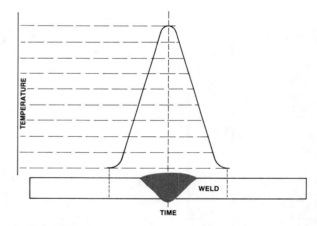

Figure 22-22   Heat distribution pattern from a moving heat source

done to produce temperature gradients for all six minutes. As the time elapsed, the heat was transferred to the cold object by conduction. For example, at point 6 (or after six minutes), there was an increase in the temperature of the cold object with a subsequent drop in the temperature of the hot object until at (a) there was a levelling or even distribution of temperature between the two objects.

Figure 22-21 shows this same situation applied to a welding operation, in which the heat source (arc or flame) is stationary. In Figure 22-22, the heat source is moving as would be the situation in a welding operation. Note that the same scales are used but the heat distribution is much narrower and the temperature gradient in that area is very high, and concentrated in a narrow band. If the heat in a welding operation was allowed to spread evenly as in Figures 22-20 and 22-21, many distortion problems would be eliminated. Unfortunately, because of the speed of welding, there are great extremes of heat and cold together. This uneven heating and cooling results in distortion, stress, and cracked welds.

22-5 STRESSES

As a result of this uneven heating and cooling, and the lack of free expansion and contraction, stresses are set up in the weld area.

There are two types of stresses in any welding process: (1) **thermal stresses**, which are set up due to the heating of the metal, and (2) **residual stresses**, which remain after cooling and give rise to most of the problems in welded assemblies. Residual stresses occur only in assemblies that have been subjected to uneven heating and cooling, as in a welding operation.

CONTROLLING RESIDUAL STRESS

Some of the more popular techniques used to control residual stresses are **peening, preheating,** and **postheating.**

Peening consists of striking the hot weld metal with a ball peen hammer. (On large assemblies an automatic hammer is usually used.) If more than one weld is deposited, each layer of weld is peened except the last, or surface, weld. When the hot metal is peened, it stretches or expands. This counteracts the contraction of weld metal which occurs upon cooling.

Preheating consists of heating the assembly before welding. A general preheat may be done, where the whole assembly is preheated, or a local preheat may be performed, where only the area in the vicinity of the weld is preheated.

Postheating consists of heating the whole assembly to a uniform temperature after welding, and allowing the assembly to cool. The equipment for preheat and postheat may range from the ordinary oxy-acetylene torch to large, sophisticated heat-treating furnaces.

DISTORTION

As you saw earlier in this chapter, longitudinal distortion is a major problem in making a butt weld. All welds shorten on cooling. In single-layer welds this may be as much as 6 mm in 2500 mm (or 1/4 in. in 1000 in.). This shortening of the metal produces buckling or warping. Figures 22-8 and 22-10 showed two methods of controlling this buckling effect. As the metal thickness increases, the buckling effect increases. At first glance, it would seem that the fastest method of welding a vee butt joint would be to use as large a welding rod as possible and to deposit as much weld metal in as short a time as possible. In fact, a number of small layers of weld will produce less longitudinal distortion than a few large weaves or beads. This will, of course, increase the efficiency of production.

In addition to longitudinal distortion, this type of joint will also be subject to angular distortion. (Methods of controlling angular distortion were shown in figures 22-8, 22-9, and 22-10.) However, it should also be noted that in welding the vee butt joint, a number of small layers will produce more angular distortion than a few

large weaves or beads. Angular distortion in tee joints is also caused by overwelding (depositing more weld metal than is necessary to produce a good sound joint).

If a choice has to be made, angular distortion is easier to control than longitudinal distortion in vee butt joints by the methods shown. Besides, by these methods of control, angular distortion can be reduced if the joint is made a double vee or double U and is welded alternately on both sides. Another method is to form the double vee or U and to have two welders work on the joint, one from each side.

JOINT ASSEMBLY: PREVENTING DISTORTION

Figure 22-23 illustrates how a problem must be carefully studied before welding begins. In this case, heavy plate has been assembled in a butt joint. In Figure 22-23A a single-vee preparation has been made. In Figure 22-23B, a single-U preparation has been formed. In Figure 22-23C the single-U has been superimposed on the single-vee, and the two triangles marked "X" show how much extra weld metal would be required to fill the joint. This would, of course, result in more lateral distortion. As the example shows, time would be saved in welding and cleaning. Less metal would be deposited (a cost saving), and less distortion would result. The single-U preparation would still allow access to the root of the weld, ensuring full penetration as in the single-vee joint, but much less weld metal would be deposited.

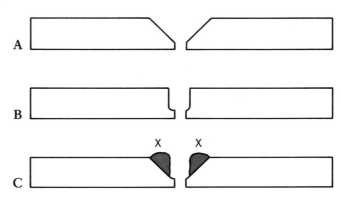

Figure 22-23　Different joint assemblies lead to different levels of distortion

POINTS TO REMEMBER

- Metal expands when heated.
- Metal contracts when cooled.
- Distortion is the end result of expansion and contraction.
- Distortion must be considered before welding is carried out on an assembly.
- It is much easier to cause distortion than to remedy it.
- The forces of expansion and contraction can also be used to help us.
- Stresses can be set up in a weld area.
- Residual stresses remain in a welding operation after cooling.
- Study a joint well before starting a welding operation.

WORDS TO REMEMBER

expansion	buckling	stress
contraction	vise	peening
distortion	shrink fit	preheating
longitudinal	wrinkle bending	postheating
angular	backstep	layers
alignment	residual	

REVIEW QUESTIONS

1. What happens to metal as it expands?
2. What happens to metal as it contracts?
3. What causes distortion?
4. What is meant by longitudinal distortion?
5. In which direction does lateral distortion occur?
6. What is meant by angular distortion?
7. Describe one method of controlling distortion in butt joints.
8. What is meant by presetting the pieces before welding?
9. Why is this presetting carried out?
10. What is meant by backstepping in welding?
11. What is meant by wrinkle bending?
12. What is thermal conductivity?
13. How is heat transmitted in solids?
14. What is meant by temperature gradient?
15. What causes stresses in the weld area?
16. Name and describe the two types of stresses that can develop in the weld area.
17. List at least three methods of controlling residual stresses.
18. What type of distortion is a major problem in butt welds?
19. Which of the two types of distortion, "angular or longitudinal," is easier to control in vee butt joints?
20. What is the main cause of angular distortion in tee joints?
21. What use does the auto body repair trade make of distortion?
22. Why is it necessary to control distortion?
23. Give an example of two metals that expand by different amounts when heated to the same temperature.
24. Would thin metal sections distort more than thick metal sections? Give reasons for your answer.

CHAPTER

23

EDGE PREPARATION

23-1 Reasons for Edge Preparation
23-2 Types of Edge Preparation

As discussed in Chapter 22, the preparation and assembly of any joint is just as important as the welding of that joint in many instances. Although welders may or may not be involved in the actual preparation of the joint or assembly, they must have knowledge of the correct assembly procedures. In the final analysis, if the assembly were to fail when in service, the welder would be at least partly responsible since he or she would have been one of the last people to work on the assembly. Apart from that, the welder who has a good knowledge of correct preparation procedures could save the employer a considerable amount of money. This would definitely be an asset if the welder were seeking promotion. In this chapter, you will find a thorough discussion of correct preparation, which should be studied carefully.

23-1 REASONS FOR EDGE PREPARATION

The careful preparation of the base metal edges is essential to successful welding. If the wrong type of joint is selected and prepared, lost time and money will result. The joint will also be weak. For **thin metal** it is possible to obtain complete penetration and full strength in the weld using any welding process with a simple square edge butt joint. It is also possible to obtain complete penetration by leaving a small gap between the pieces of metal and using a backing strip against this gap. Submerged arc welding (SAW) can also be used to penetrate a closed square edge butt joint to a considerable depth.

Nevertheless, it is sometimes necessary to prepare the edges of the metal to ensure 100% penetration of a joint. The edges of the metal to be joined can be prepared in many ways by different processes. It should be remembered, however, that this kind of work adds expense to the cost of the assembly. One should first consider whether the job can be done without edge preparation. The final decision depends on a number of factors: (1) which welding process is best suited to the job; (2) what load demands will be made on the assembly being welded; (3) the strength required for the joint; and (4) what "in service" conditions the assembly will be subject to.

Many of these types of decisions will already have been made by the designers and engineers, but it is necessary for the welder to be knowledgeable enough to give advice or make the decision if necessary. This knowledge is also useful for those who wish to move to a position beyond that of a welder.

This chapter contains descriptions of the various types of edge preparation and the joints formed by the combination of these edge preparations. Study them carefully. Careful preparation and assembly of a joint are critical if a good weld is to be made.

Bevelled edges must be uniform in depth and angle. Otherwise, the quantity of weld metal (and therefore the heat input and shrinkage on large assemblies) will vary, causing distortion. Penetration will also be irregular.

When forming a vee joint, the angle of the vee should be as small as possible in order to save metal, heat, and time and to reduce shrinkage. Yet, the angle must be large enough to permit full penetration and fusion through the full thickness of the base metal.

23-2 TYPES OF EDGE PREPARATION

As the thickness of the metal increases, it becomes increasingly difficult to obtain full penetration (Figure 23-1).

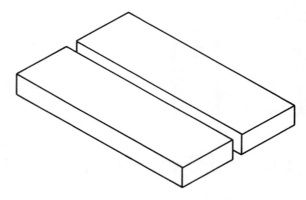

Figure 23-2   Creating a gap

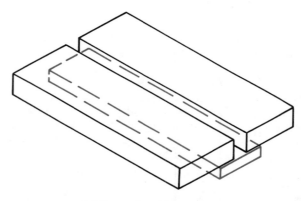

Figure 23-3   Adding a backing strip

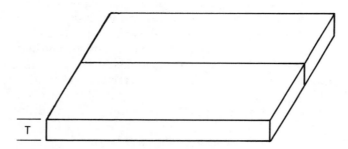

Figure 23-1   Increase in metal thickness

Placing the pieces of metal apart to create a gap (commonly referred to as the root opening) will aid in achieving full penetration when welding (Figure 23-2).

If the gap must be fairly large, a backing strip may be used (Figure 23-3).

If none of these methods will allow for complete penetration, the edges of the joint will have to be prepared. The two basic preparations used are the bevel and the

J. Many prospective welders have failed to pass tests, not because of their ability in welding, but because of poor preparation.

The single bevel is used frequently in groove joints since the angle of the bevel can be changed to suit the process being used to weld the joint. This preparation is called a **feather edge** (Figure 23-4).

Sometimes the bevel is not cut to the bottom of the metal. A small piece of metal is left uncut. This is called a **land** (Figure 23-5).

With the J preparation, a land is always left on the metal edge (Figure 23-6).

When a double bevel (Figure 23-7A) or double J (Figure 23-7B) is formed, it is formed on one piece of metal. The double bevel may or may not require a land.

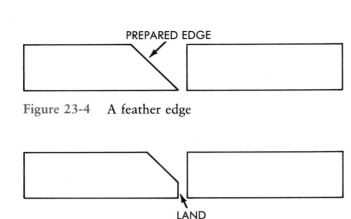

Figure 23-4   A feather edge

Figure 23-5   A land

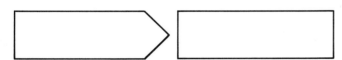

Figure 23-6   A single J

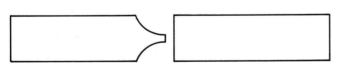

Figure 23-7A   A double bevel

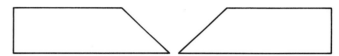

Figure 23-7B   A double J

When two single bevels are placed together, the joint is called a single vee (Figure 23-8A). The angle between the two is referred to as the included angle. The single vee may also include a land (Figure 23-8B).

When two double bevels are placed together, the joint is called a double vee (Figure 23-9).

Two single Js form a single U joint (Figure 23-10).

Two double Js will form a double U joint (Figure 23-11).

Only the vertical member is prepared in a bevel or J

for tee joints. Figure 23-12 shows different edge preparations for tee joints.

Regardless of the position of the joint, its name does not change. For example, a single vee joint is a single vee joint, whether the joint is in the flat, vertical, horizontal, or overhead position. Remember that the cost factor of joint preparation can greatly increase the cost of an assembly. In industry, the edges are prepared only when absolutely necessary. Table 23-1 gives information that should help you decide when and when not to prepare edges before welding. If you do need to prepare an edge, Figure 23-13 may help you choose the correct preparation method.

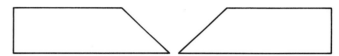

Figure 23-8A   A single vee

Figure 23-8B   A single vee with land

Figure 23-9   A double vee

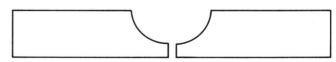

Figure 23-10   A single U

Figure 23-11   A double U

TABLE 23-1 **EDGE PREPARATION**

groove/butt	Thickness of Material	Cost of Preparation	tee
Square edge butt joint. No gap.			no preparation
Square edge butt joint. With gap. Welded one side.			single bevel
Square edge butt joint. With gap. Welded both sides.	increases decreases	increases decreases	double bevel
Single vee.			single J
Double vee.			double J
Single U.			single J
Double U.			double J

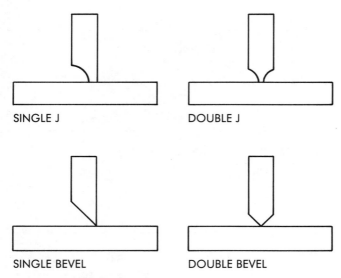

SINGLE J   DOUBLE J

SINGLE BEVEL   DOUBLE BEVEL

Figure 23-12   Edge preparation for a tee joint

POINTS TO REMEMBER

• Edges are prepared to ensure full penetration.

• The two basic preparations are the bevel and the J.
• For tee joints only the vertical member is prepared.
• Each member is prepared separately. The combination of two members forms the joint.
• The more preparation, the more expensive the assembly will be.
• If edge preparation of the base metal is needed, it must be done carefully for the weld to be successful.
• Bevelled edges must be uniform in depth and angle.

WORDS TO REMEMBER

preparation   backing   land
penetration   bevel   square

REVIEW QUESTIONS

1. What is the purpose of preparing the edges before welding?
2. Which member is prepared in tee joints?
3. What is a land?

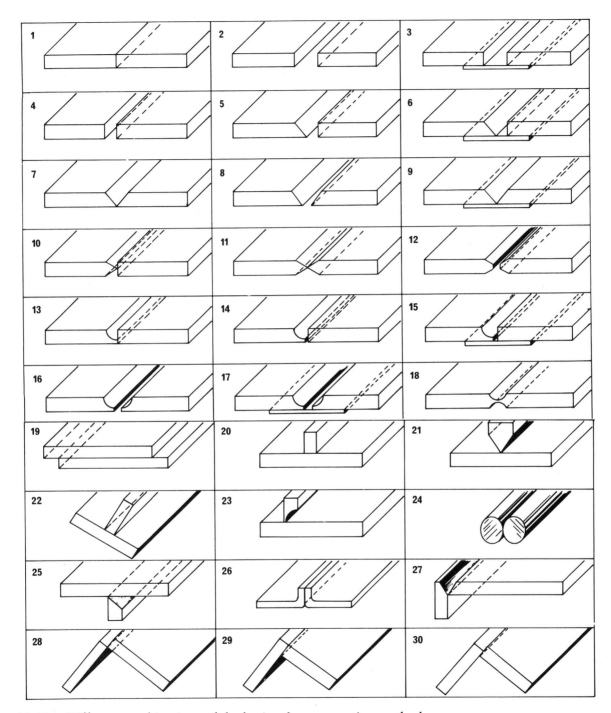

Figure 23-13 Different combinations of the basic edge preparation methods

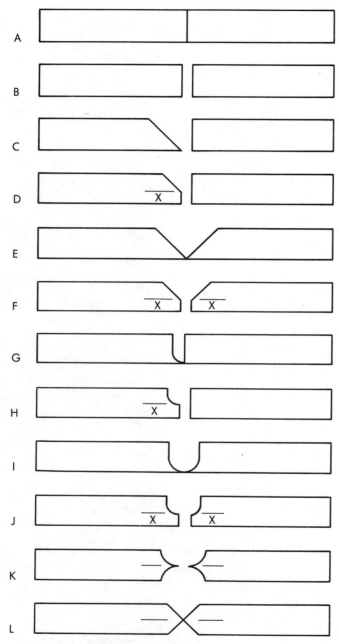

Figure 23-14   Joints to identify

4. Name the joints in Figure 23-14.
5. Draw a tee joint showing each of the following preparations:

a. Single bevel
b. Single U
c. Double bevel

6. Of the joints shown in Figure 23-13, name the following: #6, #9, #17, #21, #23, #25, and #27.
7. Describe in detail the joints shown in Figure 23-15.

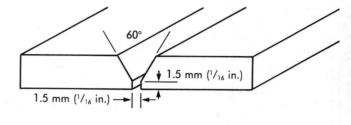

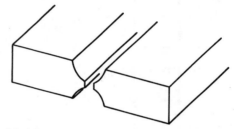

Figure 23-15   Joints to describe

8. Draw a single U butt joint with a 6 mm (1/4 in.) land and a 1.5 mm (1/16 in.) gap or root opening. The thickness of each plate is 25 mm (1 in.).
9. Draw a double vee butt joint with a 3 mm (1/8 in.) land and a root opening of 1.5 mm (1/16 in.). The included angle is 60° and the plate thickness is 25 mm (1 in.).
10. What are the recommendations regarding the angle of the vee when forming a vee joint?
11. Why is it necessary for a welder to know about edge preparation?
12. How is cost related to edge preparation?
13. What factors determine whether or not the edges of the base metal should be prepared?
14. What are the two basic edge preparations used?
15. Why must bevelled edges be uniform in depth and angle?

TESTING

When welding was in its early stages, weld quality was usually checked only by visual inspection (or perhaps by some stethoscope examination). As new materials were developed and welded assemblies were increasingly used in bridges, buildings, high-pressure operations, aircraft and ship building, testing became more sophisticated. Codes, standards, and specifications were introduced to test metals, welded joints, and the proficiency of the welding operator. Testing has become a separate field in the welding industry, and many experienced welders are employed in this area.

24-1 TESTING AGENCIES

The following is a partial list of agencies involved in testing procedures, and in setting specifications for the welding industry.

There are many others, but these are the main agencies responsible for electrodes, processes, and procedures in welding. Being certified (qualified) by one organization does not mean that you are certified by all organizations or even for all codes within the one organization. However, the more qualifications you acquire and the more

PRODUCT	AGENCY
Boilers, pressure vessels, nuclear plants	Canadian Standards Association (CSA)
	American Welding Society (AWS)
Gas and oil pipelines	CSA
	American Petroleum Industry (API)
	American Society of Mechanical Engineers (ASME)
Shipbuilding and repair	Lloyds of London
	Canadian Department of Defence
	United States Coastguard (USCG)
Bridges, structural steel	CSA
	AWS

codes for which you receive certification, the greater will be your chances of promotion, employment, and financial gain.

24-2 CHARACTERISTICS TESTED

The most common faults or defects to be checked in a weld are:

Before welding
a. Composition of base metal and filler rod
b. Welding preparation and procedure
c. Welding operator's ability

After welding
a. Welding reinforcement
b. Porosity
c. Cracks
d. Lack of fusion
e. Grain growth
f. Undercutting
g. Slag inclusions

During a welding operation, certain specific properties can be produced in a weld. For example, some welds may require hardness, and some may require strength. Others may need to be bent into certain shapes after they are completed. You should be familiar with the terms used to describe these properties. You will, in fact, be testing for some of these properties yourself.

STRENGTH

All welded joints should be as strong as or stronger than the base metal if the proper procedures have been followed. The strength of a weld is shown very clearly in Figure 24-1. Although tremendous pressure ruptured the pipe, the welds are still intact. Only the welds in line with the fracture have been forced apart. The welding was (as it should be) as strong as or stronger than the base metal.

TENSILE STRENGTH

A weld which is very strong and can resist being pulled apart is said to have a high tensile strength. Therefore, tensile strength is simply the ability of a weld to resist being pulled apart (Figure 24-2).

Courtesy of The Lincoln Electric Company

Figure 24-1 A ruptured pipe

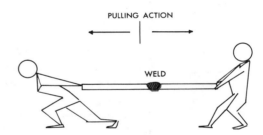

Figure 24-2 Tensile strength

Tensile test. In this test a piece of metal called a specimen is prepared to certain dimensions. The specimen is inserted into a machine which exerts a pulling action on it in opposite directions. The specimen is gripped or held in jaws or chucks and the pulling action must be steady.

This action is applied until the specimen breaks, at which point a reading is taken from the dial on the machine. This reading is the maximum tensile strength of the specimen.

DUCTILITY

A weld that can be bent and shaped without breaking is said to have good ductility. The butt joint is always tested for ductility (Figure 24-3).

Ductility test. A ductility test of a specimen may be carried out in two ways. First, the tensile test may be set up as before, but with two centre punch marks placed on the face of the specimen about 50 mm (or 2 in.) apart. After the specimen has broken apart, it is placed together and the distance between the punch marks is measured. This is actually a measure of elongation, but can be used to determine the ductility of the specimen.

The second method is more common. Again, a specimen is prepared to certain specifications. The width of the specimen, for example, might be 1.5 times the thickness and the length 10.5 times the thickness. The specimen is placed between two rollers or on a specially made female die and pressure is applied with a plunger or male die until the specimen is bent into a U shape.

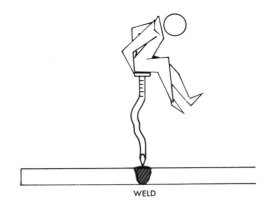

Figure 24-4   Hardness

earliest tests (Mohs scale) used the following list of materials as a gauge:

1. talc
2. gypsum
3. calcite
4. fluorite
5. apatite
6. orthoclase
7. quartz
8. topaz
9. corundum
10. diamond.

Each of these materials will scratch the one preceding it, but not the one following. Metals fall into a very narrow range somewhere between (7) and (8).

Today, sophisticated machines are used to test hardness or resistance to penetration. In the most popular of these machines, a steel ball or diamond is placed under pressure against the material being tested. Resulting indentations are very carefully checked and related to a scale which gives the metal a hardness value.

A simple shop test for hardness can be done with a file. The file is dragged, under pressure, over the surface of the metal being tested. The harder the metal, the more resistance to the file. The file will in fact slide over the hardest metals without leaving a mark.

Figure 24-3   Ductility

HARDNESS

A weld that cannot be penetrated by any other material has a high hardness quality. Such a weld, of course, would have a limited application in industry (Figure 24-4).

Hardness test. Initially, hardness was determined by the ability of a material to resist scratching. One of the

TEST YOUR KNOWLEDGE

1. Name two nondestructive tests.
2. What is meant by tensile strength?

3. What is said of a weld that can be bent or shaped without failing?

24-3 TERMS APPLIED TO A WELD

Certain terms or names are given to different parts of the weld. This makes identification of defects easier (Figure 24-5). It is simple to locate a defect when terms like "toe crack" and "root crack" are used. Although the joint shown in the figure is a lap joint, the same terms apply to any welded joint.

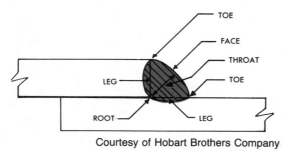

Courtesy of Hobart Brothers Company

Figure 24-5   Common terms applied to parts of a weld

DEFECTS

If the proper welding procedures are not carried out, the weld will not be as strong as the base metal. Certain flaws or defects will occur, causing the weld to fail in service. These are some of the more common defects, with explanations of their probable causes.

ADHESION

In fusion welding, if the filler metal is melted on top of the base metal before the base metal is ready to receive it, the result is poor fusion, or adhesion. This will, of course, produce a very weak weld (Figure 24-6).

CAUSE	REMEDY
Not enough heat	Use a larger tip or more amperage
Welding too quickly	Decrease speed

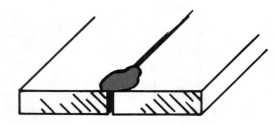

Figure 24-6   Adhesion or poor fusion

POROSITY

Gas holes in the weld are sometimes called blowholes or porosity (Figure 24-7).

CAUSE	REMEDY
Backfire	Check the torch
Allowing the tip to touch the metal	Check the distance of the tip from the metal
Dirty metal	Clean the metal before starting
Damp electrodes	Proper storage

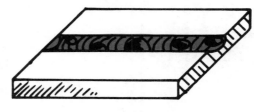

Figure 24-7   Blowholes or porosity

PENETRATION

Lack of penetration means that the joint has not been fused all the way through (Figure 24-8).

Figure 24-8   Lack of penetration

CAUSE	REMEDY
Wrong edge preparation	Check edge preparation
Not enough heat	Use a larger tip or higher amperage
Welding too quickly	Decrease speed
Wrong angle of torch	Change angle of torch
Wrong angle of electrode	Check angle of electrode

24-4 NONDESTRUCTIVE AND DESTRUCTIVE TESTS

The first test any joint receives is a visual inspection. It is checked for appearance. A good welded joint should have a neat appearance, even ripples, very little buildup, and no holes. If the joint passes the first test, it must be checked further to ensure that it is a good sound joint all the way through. This testing is carried out by both destructive and nondestructive methods.

UNDERCUT

Undercut consists of a groove that has been melted at the side of the weld. The groove has not been filled in (Figure 24-9).

NONDESTRUCTIVE TESTS

The following are some of the nondestructive tests used in industry.

Visual tests. These may be made by simply looking with the naked eye or by using devices like a magnifying glass, gauge, etc., to inspect a weld for defects.

Stethoscope or sound tests. The inspector taps the weld with a small hammer and listens with a stethoscope. The sound indicates which welds contain defects. This is similar to a doctor using a stethoscope to listen to the sounds of the human chest. Many years of experience are necessary to do this test accurately. The modern counterpart of this test is done with sonic testing equipment.

X-ray or gamma ray tests. In this test, internal photographs are taken of the weld. Defects show up in much the same manner as bone fractures show up in an X-ray of a human being. This method is usually used on large pipes and boilers.

Penetrant dyes tests. These dyes come in small aerosol cans complete with carrying case, and thus make a very portable unit. Spraying dye on the weld is an excellent method of spotting surface cracks not visible to the naked eye.

Magnetic tests. Magnetic tests are of two types:
1. Powdered iron is sprinkled on the weld. Then a magnetic charge is sent through the weld, and the iron powder gathers at the cracks or flaws.
2. Iron filings are mixed in paraffin, and this mixture is painted on the cleaned and polished surface of the weld. The weld is magnetized by a strong electric current. If there is a crack or flaw in the weld, the

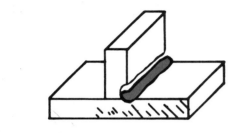

Figure 24-9 Undercut

CAUSE	REMEDY
Wrong angle of torch or electrode	Correct angle of torch or electrode
Too much heat	Use smaller tip or reduce amperage

particles of iron will cling to the edges of the crack and show up as a dark hairline mark.

Table 24-1 describes in detail the nondestructive tests, their advantages and limitations, and includes some additional remarks on each individual test.

SHOP DESTRUCTIVE TESTS

If a weld is to be part of a large assembly or fabricated item, destructive pretests may be used on test pieces similar to the actual joint. In a destructive test, the weld is bent, twisted, or pulled apart to check for flaws. These are simple tests that can be performed in any welding shop without the aid of expensive equipment. The simplest method of testing is to hold the joint on top of an anvil with a pair of pliers or to clamp it in a vise. The joint should be clamped as close to the weld as possible. After the joint has been secured as described, it is then struck a number of blows with a hammer to test the weld.

> The joint must be secured by pliers or vise to prevent it from flying off on a tangent and striking someone.

The five basic joints can be tested in the following manner:
• The corner joint should be hammered until it is flat (Figure 24-10).

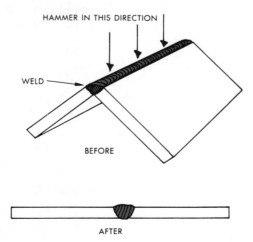

Figure 24-10   Testing a corner joint

• The butt joint should be bent until it has assumed a U shape (Figure 24-11).

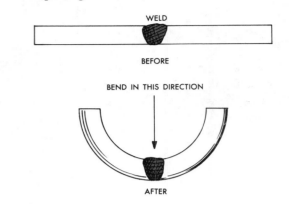

Figure 24-11   Testing a butt joint

• The tee joint should have the top or vertical piece hammered until it is flat (Figure 24-12).

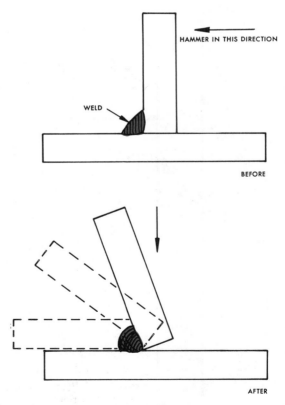

Figure 24-12   Testing a tee joint

TABLE 24-1 REFERENCE GUIDE TO MAJOR METHODS FOR THE NONDESTRUCTIVE TESTING OF WELDS

Inspection Method	Equipment Required	Enables Detection of	Advantages	Limitations	Remarks
Visual	Magnifying Glass Weld-size gauge Pocket rule Straight edge Workmanship standards	Surface flaws—cracks, porosity, unfilled craters, slag inclusions. Warpage, underwelding, overwelding, poorly formed beads, misalignments, improper fitup.	Low cost Can be applied while work is in process, permitting correction of faults. Gives indication of incorrect procedures.	Applicable to surface defects only. Provides no permanent record.	Should always be the primary method of inspection, no matter what other techniques are required. Is the only "productive" type of inspection. Is the necessary function of everyone who in any way contributes to the making of the weld.
Radiographic	Commercial X-ray or gamma units, made especially for inspecting welds, castings, and forgings. Film and processing facilities. Fluoroscopic viewing equipment.	Interior macroscopic flaws—cracks, porosity, blow holes, nonmetallic inclusions, incomplete root penetration, undercutting, icicles, and burn-through.	When the indications are recorded on film, gives a permanent record. When viewed on a fluoroscopic screen, a low-cost method of internal inspection.	Requires skill in choosing angles of exposure, operating equipment, and interpreting indications. Requires safety precautions. Not generally suitable for fillet-weld inspection.	X-ray inspection is required by many codes and specifications. Useful in qualification of welders and welding processes. Because of cost, its use should be limited to those areas where other methods will not provide the assurance required.

TABLE 24-1 (cont'd)

Method	Equipment	Detection of	Advantages	Limitations	Remarks
Magnetic particle	Special commercial equipment. Magnetic powders — dry or wet form; may be fluorescent for viewing under ultraviolet light.	Excellent for detecting surface discontinuities — especially surface cracks.	Simpler to use than radiographic inspection. Permits controlled sensitivity. Relatively low-cost method.	Applicable to ferromagnetic materials only. Requires skill in interpretation of indications and recognition of irrelevant patterns. Difficult to use on rough surfaces.	Elongated defects parallel to the magnetic field may not give pattern; for this reason the field should be applied from two directions at or near right angles to each other.
Liquid penetrant	Commercial kits, containing fluorescent or dye penetrants and developers. Application equipment for the developer. A source of ultraviolet light— if fluorescent method is used.	Surface cracks not readily visible to the unaided eye. Excellent for locating leaks in weldments.	Applicable to magnetic, nonmagnetic materials. Easy to use. Low cost.	Only surface defects are detectable. Cannot be used effectively on hot assemblies.	In thin-walled vessels, will reveal leaks not ordinarily located by usual air tests. Irrelevant surface conditions (smoke, slag) may give misleading indications.
Ultrasonic	Special commercial equipment, either of the pulse-echo or transmission type. Standard reference patterns for interpretation of RF or video patterns.	Surface and subsurface flaws, including those too small to be detected by other methods. Especially for detecting subsurface lamination-like defects.	Very sensitive. Permits probing of joints inaccessible to radiography.	Requires high degree of skill in interpreting pulse-echo patterns. Permanent record is not readily obtained.	Pulse-echo equipment is highly developed for weld inspection purposes. The transmission-type equipment simplifies pattern interpretation where it is applicable.

Courtesy of The Lincoln Electric Company

- The lap joint should be hammered until it resembles a tee joint (Figure 24-13).

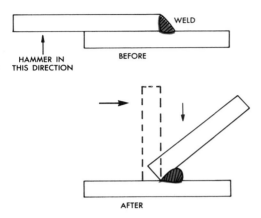

Figure 24-13   Testing a lap joint

- The edge joint should be opened and bent until it forms a U joint, similar to the butt joint (Figure 24-14).

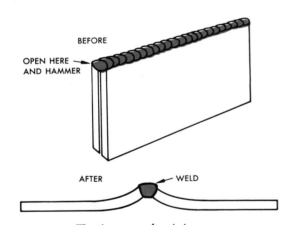

Figure 24-14   Testing an edge joint

24-5 TESTING WELDS IN INDUSTRY

In industry, the methods of testing welds are similar to the methods just described. However, they are more thorough and more sophisticated. More care is required because many of the structures and assemblies are used by the general public. Bridges, ships, high-pressure steam lines, locomotives, and office buildings fall into this category. Defective welds can result in structural failure with a possible loss of life.

A number of agencies are responsible for testing procedures in different areas of industry. Although their testing methods and procedures may vary, they are all testing for the same end result: a good sound weld, free of all defects.

As was mentioned in Chapter 8, Basic OAW Joints, approximately 70% of the joints used in industry are butt joints (or groove joints as they are sometimes called). The other 30% used in industry are tee joints. The following examples will give you some idea of the types of tests, methods of testing, and acceptable standards required by industry. Because of the variety of tests required for different applications, the following test is given for illustration only. Students interested in obtaining exact information on testing procedures should contact the appropriate testing agencies.

DESTRUCTIVE TESTS FOR BUTT WELDS

Butt or groove joint specimens for testing are usually welded on **plate** or **pipe**. Figure 24-15 shows a typical method of removing test pieces from welded plate and Figure 24-16 shows a typical method of removing test pieces from welded pipe. Figures 24-17 and 24-18 illustrate the position in which the test pieces must be welded for a welder to qualify. The most common tests carried out on these test pieces are the root bend, face bend, side bend, tensile test, reduced tensile, and impact tests. The test pieces for bending require careful preparation, and in industry, will conform to the specifications of the actual structure or assembly that is to be welded.

To carry out the root, face, and side bend tests, the guided bend test is used. In tests of solid metal, this test measures the ductility of the base metal when it is subjected to tension and compression. In tests of a welder's skill, it is used to check the soundness of the deposited weld at the face and root of the weld. Any defects at the root or face of the weld will show up as cracks. The test piece is cut and prepared to specific instructions. It may be obtained by cutting a section across the weld to test the face and root of the weld. The test piece may also

DISCARD		THIS PIECE
REDUCED SECTION		TENSILE SPECIMEN
ROOT BEND		SPECIMEN
FACE BEND		SPECIMEN
ROOT BEND		SPECIMEN
FACE BEND		SPECIMEN
REDUCED SECTION		TENSILE SPECIMEN
DISCARD		THIS PIECE

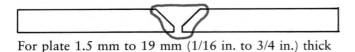

For plate 1.5 mm to 19 mm (1/16 in. to 3/4 in.) thick

DISCARD		THIS PIECE
SIDE BEND		SPECIMEN
REDUCED SECTION		TENSILE SPECIMEN
SIDE BEND		SPECIMEN
SIDE BEND		SPECIMEN
REDUCED SECTION		TENSILE SPECIMEN
SIDE BEND		SPECIMEN
DISCARD		THIS PIECE

For plate over 19 mm (3/4 in.) thick. May be used also for thicknesses from 9.5 mm to 19 mm (3/8 in. to 3/4 in.)

Courtesy of The Lincoln Electric Company

Figure 24-15   Taking test pieces from a welded plate

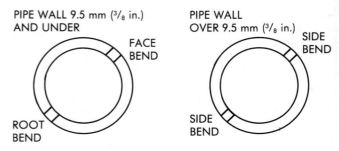

A. 1G and 2G positions

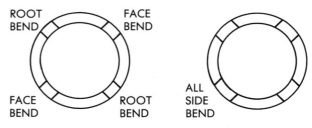

B. 5G and 6G positions

Figure 24-16   Test pieces from a welded pipe

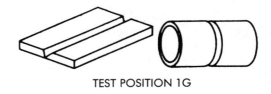

TEST POSITION 1G

TEST POSITION 2G

Figure 24-17   Test positions for butt or groove weld in pipe and plate

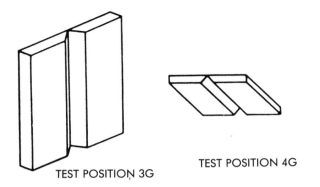

TEST POSITION 3G

TEST POSITION 4G

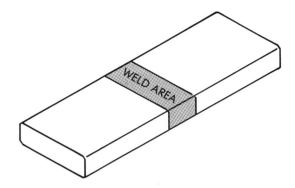

Figure 24-19   Guided bend test piece

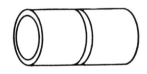

TEST POSITION 5G
Courtesy of The Lincoln Electric Company

Figure 24-17   (cont'd)

Guided Bend Test

The test fixture shown in Figure 24-20A is built to specifications based on the pieces being tested. In each test, however, the principle is the same. The fixture is usually powered by hydraulics. The former, or male die, is raised and the piece to be tested is placed across the shoulders of the female die. The former is then lowered and a steady pressure is applied to the test piece. Generally the test piece is bent until the arms are parallel, as shown in Figure 24-20B. The piece is then examined for cracks.

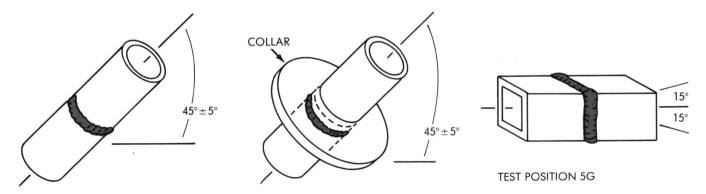

PIPE AND TUBE TEST POSITIONS

Figure 24-18   Pipe and tube test positions

be cut along the length of the weld so that it consists entirely of weld metal. Figure 24-19 shows a typical prepared specimen.

Tensile Test

Tensile strength is the ability of a metal to resist being pulled apart. This test is used to test both metals and

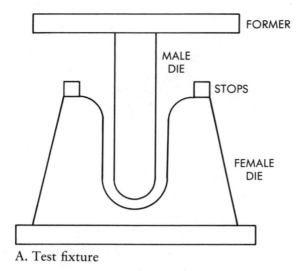

A. Test fixture

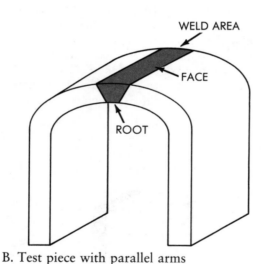

B. Test piece with parallel arms

Figure 24-20   The guided bend test

welds. Figure 24-21A shows a piece prepared for testing called a reduced tensile test piece. Another test piece used for the tensile test is the 505 specimen shown in Figure 24-21B. For weld tests, this sample is made entirely of weld metal.

The two ends of the machine used for the tensile test are equipped with jaws which grip the test specimen.

One end is movable, and it is slowly and steadily moved away, so that an even pull is exerted on the test piece. The load that is applied is registered on a dial. At the point where the metal separates, the hand on the dial stops and registers the exact load at the time of separation.

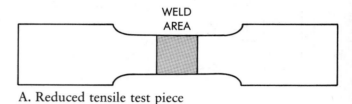

A. Reduced tensile test piece

B. A 505 tensile specimen

Figure 24-21   Pieces used for the tensile test

24-6 FILLET WELD TESTS

Figure 24-22 shows a typical fillet weld test specimen. Note that the weld has to be joined in the middle of the test piece. This stopping and starting will test the operator's ability to join one weld to another without leaving a defect such as a crater, which of course could result in a crack because of the reduced cross section of weld area at that section.

Figure 24-23 shows the four basic positions for testing fillet welds and Figure 24-24 shows the profiles that are acceptable in a fillet weld and some of the defects that can be seen visually even before any mechanical testing is carried out.

ALTERNATIVE ASSEMBLIES FOR FILLET WELD TESTS

Figure 24-25 shows some alternative assemblies for fillet weld tests. Once the initial fillet weld has been made,

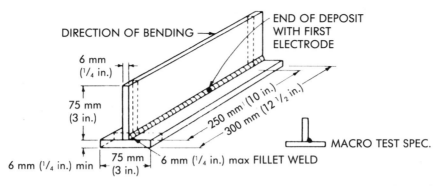

FRACTURE TEST: Maximum permissible defects such as slag, nonfusion, etc.—20% or 50 mm (2 in.). Evidence of cracking of fillet shall constitute grounds for rejection.

MACRO TEST: The fillet shall show fusion to the root of the weld but not necessarily beyond the root. Convexity and/or concavity of the fillet shall not exceed 1.5 mm ($^1/_{16}$ in.). Both legs of the fillet shall be equal to within 1.5 mm ($^1/_{16}$ in.).

Courtesy of Canadian Liquid Air Ltd.

Figure 24-22   A typical fillet weld test

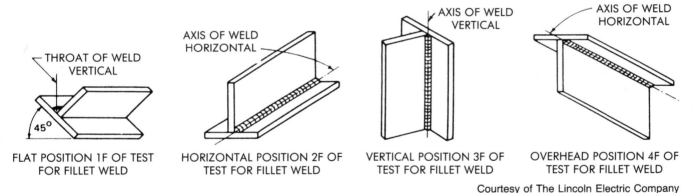

Courtesy of The Lincoln Electric Company

Figure 24-23   Four basic positions of testing fillet welds

the whole assembly can be welded in the flat position to fill up the gap. It would then be prepared and tested in the same manner as the butt weld tests on plate. The pipe shown in Figure 24-26 has a backing ring inserted between the two pieces of pipe. It is the backing ring, along with the pipe, that forms the fillet. Figure 24-27 shows the procedure for testing a tack weld on a tee joint. The tack weld is a miniature fillet weld.

Table 24-2 shows different tests that can be made on both groove and fillet joints.

POINTS TO REMEMBER

- All welded joints should be as strong as or stronger than the parent metal.
- The first test is a visual inspection.
- Poor fusion is also called adhesion.
- If possible, nondestructive tests should be used.
- In a destructive test, the weld is bent, twisted or pulled apart.
- Secure all joints before testing.

Figure 24-24
The profile standards that sectional fillet welds must meet in qualification testing

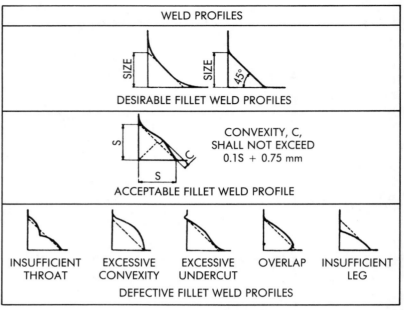

Courtesy of The Lincoln Electric Company

TABLE 24-2 TESTING DETAILS: BUTT AND FILLET WELDS

Type of Joint	Type of Test	Characteristics Being Tested	Purpose of Test	
			Operator Qualification	Procedure Qualification
G	Reduced section	Tensile strength		*
R	Free bend	Ductility		*
O	Root bend	Soundness	*	
O	Face bend	Soundness	*	
V	Side bend	Soundness	*	
E	Nick break	Soundness	*	
F	Shear	Shear strength		**
I	Free bend	Ductility		*
L	Break	Soundness	*	
L	Soundness	Soundness	**	
E				
T				

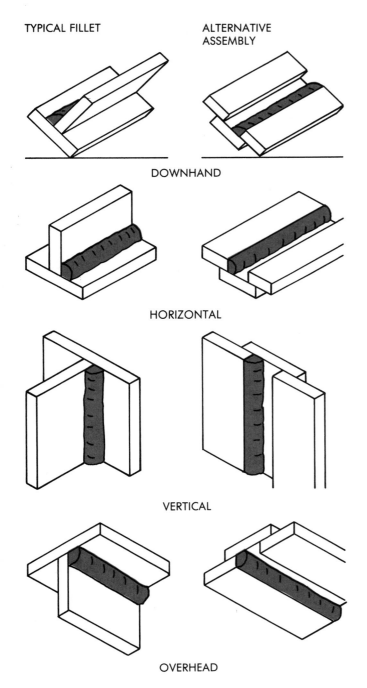

TYPICAL FILLET   ALTERNATIVE ASSEMBLY

DOWNHAND

HORIZONTAL

VERTICAL

OVERHEAD

Figure 24-25   Typical fillets and alternative assemblies for all positions

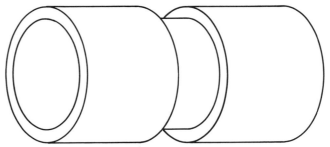

Figure 24-26   Pipe may be welded in all positions

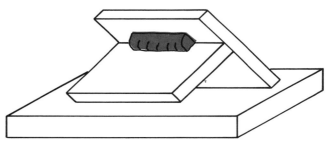

Figure 24-27   Testing a tack weld on a tee joint

- Being certified by one organization does not mean you are certified for all organizations.
- The guided bend test is a test of ductility.
- The tensile test is a test of the metal to resist being pulled apart.
- Steady pressure must be exerted when performing these tests.

WORDS TO REMEMBER

visual	destructive	qualified
tensile	groove	specimen
ductility	guided	load
hardness	profile	specifications
toe	former	root
root	die	face
adhesion	certified	

REVIEW QUESTIONS

1. What is the first test made on any joint?
2. How is destructive testing done?
3. How strong should a weld be?
4. Why are welds tested?
5. What percentage of joints in industry are butt joints?
6. List five nondestructive inspection methods.
7. List three causes of lack of penetration.
8. List three causes of undercut.
9. Describe a simple shop test for hardness.
10. List three defects that might occur in a weld.
11. What is the meaning of tensile strength?
12. What is the meaning of ductility?
13. Which agencies are responsible for the testing procedures on bridges and structural steel?
14. What are the most common tests carried out on test pieces?
15. Which test is the 505 specimen designed for?
16. Which test is used to check the soundness of a weld?
17. What is tensile strength?
18. Describe the tensile test.
19. Describe the guided bend test.
20. What do the letters CSA, AWS, API, ASME stand for?

25

BLUEPRINT READING AND WELDING SYMBOLS

Blueprints or drawings use a **universal language** made up of certain marks, lines, and symbols. Design engineers from many different countries communicate the size and shape of the product to be built with this language. Since blueprint instructions do not rely on a language like French or English or Russian, people of various nationalities can understand each other's blueprints.

It is important that a welder knows how to read blueprints, since these are the instructions for his or her job. This chapter will give the basics of reading mechanical blueprints and drawings.

25-1 LINES USED IN BLUEPRINTS

Every line on a blueprint or drawing has a purpose. A few of the most common lines are shown in Table 25-1.

25-2 VIEWS

Many objects require **three views** for their shape to be fully described. These views might show the *length, width,* and *height*; the *height, width,* and *depth*; or the *length, width,* and *thickness.* Drawings, then, use a view or views to show a three-dimensional shape on paper.

Each view is projected as though one was able to see the object from each side straight on. If one looks at a small block of steel (Figure 25-1A) from all sides as through a glass cabinet (Figure 25-1B) then one would see the sides as pictured in Figure 25-1C. This is how certain simple shapes are drawn, using the top, front, and side views. Now that we know it is a solid block of metal, we can indicate the sides that cannot be seen by using hidden lines (Figure 25-1D).

Figure 25-2A shows a drawing of a tee joint. The views are the same (top, front, side) as for the steel block, but the shape is different. One would not show a hidden line in this drawing because it would fall exactly where

TABLE 25-1 LINES USED IN BLUEPRINTS

Sample Outline	Description	What does it show?
Object line ————	heavy weight, solid	The solid line indicates the outline of the object.
Hidden line – – – – –	medium weight, broken	The broken or dotted line indicates a hidden line, the side of an object which cannot be seen.
Dimension line ←—— ——→	fine weight, arrowheads	This line is used to indicate the dimensions or the size of the object.
Extension line ————	fine weight, solid	This line, called an extension line, extends away from an object at points to be measured.
Centre line — – — —	fine weight, broken line, short and long dashes	This type of broken line is used to indicate the centre of an object.
Cutting plane line	medium to heavy weight, solid or broken	Cutting plane lines are used to indicate that the object has an imaginary cut through a certain section. The arrows indicate the face of the section that has been cut.
Long break line	medium weight, solid, break symbol	This line is called a break line and shows that an object is much longer than it appears in the drawing.
Short break line	heavy weight, solid, wavy	This indicates a *short* break line.
Leader line	fine weight, solid	This line points to a specific part or dimension on a drawing.

the solid line is. In Figure 25-2B the same tee joint is shown, but in another position, standing on its end instead of lying flat. There are still three views in the same locations in this drawing. Compare Figure 25-2A and B, using a sample tee joint to help visualize how it is shown in the drawings. In Figure 25-2C a single vee butt joint is shown in three views.

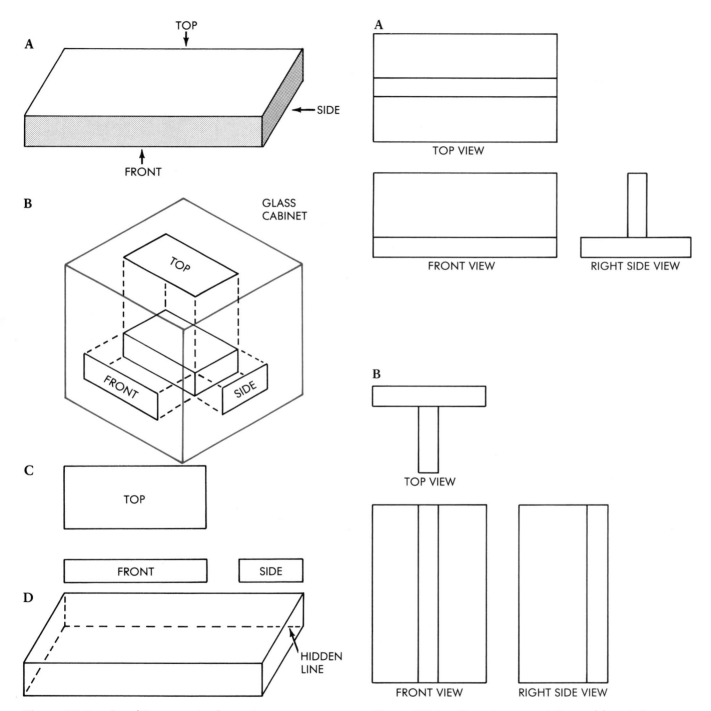

Figure 25-1　An object seen in three views

Figure 25-2　Drawing a tee joint and butt joint

C

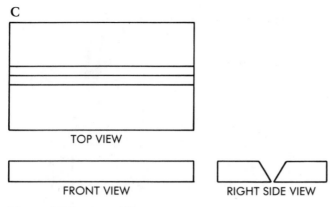

TOP VIEW

FRONT VIEW   RIGHT SIDE VIEW

Figure 25-2   (cont'd)

TEST YOUR KNOWLEDGE

1. Why are blueprints or drawings described as using a universal language?
2. What does the hidden line indicate?
3. What is the purpose of the extension line?
4. Why are views used on drawings?
5. How is each view projected?

25-3 ORTHOGRAPHIC PROJECTION

The drawings you have just looked at are all samples of **orthographic projection**, the type of drawing most commonly used for mechanical blueprints and drawings. Orthographic projection requires a certain placement of the true views of an object, so that one can easily identify which is the top view, the front view and the right side view. Three views are all that are usually needed to show the true shape of an object. However, more complex objects may require **additional views** such as a left-side view, a bottom view, and a rear view. **Auxiliary views** are used to show an additional view of a slanted surface which cannot be understood by just the three views. **Section views** are used to show the internal structure of an object. *Cutting plane lines* on the main drawing of the object show where the section view is located.

PERSPECTIVE, ISOMETRIC, AND OBLIQUE PROJECTIONS

There are other methods of drawing the exact shape of an object apart from orthographic projection. **Perspective projection**, most often used for architectural blueprints, is a perspective drawing which looks much like how one actually **sees** an object (Figure 25-3). **Isometric projection** shows the three sides of an object by using lines extending at 120° from a vertical line that is used to define the nearest corner of the object (Figure 25-4). **Oblique projection** is similar to isometric. However, one true side of an object is shown in addition to drawings showing two views set at angles of 30° or 45° (Figure 25-5).

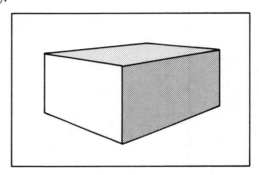

Figure 25-3   Perspective projection

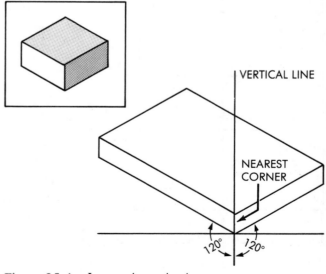

Figure 25-4   Isometric projection

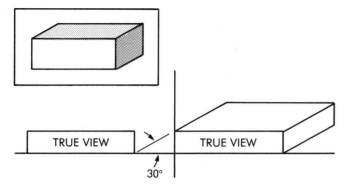

Figure 25-5 Oblique projection

PROJECTION LINES

Projection lines extend away from the corners of an object. This is how the drafter plots the views on a drawing. They are lightly drawn lines used to accurately project one view on to another (Figure 25-6). Care must be taken to keep the same dimensions. A drafting table, T-square, and set squares are useful for this operation (Figure 25-7).

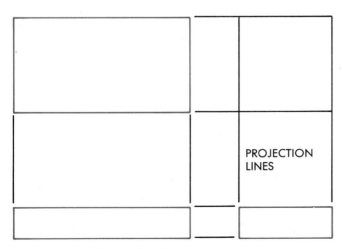

Figure 25-6 Projection lines

DIMENSIONS

Figure 25-8A shows a drawing with the dimensions length (L), width (W), and thickness (T). Other dimensions may be indicated, depending on the type of object drawn. For example, a round object requires a dimension for the diameter (D) of the circular face (Figure 25-8B). In Figure 25-8C, D stands for depth. Other dimensions are the stem (S) and the flange (F) (distance across flats), as shown in Figure 25-8D.

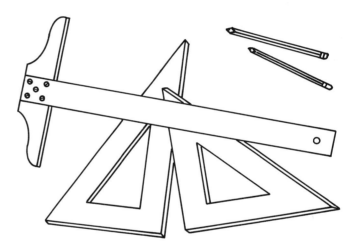

Figure 25-7 T-Square and set squares

SCALE

Since many objects and particularly whole systems with many parts are larger than a drawing, most drawings use a **reduced scale**. This means that all dimensions or lines on a drawing are reduced in length according to the scale chosen. For example, 10 mm can be used to equal 100 mm (this would be a 1/10 scale). Using 10 mm for 40 mm is using a 1/4 scale. An inch example might be 1 in. used to represent 1 ft. (a 1/12 scale). Figure 25-9 shows a half-scale (1/2 scale) drawing.

Enlarged scales are used for objects needing close views to show fine detail. If the object is drawn twice as large as it really is, the scale would be 2/1. Or if every 40 mm

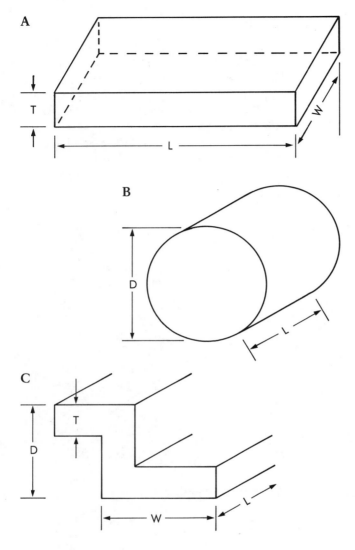

Figure 25-8   Dimensions of objects of various shapes

is equal to 10 mm, then the drafter is using a 4/1 scale.

Some drawings are equal to the actual size of the object. These are said to be **drawn to scale**. They are also called full-scale drawings.

TEST YOUR KNOWLEDGE

1. How many views are usually required to show the true shape?
2. What are section views used for?
3. Name two other methods of drawing the exact shape of an object.
4. What is the purpose of projection lines?
5. What does full scale mean?

25-4 WELDING SYMBOLS

Many signs exist in our technological society. We have signs telling us what to do and where to go, and what not to do and where not to go. Traffic signs are a good example. Many of these signs are used internationally because they eliminate lengthy explanations. Visitors from other countries can interpret them even if they do not know the language. In welding, there are signs on blueprints to indicate to the operator certain rules that must be followed even if the operator is unfamiliar with the language of engineering. The signs in welding are called **welding symbols**. Once the language of these symbols is understood, it is easy to read the signs.

Welding symbols are used in industry to represent design details that would take up too much space on a blueprint if written out in full. For example, an engineer or designer may want to convey the following information to the welding shop:

1. The location of the weld.
2. The weld is to be a fillet weld on both sides of the joint.
3. One side is to be a 12 mm (or 1/2 in.) fillet weld; the other, a 6 mm (or 1/4 in.) fillet weld.
4. Both welds have to be made with an E6014 (E41014) electrode.

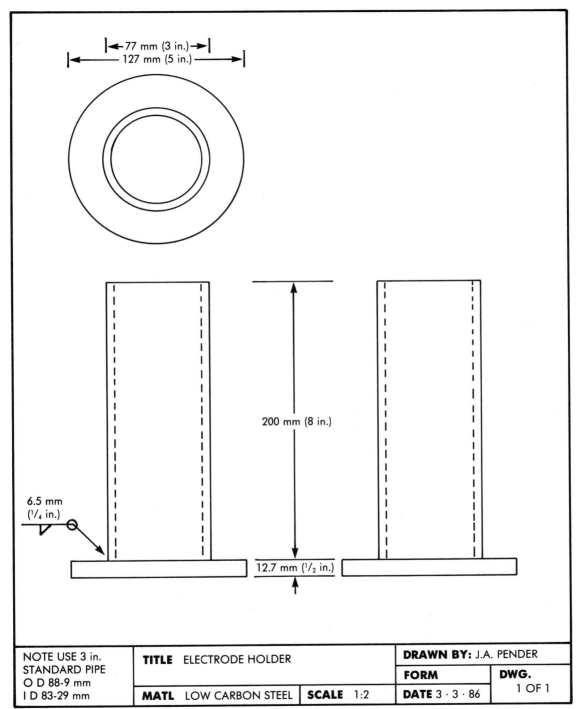

| 77 mm (3 in.) |
| 127 mm (5 in.) |

200 mm (8 in.)

6.5 mm (¹/₄ in.)

12.7 mm (¹/₂ in.)

NOTE USE 3 in. STANDARD PIPE O D 88-9 mm I D 83-29 mm	**TITLE** ELECTRODE HOLDER		**DRAWN BY:** J.A. PENDER	
			FORM	**DWG.** 1 OF 1
	MATL LOW CARBON STEEL	**SCALE** 1:2	**DATE** 3 · 3 · 86	

Figure 25-9   If the electrode holder shown in this drawing were fabricated, it could be used on the welding bench to hold full- or part-length electrodes.

5. The 12 mm (1/2 in.) fillet weld is to be ground with a grinder until all buildup and excess weld metal have been removed.

To indicate all this information, the engineer or designer merely inserts the symbol in the proper place on the blueprint, conveying the information to the welding shop (Figure 25-10). Welding symbols are as much a part of a welder's trade as running a bead or filling a joint. The American Welding Society has developed a set of standard symbols that are used in industry in both the United States and Canada to indicate and illustrate all welding information on blueprints and engineering drawings. Figure 25-11 shows the parts of a standard welding symbol.

PARTS OF THE WELDING SYMBOL

1. The reference line will always be the same in all symbols (Figure 25-12A). The arrow in the symbol shows the location of the weld (Figure 25-12B). If the weld symbol (Figure 25-12C) is below the reference line, the weld is to be made on the side of the joint to which the arrow is pointing. If the weld symbol is above the reference line, the weld is to be made on the side of the joint opposite to the side to which the arrow is pointing.

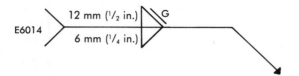

Figure 25-10   A welding symbol

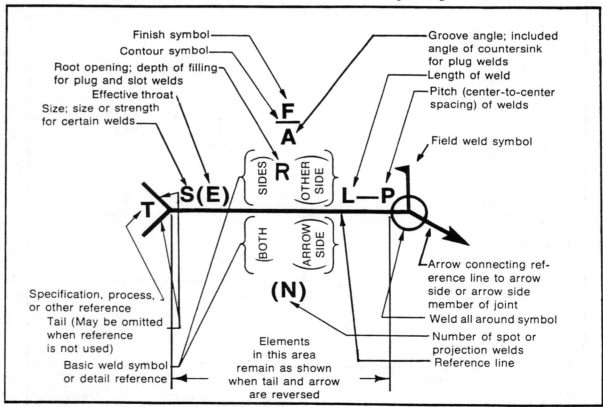

Courtesy of American Welding Society

Figure 25-11   Location of elements of a welding symbol

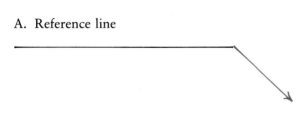

A. Reference line

B. The arrow shows the location of the weld.

C. The complete information is given on the reference line.

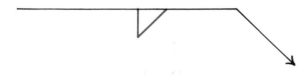

D. Arrows pointing in different directions

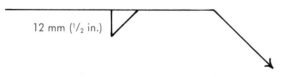

E. The weld symbol indicates the type of weld and other information on the joint.

12 mm (1/2 in.)

F. The dimensions of the particular weld are placed to the left on the weld symbol.

Figure 25-12   Parts of the welding symbol

12 mm (1/2 in.)   75 mm-150 mm (3-6 in.)   DISTANCE BETWEEN WELD CENTRES

LENGTH OF WELD

G. Additional dimensions

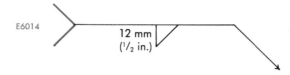

E6014   12 mm (1/2 in.)

H. The tail details special information or instructions.

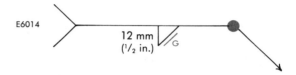

E6014   12 mm (1/2 in.)   G

I.   The supplementary symbols give extra information required to complete the job.

2. The arrow may point in different directions and may even be bent on occasion (Figure 25-12D).

3. There are many weld symbols, each corresponding to the particular weld (Figure 25-12E).

4. Dimensions are shown to the left of the weld symbol (Figure 25-12F).

5. Additional dimensions are added to the right of the symbol if the joint is to be tack welded as in the case of fillet welds. The first additional dimension in Figure 25-12G refers to the length of the weld; the second additional dimension refers to the distance between the welds (centre to centre).

6. The tail (Figure 25-12H) may contain no special information and may be omitted on occasion.

7. There are many supplementary symbols. Each has a different meaning (Figure 25-12I).

COMBINATION SYMBOL AND RESULT

Some symbols are quite complicated or seem to be at first glance, but if taken step by step, they are not difficult to understand. The first point to notice in Figure 25-13 is the double bevel part of the symbol. Double bevels

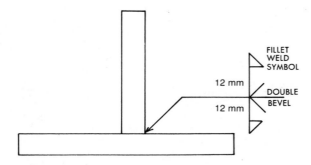

Figure 25-13   The complete symbol

are prepared on one piece of metal only, so you can proceed as in Figure 25-14A.

Next is the fillet weld symbol on both sides of the reference line. Before a fillet weld can be applied, however, there must be a vertical surface. Therefore the bevels are filled in with weld as in Figure 25-14B.

After the bevels are filled in, a 12 mm (1/2 in.) fillet weld is applied as in Figure 25-14C. This is an unusual and seldom used combination. It would be applied only where 100% strength and penetration are required. It is used here simply as an example to show the steps in reading symbols.

A large number of combinations may be used, but the basic weld symbols and the supplementary symbols shown in figures 25-15 and 25-16 and tables 25-2 to 25-4 are the most important ones.

APPLICATION OF WELDING SYMBOLS

The preceding illustrations show very basic welding symbols and their applications. However, it must be remembered that these are simple illustrations and they would probably contain more information if they were part of an actual drawing.

TEST YOUR KNOWLEDGE

1. What is the difference between a weld symbol and a welding symbol?
2. What is the purpose of welding symbols?

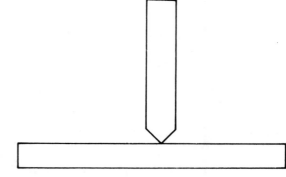

A. Vertical piece bevelled

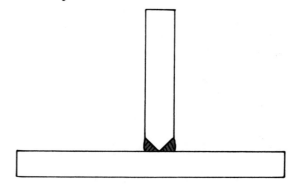

B. The bevels filled in

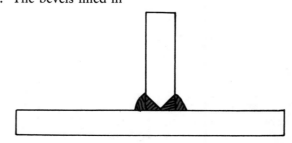

C. Completed weld

Figure 25-14   Interpreting the welding symbol

3. What is the purpose of the reference line?
4. Which part shows the location of the weld?
5. If the weld symbol is below the reference line, on which side of the joint is the weld to be made?

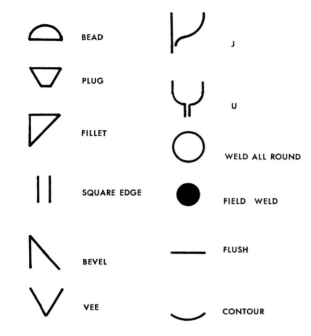

BEAD

PLUG

FILLET

SQUARE EDGE

BEVEL

VEE

J

U

WELD ALL ROUND

FIELD WELD

FLUSH

CONTOUR

Figure 25-15   Basic welding symbols

POINTS TO REMEMBER

- Every line in a blueprint drawing has a definite purpose.
- The solid line indicates the outline of an object.
- The dotted line, indicating hidden information, is called a hidden line.
- Simple drawings usually have three views in an orthographic drawing.
- These views are top, front, and side (usually the right side).
- The location of the three views does not change on a drawing.
- Welding symbols represent design details on blueprints or drawings.
- Welding symbols are used, rather than repeating standard instructions.
- The arrow on a welding symbol may point in different directions.

TABLE 25-2   SYMBOLS FOR TEE JOINTS

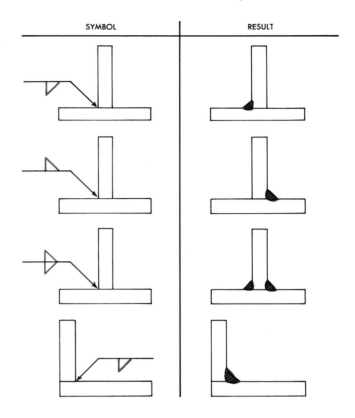

SYMBOL	RESULT

TABLE 25-3   SYMBOLS FOR LAP JOINTS

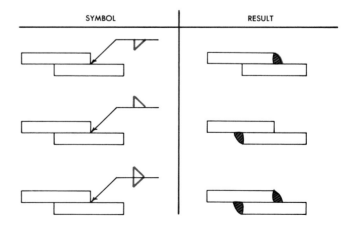

SYMBOL	RESULT

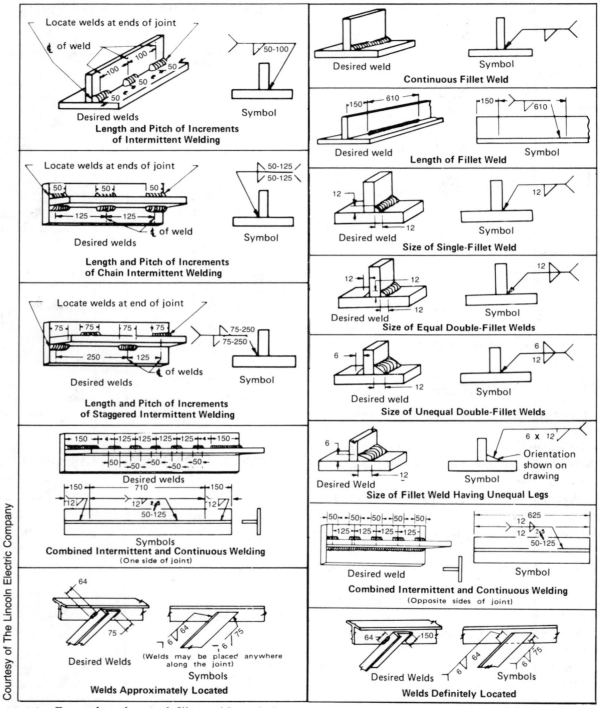

Figure 25-16   Examples of typical fillet weld symbols

TABLE 25-4   SYMBOLS FOR BUTT JOINTS

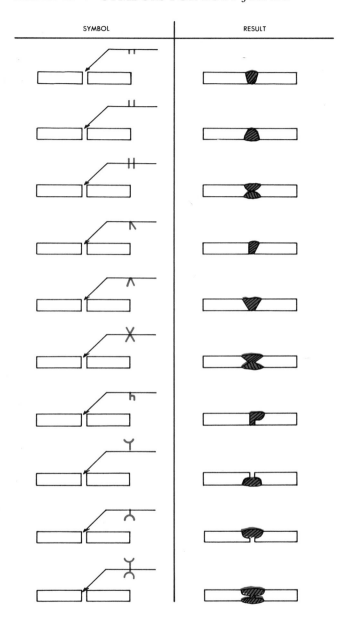

SYMBOL	RESULT

- The tail of the symbol may be omitted on occasions.
- Symbols are not complicated if they are examined one step at a time.

WORDS TO REMEMBER

blueprint	tail	isometric
extension	auxiliary	section
symbols	universal	dimensions
view	orthographic	projection
designer	reference line	scale

REVIEW QUESTIONS

1. List and explain the purpose of lines found in a drawing or blueprint.
2. Why would a photograph of an object not give sufficient information?
3. How many views are on a simple drawing? Name these views.
4. Why are welding symbols used in industry?
5. If dimensions are placed to the right of the weld symbol, what do they indicate?
6. Draw any five joints, complete with welding symbols of your choice, and explain each one.
7. Apply the correct weld shape or draw in the joints as indicated by the welding symbols shown in Figure 25-17.

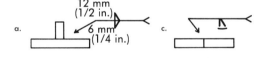
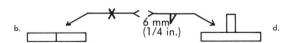

Figure 25-17   Welding symbols

8. What is the purpose of the arrow?
9. What does the weld symbol indicate?
10. Where is special information placed?
11. Describe the information that is indicated if the weld symbol is:
    a. above the reference line
    b. below the reference line
12. Where are the dimensions normally placed in the welding symbol?

PRACTICAL ASSIGNMENTS

Part 6 consists of a number of assignments that you can do after you have studied and practised the skills described in the preceding chapters. These assignments are similar to many of the actual tests a welder would be expected to perform in industry. The **guided bend test** is one of the most widely used tests to check the welder's abilities and to make sure that the correct electrode is being used for each operation. If equipment is available, test as many different welds as possible with this test. Both the **face bend** and the **root bend test** should be used to check the soundness of the weld.

Measurements given for amperages, gas flow, etc., are included only as general guidelines. Adjustments will have to be made to suit the particular equipment being used or specific instructions given by your instructor. One often has to adapt to particular conditions and equipment on the job. By using the student progress chart which appears at the end of Part 6, you can ensure that you have had practise in all the important areas of study that will lead to a welding career. The progress chart is laid out in a logical sequence for practical study to provide you with the best possible route to success.

PRACTICAL WELDING ASSIGNMENT NO. 1

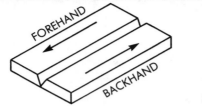
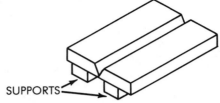

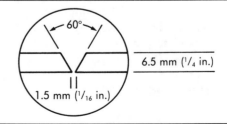

Process	OAW
Type of Joint	single–vee butt joint
Metal	low carbon steel (LCS) 6.5 mm (1/4 in.)
No. of Pieces	2
Size of Pieces	75 mm × 150 mm (3 in. × 6 in.)
Position	flat (downhand)
Amperage	n/a
Voltage	n/a
Polarity	n/a
High Frequency	n/a
Welding Rod/Wire	5.0 mm (3/16 in.) RG410 (RG60)
Tip Size	Use tip size recommended by manufacturer of your torch.
Gas Flow	Gas flow will correspond to size of tip being used.
Finish	Grind welds flush; cut two 38 mm (1 1/2 in.) strips across weld.
Testing	Face and Root Bend Test
Reference	Chapters 8, 19, 23, 24

Additional Remarks

Use a neutral flame; maintain torch/rod angles.
Do one joint forehand and one joint backhand.
Support the joint so that root of the joint is clear of bench.

PRACTICAL WELDING ASSIGNMENT NO. 2

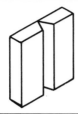 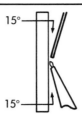

Process	OAW
Type of Joint	single–vee butt joint
Metal	low carbon steel (LCS) 6.5 mm (1/4 in.)
No. of Pieces	2
Size of Pieces	75 mm × 150 mm (3 in. × 6 in.)
Position	vertical up (1 pass)
Amperage	n/a
Voltage	n/a
Polarity	n/a
High Frequency	n/a
Welding Rod/Wire	5.0 mm (3/16 in.) RG410 (RG60)
Tip Size	Use tip size recommended by manufacturer of your torch.
Gas Flow	Gas flow will correspond to size of tip being used.
Finish	Grind welds flush; cut 38 mm (1 1/2 in.) strips across weld.
Testing	Face and Root Guided Bend Test
Reference	Chapters 8, 19, 23, 24

Additional Remarks

Use a neutral flame. Torch and rod angles are important to maintain.

Do not let puddle become too fluid.

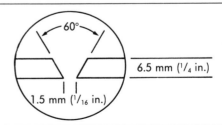

PRACTICAL WELDING ASSIGNMENT NO. 3

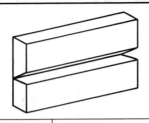

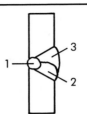

Process	OAW
Type of Joint	single–vee butt joint
Metal	low carbon steel (LCS) 6.5 mm (1/4 in.)
No. of Pieces	2
Size of Pieces	75 mm × 150 mm (3 in. × 6 in.)
Position	horizontal (3 pass)
Amperage	n/a
Voltage	n/a
Polarity	n/a
High Frequency	n/a
Welding Rod/Wire	3.2 mm (1/8 in.) RG410 (RG60)
Tip Size	Use tip size recommended by manufacturer of your torch.
Gas Flow	Gas flow will correspond to tip size being used.
Finish	Grind welds flush; cut two 38 mm (1 1/2 in.) strips across weld.
Testing	1 Face Bend and 1 Root Bend Test
Reference	Chapters 8, 19, 23, 24

Additional Remarks

Feed the rod into the top of the molten puddle.
Point the torch 10° upward.

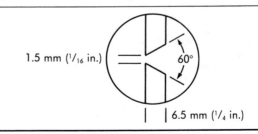

PRACTICAL WELDING ASSIGNMENT NO. 4

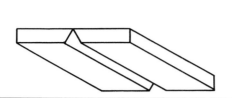

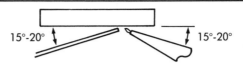

Process	OAW
Type of Joint	single–vee butt joint
Metal	low carbon steel (LCS) 6.5 mm (1/4 in.)
No. of Pieces	2
Size of Pieces	75 mm × 150 mm (3 in. × 6 in.)
Position	overhead (2 pass)
Amperage	n/a
Voltage	n/a
Polarity	n/a
High Frequency	n/a
Welding Rod/Wire	5.0 mm (3/16 in.) RG410 (RG60)
Tip Size	Use tip size recommended by manufacturer of your torch.
Gas Flow	Gas flow will correspond to size of tip being used.
Finish	Grind welds flush; cut two 38 mm (1 1/2 in.) strips across weld.
Testing	1 Face Bend and 1 Root Bend Test
Reference	Chapters 8, 19, 23, 24

Additional Remarks

Use a neutral flame. Do not let puddle become too fluid.

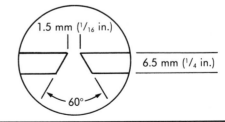

PRACTICAL WELDING ASSIGNMENT NO. 5

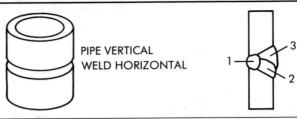

PIPE VERTICAL
WELD HORIZONTAL

Process	OAW
Type of Joint	single–vee butt joint
Metal	schedule 40 pipe 150 mm (6 in.) dia. 6.5 mm (1/4 in.) wall
No. of Pieces	2
Size of Pieces	150 mm (6 in.) long
Position	horizontal (3 pass)
Amperage	n/a
Voltage	n/a
Polarity	n/a
High Frequency	n/a
Welding Rod/Wire	3.2 mm (1/8 in.) RG410 (RG60)
Tip Size	Use tip size recommended by manufacturer of your torch.
Gas Flow	Gas flow will correspond to tip size.
Finish	Grind flush; cut four 38 mm (1 1/2 in.) strips across weld.
Testing	2 Face Bend and 2 Root Bend Tests
Reference	Chapters 8, 19, 23, 24

Additional Remarks

The pipe must be fixed in the vertical position with the axis of
the weld in the horizontal position.
The pipe must not be moved during welding.

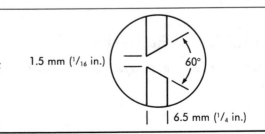

PRACTICAL WELDING ASSIGNMENT NO. 6

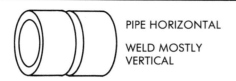

PIPE HORIZONTAL

WELD MOSTLY VERTICAL

START WELD AT BOTTOM AND WELD IN DIRECTION OF ARROW

Process	OAW
Type of Joint	single–vee butt joint
Metal	schedule 40 pipe 150 mm (6 in.) dia. 6.5 mm (1/4 in.) wall
No. of Pieces	2
Size of Pieces	150 mm (6 in.) long
Position	fixed (2 pass)
Amperage	n/a
Voltage	n/a
Polarity	n/a
High Frequency	n/a
Welding Rod/Wire	3.2 mm (1/8 in.) RG410 (RG60)
Tip Size	Use tip size recommended by manufacturer of your torch.
Gas Flow	Gas flow will correspond to tip size.
Finish	Grind flush; cut four 38 mm (1 1/2 in.) strips across weld
Testing	2 Face Bend and 2 Root Bend Tests
Reference	Chapters 8, 19, 23, 24

Additional Remarks

The pipe must be fixed in the horizontal position with the axis of the weld in the vertical position.
The pipe must not be rotated.
Weld vertical up from the bottom on both sides.
The angle of torch and rod must be changed continually.

PRACTICAL WELDING ASSIGNMENT NO. 7

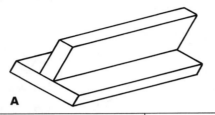

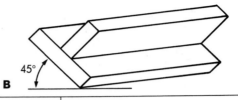

Process	SMAW	SMAW
Type of Joint	tee joint	tee joint
Metal	LCS 9.5 mm (3/8 in.) thick	LCS 9.5 mm (3/8 in.) thick
No. of Pieces	2	2
Size of Pieces	76 mm × 203 mm (3 in. × 8 in.)	76 mm × 203 mm (3 in. × 8 in.)
Position	horizontal (1 pass)	flat (downhand) (1 pass)
Amperage	300 A–410A	300 A–410 A
Voltage	n/a	n/a
Polarity	AC	AC
High Frequency	n/a	n/a
Welding Rod/Wire	6.0 mm (1/4 in.) E48024 (E7024)	6.0 mm (1/4 in.) E48024 (E7024)
Tip Size	n/a	n/a
Gas Flow	n/a	n/a
Finish	Chip and wire brush clean.	
Testing	Visual and Break Tests, or Etch Test	
Reference	Chapters 13, 15, 24	

Additional Remarks

Try making multiple passes as in Figures A, B, and C.

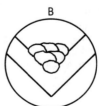

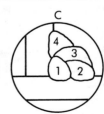

PRACTICAL WELDING ASSIGNMENT NO. 8

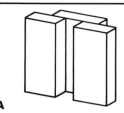
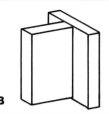

A   **B**

	A	B
Process	SMAW	SMAW
Type of Joint	lap joint with 19.1 mm (3/4 in.) gap.	tee joint
Metal	LCS 9.5 mm (3/8 in.) thick	LCS 9.5 mm (3/8 in.) thick
No. of Pieces	3	2
Size of Pieces	76 mm × 203 mm (3 in. × 8 in.)	76 mm × 203 mm (3 in. × 8 in.)
Position	vertical up (3 pass)	vertical up (1 pass)
Amperage	120 A–160 A	120 A–145 A
Voltage	n/a	n/a
Polarity	AC or DCRP	DCRP
High Frequency	n/a	n/a
Welding Rod/Wire	4.0 mm (5/32 in.) E48018 (E7018)	4.0 mm (5/32 in.) E41010 (E6010)
Tip Size	n/a	n/a
Gas Flow	n/a	n/a
Finish	Chip and wire brush clean.	
Testing	Visual and Break Tests.	
Reference	Chapters 13, 19, 24	

Additional Remarks

Use a short whipping motion for E41010 (E6010)
Use a triangular motion for E48018 (E7018)
Check angles frequently to avoid undercut.
Last pass on lap joint will be a weave.

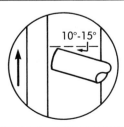

PRACTICAL WELDING ASSIGNMENT NO. 9

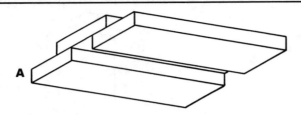
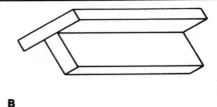

Process	SMAW	SMAW
Type of Joint	lap joint with 19.1 mm (3/4 in.) gap.	tee joint
Metal	LCS 9.5 mm (3/8 in.) thick	LCS 9.5 mm (3/8 in.) thick
No. of Pieces	3	2
Size of Pieces	76 mm × 203 mm (3 in. × 8 in.)	76 mm × 203 mm (3 in. × 8 in.)
Position	overhead (multiple passes)	overhead (1 pass)
Amperage	150 A–210 A	120 A–145 A
Voltage	n/a	n/a
Polarity	AC or DCRP	AC or DCRP
High Frequency	n/a	n/a
Welding Rod/Wire	4 mm (5/32 in.) E48018 (E7018)	4 mm (5/32 in.) E41011 (E6011)
Tip Size	n/a	n/a
Gas Flow	n/a	n/a
Finish	Chip and wire brush clean.	
Testing	Visual and Break Tests.	
Reference	Chapters 13, 19, 24	

Additional Remarks

Use stringer beads. Do not weave.
With E48018 (E7018) use a short arc and no whipping.
For multiple passes, use the sequence shown in Figure A.

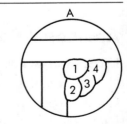

PRACTICAL WELDING ASSIGNMENT NO. 10

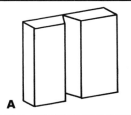
A

TRIANGULAR WEAVE

WHIP

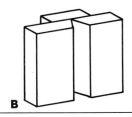
B

	A	B
Process	SMAW	SMAW
Type of Joint	single–vee butt joint	single–vee butt joint with backing
Metal	LCS 9.5 mm (3/8 in.) thick	LCS 9.5 mm (3/8 in.) thick
No. of Pieces	2	3
Size of Pieces	76 mm × 203 mm (3 in. × 8 in.)	76 mm × 203 mm (3 in. × 8 in.)
Position	vertical up (multiple passes)	vertical up (multiple passes)
Amperage	100 A–160 A	90 A–150 A
Voltage	n/a	n/a
Polarity	AC or DCRP	DCRP
High Frequency	n/a	n/a
Welding Rod/Wire	3.2 mm (1/8 in.) E48018 (E7018); 4 mm (5/32 in.) E48018 (E7018)	3.2 mm (1/8 in.) (E41010) E6010; 4 mm (5/32 in.) (E41010) E6010
Tip Size	n/a	n/a
Gas Flow	n/a	n/a
Finish	Grind flush.	Remove backing; grind flush.
Testing	Face and Root Guided Bend Tests.	
Reference	Chapters 11, 13, 19, 23, 24	

Additional Remarks

On first pass: when using E48018 (E7018) use a triangular weave; when using E41010 (E6010) use a short whipping motion.

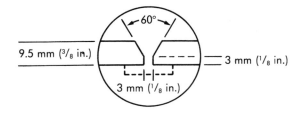

PRACTICAL WELDING ASSIGNMENT NO. 11

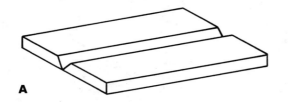

A

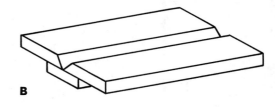

B

Process	SMAW	SMAW
Type of Joint	single–vee butt joint	single–vee butt joint with backing
Metal	LCS 9.5 mm (3/8 in.) thick	LCS 9.5 mm (3/8 in.) thick
No. of Pieces	2	3
Size of Pieces	76 mm × 203 mm (3 in. × 8 in.)	76 mm × 203 mm (3 in. × 8 in.)
Position	flat (downhand) (3 pass)	flat (downhand) (3 pass)
Amperage	1st pass 120 A–180 A	1st pass 110 A–160A
	2nd/3rd pass 150 A–230 A	2nd/3rd pass 120 A–240 A
Voltage	n/a	n/a
Polarity	DCRP	AC
High Frequency	n/a	n/a
Welding Rod/Wire	1st pass 4.0 mm (5/32 in.)	1st pass 4.0 mm (5/32 in.)
	E41010 (E6010)	E41011 (E6011)
	2nd/3rd pass 5.0 mm (3/16 in.)	2nd/3rd pass 4.0 mm (5/32 in.)
	E41010 (E6010)	E41027 (E6027)
Tip Size	n/a	n/a
Gas Flow	n/a	n/a
Finish	Grind or machine finish.	Remove backing; grind or machine finish.
Testing	Face and Root Guided Bend Tests.	
Reference	Chapters 15, 19, 23, 24	

Additional Remarks

With E41010 (E6010) only: on the first pass use a short back and forward whipping motion *or* set the machine at high end of amperage; establish a keyhole, hold a very short arc and move rapidly enough to maintain the keyhole (*on joint without backing*).

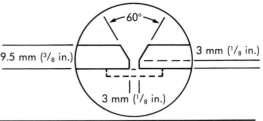

PRACTICAL WELDING ASSIGNMENT NO. 12

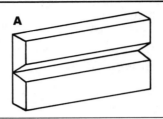

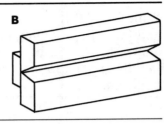

	A	B
Process	SMAW	SMAW
Type of Joint	single–vee butt joint	single–vee butt joint wih backing
Metal	LCS 9.5 mm (3/8 in.) thick	LCS 9.5 mm (3/8 in.) thick
No. of Pieces	2	3
Size of Pieces	76 mm × 203 mm (3 in. × 8 in.)	76 mm × 203 mm (3 in. × 8 in.)
Position	horizontal (multiple passes)	horizontal (multiple passes)
Amperage	90 A–150 A	100 A–170 A
Voltage	n/a	n/a
Polarity	DCRP	AC or DCRP
High Frequency	n/a	n/a
Welding Rod/Wire	3.2 mm (1/8 in.) E41010 (E6010)	3.2 mm (1/8 in.) E48018 (E7018)
	4 mm (5/32 in.) E41010 (E6010)	4 mm (5/32 in.) E48018 (E7018)
Tip Size	n/a	n/a
Gas Flow	n/a	n/a
Finish	Grind flush.	Remove backing; grind flush.
Testing	Face and Root Guided Bend Tests.	
Reference	Chapters 11, 13, 19, 23, 24	

Additional Remarks

Use single passes only: Do not weave.

When using E41010 (E6010), use a short back and forward whipping motion.

When using E48018, use a short arc with a straight forward progression in the direction of travel.

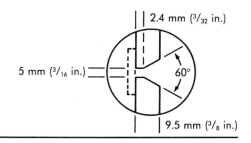

PRACTICAL WELDING ASSIGNMENT NO. 13

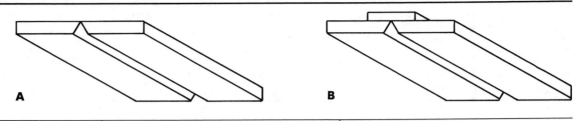

A   B

Process	SMAW	SMAW
Type of Joint	single–vee butt joint	single–vee butt joint with backing
Metal	LCS 9.5 mm (3/8 in.) thick	LCS 9.5 mm (3/8 in.)
No. of Pieces	2	3
Size of Pieces	76 mm × 203 mm (3 in. × 8 in.)	76 mm × 203 mm (3 in. × 8 in.)
Position	overhead (multiple passes)	overhead (multiple passes)
Amperage	90 A–160 A	120 A–210 A
Voltage	n/a	n/a
Polarity	DCRP	AC or DCRP
High Frequency	n/a	n/a
Welding Rod/Wire	3.2 mm (1/8 in.) E41010 (E6010)	3.2 mm (1/8 in.) E48018 (E7018)
	4 mm (5/32 in.) E41010 (E6010)	4 mm (5/32 in.) E48018 (E7018)
Tip Size	n/a	n/a
Gas Flow	n/a	n/a
Finish	Grind flush.	Remove backing; grind flush.
Testing	Face and Root Guided Bend Tests.	
Reference	Chapters 11, 13, 19, 23, 24	

Additional Remarks

When using E48018 (E7018), use stringer beads, not weaves.
When using E41010 (E6010) (first pass), use a short whip.
When using E48018 (E7018), hold a short arc; do not whip.

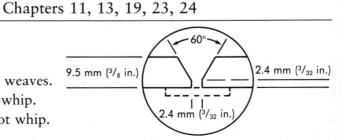

9.5 mm (³/₈ in.)   60°   2.4 mm (³/₃₂ in.)

2.4 mm (³/₃₂ in.)

PRACTICAL WELDING ASSIGNMENT NO. 14

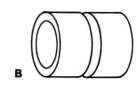

A B

Process	SMAW	SMAW
Type of Joint	single–vee butt joint	single–vee butt joint
Metal	schedule 60 LCS pipe	schedule 60 LCS pipe
No. of Pieces	(2 for each assembly)	(2 for each assembly)
Size of Pieces	203 mm dia. × 102 mm long (8 in. × 4 in.); 10.3 mm (13/32 in.) thick	203 mm dia. × 102 mm long (8 in. × 4 in.); 10.3 mm (13/32 in.) thick
Position	horizontal	all positions (fixed)
Amperage	80 A–130 A	100 A–130 A
Voltage	n/a	n/a
Polarity	DCRP	AC or DCRP
High Frequency	n/a	n/a
Welding Rod/Wire	3.2 mm (1/8 in.) E41010 (E6010)	3.2 mm (1/8 in.) E48018 (E7018)
Tip Size	n/a	n/a
Gas Flow	n/a	n/a
Finish	Cut test pieces the full length of the pipe and grind welds flush.	
Testing	Visual inspection before cutting then Face and Root Bend Tests.	
Reference	Chapters 11, 13, 19, 23, 24	

Additional Remarks

The pipe must not be rotated. The fit–up of the joint is critical.
The angle of the electrode must be constantly adjusted.
When confident, use a 3.2 mm (1/8 in.) electrode for the first
pass and a 4.0 mm (5/32 in.) electrode for all others.

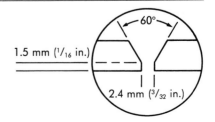

PRACTICAL WELDING ASSIGNMENT NO. 15

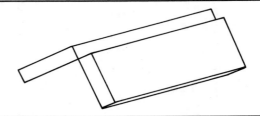

Process	GTAW
Type of Joint	open corner joint
Metal	1100 series aluminum 3.2 mm (1/8 in.) thick
No. of Pieces	2
Sizes of Pieces	76 mm × 203 mm (3 in. × 8 in.)
Position	downhand
Amperage	110 A–150 A
Voltage	n/a
Polarity	AC
High Frequency	continuous
Welding Rod/Wire	2.4 mm (3/32 in.) ER4043 welding rod; 3.2 mm (1/8 in.) pure tungsten.
Tip Size	9.5 mm (3/8 in.) dia. gas nozzle
Gas Flow	argon: 7.5–9.4 L/m (16–20 cu. ft./hr.)
Finish	as is
Testing	Visual: hammer flat.
Reference	Chapters 8, 16, 24

Additional Remarks

Weld the joint with and without a welding rod.

PRACTICAL WELDING ASSIGNMENT NO. 16

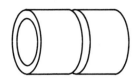

Process	GTAW
Type of Joint	single–vee butt joint 2 pass
Metal	6061 series aluminum schedule 40 pipe
No. of Pieces	2
Size of Pieces	152 mm × 100 mm (6 in. × 4 in. long)
Position	all positions
Amperage	200 A–240 A
Voltage	n/a
Polarity	AC
High Frequency	continuous
Welding Rod/Wire	4.0 mm (5/32 in.) ER4043 welding rod; 5.0 mm (3/16 in.) pure tungsten.
Tip Size	9.5 mm (3/8 in.) dia. gas nozzle
Gas Flow	argon: 16.5 L/m (35 cu. ft./hr.)
Finish	Cut 37 mm (1 1/2 in.) wide strips the full length of the pipe and machine welds flush.
Testing	Face and Root Guided Bend Tests.
Reference	Chapters 16, 23, 24

Additional Remarks

The angle of the torch must be continually adjusted as you move around the circumference of the pipe. The pipe must not be turned; it must be welded in the fixed position.

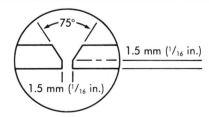

PRACTICAL WELDING ASSIGNMENT NO. 17

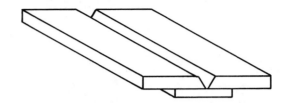

Process	GMAW
Type of Joint	single–vee butt joint (with backing)
Metal	1100 series aluminum, 9.5 mm (3/8 in.) thick
No. of Pieces	3
Size of Pieces	76 mm × 203 mm (3 in. × 8 in.)
Position	flat (downhand) (3 pass)
Amperage	230 A–300 A
Voltage	28 V–30 V
Polarity	DCRP
High Frequency	n/a
Welding Rod/Wire	1.5 mm (1/16 in.) ER1100 or ER4043 welding rod
Tip Size	16 mm (5/8 in.) nozzle
Gas Flow	argon: 18.8 L/min–28.3 L/m (40–60 cu. ft./hr.)
Finish	Remove backing; machine weld surfaces flush.
Testing	Face and Root Guided Bend Tests.
Reference	Chapters 8, 17, 23, 24

Additional Remarks

Weld in a forehand direction.

Point the gun in the direction of travel and incline the gun 5° to 20° from a vertical position.

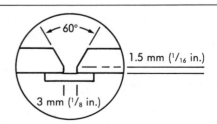

PRACTICAL WELDING ASSIGNMENT NO. 18

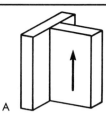 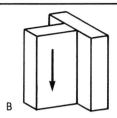

Process	GMAW
Type of Joint	tee joint
Metal	LCS 3.2 mm (1/8 in.) thick
No. of Pieces	2
Size of Pieces	76 mm × 203 mm (3 in. × 8 in.)
Position	vertical up 2 passes
Amperage	120 A–130 A
Voltage	20 V–23 V
Polarity	DCRP
High Frequency	n/a
Welding Rod/Wire	E480S–3 (E70S–3) welding rod; 0.9 mm (0.35 in.)
Tip Size	n/a
Gas Flow	CO_2 or CO_2/A 10.4 L/m (22 cu. ft./hr.)
Finish	as is
Testing	Visual and Break Tests.
Reference	Chapters 17, 19, 24

Additional Remarks

The gun should be pointing directly into the joint, but inclined slightly in an upward direction. Use a triangular motion on the first pass and a straight weaving motion for the second pass. Try a vertical down pass; use the same angles, gas flow, etc., as vertical up, but this time use a straight down motion with no weaving or moving.

SECTION 1 OXYFUEL WELDING AND CUTTING

EXERCISES

PURPOSE

A OXYFUEL SAFETY	SETTING UP THE EQUIPMENT	SHUTTING DOWN THE EQUIPMENT	TESTING FOR LEAKS	LIGHTING THE TORCH

TO BECOME FAMILIAR WITH OXYFUEL EQUIPMENT

B FLAME ADJUSTMENT	LINE OF FUSION NO ROD	LINE OF FUSION WITH ROD	CORNER JOINT NO ROD	CORNER JOINT WITH ROD

TO PRACTISE TORCH/ROD MANIPULATION

C BUTT JOINT FLAT POSITION	TEE JOINT HORIZONTAL POSITION	LAP JOINT HORIZONTAL POSITION	TEE JOINT FLAT POSITION	SINGLE VEE BUTT JOINT FLAT POSITION

TO FUSION WELD JOINTS

D BRAZE WELD LAP JOINT HORIZONTAL POSITION	BRAZE WELD TEE JOINT FLAT POSITION	BRAZE WELD SINGLE VEE JOINT FLAT POSITION	BRAZE WELD SINGLE VEE JOINT VERTICAL POSITION	SILVER BRAZE LAP JOINT HORIZONTAL POSITION

TO BRAZE WELD

E BEADS VERTICAL POSITION	BUTT JOINT VERTICAL POSITION	CORNER JOINT VERTICAL POSITION	LAP JOINT VERTICAL POSITION	TEE JOINT VERTICAL POSITION

TO PRACTISE VERTICAL POSITION WELDING

F SINGLE VEE BUTT JOINT HORIZONTAL POSITION	SINGLE VEE BUTT JOINT VERTICAL POSITION	SINGLE VEE BUTT JOINT OVERHEAD POSITION	TEE JOINT OVERHEAD POSITION	LAP JOINT OVERHEAD POSITION

TO PRACTISE OVERHEAD/VERTICAL HORIZONTAL POSITION WELDING

G WELDING PIPE IN THE FLAT POSITION (ROLLED)	WELDING PIPE IN THE FIXED HORIZONTAL POSITION	WELDING PIPE IN THE FIXED VERTICAL POSITION	WELDING PIPE WITH BACKING RING	WELDING BOX ASSEMBLY ALL POSITION

TO WELD PIPE ALL POSITION

H OXYFUEL CUTTING SAFETY	CUTTING A STRAIGHT LINE	PIERCING A HOLE	CUTTING A CIRCLE	CUTTING BEVELS

TO PRACTISE OXY FUEL CUTTING

SECTION 2 SMAW

EXERCISES

PURPOSE

A	SAFETY	SETTING UP EQUIPMENT	STRIKING AN ARC	STOP/START RUNNING BEADS DOWNHAND POSITION	WEAVING IN THE DOWNHAND POSITION
					TO BECOME FAMILIAR WITH THE SMAW PROCESS

B	TO WELD BEADS IN THE HORIZONTAL POSITION	TO WELD BEADS IN THE VERTICAL UP POSITION	TO WELD BEADS IN THE VERTICAL DOWN POSITION	TO WELD BEADS IN THE OVERHEAD POSITION	SAVE THESE PIECES FOR FUTURE ASSEMBLIES AND FUTURE PRACTICE
					TO PRACTICE ROD AND PUDDLE MANIPULATION IN ALL POSITIONS

C	TO PAD OR BUILDUP IN THE DOWNHAND POSITION	TO WELD A CORNER JOINT WITH SINGLE AND MULTIPLE PASS WELDS DOWNHAND	TO WEAVE IN THE VERTICAL POSITION	TO WEAVE IN THE OVERHEAD POSITION	SAVE THESE PIECES FOR FUTURE ASSEMBLIES
					TO PERFECT ROD AND PUDDLE CONTROL IN ALL POSITIONS

D	TO WELD A LAP JOINT IN THE OVERHEAD POSITION	TO WELD A TEE JOINT IN THE OVERHEAD POSITION	TO WELD A SQUARE EDGE BUTT JOINT IN THE OVERHEAD POSITION	TO WELD A SINGLE VEE BUTT JOINT IN THE OVERHEAD POSITION	TO WELD MULTI PASS WELDS ON LAP/TEE JOINTS IN OVERHEAD POSITION
					TO PRACTICE WELDING IN THE OVERHEAD POSITION

E	TO WELD PIPE IN THE FLAT DOWNHAND POSITION (ROLLED)	TO WELD PIPE IN THE HORIZONTAL FIXED POSITION	TO WELD PIPE IN THE FIXED VERTICAL POSITION	TO WELD BOX ASSEMBLY ALL POSITION	TO WELD A SINGLE VEE BUTT JOINT IN DOWNHAND POSITIONS
					TO WELD PIPE AND PLATE ALL POSITIONS

SECTION 3 GTAW

EXERCISES

PURPOSE

A

SAFETY	SETTING UP EQUIPMENT	SELECTING ELECTRODE AND FILLER ROD	SELECTING CORRECT GAS SUPPLY	STRIKING THE ARC AC

TO BECOME FAMILIAR WITH THE GTAW PROCESS

B

STRIKING THE ARC DC	STOP/START JOINING WELDS	RUNNING BEADS DOWNHAND POSITION NO ROD	RUNNING BEADS DOWNHAND POSITION WITH ROD	MAKING TACK WELDS

TO PRACTISE TORCH AND ROD MANIPULATION

C

TO WELD A LAP/TEE JOINT DOWNHAND POSITION ON ALUMINUM	TO WELD A LAP/TEE JOINT HORIZONTAL POSITION ON ALUMINUM	TO WELD MULTIPASS WELDS ON LAP/TEE JOINTS ON ALUMINUM	REPEAT LAP/TEE WELDS ON LOW CARBON STEEL	REPEAT LAP/TEE WELDS ON STAINLESS STEEL

TO WELD FILLET WELDS IN HORIZONTAL AND DOWNHAND POSITION ON VARIOUS METALS

D

TO WELD LAP/TEE JOINT VERTICAL UP POSITION ON ALUMINUM	TO WELD MULTIPASS WELDS ON LAP/TEE JOINT VERTICAL UP ON ALUMINUM	TO WELD LAP/TEE JOINT VERTICAL DOWN POSITION	TO WELD SQUARE EDGE BUTT JOINT IN VERTICAL POSITION	TO WELD SINGLE VEE BUTT JOINT IN VERTICAL UP POSITION

TO WELD IN THE VERTICAL POSITION. EXERCISES SHOULD BE REPEATED ON SS AND LCS

E

TO WELD LAP/TEE JOINT OVERHEAD POSITION ON ALUMINUM	TO WELD MULTIPASS WELDS ON LAP/TEE JOINTS OVERHEAD ON ALUMINUM	TO WELD A SQUARE EDGE BUTT JOINT IN OVERHEAD POSITION ON ALUMINUM	TO WELD SINGLE VEE BUTT JOINT ON ALUMINUM OVERHEAD POSITION	TO REPEAT THESE EXERCISES ON STAINLESS AND LOW CARBON STEEL

TO WELD IN THE OVERHEAD POSITION ON VARIOUS METALS

F

TO WELD SQUARE EDGE BUTT JOINT HORIZONTAL POSITION ON AL. SS. LCS.	TO WELD A SINGLE VEE BUTT JOINT HORIZONTAL POSITION ON AL. SS. LCS	TO WELD PIPE IN THE HORIZONTAL FIXED POSITION ON AL. SS. LCS.	TO WELD PIPE IN THE FIXED VERTICAL POSITION ON AL. SS. LCS.	TO WELD BOX ASSEMBLY ALL POSITIONS ON AL. SS. LCS.

TO WELD PLATE/PIPE ALL POSITIONS ON VARIOUS METALS

SECTION 4 GMAW

EXERCISES   ## PURPOSE

A

SAFETY	SETTING UP EQUIPMENT	SELECTING PROCESS AND WELDING ROD (WIRE)	SELECTING CORRECT GAS SUPPLY	STRIKING THE ARC

TO BECOME FAMILIAR WITH THE GMAW PROCESS

B

STOP/START	RUNNING BEADS DOWNHAND POSITION	JOINING BEADS DOWNHAND POSITION	WEAVING DOWNHAND POSITION	MAKING TACK WELDS

TO PRACTISE GUN AND WIRE MANIPULATION

C

TO WELD LAP/TEE/VEE JOINT DOWNHAND POSITION ON AL	TO WELD LAP/TEE JOINT HORIZONTAL POSITION ON AL	TO WELD MULTIPASS WELDS ON LAP/TEE JOINTS ON AL	REPEAT LAP/TEE WELDS ON LOW CARBON STEEL	REPEAT LAP/TEE WELDS ON STAINLESS STEEL

TO WELD FILLET WELDS IN HORIZONTAL AND DOWNHAND POSITION ON VARIOUS METALS

D

TO WELD LAP/TEE JOINTS VERTICAL UP POSITION ON AL	TO WELD MULTIPASS WELDS ON LAP/TEE JOINTS VERTICAL UP ON AL	TO WELD LAP/TEE JOINTS VERTICAL DOWN POSITION ON AL	TO WELD SQUARE EDGE BUTT JOINT VERTICAL POSITION ON AL	TO WELD SINGLE VEE BUTT JOINT VERTICAL UP POSITION ON AL

TO WELD IN THE VERTICAL POSITION. EXERCISES SHOULD BE REPEATED ON SS.—LCS.

E

TO WELD LAP/TEE JOINT OVERHEAD POSITION ON AL	TO WELD MULTIPASS WELDS ON LAP/TEE JOINTS OVERHEAD ON AL	TO WELD A SQUARE EDGE BUTT JOINT OVERHEAD POSITION ON AL	TO WELD SINGLE VEE BUTT JOINT OVERHEAD POSITION ON AL	TO REPEAT THESE EXERCISES ON SS.-LCS

TO WELD IN THE OVERHEAD POSITION ON VARIOUS METALS

F

TO WELD SQUARE EDGE BUTT JOINT HORIZONTAL POSITION ON AL. SS. LCS.	TO WELD A SINGLE VEE BUTT JOINT HORIZONTAL POSITION ON AL. SS. LCS.	TO WELD PIPE IN THE FIXED HORIZONTAL POSITION ON AL. SS. LCS.	TO WELD PIPE IN THE FIXED VERTICAL POSITION ON AL. SS. LCS.	TO WELD BOX ASSEMBLY ALL POSITIONS ON AL. SS. LCS.

TO WELD PLATE/PIPE ALL POSITION ON VARIOUS METALS

SECTION 5 JOINT PREPARATION

EXERCISE

PURPOSE

A

TO PREPARE A SINGLE BEVEL NO LAND	TO PREPARE A SINGLE BEVEL WITH LAND	TO PREPARE A DOUBLE BEVEL NO LAND	TO PREPARE A DOUBLE BEVEL WITH LAND	TO CONSERVE MATERIAL USE SCRAP METAL FOR PRACTICE

TO PREPARE BEVEL SPECIMENS

B

TO PREPARE A SINGLE J WITH LAND	TO PREPARE A DOUBLE J WITH LAND	TO PREPARE A SINGLE U WITH LAND	TO PREPARE A DOUBLE U WITH LAND	SAVE THESE PIECES FOR FUTURE ASSEMBLY

TO PREPARE J AND U SPECIMENS

C

TO PREPARE A SINGLE VEE NO LAND	TO PREPARE A SINGLE VEE WITH LAND	TO PREPARE A DOUBLE VEE NO LAND	TO PREPARE A DOUBLE VEE WITH LAND	SAVE THESE PIECES FOR FUTURE ASSEMBLY

TO PREPARE VEE SPECIMENS

D

TO PREPARE A TEE/ JOINT WITH A SINGLE BEVEL	TO PREPARE A TEE JOINT WITH DOUBLE BEVEL	TO PREPARE A TEE JOINT WITH A SINGLE J	TO PREPARE A TEE JOINT WITH A DOUBLE J	JOINTS TO BE COMPLETELY ASSEMBLED AND TACK WELDED

TO PREPARE TEE JOINT SPECIMENS

E

TO PREPARE A SINGLE VEE JOINT WITH LAND AND BACKING	TO PREPARE A SINGLE VEE JOINT NO LAND WITH BACKING	TO PREPARE A SINGLE U JOINT WITH WITH LAND AND BACKING	TO PREPARE A SINGLE U JOINT WITH LAND NO BACKING	JOINTS TO BE COMPLETELY ASSEMBLED AND TACK WELDED

TO PREPARE GROOVE OR BUTT JOINTS WITH AND WITHOUT BACKING

F

TO PREPARE AND TEST A SQUARE EDGE BUTT JOINT	TO PREPARE AND TEST A CORNER JOINT	TO PREPARE AND TEST A TEE JOINT	TO PREPARE AND TEST A FLANGE OR EDGE JOINT	OBSERVE ALL SAFETY PRECAUTIONS

TO PREPARE AND TEST BASIC JOINTS

G

TO PREPARE A GUIDED BEND TEST SPECIMEN	TO TEST A FACE BEND	TO TEST A ROOT BEND	TO TEST A TEE JOINT DESTRUCTIVE	TO TEST A TEE JOINT NON- DESTRUCTIVE

TO PREPARE AND TEST WELD SPECIMENS

INDEX